P9-DEP-000

THE BEDFORD SERIES IN HISTORY AND CULTURE

Abraham Lincoln, Slavery, and the Civil War

Selected Writings and Speeches

Related Titles in
THE BEDFORD SERIES IN HISTORY AND CULTURE
Advisory Editors: Lynn Hunt, *University of California, Los Angeles*
David W. Blight, *Yale University*
Bonnie G. Smith, *Rutgers University*
Natalie Zemon Davis, *Princeton University*
Ernest R. May, *Harvard University*

Narrative of the Life of Frederick Douglass, An American Slave, Written by Himself
Edited with an Introduction by David W. Blight, *Amherst College*

William Lloyd Garrison and the Fight against Slavery: Selections from The Liberator
Edited with an Introduction by William E. Cain, *Wellesley College*

Defending the Cornerstone: Proslavery Arguments in the American South (forthcoming)
Paul Finkelman, *University of Tulsa College of Law*

Dred Scott v. Sanford: A Brief History with Documents
Paul Finkelman, *University of Tulsa College of Law*

African American Perspectives on the Civil War and Reconstruction (forthcoming)
Michael P. Johnson, *Johns Hopkins University*

THE BEDFORD SERIES IN HISTORY AND CULTURE

Abraham Lincoln, Slavery, and the Civil War

Selected Writings and Speeches

Edited by

Michael P. Johnson

Johns Hopkins University

BEDFORD/ST. MARTIN'S   Boston   ♦   New York

To the memory of Howard and Maybelle Johnson, my parents.

For Bedford/St. Martin's

Executive Editor, History and Political Science: Katherine E. Kurzman
Developmental Editor: Louise Townsend
Editorial Assistant: Jamie Farrell
Senior Production Supervisor: Cheryl Mamaril
Project Management: Books By Design, Inc.
Text Design: Claire Seng-Niemoeller
Indexer: Books By Design, Inc.
Cover Design: Richard Emery
Cover Photo: Mathew Brady, *President Abraham Lincoln,* 1864. National Archives.
Composition: Stratford Publishing Services
Printing and Binding: Haddon Craftsmen, an R. R. Donnelley & Sons Company

President: Charles H. Christensen
Editorial Director: Joan E. Feinberg
Director of Marketing: Karen R. Melton
Director of Editing, Design, and Production: Marcia Cohen
Manager, Publishing Services: Emily Berleth

Library of Congress Control Number: 00-104126

6
f e d c

For information, write: Bedford/St. Martin's, 75 Arlington Street, Boston, MA 02116
(617-399-4000)

ISBN-10: 0-312-20854-5 (paperback)
        0-312-22763-9 (hardcover)
ISBN-13: 978-0-312-20854-7

Foreword

The Bedford Series in History and Culture is designed so that readers can study the past as historians do.

The historian's first task is finding the evidence. Documents, letters, memoirs, interviews, pictures, movies, novels, or poems can provide facts and clues. Then the historian questions and compares the sources. There is more to do than in a courtroom, for hearsay evidence is welcome, and the historian is usually looking for answers beyond act and motive. Different views of an event may be as important as a single verdict. How a story is told may yield as much information as what it says.

Along the way the historian seeks help from other historians and perhaps from specialists in other disciplines. Finally, it is time to write, to decide on an interpretation and how to arrange the evidence for readers.

Each book in this series contains an important historical document or group of documents, each document a witness from the past and open to interpretation in different ways. The documents are combined with some element of historical narrative—an introduction or a biographical essay, for example—that provides students with an analysis of the primary source material and important background information about the world in which it was produced.

Each book in the series focuses on a specific topic within a specific historical period. Each provides a basis for lively thought and discussion about several aspects of the topic and the historian's role. Each is short enough (and inexpensive enough) to be a reasonable one-week assignment in a college course. Whether as classroom or personal reading, each book in the series provides firsthand experience of the challenge—and fun—of discovering, re-creating, and interpreting the past.

Lynn Hunt
David W. Blight
Bonnie G. Smith
Natalie Zemon Davis
Ernest R. May

115596

Preface

This book makes Abraham Lincoln's most important writings and speeches about slavery and the Civil War readily available to any interested reader. From approximately 120,000 documents in the ten volumes of Lincoln's collected works, I have selected more than 170 letters, speeches, and other writings that portray the range and depth of Lincoln's thought about the issues that defined his times, his presidency, and his place in history.

Rather than a little of all of Lincoln, this collection features most of the essential Lincoln. Lincoln was so influential in the history of slavery and the Civil War that neither can be fully understood apart from him, nor can the major contours of his life and thought be separated from these matters, which preoccupied him during his last eleven years, especially during his presidency. The focus on slavery and the Civil War means that this collection necessarily slights other interesting features of Lincoln's experience: his family life, his congressional career, his years as an Illinois lawyer and politician before 1854, his legendary wit, and his endless supply of funny stories. That is, this edition of Lincoln's words makes no attempt to be a documentary biography. Such a project would require a far longer book and less concentrated attention to the central issues of slavery and the Civil War. What this edition sacrifices in the range of topics covered is recompensed by thorough, though still selective, coverage of topics at the core of Lincoln's historical significance.

The documents are arranged in ten chapters organized thematically and more or less chronologically. The first three chapters survey Lincoln's early life and his emergence as a leader of the new Republican party, first in Illinois, then in the North, and finally as president-elect. The remaining seven chapters chronicle Lincoln's attempt to preserve the Union during the bloody war that dominated his four years as president. They illustrate the evolution of Lincoln's political and military policies to place the war aim of freedom alongside that of union. Taken together, the documents provide an extended historical commentary, in Lincoln's own words, on his statement early in 1865 that the Emancipation Proclamation was "the central act of my administration and the great event of the nineteenth century."[1]

To make Lincoln's words more accessible, brief headnotes give sufficient information to allow readers to understand the historical context and significance of each document. By supplying connections between documents, the headnotes help readers follow the development of Lincoln's ideas. They also permit otherwise disconnected documents to be read as episodes in a continuous historical narrative, capturing some of the drama, uncertainty, and contingency of Lincoln's experience. Footnotes identify the people, places, and events that Lincoln mentions but that are unfamiliar to most readers today. Quotations from Lincoln's correspondents and from his spoken comments to his contemporaries frequently supplement the footnotes and the headnotes. Other editorial features designed to assist readers include maps and photographs, a chronology, questions to provoke reflection on Lincoln's thought, a selected bibliography of sources for further study, and a comprehensive index. In all, the editorial apparatus offers an array of concise, detailed information to help readers explore the many levels of meaning in Lincoln's words.

ACKNOWLEDGMENTS

In the preparation of this book I have been the beneficiary of knowledge, insight, and support from many people. Anne Johnson lovingly helped and sustained me, as always. For years, students at Johns Hopkins and the University of California, Irvine, have indulged my curiosity about Lincoln and his world. Friends James Roark and David Rankin endured numerous conversations about Lincoln, kindly read an early draft, and helped identify mistakes and blind spots. Edward Ayers, Jean Baker, Michael Burlingame, Drew Faust, and two anonymous readers saved me from embarrassing errors of commission and omission. At Bedford, sponsoring editor Katherine Kurzman and president Chuck Christensen welcomed this project from the outset. Louise Townsend made this a much better book with her sharp editorial eye and balanced historical judgment. Gerry McCauley put the contractual arrangements in place with his customary skill. I have had the

---

[1]Francis B. Carpenter, "Anecdotes and Reminiscences," in Henry J. Raymond, *The Life and Public Services of Abraham Lincoln* (New York, 1865), 764.

luxury of making revisions while a Fellow at the Center for Advanced Study in the Behavioral Sciences, supported in part by the Andrew W. Mellon Foundation. In addition to all of this indispensable help, I have benefited beyond measure from the writings of Lincoln scholars past and present, to whom all who share an interest in Lincoln, slavery, and the Civil War are permanently indebted. In 1876, Frederick Douglass declared, "Any man can say things that are true of Abraham Lincoln, but no man can say anything that is new of Abraham Lincoln."[2] Shelves of fascinating books and articles about Lincoln published since 1876 prove that Douglass spoke prematurely.

Michael P. Johnson

[2]Frederick Douglass, "Oration in Memory of Abraham Lincoln," Apr. 14, 1876, in Philip S. Foner, ed., *The Life and Writings of Frederick Douglass* (4 vols.; New York, 1955), IV, 315.

Maps and Illustrations

Contents

(See following pages.)

Map 1.   Major Union Campaigns of the Civil War, 1861–1865

Lincoln's homes in Kentucky, Indiana, and Illinois straddled the legal boundary of slave and free states that the Civil War and the Thirteenth Amendment ultimately erased. Although the war was truly continental in scope, major battles often occurred at important sites of water, rail, or road transportation, testimony to the significance of the movement of men and goods to both the Union and the Confederacy.

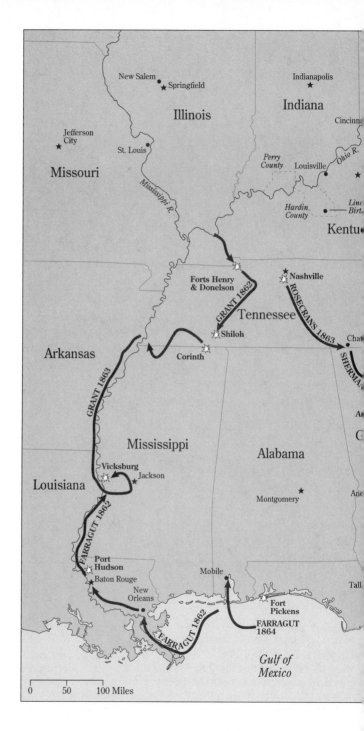

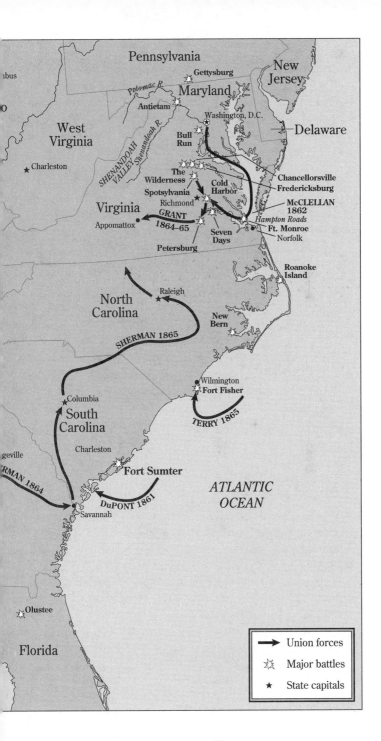

Introduction:
Abraham Lincoln, Wordsmith

In the early morning hours of November 7, 1860, after spending the evening listening to election returns clatter into the telegraph office in Springfield, Illinois, Abraham Lincoln went home, knowing he had received enough popular votes to win a comfortable electoral majority and become the next president of the United States. Since the days of George Washington, twelve other men had been elected to the nation's highest office and had prepared themselves to take the reins of power from an incumbent. Each time the transition from the old president to the new one was peaceful and without incident. Power transferred smoothly even when the incumbent and the newly elected president were partisan enemies—as in 1801, for example, when Federalist John Adams relinquished presidential authority to Democratic-Republican Thomas Jefferson. Lincoln had every reason to suppose that his election—the first for a member of the relatively new Republican party—would follow the pattern well established by his predecessors: He would take over the presidency from the Democratic incumbent, James Buchanan, and those who lost the election would regroup and try to win the next time, four years later.

On March 4, 1861, Buchanan stepped aside, as all other outgoing presidents had, and Lincoln was inaugurated in an orderly and routine ceremony. But by this time, unlike the immediate aftermath of any previous presidential election, seven slave states had declared their secession from the Union. No other presidential election, before or since, has had such violent and ultimately transforming consequences for the nation. During his campaign for the presidency and even during the four-month interval between his election and his inauguration, Lincoln never seriously contemplated civil war or the emancipation of four million slaves. But between his inauguration and his assassination four years later, Lincoln was preoccupied with the Civil War and slavery. His presidency permanently changed the course of American history.

Of course, Lincoln alone did not win the war and free the slaves. Such massive events involved the efforts of millions of Americans, soldiers and civilians, men and women, blacks and whites, northerners and southerners. Lincoln understood the considerable scope of his presidential powers, but he also realized that those powers had severe limits. He knew that he could not effectively exercise his presidential authority without mobilizing the consent of millions of ordinary Americans. He needed their consent in the form of their votes, their men of military age, their trust, and their willingness to sacrifice. A political creature to the tips of his toes, Lincoln worked hard to create that consent. Elected with slightly less than 40 percent of the popular vote, he needed no reminder of the nation's deep and bitter divisions, not only between, but also within, the North and the South. As a lawyer and politician in Illinois, Lincoln had years of experience confronting people with opposing views, dissecting their arguments, and advocating his own. But until he became president, he had never been required to generate consent for the kinds of personal commitment demanded by civil war. No other American president ever faced such a formidable challenge. To build and maintain popular consent—that is, to govern, to win the war, and to save the Union—Lincoln relied on both deeds and words, particularly words that persuaded many Americans to consent to his presidential deeds.[1]

Since boyhood, Lincoln had honed his skill with words. He is often thought of as a backwoods rail-splitter, a farm boy who became president by pluck and luck. It is true that he worked on his father's farm—first in Kentucky, then in Indiana, and finally in Illinois—and that he split logs into the fence rails immortalized in his 1860 presidential campaign. But farmwork convinced Lincoln that he wanted to do something else, almost anything else, when he came of age. He told a farmer who hired him in 1829 that "his father taught him to work but never learned him to love it."[2] In 1831, when he was twenty-two, he left his father's farm, moved to the small village of New Salem, Illinois, and began to try his hand at one thing after another—store clerk, merchant, surveyor, postmaster—but never farmer. Barely mak-

---

[1]See James M. McPherson, "How Lincoln Won the War with Metaphors," in McPherson, *Abraham Lincoln and the Second American Revolution* (New York, 1990), 93–112; Paul M. Angle, "Lincoln's Power with Words," *Papers of the Abraham Lincoln Association*, 3 (1981), 9–93.

[2]John Romine interview, September 14, 1865, in Douglas L. Wilson and Rodney O. Davis, eds., *Herndon's Informants: Letters, Interviews, and Statements about Abraham Lincoln* (Urbana, 1998), 118. This invaluable volume is cited hereafter as *Herndon's Informants*.

ing ends meet, Lincoln also explored two other occupations that became his lifelong pursuits: lawyer and politician. Both required skill with words, head-work rather than handwork. His ultimate achievements depended far more on his ability to turn a phrase, craft a sentence, and construct an argument than to handle an ax or plow. In fact, Lincoln made his living with words.

Like many Americans of his time, Lincoln was born into a poor family almost bereft of formal learning. Lincoln's mother could neither read nor write; his father could write his signature, but little else. Looking back on his youth, Lincoln recalled, "There was absolutely nothing to excite ambition for education."[3] One of Lincoln's Illinois neighbors remembered, "We all [were] low flung Could Neither read or Write."[4] Rather than learn the skills of literacy, most of Lincoln's neighbors trained their eyes on the unforgiving tasks of farming. "I had no books in my house," said another of Lincoln's Illinois friends, "loaned him none—we didn't think about books—papers—We worked—had to live."[5]

Lincoln worked, too, but he stole time before, during, and after work to read and write. His stepmother, Sarah Lincoln, recalled that he "studied in the daytime—didnt after night much—went to bed Early—got up Early & then read—Eat his breakfast—go to work in the field with the men."[6] Making time to read while six or seven others in a crowded one-room cabin were still asleep or just stirring to begin the day is a measure of Lincoln's appetite for learning. Even at work Lincoln found time to read. One neighbor remembered that when Lincoln "went out to work any where [he] would Carry his books with and would always read whilst resting."[7] After work when Lincoln "returned to the house," a relative said, "he would go to the Cupboard—Snatch a piece of Corn bread—take down a book—Sit down on a chair—Cock his legs up as high as his head and read. . . . He was a Constant and voracious reader."[8]

Although Sarah Lincoln was illiterate, she brought along several books when she moved into the Lincoln cabin, among them a Bible, *Aesop's Fables,* John Bunyan's *The Pilgrim's Progress,* and William Scott's *Lessons in Elocution,* which included passages from Shakespeare.[9] Lincoln read them all, plus books he obtained from friends and neighbors, such as Parson

[3]See Lincoln to Jesse W. Fell, December 20, 1859, in chapter 1. *CW,* III, 511.
[4]Abner Y. Ellis statement, [January 1866], *Herndon's Informants,* 173.
[5]Hannah Armstrong interview, [1866], *Herndon's Informants,* 526.
[6]Sarah Lincoln interview, September 8, 1865, *Herndon's Informants,* 107.
[7]Nathaniel Grigsby interview, September 12, 1865, *Herndon's Informants,* 112–13.
[8]John Hanks interview, [1865–66], *Herndon's Informants,* 455.
[9]David Herbert Donald, *Lincoln* (New York, 1995), 28–29.

Weems's *Life of George Washington,* Daniel Defoe's *Robinson Crusoe,* and *The Columbian Orator,* a collection of famous speeches.[10] He worked his way through "an old dog-eared arithmetic" book, and as Sarah recalled, he "was a Constant reader" of newspapers.[11]

Lincoln's reading led his cousin and childhood pal Dennis Hanks, among many others, to say that "Lincoln was lazy—a very lazy man—He was always reading—scribbling—writing—Ciphering—writing Poetry."[12] Hanks recalled that because Lincoln was "a Constant and I m[a]y Say Stubborn reader, his father ... Sometimes [had] to slash him for neglecting his work by reading."[13] When Lincoln could be spared from farmwork, he attended school a month or so at a time; in all, he had less than a year of formal schooling. For the most part, he educated himself, starting with disciplined reading.

With access to few books as a youngster, Lincoln developed reading habits that he used throughout his life. An Indiana neighbor remembered, "What Lincoln read he read and re-read—read and Studied thoroughly."[14] William H. Herndon, Lincoln's law partner in Springfield for two decades, claimed that "Mr. Lincoln read *less* and thought *more* than any man in his sphere in America."[15] In part, Herndon's remark reflected the narrowing in Lincoln's reading that occurred after 1836 when he began to practice law. Although Lincoln concentrated more on legal texts, he never stopped reading newspapers and books. Even while distracted by the endless responsibilities of his presidency, Lincoln borrowed more than 125 items from the Library of Congress on topics ranging from Shakespeare to military tactics.[16]

Lincoln read as if printed words were scarce victuals to be savored and devoured. He had little interest in owning books and never collected a sizable personal library, even after his law practice prospered in the 1850s.[17]

[10]Lincoln's Address to the New Jersey Senate, February 21, 1861, *CW,* IV, 235–36; Dennis Hanks interview, September 8, 1865, *Herndon's Informants,* 105.

[11]Allen Thorndike Rice, ed., *Reminiscences of Abraham Lincoln by Distinguished Men of His Time* (New York, 1886), 457–58; Sarah Lincoln interview, September 8, 1865, *Herndon's Informants,* 107.

[12]Dennis Hanks interview, September 8, 1865, *Herndon's Informants,* 104.

[13]Dennis Hanks interview, June 13, 1865, *Herndon's Informants,* 41.

[14]David Turnham interview, September 15, 1865, *Herndon's Informants,* 121.

[15]William H. Herndon, "The Analysis of Mr. Lincoln's Character," in Osborn H. Oldroyd, ed., *The Lincoln Memorial: Album-Immortelles* (New York, 1882), 533.

[16]David C. Mearns, "Mr. Lincoln and the Books He Read," in Arthur Bestor, David C. Mearns, and Jonathan Daniels, *Three Presidents and Their Books: The Reading of Jefferson, Lincoln, and Franklin D. Roosevelt* (Urbana, 1955), 68.

[17]Ibid., 63–64. See also Douglas L. Wilson, "The Frigate and the Frugal Chariot: Jefferson and Lincoln as Readers," in Wilson, *Lincoln before Washington: New Perspectives on the Illinois Years* (Urbana, 1997), 3–17.

Instead, he made a text his by reading and writing. Sarah Lincoln explained that when he "came across a passage that Struck him he would write it down on boards if he had no paper & keep it there till he did get paper—then he would rewrite it—look at it repeat it.... And when the board would get too black he would shave it off with a drawing knife and go on again."[18] An acquaintance from New Salem reported that a decade or so later Lincoln's "practice was, when He wished to indelibly fix any thing he was reading or studying on his mind, to write it down, have known him to write whole pages of books he was reading."[19]

In addition to writing out the core of his reading, Lincoln usually read aloud. This habit often annoyed Herndon, who found it distracting in their small law office. Lincoln explained why he did it: "When I read aloud, two senses catch the idea: first, I see what I read; second, I hear it, and therefore can remember it better."[20]

Reading aloud and writing out passages imprinted ideas in Lincoln's mind. Associates marveled at the power of his memory. When a friend mentioned that it seemed easy for Lincoln to remember things, he responded, "No ... you are mistaken—I am slow to learn and slow to forget that which I have learned—My mind is like a piece of steel, very hard to scratch any thing on it and almost impossible after you get it there to rub it out."[21]

The words engraved on Lincoln's mind came as much from listening as from reading. To a great extent, Lincoln's reading habits grew out of keen listening. In a sense, he listened to books as he did conversations. As president he told an acquaintance that "after hearing the neighbors talk of an evening with my father ... I can remember going to my little bedroom, and spending the night ... trying to make out what was the exact meaning of some of their, to me, dark sayings. I could not sleep ... until I had put it in language plain enough, as I thought, for any boy I knew to comprehend. This was a kind of passion with me, and it has stuck by me."[22]

Of course, Lincoln did not confine his listening to the log cabin. "He would hear sermons preached," Sarah Lincoln remembered, "come home—take the children out—get on a stump or log and almost repeat it word for

[18]Sarah Lincoln interview, September 8, 1865, *Herndon's Informants,* 107.

[19]Robert B. Rutledge to William H. Herndon, December 4, 1866, *Herndon's Informants,* 497.

[20]William H. Herndon and Jesse K. Weik, *Herndon's Lincoln: The True Story of a Great Life* (3 vols.; Chicago, 1889), II, 332.

[21]Joshua F. Speed to William H. Herndon, December 8, 1866, *Herndon's Informants,* 499.

[22]Francis B. Carpenter, *Six Months at the White House with Abraham Lincoln: The Story of a Picture* (New York, 1866), 312–13.

word."[23] By dramatizing his command of language, Lincoln pretended to exhort his small flock with holy words. The fun and glory were irresistible, as was the welcome alternative to farmwork. By stump preaching, Lincoln launched his apprenticeship as a wordsmith.

Lincoln's apprenticeship took him wherever he could hear people talking, arguing, and laughing. He listened to his father and other men swap tales at the stable, the mill, the spring, the crossroads, and the whiskey barrel. He crowded into rustic courtrooms and listened to people plead their cases, parsing their personal stories by rules of law and local standards of justice. He listened to politicians explain why they deserved to be elected. Dennis Hanks said that he and Lincoln "learned by sight—scent & hearing—We heard all that was said & talked over & over the questions [we] heard—wore them slick—greasy and threadbare."[24]

Not satisfied to listen and discuss, Lincoln projected himself into the leading role of persuader, just as he had after church. A relative recalled that Lincoln "would gather the children together Mount a stump or Log & harang his juvenile audience" with a political speech.[25] Lincoln's long apprenticeship at stump speaking meant that in 1832, when he first ran for the Illinois legislature, he had plenty of practice giving, according to a friend, "what the world would call an awkward speech, but . . . a powerful one, cutting the centre Evry shot."[26]

Not content to stand in the back of a courtroom listening to lawsuits, Lincoln began to "Pettifog before [the] Justice of the Peace" shortly after moving to New Salem.[27] Although he had no legal credentials, an old book of Illinois laws and the countless disputes he had witnessed made him enough of a lawyer to argue cases for his neighbors, for free. A New Salem resident recalled that "the manner in which . . . [Lincoln] used to force his law arguments upon . . . [the local magistrate] was both amuseing and instructive, so laconic often as to produce a spasmatic shaking of the verry fat sides of the old law functionary of New Salem . . . but in a short time [the magistrate] was led to pay great respect to [Lincoln's] powers of mind in a forensic point of view."[28]

A courtroom advocate long before he was a lawyer, a stump speaker

[23]Ibid.
[24]Dennis Hanks interview, September 8, 1865, *Herndon's Informants,* 105.
[25]A. H. Chapman statement, before September 8, 1865, *Herndon's Informants,* 102.
[26]William G. Greene interview, May 30, 1865, *Herndon's Informants,* 20.
[27]Ibid.
[28]Jason Duncan to William H. Herndon, [late 1866-early 1867], *Herndon's Informants,* 540.

long before he was a political candidate, Lincoln also had a long apprenticeship in the art of storytelling. He soaked up jokes, yarns, and scandals from every source. He drew from his bottomless reservoir of stories all his life, on the stump, in the courtroom, and later in the White House. More than any other single trait, Lincoln's associates recalled his ability to tell a funny story. He once described laughter as "the joyous, beautiful, universal evergreen of life."[29] He delighted in condensing a telling observation into a witty quip. For example, he described a lawyer blathering to a Chicago jury as a person who "can concentrate more words into the fewest ideas of any man I ever knew."[30] In 1862, when a friend described General George B. McClellan's massive encampment as the Army of the Potomac, Lincoln replied, "No, you are mistaken; that is General McClellan's bodyguard."[31] In 1863, he told one of his secretaries that he intended to pardon soldiers sentenced to be executed for cowardice because "it would frighten the poor devils too terribly to shoot them."[32]

Beyond sharing a laugh with his audience, Lincoln used stories to illustrate his ideas. An Indiana neighbor pointed out that Lincoln "argued much from Analogy and Explained things hard for us to understand by stories ... that we might instantly see the force & bearing of what he said."[33] Lincoln's stories bridged the abstract ideas of books and laws to everyday lives. Stories made common sense out of uncommon ideas. Stories deployed a vocabulary of experience rather than professional expertise. With stories, Lincoln built the foundation for persuasion and consent. During the Civil War, he told a Republican leader, "I have found in the course of a long experience that common people ... are more easily influenced and informed through the medium of a broad illustration than in any other way, and as to what the hyper-critical few may think, I don't care."[34]

Lincoln's stories contributed to the frequent impression among genteel, educated people that he was a hayseed, an impression reinforced by his mannerisms and appearance. Even in rustic New Salem, Lincoln's "Manors

[29]John G. Nicolay, "Lincoln's Literary Experiments," *Century Magazine,* 47 (April 1894), 832.

[30]John M. Palmer, ed., *The Bench and Bar of Illinois* (2 vols.; Chicago, 1899), II, 642–43.

[31]Lincoln quoted in Don E. Fehrenbacher and Virginia Fehrenbacher, eds., *Recollected Words of Abraham Lincoln* (Stanford, 1996), 201.

[32]Tyler Dennet, ed., *Lincoln and the Civil War in the Diaries and Letters of John Hay* (New York, 1939), 68–69.

[33]Nathaniel Grigsby interview, September 12, 1865, *Herndon's Informants,* 114–15.

[34]Quoted in Herbert Joseph Edwards and John Erskine Hankins, *Lincoln the Writer* (Orono, Maine, 1962), 26.

wer what might be termined Back[w]oodish," one of the village's one hundred residents remembered.[35] A lawyer recalled that when he first saw Lincoln in court in 1854, "he had the appearance of a rough intelligent farmer."[36] Lincoln sometimes poked fun at his looks. In 1863 when a photographer at Mathew Brady's studio asked Lincoln to just look natural, Lincoln quipped, "That is what I would like to avoid."[37]

Appearances, of course, can be deceiving. Leonard Swett, an eminent Illinois attorney and Lincoln's longtime friend and frequent courtroom adversary, declared that Lincoln was "considered by the people of this country as a frank, guileless, unsophisticated man. There never was a greater mistake."[38] As another lawyer and old friend said, Lincoln "was an artful man and yet his art had all the appearance of simple mindedness."[39] Having witnessed Lincoln try many cases, Swett observed, "Any man who took Lincoln for a simple minded man would very soon wake [up] with his back in a ditch."[40]

Behind Lincoln's courtroom artfulness lay careful preparation that continued through his presidential years. Swett noted that when Lincoln appeared in court, "the first impression he generally conveyed was, that he had stated the case of his adversary better and more forcibly, than his opponent could state it himself. . . . The force of his logic was in conveying to the minds of others the same clear and thorough analysis he had in his own."[41] In many ways, Lincoln's style of argument was an outgrowth of his reading habit of distilling every subject to its essence. He confided to a congressman in 1863 that "a peculiarity of his own life from his earliest manhood had been that he habitually studied the opposite side of every disputed question, of every law case, of every political issue, more exhaustively, if possible, than his own side . . . [with] the result . . . that in all his long practice at the bar he had never once been surprised in court by the strength of his adversary's case, often finding it much weaker than he had feared."[42]

The style of analysis Lincoln deployed in his legal arguments pervaded his writings and speeches. In an age of inflated political rhetoric, Lincoln

[35]William G. Greene to William H. Herndon, December 20, 1865, *Herndon's Informants,* 145.
[36]Henry C. Whitney statement, [1887?], *Herndon's Informants,* 648.
[37]Lincoln quoted in Fehrenbacher and Fehrenbacher, eds., *Recollected Words,* 126.
[38]Leonard Swett to William H. Herndon, January 17, 1866, *Herndon's Informants,* 168.
[39]Joseph Gillespie to William H. Herndon, December 8, 1866, *Herndon's Informants,* 507.
[40]Leonard Swett statement included in Henry C. Whitney to William H. Herndon, August 29, 1887, *Herndon's Informants,* 636.
[41]Leonard Swett to William H. Herndon, January 17, 1866, *Herndon's Informants,* 167.
[42]Rice, ed., *Reminiscences of Abraham Lincoln,* 333–34.

valued reason. "Reason," he declared in a speech in 1838, "cold, calculating, unimpassioned reason, must furnish all the materials for our future support and defence."[43] Although Lincoln was capable of unsurpassed eloquence—in the Gettysburg Address and Second Inaugural, for example—for the most part his language was lean, plain, and direct. As a lawyer friend observed, Lincoln "confined himself to a dry bold statement of his point and then worked away with sledge hammer logic at making out his case."[44] Lincoln's rhetorical style reflected the clarity and precision of his thought. In general, he chose words with unusual care to say just what he meant, no more, no less. During his presidency, Lincoln commented, "It is very common in this country to find great facility of expression and less common to find great lucidity of thought. The combination of the two in one person is very uncommon but whenever you do find it, you have a great man."[45] Perhaps half-consciously, Lincoln described himself.

Lincoln's lifelong habit of writing contributed to the clarity of his thought. In addition to writing out passages from his reading, Lincoln told a New Salem friend that "the way he learned to write so well & so distinctly & precisely" was by writing "friendly confidential letters" for illiterate neighbors after the Lincolns moved from Kentucky to Indiana. By writing those letters, he said, "his perceptions were sharpened—he learnd to see other people['s] thoughts and feelings and ideas."[46] During his presidency, Lincoln often crystallized his thoughts by writing them down. Major speeches he painstakingly wrote and rewrote.[47] He never wrote a book, although his famous debates with Stephen A. Douglas were published in book form. He wrote a number of anonymous, mostly satirical pieces for the Springfield newspaper.[48] But mostly he wrote speeches, letters, and—once he became president—official documents.

[43]See Lincoln's "Address to the Young Men's Lyceum of Springfield, Illinois," January 27, 1838, in chapter 1. *CW,* I, 115.

[44]Joseph Gillespie to William H. Herndon, December 8, 1866, *Herndon's Informants,* 508. On the utilitarian nature of Lincoln's rhetoric as well as the difficulty of determining precisely what he said, see Don E. Fehrenbacher, "The Words of Lincoln," in Fehrenbacher, *Lincoln in Text and Context: Collected Essays* (Stanford, 1987), 270–86.

[45]Edward Dicey, "Washington during the War," *Macmillan's Magazine,* 6 (May 1862), 24.

[46]Mentor Graham interview, [1865–66], *Herndon's Informants,* 450.

[47]See, for example, Harold Holzer, "Avoid Saying 'Foolish Things': The Legacy of Lincoln's Impromptu Oratory," in James M. McPherson, ed., *"We Cannot Escape History": Lincoln and the Last Best Hope of Earth* (Urbana, 1995), 105–23; Roy P. Basler, "Lincoln's Development as a Writer," in Basler, *Abraham Lincoln: His Speeches and Writings* (Cleveland, 1946), 1–49.

[48]See, for example, Douglas L. Wilson, *Honor's Voice: The Transformation of Abraham Lincoln* (New York, 1998), 298–304.

Lincoln declared that writing—"the art of communicating thoughts to the mind, through the eye—is the great invention of the world ... great, very great in enabling us to converse with the dead, the absent, and the unborn, at all distances of time and space."[49] Printing enormously expanded the range of writing by communicating to thousands what had been previously available only to a few. Before printing, Lincoln declared, "the great mass of men ... were utterly unconscious, that their conditions, or their minds were capable of improvement.... To immancipate the mind from this false and under estimate of itself, is the great task which printing came into the world to perform."[50]

Most Americans, of course, never saw Lincoln or heard him speak. But printing brought his ideas to millions. Published in newspapers throughout the North, Lincoln's writings and speeches were widely read, discussed, and criticized. "The image of the man went out with his words," the famous abolitionist Frederick Douglass observed, "and those who read them knew him."[51] If Lincoln had not become president, he would have remained a gifted but obscure Illinois lawyer, forgotten by all but a small circle of friends and relatives. Yet Lincoln's words, along with a concatenation of many other developments, elevated him to the presidency. In the Civil War's fourth year, Lincoln mused, "It is strange that I, a boy brought up in the woods, and seeing, as it were, but little of the world, should be drifted to the very apex of this great event."[52] That boy brought up in the woods had become a master wordsmith by a lifelong apprenticeship of reading, speaking, and writing. Because he was president, his words about slavery and the Civil War had profound influence then and still. Above all, his words helped fashion the popular consent upon which his presidency depended. Rather than a rail-splitter, Lincoln should be remembered as a wordsmith whose language did more than that of any president since Thomas Jefferson to define the meaning of America.

[49]"Second Lecture on Discoveries and Inventions," February 11, 1859, *CW,* 359–60.
[50]Ibid., 362–63.
[51]Frederick Douglass, "Oration in Memory of Abraham Lincoln," April 14, 1876, in Philip S. Foner, ed., *The Life and Writings of Frederick Douglass* (4 vols.; New York, 1955), IV, 315. I am indebted to David Rankin for this quotation.
[52]Lincoln quoted in Fehrenbacher and Fehrenbacher, eds., *Recollected Words,* 31.

A NOTE ABOUT THE TEXT

The texts reprinted here follow the superb edition of Lincoln's works prepared by Roy P. Basler and published nearly a half-century ago in 1953.[53] Basler's edition was the first to have access to the massive collection of Lincoln papers, which were not made available for study until July 26, 1947, twenty-one years after the death of Lincoln's son, Robert Todd Lincoln.[54] Scholars accept Basler's edition as definitive except for a few relatively minor typographic or transcription errors. Many documents are published here in full, but to conserve space I have often abridged documents, trying always to preserve both the substance and the flavor of the complete text. Lincoln's spelling was better than that of most Americans in the mid-nineteenth century, but incorrectly spelled words repeatedly crept into his writing. For example, he frequently wrote the contraction *it's* when the context makes clear that he meant the possessive form, *its.* Throughout this volume, I have preserved Lincoln's spelling as presented in Basler's *Collected Works* and have not used [sic] to alert readers that I am aware of a misspelled word. When Basler suggests alternative readings of a word or phrase, I have silently chosen one that seems to me preferable. For purposes of clarity, I have occasionally inserted a word or two in brackets— [for example]—into Lincoln's text. While remaining faithful to Lincoln's words, punctuation, and capitalization, I have made the following alterations to the format of the documents: each date has been standardized to a month, day, and year style (for example, July 4, 1863) and raised above the text of the document; the place from which Lincoln wrote a document (for example, Washington, D.C.) has been printed flush to the right margin; if Lincoln used a closing in a document (for example, *Yours truly*), it has been placed flush to the right margin; if Lincoln signed a document, his signature has been printed in small capital letters below his closing (if there is one) and flush to the right margin. Readers can easily consult the full text of any document abridged in this collection or omitted from it since the Basler edition is widely available in libraries large and small.

[53]Roy P. Basler, Marion Dolores Pratt, and Lloyd A. Dunlap, eds., *The Collected Works of Abraham Lincoln* (8 vols.; New Brunswick, N.J., 1953); Roy P. Basler, ed., *The Collected Works of Abraham Lincoln, Supplement, 1832–1865* (Westport, Conn., 1974); Roy P. Basler and Christian O. Basler, eds., *The Collected Works of Abraham Lincoln, Second Supplement, 1848–1865* (New Brunswick, N.J., 1990). Hereafter, *The Collected Works* are cited in abbreviated form as *CW,* with the appropriate volume and page numbers.

[54]See Merrill D. Peterson, *Lincoln in American Memory* (New York, 1994), 258–70, 327–28.

In addition, all of Lincoln's collected works are available on-line at *<www. alincolnassoc.com>*. A great deal of related material can also be found at Lincoln/Net (*<lincoln.lib.niu.edu>*), the creation of a consortium of research institutions headquartered at Northern Illinois University. Ideally, this edition of Lincoln's writings and speeches will stimulate readers to turn to these and other resources to learn more about Lincoln and his times.

1

Lessons of Life

Like most people, Abraham Lincoln translated his personal experiences into basic rules for living. And like most people, Lincoln did not jot down the rules in a diary or preserve them in a memoir. Instead, he tried to live by them. But certain lessons of life were so central to Lincoln's understanding of himself and his world that they surfaced in his public speeches and private correspondence. The documents in this chapter disclose some of the most important lessons Lincoln learned from life.

Lincoln tended to view his life as a source of lessons for other Americans. Like him, most Americans had not been born into families that enjoyed wealth, privilege, or security. His achievements, he believed, exemplified what a white man could make of himself in the free society of the United States. Although Lincoln was not a self-righteous, preachy, or moralistic person, he believed that other people could succeed if they behaved more or less as he did. Lincoln interpreted his life history—which he acknowledged was a story of both disappointments and successes—as a template for farmers and common laborers, the penniless and the uneducated. Part of Lincoln's political appeal came from his ability to put into words his deep faith that work, education, and freedom would overcome setbacks—a faith shared by many other Americans.

AUTOBIOGRAPHIES

Lincoln wrote two autobiographical statements on the eve of the 1860 presidential campaign. He composed the first just before Christmas 1859 when he was being mentioned as a possible presidential candidate. In response to a request from Jesse W. Fell, an old acquaintance from Illinois, Lincoln penned a brief summary of his life that was published in a Pennsylvania newspaper in February 1860 and was subsequently copied by many other

Republican newspapers. Fell's inquiry and the eager reprinting of the information it elicited show that Lincoln was not yet well known outside Illinois.

Six months later, a few weeks after he had been chosen as the Republican nominee for president, Lincoln wrote a second, more detailed autobiography. Now, he needed to introduce himself to citizens throughout the nation. He prepared this account for a campaign biography, to be published by the *Chicago Press and Tribune,* that would circulate widely during the presidential contest.

Both autobiographies reveal something of Lincoln's attitudes about his early life and his determination to escape it. Both describe his humble origins and quietly call attention to his remarkable ascent to political prominence. Both display his disarming, self-deprecating charm. Scholars have corroborated the accuracy of Lincoln's accounts, but readers should remain alert to what he left vague or unsaid as well as what he chose to emphasize. After all, both autobiographies craft some of the facts of Lincoln's life into a political statement intended to appeal to the electorate. Note, for example, what Lincoln chose to say about his thriving law practice and about his experience with slaves.

Letter to Jesse W. Fell
December 20, 1859

                                                        Springfield, [Illinois]
J. W. Fell, Esq
My dear Sir:
Herewith is a little sketch, as you requested. There is not much of it, for the reason, I suppose, that there is not much of me.

If any thing be made out of it, I wish it to be modest, and not to go beyond the material. If it were thought necessary to incorporate any thing from any of my speeches, I suppose there would be no objection. Of course it must not appear to have been written by myself.

                                                        Yours very truly
                                                        A. LINCOLN

I was born Feb. 12, 1809, in Hardin County, Kentucky. My parents were both born in Virginia, of undistinguished families—second families, perhaps I should say. My mother, who died in my tenth year, was of a family of the name of Hanks, some of whom now reside in Adams, and others in Macon counties, Illinois. My paternal grandfather, Abraham Lincoln, emigrated from Rockingham County, Virginia, to Kentucky, about 1781 or 2, where, a year or two later, he was killed by indians, not in battle, but by stealth, when he was laboring to open a farm in the forest. His ancestors, who were quakers, went to Virginia from Berks County, Pennsylvania. . . .

My father, at the death of his father, was but six years of age; and he grew up, litterally without education. He removed from Kentucky to what is now Spencer county, Indiana, in my eighth year. We reached our new home about the time the State came into the Union. It was a wild region, with many bears and other wild animals still in the woods. There I grew up. There were some schools, so called; but no qualification was ever required of a teacher, beyond *"readin, writin, and cipherin,"* to the Rule of Three.[1] If a straggler supposed to understand latin, happened to sojourn in the neighborhood, he was looked upon as a wizzard. There was absolutely nothing to excite ambition for education. Of course when I came of age I did not know much. Still somehow, I could read, write, and cipher to the Rule of Three; but that was all. I have not been to school since. The little advance I now have upon this store of education, I have picked up from time to time under the pressure of necessity.

I was raised to farm work, which I continued till I was twenty two. At twenty one I came to Illinois, and passed the first year in Illinois—Macon county. Then I got to New-Salem, (at that time in Sangamon, now in Menard county [Illinois]), where I remained a year as a sort of Clerk in a store. Then came the Black-Hawk war;[2] and I was elected a Captain of Volunteers—a success which gave me more pleasure than any I have had since. I went the campaign, was elated, ran for the Legislature the same year (1832) and was beaten—the only time I have been beaten by the people. The next, and three succeeding biennial elections, I was elected to the Legislature. I was not a candidate afterwards. During this Legislative period I had studied law, and removed to Springfield to practice it. In 1846 I was once elected to the lower House of Congress. Was not a candidate for re-election. From 1849 to 1854, both inclusive, practiced law more assiduously than ever before. Always a whig in politics, and generally on the whig electoral tickets, making active canvasses. I was losing interest in politics, when the repeal of the Missouri Compromise[3] aroused me again. What I have done since then is pretty well known.

[1] The Rule of Three involved an understanding of fractions and ratios.

[2] The Black Hawk War resulted from the encroachment of white settlers on land west of the Mississippi that an 1830 treaty had reserved for the Sauk and Fox Indians. Led by Black Hawk, the Sauk and Fox refused to cede their land, triggering a war that ended with the massacre of the Indians.

[3] The Missouri Compromise of 1820 outlawed slavery north of 36° 30' latitude in territory acquired in the Louisiana Purchase. In 1854, Stephen A. Douglas, U.S. senator from Illinois, sponsored passage of the Kansas-Nebraska Act, which repealed the prohibition of slavery in this territory.

If any personal description of me is thought desirable, it may be said, I am, in height, six feet, four inches, nearly; lean in flesh, weighing, on an average, one hundred and eighty pounds; dark complexion, with coarse black hair, and grey eyes—no other marks or brands recollected.

Yours very truly
A. Lincoln

Autobiography Written for the 1860 Presidential Campaign

Circa June 1860

Abraham Lincoln was born Feb. 12, 1809, then in Hardin, now in the more recently formed county of Larue, Kentucky. His father, Thomas, & grandfather, Abraham, were born in Rockingham county Virginia, whither their ancestors had come from Berks county Pennsylvania. His lineage has been traced no farther back than this. The family were originally quakers, though in later times they have fallen away from the peculiar habits of that people. . . . Abraham, grandfather of the subject of this sketch, came to Kentucky, and was killed by indians about the year 1784. He left a widow, three sons and two daughters. . . . Thomas, the youngest son, and father of the present subject, by the early death of his father, and very narrow circumstances of his mother, even in childhood was a wandering laboring boy, and grew up litterally without education. He never did more in the way of writing than to bunglingly sign his own name. Before he was grown, he passed one year as a hired hand with his uncle Isaac on Wataga, a branch of the Holsteen River [in southwestern Virginia]. Getting back into Kentucky, and having reached his 28th. year, he married Nancy Hanks—mother of the present subject—in the year 1806. She also was born in Virginia; and relatives of hers of the name of Hanks, and of other names, now reside in Coles, in Macon, and in Adams counties, Illinois, and also in Iowa. The present subject has no brother or sister of the whole or half blood. He had a sister,[4] older than himself, who was grown and married, but died many years ago, leaving no child. Also a brother,[5] younger than himself, who died in infancy. Before leaving Kentucky he and his sister were sent for short periods, to A.B.C. schools.[6] . . .

At this time his father resided on Knob-creek, on the road from Bardstown Ky. to Nashville Tenn. at a point three, or three and a half miles South or South-West of Atherton's ferry on the Rolling Fork. From this place he removed to what is now Spencer county Indiana, in the autumn of 1816, A.

[4]Sarah Lincoln, born in 1807, died during childbirth in 1828.
[5]Thomas Lincoln died in 1812, the year of his birth.
[6]That is, schools that taught the alphabet and elementary reading and writing.

then being in his eigth year. This removal was partly on account of slavery; but chiefly on account of the difficulty in land titles in Ky. He settled in an unbroken forest; and the clearing away of surplus wood was the great task a head. A. though very young, was large of his age, and had an axe put into his hands at once; and from that till within his twentythird year, he was almost constantly handling that most useful instrument—less, of course, in plowing and harvesting seasons. At this place A. took an early start as a hunter, which was never much improved afterwards. (A few days before the completion of his eigth year, in the absence of his father, a flock of wild turkeys approached the new log-cabin, and A. with a rifle gun, standing inside, shot through a crack, and killed one of them. He has never since pulled a trigger on any larger game.) In the autumn of 1818 his mother died; and a year afterwards his father married Mrs. Sally Johnston, at Elizabeth-Town, Ky—a widow, with three children of her first marriage.[7] She proved a good and kind mother to A. and is still living in Coles Co. Illinois. There were no children of this second marriage. His father's residence continued at the same place in Indiana, till 1830. While here A. went to A.B.C. schools by littles. . . . A. now thinks that the agregate of all his schooling did not amount to one year. He was never in a college or Academy as a student; and never inside of a college or accademy building till since he had a law-license. What he has in the way of education, he has picked up. After he was twenty-three, and had separated from his father, he studied English grammar, imperfectly of course, but so as to speak and write as well as he now does. He studied and nearly mastered the Six-books of Euclid, since he was a member of Congress. He regrets his want of education, and does what he can to supply the want. In his tenth year he was kicked by a horse, and apparently killed for a time. When he was nineteen, still residing in Indiana, he made his first trip upon a flat-boat to New-Orleans. He was a hired hand merely; and he and a son of the owner, without other assistance, made the trip. The nature of part of the cargo-load, as it was called—made it necessary for them to linger and trade along the Sugar coast[8]—and one night they were attacked by seven negroes with intent to kill and rob them. They were hurt some in the melee, but succeeded in driving the negroes from the boat, and then "cut cable" "weighed anchor" and left.

March 1st. 1830—A. having just completed his 21st. year, his father and family, with the families of the two daughters and sons-in-law, of his step-mother, left the old homestead in Indiana, and came to Illinois. Their mode of conveyance was waggons drawn by ox-teams, or A. drove one of the teams. They reached the county of Macon, and stopped there some time within the same month of March. His father and family settled a new place on the North side of the Sangamon river, at the junction of the timber-land and prairie, about ten miles Westerly from Decatur. Here they built a log-cabin,

[7]Sarah (Sally) Bush Johnston's three children were Elizabeth Johnston (born 1807), John D. Johnston (born 1810), and Matilda Johnston (born 1811).
[8]Sugar plantations lined the lower Mississippi in Louisiana.

into which they removed, and made sufficient of rails to fence ten acres of ground, fenced and broke the ground, and raised a crop of sown corn upon it the same year. These are, or are supposed to be, the rails about which so much is being said just now, though they are far from being the first, or only rails ever made by A.

The sons-in-law were temporarily settled at other places in the county. In the autumn all hands were greatly afflicted with augue and fever, to which they had not been used, and by which they were greatly discouraged—so much so that they determined on leaving the county. They remained however, through the succeeding winter, which was the winter of the very celebrated "deep snow" of Illinois. During that winter, A. together with his step-mother's son, John D. Johnston, and John Hanks,[9] yet residing in Macon county, hired themselves to one Denton Offutt, to take a flat boat from Beardstown Illinois to New-Orleans; and for that purpose, were to join him— Offut—at Springfield, Ills so soon as the snow should go off. When it did go off which was about the 1st. of March 1831—the county was so flooded, as to make traveling by land impracticable; to obviate which difficulty they purchased a large canoe and came down the Sangamon river in it. This is the time and the manner of A's first entrance into Sangamon County. They found Offutt at Springfield, but learned from him that he had failed in getting a boat at Beardstown. This lead to their hiring themselves to him at $12 per month, each; and getting the timber out of the trees and building a boat at old Sangamon Town on the Sangamon river, seven miles N.W. of Springfield, which boat they took to New-Orleans, substantially upon the old contract. It was in connection with this boat that occurred the ludicrous incident of sewing up the hogs eyes. Offutt bought thirty odd large fat live hogs, but found difficulty in driving them from where he purchased them to the boat, and thereupon conceived the whim that he could sew up their eyes and drive them where he pleased. No sooner thought of than decided, he put his hands, including A. at the job, which they completed—all but the driving. In their blind condition they could not be driven out of the lot or field they were in. This expedient failing, they were tied and hauled on carts to the boat. It was near the Sangamon River, within what is now Menard county.

During this boat enterprize acquaintance with Offutt, who was previously an entire stranger, he conceved a liking for A. and believing he could turn him [Lincoln] to account, he contracted with him [Lincoln] to act as clerk for him, on his return from New-Orleans, in charge of a store and Mill at New-Salem, then in Sangamon, now in Menard county. . . . A's father, with his own family & others mentioned, had, in pursuance of their intention, removed from Macon to Coles county. John D. Johnston, the step-mother's son, went to them; and A. stopped indefinitely, and, for the first time, as it were, by himself at New-Salem. . . . This was in July 1831. Here he rapidly made acquaintances and friends. In less than a year Offutt's business was failing—had

[9]Hanks was Lincoln's cousin.

almost failed,—when the Black-Hawk war of 1832—broke out. A joined a volunteer company, and to his own surprize, was elected captain of it. He says he has not since had any success in life which gave him so much satisfaction. He went the campaign, served near three months, met the ordinary hardships of such an expedition, but was in no battle. He now owns in Iowa, the land upon which his own warrants for this service, were located. Returning from the campaign, and encouraged by his great popularity among his immediate neighbors, he, the same year, ran for the Legislature and was beaten—his own precinct, however, casting it's votes 277 for and 7, against him. And this too while he was an avowed Clay[10] man, and the precinct the autumn afterwards, giving a majority of 115 to Genl. Jackson[11] over Mr. Clay. This was the only time A was ever beaten on a direct vote of the people. He was now without means and out of business, but was anxious to remain with his friends who had treated him with so much generosity, especially as he had nothing elsewhere to go to. He studied what he should do—thought of learning the black-smith trade—thought of trying to study law—rather thought he could not succeed at that without a better education. Before long, strangely enough, a man offered to sell and did sell, to A. and another as poor as himself, an old stock of goods, upon credit. They opened as merchants; and he says that was *the* store. Of course they did nothing but get deeper and deeper in debt. He was appointed Postmaster at New-Salem—the office being too insignificant, to make his politics an objection. The store winked out. The Surveyor of Sangamon, offered to depute to A that portion of his work which was within his part of the county. He accepted, procured a compass and chain, studied Flint, and Gibson[12] a little, and went at it. This procured bread, and kept soul and body together. The election of 1834 came, and he was then elected to the Legislature by the highest vote cast for any candidate. Major John T. Stuart,[13] then in full practice of the law, was also elected. During the canvass, in a private conversation he encouraged A. to study law. After the election he borrowed books of Stuart, took them home with him, and went at it in good earnest. He studied with nobody. He still mixed in the surveying to pay board and clothing bills. When the Legislature met, the law books were dropped, but were taken up again at the end of the session. He was re-elected in 1836, 1838, and 1840. In the autumn of 1836 he obtained a law licence, and on April 15, 1837 removed to Springfield, and commenced the practice, his old friend, Stuart taking him into partnership. March 3rd. 1837, by a protest entered upon the Ills. House Journal of that date ... A. with Dan Stone, another representative of Sangamon, briefly defined his position on

[10]Henry Clay was the Whig candidate in the 1832 presidential election.

[11]Andrew Jackson, a Democrat, was re-elected president in 1832.

[12]Flint and Gibson authored practical guides to surveying.

[13]During the Black Hawk War, Lincoln served in the same battalion as Stuart, an established lawyer in Springfield.

the slavery question; and so far as it goes, it was then the same that it is now.[14] ... In 1838, & 1840 Mr. L's party in the Legislature voted for him as Speaker; but being in the minority, he was not elected. After 1840 he declined a re-election to the Legislature. He was on the Harrison[15] electoral ticket in 1840, and on that of Clay[16] in 1844, and spent much time and labor in both those canvasses. In Nov. 1842 he was married to Mary,[17] daughter of Robert S. Todd, of Lexington, Kentucky. They have three living children, all sons— one[18] born in 1843, one[19] in 1850, and one[20] in 1853. They lost one,[21] who was born in 1846. In 1846, he [Lincoln] was elected to the lower House of Congress, and served one term only, commencing in Dec. 1847 and ending with the inauguration of Gen. Taylor,[22] in March 1849. All the battles of the Mexican war had been fought before Mr. L. took his seat in congress, but the American army was still in Mexico, and the treaty of peace was not fully and formally ratified till the June afterwards. Much has been said of his course in Congress in regard to this war. A careful examination of the Journals and Congressional Globe shows, that he voted for all the supply measures which came up, and for all the measures in any way favorable to the officers, soldiers, and their families, who conducted the war through; with this exception that some of these measures passed without yeas and nays, leaving no record as to how particular men voted. The Journals and Globe also show him voting that the war was unnecessarily and unconstitutionally begun by the President[23] of the United States. This is the language of Mr. Ashmun's[24] amendment, for which Mr. L. and nearly or quite all, other whigs of the H. R.[25] voted.

Mr. L's reasons for the opinion expressed by this vote were briefly that the President had sent Genl. Taylor into an inhabited part of the country belonging to Mexico, and not to the U.S. and thereby had provoked the first

[14]The protest filed by Lincoln and Stone declared, "They believe that the institution of slavery is founded on both injustice and bad policy; but that the promulgation of abolition doctrines tends rather to increase than to abate its evils. They believe that the Congress of the United States has no power, under the constitution, to interfere with the institution of slavery in the different States. They believe that the Congress of the United States has the power, under the constitution to abolish slavery in the District of Columbia; but that that power ought not to be exercised unless at the request of the people of said District." *CW,* I, 74–75.

[15]William Henry Harrison was the Whig candidate in the 1840 presidential election.

[16]Henry Clay was the Whig candidate in the 1844 presidential election.

[17]Mary Ann Todd was born in Kentucky in 1818; her parents were socially prominent and owned numerous slaves.

[18]Robert Todd Lincoln.

[19]William (Willie) Wallace Lincoln.

[20]Thomas (Tad) Lincoln.

[21]Edward Baker Lincoln died in 1850.

[22]Zachary Taylor, the Whig candidate, was elected president in 1848.

[23]James K. Polk, a Democrat, was elected president in 1844.

[24]George Ashmun was a congressman from Massachusetts.

[25]House of Representatives.

act of hostility—in fact the commencement of the war; that the place, being the country bordering on the East bank of the Rio Grande, was inhabited by native Mexicans, born there under the Mexican government; and had never submitted to, nor been conquered by Texas, or the U.S. nor transferred to either by treaty—that although Texas claimed the Rio Grande as her boundary, Mexico had never recognized it, the people on the ground had never recognized it, and neither Texas nor the U.S. had ever enforced it—that there was a broad desert between that, and the country over which Texas had actual control—that the country where hostilities commenced, having once belonged to Mexico, must remain so, until it was somehow legally transferred, which had never been done.

Mr. L. thought the act of sending an armed force among the Mexicans, was *unnecessary,* inasmuch as Mexico was in no way molesting, or menacing the U.S. or the people thereof; and that it was *unconstitutional,* because the power of levying war is vested in Congress, and not in the President. He thought the principal motive for the act, was to divert public attention from the surrender of "Fifty-four, forty, or fight" to Great Brittain, on the Oregon boundary question.[26]

Mr. L. was not a candidate for re-election. This was determined upon, and declared before he went to Washington, in accordance with an understanding among whig friends. . . .

In 1848, during his term in congress, he advocated Gen. Taylor's nomination for the Presidency, in opposition to all others, and also took an active part for his election, after his nomination—speaking a few times in Maryland, near Washington, several times in Massachusetts, and canvassing quite fully his own district in Illinois, which was followed by a majority in the district of over 1500 for Gen. Taylor.

Upon his return from Congress he went to the practice of the law with greater earnestness than ever before. In 1852 he was upon the Scott[27] electoral ticket, and did something in the way of canvassing, but owing to the hopelessness of the cause in Illinois, he did less than in previous presidential canvasses.

In 1854, his profession had almost superseded the thought of politics in his mind, when the repeal of the Missouri compromise aroused him as he had never been before.

In the autumn of that year he took the stump with no broader practical aim or object than to secure, if possible, the re-election of Hon Richard Yates[28] to congress. His speeches at once attracted a more marked attention than they had ever before done. As the canvass proceeded, he was drawn to

[26] An 1846 treaty between Britain and the United States set the northern boundary of Oregon territory at 49° latitude, rather than much farther north at 54°40' latitude, deeper into land claimed by the British.

[27] Winfield Scott was the Whig candidate in the 1852 presidential election.

[28] Richard Yates was an Illinois Whig who opposed the Kansas-Nebraska Act.

different parts of the state, outside of Mr. Yates' district. He did not abandon the law, but gave his attention, by turns, to that and politics....

AMBITION

In his autobiographies, Lincoln portrayed himself as a self-made man who overcame the poverty and ignorance that handicapped so many Americans. He did not emphasize the ambition that drove him to better himself or the tireless work with which he pursued his goals. His law partner in Springfield, William H. Herndon, called Lincoln's ambition "a little engine that knew no rest."[29] Lincoln himself seldom spoke candidly about his relentless drive. For the most part, his behavior did the talking. But more than two decades before he wrote his autobiographies, Lincoln discussed ambition in two statements that revealed both his longings and his concerns.

In March 1832, less than a month after his twenty-third birthday and only six months after arriving in New Salem, Lincoln announced his candidacy for the Illinois legislature in his first known published writing, which appeared in the *Sangamo Journal*. He declared his support for making the Sangamon River navigable, controlling interest rates on loans, and providing public education. He concluded with a blunt assessment of his aims and prospects.

[29]Paul M. Angle, ed., *Herndon's Life of Lincoln* (New York, 1930), 304.

To the People of Sangamo County
March 9, 1832

New Salem
... Every man is said to have his peculiar ambition. Whether it be true or not, I can say for one that I have no other so great as that of being truly esteemed of my fellow men, by rendering myself worthy of their esteem. How far I shall succeed in gratifying this ambition, is yet to be developed. I am young and unknown to many of you. I was born and have ever remained in the most humble walks of life. I have no wealthy or popular relations to recommend me. My case is thrown exclusively upon the independent voters of this county, and if elected they will have conferred a favor upon me, for which I shall be unremitting in my labors to compensate. But if the good

people in their wisdom shall see fit to keep me in the background, I have been too familiar with disappointments to be very much chagrined.

Your friend and fellow-citizen,

A. Lincoln.

Almost six years later, in January 1838, after Lincoln had given numerous speeches in two successful campaigns for election to the Illinois House of Representatives, he spoke to the Young Men's Lyceum in Springfield. He had lived in Springfield about nine months, having moved there in April 1837 to practice law. The Lyceum provided a forum for Springfield's aspiring leaders to address important issues of the day. In his speech, Lincoln explained the historical task bequeathed to his generation by the Founders. He contemplated the threats to that legacy posed by ambitious men and by lawless mobs, such as the one that had murdered the abolitionist Elijah Lovejoy in Alton, Illinois, the previous November. Lincoln emphasized that only law and reason could defend democracy. His descriptions of both threats and remedies reveal his view of the profound value of his chosen profession and of the grave danger of unrestrained ambition. The *Sangamo Journal* printed the address in early February 1838, shortly before Lincoln's twenty-ninth birthday.

Address to the Young Men's Lyceum of Springfield, Illinois

January 27, 1838

The Perpetuation of Our Political Institutions

As a subject for the remarks of the evening, *the perpetuation of our political institutions,* is selected.

In the great journal of things happening under the sun, we, the American People, find our account running, under date of the nineteenth century of the Christian era. We find ourselves in the peaceful possession, of the fairest portion of the earth, as regards extent of territory, fertility of soil, and salubrity of climate. We find ourselves under the government of a system of political institutions, conducing more essentially to the ends of civil and religious liberty, than any of which the history of former times tells us. We, when mounting the stage of existence, found ourselves the legal inheritors of these fundamental blessings. We toiled not in the acquirement or establishment of them—they are a legacy bequeathed us, by a *once* hardy, brave, and patriotic, but *now* lamented and departed race of ancestors. Their's was the task (and nobly they performed it) to possess themselves, and through themselves, us, of this goodly land; and to uprear upon its hills and its valleys, a political edifice of liberty and equal rights; 'tis ours only, to transmit these, the former, unprofaned by the foot of an invader; the latter, undecayed by the lapse of time, and untorn by usurpation—to the latest generation that fate shall permit the world to know. This task of gratitude to our fathers, justice to ourselves, duty to posterity, and love for our species in general, all imperatively require us faithfully to perform.

How, then, shall we perform it? At what point shall we expect the approach of danger? By what means shall we fortify against it? Shall we expect some transatlantic military giant, to step the Ocean, and crush us at a blow? Never! All the armies of Europe, Asia and Africa combined, with all the treasure of the earth (our own excepted) in their military chest; with a Buonaparte for a commander, could not by force, take a drink from the Ohio, or make a track on the Blue Ridge, in a trial of a thousand years.

At what point then is the approach of danger to be expected? I answer, if it ever reach us, it must spring up amongst us. It cannot come from abroad. If destruction be our lot, we must ourselves be its author and finisher. As a nation of freemen, we must live through all time, or die by suicide.

I hope I am over wary; but if I am not, there is, even now, something of ill-omen amongst us. I mean the increasing disregard for law which pervades the country; the growing disposition to substitute the wild and furious passions, in lieu of the sober judgement of Courts; and the worse than savage mobs, for the executive ministers of justice. This disposition is awfully fearful in any community; and that it now exists in ours, though grating to our feelings to admit, it would be a violation of truth, and an insult to our intelligence, to deny. Accounts of outrages committed by mobs, form the everyday news of the times. They have pervaded the country, from New England to Louisiana;—they are neither peculiar to the eternal snows of the former, nor the burning suns of the latter;—they are not the creature of climate—neither are they confined to the slaveholding, or the non-slaveholding States. Alike, they spring up among the pleasure hunting masters of Southern slaves, and the order loving citizens of the land of steady habits. Whatever, then, their cause may be, it is common to the whole country.

It would be tedious, as well as useless, to recount the horrors of all of them. Those happening in the State of Mississippi, and at St. Louis, are, perhaps, the most dangerous in example, and revolting to humanity. In the Mississippi case, they first commenced by hanging the regular gamblers: a set of men, certainly not following for a livelihood, a very useful, or very honest occupation; but one which, so far from being forbidden by the laws, was actually licensed by an act of the Legislature, passed but a single year before. Next, negroes, suspected of conspiring to raise an insurrection, were caught up and hanged in all parts of the State: then, white men, supposed to be leagued with the negroes; and finally, strangers, from neighboring States, going thither on business, were, in many instances, subjected to the same fate. Thus went on this process of hanging, from gamblers to negroes, from negroes to white citizens, and from these to strangers; till, dead men were seen literally dangling from the boughs of trees upon every road side; and in numbers almost sufficient, to rival the native Spanish moss of the country, as a drapery of the forest.

Turn, then, to that horror-striking scene at St. Louis. A single victim was only sacrificed there. His story is very short; and is, perhaps, the most highly tragic, of any thing of its length, that has ever been witnessed in real life. A mulatto man, by the name of McIntosh, was seized in the street, dragged to the suburbs of the city, chained to a tree, and actually burned to death; and all within a single hour from the time he had been a freeman, attending to his own business, and at peace with the world.

Such are the effects of mob law; and such are the scenes, becoming more and more frequent in this land so lately famed for love of law and order; and the stories of which, have even now grown too familiar, to attract any thing more, than an idle remark.

But you are, perhaps, ready to ask, "what has this to do with the perpetuation of our political institutions?" I answer, it has much to do with it. Its direct consequences are, comparatively speaking, but a small evil; and much of its danger consists, in the proneness of our minds, to regard its direct, as its only consequences. Abstractly considered, the hanging of the gamblers at Vicksburg, was of but little consequence. They constitute a portion of population, that is worse than useless in any community; and their death, if no pernicious example be set by it, is never matter of reasonable regret with any one. If they were annually swept, from the stage of existence, by the plague or small pox, honest men would, perhaps, be much profited, by the operation. Similar too, is the correct reasoning, in regard to the burning of the negro at St. Louis. He had forfeited his life, by the perpetration of an outrageous murder, upon one of the most worthy and respectable citizens of the city; and had he not died as he did, he must have died by the sentence of the law, in a very short time afterwards. As to him alone, it was as well the way it was, as it could otherwise have been. But the example in either case, was fearful. When men take it in their heads to day, to hang gamblers, or burn murderers, they should recollect, that, in the confusion usually attending such transactions, they will be as likely to hang or burn some one, who is neither a gambler nor a murderer as one who is; and that, acting upon the example they set, the mob of to-morrow, may, and probably will, hang or burn some of them, by the very same mistake. And not only so; the innocent, those who have ever set their faces against violations of law in every shape, alike with the guilty, fall victims to the ravages of mob law; and thus it goes on, step by step, till all the walls erected for the defence of the persons and property of individuals, are trodden down, and disregarded. But all this even, is not the full extent of the evil. By such examples, by instances of the perpetrators of such acts going unpunished, the lawless in spirit, are encouraged to become lawless in practice; and having been used to no restraint, but dread of punishment, they thus become, absolutely unrestrained. Having ever regarded Government as their deadliest bane, they make a jubilee of the suspension of its operations; and pray for nothing so much, as its total annihilation. While, on the other hand, good men, men who love tranquility, who desire to abide by the laws, and enjoy their benefits, who would gladly spill their blood in the defence of their country; seeing their property destroyed; their families insulted, and their lives endangered; their persons injured; and seeing nothing in prospect that forebodes a change for the better; become tired of; and disgusted with, a Government that offers them no protection; and are not much averse to a change in which they imagine they have nothing to lose. Thus, then, by the operation of this mobocratic spirit, which all must admit, is now abroad in the land, the strongest bulwark of any Government, and particularly of those constituted like ours, may effectually be broken down and destroyed—I mean the *attachment* of the People. Whenever this effect shall be produced among us; whenever the vicious portion of population shall be permitted to gather in bands of hundreds and thousands, and burn churches, ravage and rob provision stores, throw printing presses into rivers, shoot editors, and hang and burn obnoxious persons at pleasure, and with impunity; depend on it, this Government cannot last. By such things, the feelings of the best citizens will become more or less alienated from it; and thus it will be left without friends, or with too few, and those few too weak, to make their friendship effectual. At such a time and under such circumstances, men of sufficient talent and ambition will not be wanting to seize the opportunity, strike the blow, and overturn that fair fabric, which for the last half century, has been the fondest hope, of the lovers of freedom, throughout the world.

I know the American People are *much* attached to their Government;—I know they would suffer *much* for its sake;—I know they would endure evils long and patiently, before they would ever think of exchanging it for another. Yet, notwithstanding all this, if the laws be continually despised and disregarded, if their rights to be secure in their persons and property, are held by no better tenure than the caprice of a mob, the alienation of their affections from the Government is the natural consequence; and to that, sooner or later, it must come.

Here then, is one point at which danger may be expected.

The question recurs "how shall we fortify against it?" The answer is simple. Let every American, every lover of liberty, every well wisher to his posterity, swear by the blood of the Revolution, never to violate in the least particular, the laws of the country; and never to tolerate their violation by others. As the patriots of seventy-six did to the support of the Declaration of Independence, so to the support of the Constitution and Laws, let every American pledge his life, his property, and his sacred honor;—let every man remember that to violate the law, is to trample on the blood of his father, and to tear the character of his own, and his children's liberty. Let reverence for the laws, be breathed by every American mother, to the lisping babe, that prattles on her lap—let it be taught in schools, in seminaries, and in colleges;—let it be written in Primmers, spelling books, and in Almanacs;—let it be preached from the pulpit, proclaimed in legislative halls, and enforced in courts of justice. And, in short, let it become the *political religion* of the nation; and let the old and the young, the rich and the poor, the grave and the gay, of all sexes and tongues, and colors and conditions, sacrifice unceasingly upon its altars.

While ever a state of feeling, such as this, shall universally, or even, very generally prevail throughout the nation, vain will be every effort, and fruitless every attempt, to subvert our national freedom.

When I so pressingly urge a strict observance of all the laws, let me not be understood as saying there are no bad laws, nor that grievances may not arise, for the redress of which, no legal provisions have been made. I mean to say no such thing. But I do mean to say, that, although bad laws, if they exist, should be repealed as soon as possible, still while they continue in force, for the sake of example, they should be religiously observed. So also in unprovided cases. If such arise, let proper legal provisions be made for them with the least possible delay; but, till then, let them if not too intolerable, be borne with.

There is no grievance that is a fit object of redress by mob law. In any case that arises, as for instance, the promulgation of abolitionism, one of two positions is necessarily true; that is, the thing is right within itself, and therefore deserves the protection of all law and all good citizens; or, it is wrong, and therefore proper to be prohibited by legal enactments; and in neither case, is the interposition of mob law, either necessary, justifiable, or excusable.

But, it may be asked, why suppose danger to our political institutions? Have we not preserved them for more than fifty years? And why may we not for fifty times as long?

We hope there is no *sufficient* reason. We hope all dangers may be overcome; but to conclude that no danger may ever arise, would itself be extremely dangerous. There are now, and will hereafter be, many causes, dangerous in their tendency, which have not existed heretofore; and which are not too insignificant to merit attention. That our government should have been maintained in its original form from its establishment until now, is not much to be wondered at. It had many props to support it, through that period, which now are decayed, and crumbled away. Through that period, it was felt by all, to be an undecided experiment; now, it is understood to be a successful one. Then, all that sought celebrity and fame, and distinction, expected to find them in the success of that experiment. Their *all* was staked upon it:—their destiny was *inseparably* linked with it. Their ambition aspired to display before an admiring world, a practical demonstration of the truth of a proposition, which had hitherto been considered, at best no better, than problematical; namely, *the capability of a people to govern themselves.* If they succeeded, they were to be immortalized; their names were to be transferred to counties and cities, and rivers and mountains; and to be revered and sung, and toasted through all time. If they failed, they were to be called knaves and fools, and fanatics for a fleeting hour; then to sink and be forgotten. They succeeded. The experiment is successful; and thousands have won their deathless names in making it so. But the game is caught; and I believe it is true, that with the catching, end the pleasures of the chase. This field of glory is harvested, and the crop is already appropriated. But new reapers will arise, and *they,* too, will seek a field. It is to deny, what the history of the world tells us is true, to suppose that men of ambition and talents will not continue to spring up amongst us. And, when they do, they will as naturally seek the gratification of their ruling passion, as others have *so* done before them. The question then, is, can that gratification be found in supporting and maintaining an edifice that has been erected by others? Most certainly it cannot. Many great and good men sufficiently qualified for any task they should undertake, may ever be found, whose ambition would aspire to nothing beyond a seat in Congress, a gubernatorial or a presidential chair; *but such belong not to the family of the lion, or the tribe of the eagle.* What! think you these places would satisfy an Alexander, a Caesar, or a Napoleon? Never! Towering genius disdains a beaten path. It seeks regions hitherto unexplored. It sees *no distinction* in adding story to story, upon the monuments of fame, erected to the memory of others. It *denies* that it is glory enough to serve under any chief. It *scorns* to tread in the footsteps of *any* predecessor, however illustrious. It thirsts and burns for distinction; and, if possible, it will have it, whether at the expense of emancipating slaves, or enslaving freemen. Is it unreasonable then to expect, that some man possessed of the loftiest genius, coupled with ambition sufficient to push it to its utmost stretch, will at some time, spring up among us? And when such a one does, it will require the people to be united with each other, attached to the government and laws, and generally intelligent, to successfully frustrate his designs.

Distinction will be his paramount object; and although he would as willingly, perhaps more so, acquire it by doing good as harm; yet, that opportunity being past, and nothing left to be done in the way of building up, he would set boldly to the task of pulling down.

Here then, is a probable case, highly dangerous, and such a one as could not have well existed heretofore.

Another reason which *once was;* but which, to the same extent, is *now no more,* has done much in maintaining our institutions thus far. I mean the powerful influence which the interesting scenes of the revolution had upon the *passions* of the people as distinguished from their judgment. By this influence, the jealousy, envy, and avarice, incident to our nature, and so common to a state of peace, prosperity, and conscious strength, were, for the time, in a great measure smothered and rendered inactive; while the deep rooted principles of *hate,* and the powerful motive of *revenge,* instead of being turned against each other, were directed exclusively against the British nation. And thus, from the force of circumstances, the basest principles of our nature, were either made to lie dormant, or to become the active agents in the advancement of the noblest of cause—that of establishing and maintaining civil and religious liberty.

But this state of feeling *must fade, is fading, has faded,* with the circumstances that produced it.

I do not mean to say, that the scenes of the revolution *are now* or *ever will be* entirely forgotten; but that like every thing else, they must fade upon the memory of the world, and grow more and more dim by the lapse of time. In history, we hope, they will be read of, and recounted, so long as the bible shall be read;—but even granting that they will, their influence *cannot be* what it heretofore has been. Even then, they *cannot be* so universally known, nor so vividly felt, as they were by the generation just gone to rest. At the close of that struggle, nearly every adult male had been a participator in some of its scenes. The consequence was, that of those scenes, in the form of a husband, a father, a son or a brother, a *living history was* to be found in every family—a history bearing the indubitable testimonies of its own authenticity, in the limbs mangled, in the scars of wounds received, in the midst of the very scenes related—a history, too, that could be read and understood alike by all, the wise and the ignorant, the learned and the unlearned. But *those* histories are gone. They *can* be read no more forever. They *were* a fortress of strength; but, what invading foemen could *never do,* the silent artillery of time *has done;* the levelling of its walls. They are gone. They *were* a forest of giant oaks; but the all-resistless hurricane has swept over them, and left only, here and there, a lonely trunk, despoiled of its verdure, shorn of its foliage; unshading and unshaded, to murmur in a few more gentle breezes, and to combat with its mutilated limbs, a few more ruder storms, then to sink, and be no more.

They *were* the pillars of the temple of liberty; and now, that they have crumbled away, that temple must fall, unless we, their descendants, supply their places with other pillars, hewn from the solid quarry of sober reason. Passion has helped us; but can do so no more. It will in future be our enemy. Reason, cold, calculating, unimpassioned reason, must furnish all the materials for our future support and defence. Let those materials be moulded into *general intelligence, sound morality* and, in particular, *a reverence for the constitution and laws;* and, that we improved to the last; that we remained free to the last; that we revered his name to the last; that, during his long sleep, we permitted no hostile foot to pass over or desecrate his resting place; shall be that which to learn the last trump shall awaken our WASHINGTON.

Upon these let the proud fabric of freedom rest, as the rock of its basis; and as truly as has been said of the only greater institution, *"the gates of hell shall not prevail against it."*

WORK

Lincoln believed that ambitions could be realized only through work. His ascent from a log cabin to Congress proved to him that Americans who worked hard could achieve seemingly impossible goals. People who did not work hard enough had only themselves to blame for their lack of success. Although Lincoln tended to be tolerant of weaknesses in others, he did not mince words in expressing his opinion of the slack work habits of his step-brother, John D. Johnston. Lincoln knew Johnston well, having grown up with him until 1831, when Johnston and Lincoln's father moved to Coles County, Illinois, and Lincoln went his own way. By the time Lincoln wrote the following letters, Johnston was still trying to farm in Coles County, while Lincoln was a prominent attorney routinely arguing cases before the Illinois Supreme Court.

Letter to John D. Johnston
December 24, 1848

Washington, [D.C.]

Dear Johnston:

Your request for eighty dollars, I do not think it best, to comply with now. At the various times when I have helped you a little, you have said to me "We can get along very well now" but in a very short time I find you in the same difficulty again. Now this can only happen by some defect in your *conduct.* What that defect is, I think I know. You are not *lazy,* and still you *are* an *idler.* I doubt whether since I saw you, you have done a good whole day's work, in any one day. You do not very much dislike to work; and still you do not work much, merely because it does not seem to you that you could get much for it. This habit of uselessly wasting time, is the whole difficulty; and it is vastly important to you, and still more so to your children that you should break this habit. It is more important to them, because they have longer to live, and can keep out of an idle habit before they are in it; easier than they can get out after they are in.

You are now in need of some ready money; and what I propose is, that you shall go to work, "tooth and nails" for some body who will give you money for it. Let father [Thomas Lincoln] and your boys take charge of things at home—prepare for a crop, and make the crop; and you go to work for the best money wages, or in discharge of any debt you owe, that you can get. And to secure you a fair reward for your labor, I now promise you, that for every dollar you will, between this and the first of next May, get for your

Figure 1. Congressman-Elect

The first known photograph of Lincoln, this portrait was made in Springfield in 1846, shortly after his election to Congress. It portrays the successful young lawyer and Whig politician in splendid clothing that betrays no hint of his log cabin origins.

own labor, either in money, or in your own indebtedness, I will then give you one other dollar. By this, if you hire yourself at ten dollars a month, from me you will get ten more, making twenty dollars a month for your work. In this, I do not mean you shall go off to St. Louis, or the lead mines, or the gold mines, in California, but I mean for you to go at it for the best wages you can get close to home in Coles county. Now if you will do this, you will soon be out of debt, and what is better, you will have a habit that will keep you from getting in debt again. But if I should now clear you out, next year you will be just as deep in as ever. You say you would almost give your place in Heaven for $70 or $80. Then you value your place in Heaven very cheaply for I am sure you can with the offer I make you get the seventy or eighty dollars for four or five months work. You say if I furnish you the money you will deed me the land, and, if you dont pay the money back, you will deliver possession [of the land]. Nonsense! If you cant now live *with* the land, how will you then live without it? You have always been kind to me, and I do not now mean to be unkind to you. On the contrary, if you will but follow my advice, you will find it worth more than eight times eighty dollars to you.

Affectionately Your brother

A. LINCOLN

Letter to John D. Johnston

November 4, 1851

Shelbyville, [Illinois]

Dear Brother:

When I came into Charleston [Illinois] day-before yesterday I learned that you are anxious to sell the land where you live, and move to Missouri. I have been thinking of this ever since; and can not but think such a notion is utterly foolish. What can you do in Missouri, better than here? Is the land any richer? Can you there, any more than here, raise corn, & wheat & oats, without work? Will any body there, any more than here, do your work for you? If you intend to go to work, there is no better place than right where you are; if you do not intend to go to work, you can not get along any where. Squirming & crawling about from place to place can do no good. You have raised no crop this year, and what you really want is to sell the land, get the money and spend it—part with the land you have, and my life upon it, you will never after, own a spot big enough to bury you in. Half you will get for the land, you spend in moving to Missouri, and the other half you will eat and drink, and wear out, & no foot of land will be bought. Now I feel it is my duty to have no hand in such a piece of foolery. . . .

Now do not misunderstand this letter. I do not write it in any unkindness. I write it in order, if possible, to get you to *face* the truth—which truth is, you are destitute because you have *idled* away all your time. Your thousand pretences for not getting along better, are all non-sense—they deceive no body but yourself. *Go to work* is the only cure for your case. . . .

A. LINCOLN

Lincoln firmly believed in the profound social, political, and moral virtues of work. In a speech to the Wisconsin State Agricultural Society in the fall of 1859, excerpted below, he explained that work was the foundation of the free labor system, in contrast to what he termed the "mud-sill theory" that defended slave labor. Lincoln's speech outlined a general social philosophy based on the conviction that his personal experience was typical and that it demonstrated the immense promise of the free labor system. Those who failed to realize that promise, like John D. Johnston, were not victims of the system but of their individual shortcomings. Lincoln's speech, which was quickly published by Milwaukee and Chicago newspapers, echoed many Americans' faith in work, education, social mobility, competition, and progress. Delivered when Lincoln was attracting attention as a potential presidential candidate, the speech is one of the best brief statements of the free labor ideology that was a hallmark of the Republican party. Note, however, that Lincoln declares that free labor was not confined to one political party or geographic region but was instead practiced by "a large majority" throughout the nation. In effect, Lincoln proclaimed free labor the truly American system.

Address to the Wisconsin State Agricultural Society, Milwaukee, Wisconsin

September 30, 1859

. . . The world is agreed that *labor* is the source from which human wants are mainly supplied. There is no dispute upon this point. From this point, however, men immediately diverge. Much disputation is maintained as to the best way of applying and controlling the labor element. By some it is assumed that labor is available only in connection with capital—that nobody labors, unless somebody else, owning capital, somehow, by the use of that capital, induces him to do it. Having assumed this, they proceed to consider whether it is best that capital shall *hire* laborers, and thus induce them to work by their own consent; or *buy* them, and drive them to it without their consent.

Having proceeded so far they naturally conclude that all laborers are necessarily either *hired* laborers, or *slaves.* They further assume that whoever is once a *hired* laborer, is fatally fixed in that condition for life; and thence again that his condition is as bad as, or worse than that of a slave. This is the *"mud-sill"*[30] theory.

But another class of reasoners hold the opinion that there is no *such* relation between capital and labor, as assumed; and that there is no such thing as a freeman being fatally fixed for life, in the condition of a hired laborer, that both these assumptions are false, and all inferences from them groundless. They hold that labor is prior to, and independent of, capital; that, in fact, capital is the fruit of labor, and could never have existed if labor had not *first* existed—that labor can exist without capital, but that capital could never have existed without labor. Hence they hold that labor is the superior—greatly the superior—of capital.

They do not deny that there is, and probably always will be, *a* relation between labor and capital. The error, as they hold, is in assuming that the *whole* labor of the world exists within that relation. A few men own capital; and that few avoid labor themselves, and with their capital, hire, or buy, another few to labor for them. A large majority belong to neither class—neither work for others, nor have others working for them. Even in all our slave States, except South Carolina, a majority of the whole people of all colors, are neither slaves nor masters. In these Free States, a large majority are neither *hirers* nor *hired.* Men, with their families—wives, sons and daughters—work for themselves, on their farms, in their houses and in their shops, taking the whole product to themselves, and asking no favors of capital on the one hand, nor of hirelings or slaves on the other. It is not forgotten that a considerable number of persons mingle their own labor with capital; that is, labor with their own hands, and also buy slaves or hire freemen to labor for them; but this is only a *mixed,* and not a *distinct* class. No principle stated is disturbed by the existence of this mixed class. Again, as has already been said, the opponents of the *"mud-sill"* theory insist that there is not, of necessity, any such thing as the free hired laborer being fixed to that condition for life. There is demonstration for saying this. Many independent men, in this assembly, doubtless a few years ago were hired laborers. And their case is almost if not quite the general rule.

The prudent, penniless beginner in the world, labors for wages awhile, saves a surplus with which to buy tools or land, for himself; then labors on his own account another while, and at length hires another new beginner to help him. This, say its advocates, is *free* labor—the just and generous, and prosperous system, which opens the way for all—gives hope to all, and energy, and progress, and improvement of condition to all. If any continue through life in the condition of the hired laborer, it is not the fault of the sys-

[30]*Mud-sill* refers to the lowest stratum of society, permanently on the bottom, in the mud.

tem, but because of either a dependent nature which prefers it, or improvidence, folly, or singular misfortune. I have said this much about the elements of labor generally, as introductory to the consideration of a new phase which that element is in process of assuming. The old general rule was that *educated* people did not perform manual labor. They managed to eat their bread, leaving the toil of producing it to the uneducated. This was not an insupportable evil to the working bees, so long as the class of drones remained very small. But *now,* especially in these free States, nearly all are educated—quite too nearly all, to leave the labor of the uneducated, in any wise adequate to the support of the whole. It follows from this that henceforth educated people must labor. Otherwise, education itself would become a positive and intolerable evil. No country can sustain, in idleness, more than a small per centage of its numbers. The great majority must labor at something productive. From these premises the problem springs, "How can *labor* and *education* be the most satisfactorily combined?"

By the *"mud-sill"* theory it is assumed that labor and education are incompatible; and any practical combination of them impossible. According to that theory, a blind horse upon a tread-mill, is a perfect illustration of what a laborer should be—all the better for being blind, that he could not tread out of place, or kick understandingly. According to that theory, the education of laborers, is not only useless, but pernicious, and dangerous. In fact, it is, in some sort, deemed a misfortune that laborers should have heads at all. Those same heads are regarded as explosive materials, only to be safely kept in damp places, as far as possible from that peculiar sort of fire which ignites them. A Yankee who could invent a strong *handed* man without a head would receive the everlasting gratitude of the "mud-sill" advocates.

But Free Labor says "no!" Free Labor argues that, as the Author of man makes every individual with one head and one pair of hands, it was probably intended that heads and hands should cooperate as friends; and that that particular head, should direct and control that particular pair of hands. As each man has one mouth to be fed, and one pair of hands to furnish food, it was probably intended that that particular pair of hands should feed that particular mouth—that each head is the natural guardian, director, and protector of the hands and mouth inseparably connected with it; and that being so, every head should be cultivated, and improved, by whatever will add to its capacity for performing its charge. In one word Free Labor insists on universal education.

... Let us hope ... that by the best cultivation of the physical world, beneath and around us; and the intellectual and moral world within us, we shall secure an individual, social, and political prosperity and happiness, whose course shall be onward and upward, and which, while the earth endures, shall not pass away.

RELIGION

Lincoln's religious ideas did not conform to the conventional Christian orthodoxies of the Baptists, Methodists, and Presbyterians among his neighbors in Illinois. He did not attend church regularly, unlike many other Americans. As a young man in New Salem, he often discussed such topics as the literal truth of the Bible and the divinity of Christ with a few free-thinking friends. Years later, in 1846, when he campaigned for election to Congress against Peter Cartwright, a Methodist preacher and politician, Lincoln responded to damaging rumors about his unorthodox views by publishing a handbill. Although Lincoln often referred to God in his speeches, especially after he became president, this handbill was the only time he publicly described his religious convictions.

Handbill on Religion: To the Voters of the Seventh Congressional District

July 31, 1846

FELLOW CITIZENS:

A charge having got into circulation in some of the neighborhoods of this District, in substance that I am an open scoffer at Christianity, I have by the advice of some friends concluded to notice the subject in this form. That I am not a member of any Christian Church, is true; but I have never denied the truth of the Scriptures; and I have never spoken with intentional disrespect of religion in general, or of any denomination of Christians in particular. It is true that in early life I was inclined to believe in what I understand is called the "Doctrine of Necessity"—that is, that the human mind is impelled to action, or held in rest by some power, over which the mind itself has no control; and I have sometimes (with one, two or three, but never publicly) tried to maintain this opinion in argument. The habit of arguing thus however, I have, entirely left off for more than five years. And I add here, I have always understood this same opinion to be held by several of the Christian denominations. The foregoing, is the whole truth, briefly stated, in relation to myself, upon this subject.

I do not think I could myself, be brought to support a man for office, whom I knew to be an open enemy of, and scoffer at, religion. Leaving the higher matter of eternal consequences, between him and his Maker, I still do not think any man has the right thus to insult the feelings, and injure the morals, of the community in which he may live. If, then, I was guilty of such conduct, I should blame no man who should condemn me for it; but I do blame those, whoever they may be, who falsely put such a charge in circulation against me.

A. LINCOLN

2

Becoming a Republican

Abraham Lincoln spent most of his political life as a loyal member of the Whig party. From the time he first stepped forward as a candidate for political office in 1832, Lincoln declared his support for policies that would aid economic development, policies endorsed by Whigs throughout the nation. He believed internal improvements—roads, canals, and railroads—should be built to connect inland farms, towns, navigable waterways, and more distant markets; he favored tariffs to provide revenues to fund internal improvements and to protect American manufacturers from foreign competition; he advocated banks to help capitalize these improvements and to make credit more readily available to borrowers. Henry Clay, the national leader of the Whig party, termed these central tenets of Whig faith "the American System." Clay and other Whigs believed that the American System would create an economic infrastructure that would produce prosperity and strengthen the nation by encouraging trade among people in the North, South, and West, thereby making the sections interdependent.

As a Whig, Lincoln was elected to four terms in the Illinois legislature between 1834 and 1840 and to one term in Congress in 1846. He campaigned energetically for other Whig candidates, including Henry Clay. But after the Mexican War, when the status of slavery in the newly acquired territories became controversial, Whig party ties began to fray. Southern Whigs tended to claim that the new territories should be open to slavery; most northern Whigs argued that slavery should be barred. Slavery and questions of sectional loyalty began to crowd the economic issues of the American System out of the political spotlight, weakening the Whig party's national appeal. Whigs were still strong enough, however, for Henry Clay to play a major role in crafting the Compromise of 1850, which seemed to settle the question of slavery in the territories once and for all. In addition to defining the boundary between Texas and New Mexico and paying certain Texas debts, the Compromise balanced the admission of

California as a free state and the elimination of the buying and selling of slaves in the District of Columbia with the organization of the Utah and New Mexico territories without specifying the status of slavery and a new fugitive slave law that favored slaveholders by, among other provisions, increasing punishments for aiding slaves to escape and requiring northern citizens to help catch runaway slaves. Finally, it seemed, the compromise had removed the troublesome question of slavery from political contention.

In 1854, the Kansas-Nebraska Act (discussed later in this chapter) exploded the Whig party and blasted deep fissures among Democrats, permanently altering the nation's political landscape. In flight from the Whig party, whose southern wing endorsed Kansas-Nebraska, many northern Whigs began to align themselves with the newly formed Republican party. The Republicans, who nominated John C. Frémont as their first presidential candidate in 1856, represented the coalescence of a truly sectional party. In the 1856 election, Frémont carried all but five free states: New Jersey, Pennsylvania, Indiana, Illinois, and California. James Buchanan, the Democratic candidate, was elected president with majorities in every slave state but Maryland.

The Kansas-Nebraska Act provoked Lincoln into renewed political activity. At first reluctant to abandon his roots in the Whig party, he soon emerged as an important Republican spokesman in Illinois. In the heat of partisan battle, Lincoln repeatedly addressed questions of the place of slavery and black people in American society, of the meaning of freedom in the life of the republic, and of the profound value of the Constitution and the Union in preserving the nation's experiment in self-government—all issues that Lincoln believed distinguished his political allies (first Whigs, then Republicans) from their foes in the Democratic party. The speeches and writings in this chapter document Lincoln's careful explanation of the ideas that defined his Republican convictions and, ultimately, his policies as president.

HENRY CLAY, WHIG STATESMAN

Lincoln worshiped Henry Clay, whom he considered a model Whig statesman. Clay's long political career lasted nearly half a century, beginning in 1803 when he was first elected to the Kentucky legislature; it included repeated terms in Congress as Speaker of the House and U.S. senator from Kentucky, as well as service as secretary of state under John Quincy

Adams and campaigns for the presidency in 1824, 1832, and 1844. After Clay's death in 1852, Lincoln delivered a eulogy, subsequently published in the *Illinois State Journal,* that put into words the qualities he most valued about Clay and the Whig party. The following selection from the eulogy discloses traits Lincoln admired in Clay and aspired to emulate in his own political career. An ardent Whig at the time of the eulogy, Lincoln remained committed for the rest of his life to the ideals he believed Clay exemplified.

Eulogy on Henry Clay
July 6, 1852

Springfield, Illinois

On the fourth day of July, 1776, the people of a few feeble and oppressed colonies of Great Britain, inhabiting a portion of the Atlantic coast of North America, publicly declared their national independence, and made their appeal to the justice of their cause, and to the God of battles, for the maintenance of that declaration. That people were few in numbers, and without resources, save only their own wise heads and stout hearts. Within the first year of that declared independence, and while its maintenance was yet problematical—while the bloody struggle between those resolute rebels, and their haughty would-be-masters, was still waging, of undistinguished parents, and in an obscure district of one of those colonies, Henry Clay was born. The infant nation, and the infant child began the race of life together. For three quarters of a century they have travelled hand in hand. They have been companions ever. The nation has passed its perils, and is free, prosperous, and powerful. The child has reached his manhood, his middle age, his old age, and is dead. In all that has concerned the nation the man ever sympathised; and now the nation mourns for the man.

... Henry Clay was born on the 12th of April 1777, in Hanover county, Virginia. Of his father, who died in the fourth or fifth year of Henry's age, little seems to be known, except that he was a respectable man, and a preacher of the baptist persuasion. Mr. Clay's education, to the end of his life, was comparatively limited. I say *"to the end of his life,"* because I have understood that, from time to time, he added something to his education during the greater part of his whole life. Mr. Clay's lack of a more perfect early education, however it may be regretted generally, teaches at least one profitable lesson; it teaches that in this country, one can scarcely be so poor, but that, if he *will,* he *can* acquire sufficient education to get through the world respectably. In his twenty-third year Mr. Clay was licenced to practice law, and emigrated to Lexington, Kentucky. Here he commenced and continued the practice till the year 1803, when he was first elected to the Kentucky Legislature. . . .

In all the great questions which have agitated the country, and particularly in those great and fearful crises, the Missouri question—the Nullification question, and the late slavery question, as connected with the newly acquired territory, involving and endangering the stability of the Union, his has been the leading and most conspicuous part.[1] In 1824 he was first a candidate for the Presidency, and was defeated; and, although he was successively defeated for the same office in 1832, and in 1844, there has never been a moment since 1824 till after 1848 when a very large portion of the American people did not cling to him with an enthusiastic hope and purpose of still elevating him to the Presidency. With other men, to be defeated, was to be forgotten; but to him, defeat was but a trifling incident, neither changing him, or the world's estimate of him. Even those of both political parties, who have been preferred to him for the highest office, have run far briefer courses than he, and left him, still shining, high in the heavens of the political world. . . . The spell—the long enduring spell—with which the souls of men were bound to him, is a miracle. Who can compass it? It is probably true he owed his pre-eminence to no one quality, but to a fortunate combination of several. He was surpassingly eloquent; but many eloquent men fail utterly; and they are not, as a class, generally successful. His judgment was excellent; but many men of good judgment, live and die unnoticed. His will was indomitable; but this quality often secures to its owner nothing better than a character for useless obstinacy. These then were Mr. Clay's leading qualities. No one of them is very uncommon; but all taken together are rarely combined in a single individual; and this is probably the reason why such men as Henry Clay are so rare in the world.

Mr. Clay's eloquence did not consist, as many fine specimens of eloquence does, of types and figures—of antithesis, and elegant arrangement of words and sentences; but rather of that deeply earnest and impassioned tone, and manner, which can proceed only from great sincerity and a thorough conviction, in the speaker of the justice and importance of his cause. This it is, that truly touches the chords of human sympathy; and those who heard Mr. Clay, never failed to be moved by it, or ever afterwards, forgot the impression. All his efforts were made for practical effect. He never spoke merely to be heard. He never delivered a Fourth of July Oration, or an eulogy on an occasion like this. As a politician or statesman, no one was so habitually careful to avoid

---

[1] The Missouri Compromise of 1820 settled the question of the status of slavery in the territory acquired in the Louisiana Purchase. The 1832 nullification controversy pitted South Carolina—which declared the federal tariff law null and void—against President Andrew Jackson and the federal government. When Clay engineered a reduced tariff and Jackson and Congress threatened to use force to collect it, South Carolina rescinded nullifaction. The *late slavery question* refers to the status of slavery in the territory acquired after the Mexican War, which Clay helped resolve with the Compromise of 1850.

all sectional ground. Whatever he did, he did for the whole country. In the construction of his measures he ever carefully surveyed every part of the field, and duly weighed every conflicting interest. Feeling, as he did, and as the truth surely is, that the world's best hope depended on the continued Union of these States, he was ever jealous of, and watchful for, whatever might have the slightest tendency to separate them.

Mr. Clay's predominant sentiment, from first to last, was a deep devotion to the cause of human liberty—a strong sympathy with the oppressed every where, and an ardent wish for their elevation. With him, this was a primary and all controlling passion. Subsidiary to this was the conduct of his whole life. He loved his country partly because it was his own country, but mostly because it was a free country; and he burned with a zeal for its advancement, prosperity and glory, because he saw in such, the advancement, prosperity and glory, of human liberty, human right and human nature. He desired the prosperity of his countrymen partly because they were his countrymen, but chiefly to show to the world that freemen could be prosperous. . . .

A free people, in times of peace and quiet—when pressed by no common danger—naturally divide into parties. At such times, the man who is of neither party, is not—cannot be, of any consequence. Mr. Clay, therefore, was of a party.[2] . . .

He ever was, on principle and in feeling, opposed to slavery. The very earliest, and one of the latest public efforts of his life, separated by a period of more than fifty years, were both made in favor of gradual emancipation of the slaves in Kentucky. He did not perceive, that on a question of human right, the negroes were to be excepted from the human race. And yet Mr. Clay was the owner of slaves. Cast into life where slavery was already widely spread and deeply seated, he did not perceive, as I think no wise man has perceived, how it could be at *once* eradicated, without producing a greater evil, even to the cause of human liberty itself. His feeling and his judgment, therefore, ever led him to oppose both extremes of opinion on the subject. Those who would shiver into fragments the Union of these States; tear to tatters its now venerated constitution; and even burn the last copy of the Bible, rather than slavery should continue a single hour, together with all their more halting sympathisers, have received, and are receiving their just execration; and the name, and opinions, and influence of Mr. Clay, are fully, and, as I trust, effectually and enduringly, arrayed against them. But I would also, if I could, array his name, opinions, and influence against the opposite extreme—against a few, but an increasing number of men, who, for the sake of perpetuating slavery, are beginning to assail and to ridicule the white-man's charter of freedom—the declaration that "all men are created free and equal." . . .

The American Colonization Society was organized in 1816. Mr. Clay, though not its projector, was one of its earliest members; and he died, as for

[2]That is, the Whig party.

the many preceding years he had been, its President. It was one of the most cherished objects of his direct care and consideration; and the association of his name with it has probably been its very greatest collateral support. He considered it no demerit in the society, that it tended to relieve slave-holders from the troublesome presence of the free negroes; but this was far from being its whole merit in his estimation.... [H]e says: "There is a moral fitness in the idea of returning to Africa her children, whose ancestors have been torn from her by the ruthless hand of fraud and violence. Transplanted in a foreign land, they will carry back to their native soil the rich fruits of religion, civilization, law and liberty. May it not be one of the great designs of the Ruler of the universe, (whose ways are often inscrutable by short-sighted mortals,) thus to transform an original crime, into a signal blessing to that most unfortunate portion of the globe?" This suggestion of the possible ultimate redemption of the African race and African continent, was made twenty-five years ago. Every succeeding year has added strength to the hope of its realization. May it indeed be realized! Pharaoh's country was cursed with plagues, and his hosts were drowned in the Red Sea for striving to retain a captive people who had already served them more than four hundred years. May like disasters never befall us! If as the friends of colonization hope, the present and coming generations of our countrymen shall by any means, succeed in freeing our land from the dangerous presence of slavery; and, at the same time, in restoring a captive people to their long-lost father-land, with bright prospects for the future; and this too, so gradually, that neither races nor individuals shall have suffered by the change, it will indeed be a glorious consummation. And if, to such a consummation, the efforts of Mr. Clay shall have contributed, it will be what he most ardently wished, and none of his labors will have been more valuable to his country and his kind.

But Henry Clay is dead. His long and eventful life is closed. Our country is prosperous and powerful; but could it have been quite all it has been, and is, and is to be, without Henry Clay? Such a man the times have demanded, and such, in the providence of God was given us. But he is gone. Let us strive to deserve, as far as mortals may, the continued care of Divine Providence, trusting that, in future national emergencies, He will not fail to provide us the instruments of safety and security.

THE KANSAS-NEBRASKA ACT

Passage of the Kansas-Nebraska Act in May 1854 ignited a political firestorm. James M. McPherson, one of the foremost historians of the Civil War, declares that the "law may have been the most important single event

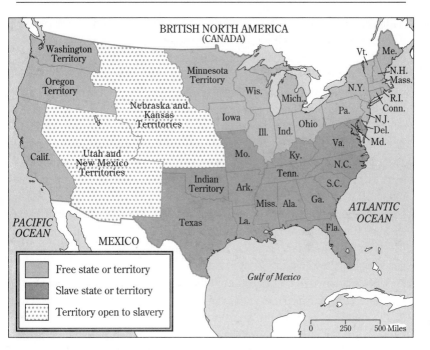

Map 2.   The Kansas-Nebraska Act, 1854

Compared to the states east of the Mississippi River, the immense size of the Kansas and Nebraska territories roughly equaled all the free states or all the slave states, an illustration of the high stakes in the Kansas-Nebraska controversy.

pushing the nation toward civil war."[3] But why did a single piece of congressional legislation about a thinly populated region most Americans had no desire to settle or even to visit cause such an uproar?

The major reason the Kansas-Nebraska Act created controversy was that it repealed the provision of the Missouri Compromise that prohibited slavery from the Kansas-Nebraska region, overturning the long-standing political settlement of the status of slavery in this territory. In effect, the Kansas-Nebraska Act opened to slavery land that had previously been closed, which outraged many northerners, especially northern Whigs like Lincoln. Stephen A. Douglas, U.S. senator from Illinois and architect of the Kansas-Nebraska Act, agreed to repeal the Missouri Compromise because,

[3] James M. McPherson, *Battle Cry of Freedom: The Civil War Era* (New York, 1988), 121.

without repeal, southern representatives in Congress refused to support the Kansas-Nebraska legislation. Douglas wanted to organize the Kansas-Nebraska territory in order to encourage settlement and, ideally, to permit a transcontinental railroad to be built through the region, with its eastern terminus in his home state at Chicago. Douglas argued that repeal of the Missouri Compromise did not matter much. For one thing, few masters would bring their slaves into the territory because the climate and topography were far from ideal for slave-grown crops like cotton and tobacco. More important, Douglas pointed out, the Kansas-Nebraska Act permitted settlers to decide for themselves all questions regarding slavery in the region. If they wanted to prohibit slavery, they could vote to do so. What could be more democratic? This doctrine of popular sovereignty had been approved by Congress in the Compromise of 1850 for settling the question of slavery in the Utah and New Mexico territories. Why should it cause such turmoil now, just four years later?

Lincoln addressed that question in the fall of 1854 when, in a prelude to the more famous Lincoln-Douglas debates of 1858, he confronted Douglas at Bloomington, Springfield, and finally at Peoria. Lincoln's speeches signaled both his opposition to Kansas-Nebraska and his ambition to be elected to the U.S. Senate to take the seat currently held by the Democratic incumbent James Shields, an election he eventually lost to Lyman Trumbull, a Democrat who also opposed Kansas-Nebraska. At Peoria, Douglas spoke first for more than three hours, then after a dinner break, Lincoln launched an equally long oration, later published in the *Illinois State Journal,* that examined the history of disputes about the status of slavery in the territories and explained why the Kansas-Nebraska Act was so wrong and so dangerous. In the following selection, Lincoln outlined themes that remained central to his thinking about slavery, freedom, African Americans, the Constitution, and the Union. His speech also illustrated why Kansas-Nebraska drove many northern Whigs to look for a new political home. In Congress, for example, almost three out of four southern Whigs voted in favor of Kansas-Nebraska, while every northern Whig voted against it. For Lincoln and many other northerners, Kansas-Nebraska initiated the metamorphosis of old Whigs into new Republicans.

Speech on the Kansas-Nebraska Act at Peoria, Illinois
October 16, 1854

... Preceding the Presidential election of 1852, each of the great political parties, democrats and whigs, met in convention, and adopted resolutions endorsing the compromise of '50; as a "finality," a final settlement, so far as these parties could make it so, of all slavery agitation. ...

During this long period of time Nebraska had remained, substantially an uninhabited country, but now emigration to, and settlement within it began to take place. It is about one third as large as the present United States, and its importance so long overlooked, begins to come into view. The restriction of slavery by the Missouri Compromise directly applies to it; in fact, was first made, and has since been maintained, expressly for it. ... On January 4th, 1854, Judge Douglas[4] introduces a new bill to give Nebraska territorial government. He accompanies this bill with a report, in which last, he expressly recommends that the Missouri Compromise shall neither be affirmed nor repealed.

Before long the bill is so modified as to make two territories instead of one; calling the Southern one Kansas.

Also, about a month after the introduction of the bill, on the judge's own motion, it is so amended as to declare the Missouri Compromise inoperative and void; and, substantially, that the People who go and settle there may establish slavery, or exclude it, as they may see fit. In this shape the bill passed both branches of congress, and became a law.

This is the *repeal* of the Missouri Compromise. ... I think, and shall try to show, that it is wrong; wrong in its direct effect, letting slavery into Kansas and Nebraska—and wrong in its prospective principle, allowing it to spread to every other part of the wide world, where men can be found inclined to take it.

This *declared* indifference, but as I must think, covert *real* zeal for the spread of slavery, I can not but hate. I hate it because of the monstrous injustice of slavery itself. I hate it because it deprives our republican example of its just influence in the world—enables the enemies of free institutions, with plausibility, to taunt us as hypocrites—causes the real friends of freedom to doubt our sincerity, and especially because it forces so many really good men amongst ourselves into an open war with the very fundamental principles of civil liberty—criticising the Declaration of Independence, and insisting that there is no right principle of action but *self-interest.*

Before proceeding, let me say I think I have no prejudice against the Southern people. They are just what we would be in their situation. If slavery

---

[4]Although Douglas was a U.S. senator, Lincoln refers to him as "Judge" because he served on the Illinois Supreme Court for two years before he was elected to Congress in 1843.

did not now exist amongst them, they would not introduce it. If it did now exist amongst us, we should not instantly give it up. This I believe of the masses north and south. Doubtless there are individuals, on both sides, who would not hold slaves under any circumstances; and others who would gladly introduce slavery anew, if it were out of existence. We know that some southern men do free their slaves, go north, and become tip-top abolitionists; while some northern ones go south, and become most cruel slavemasters.

When southern people tell us they are no more responsible for the origin of slavery, than we; I acknowledge the fact. When it is said that the institution exists; and that it is very difficult to get rid of it, in any satisfactory way, I can understand and appreciate the saying. I surely will not blame them for not doing what I should not know how to do myself. If all earthly power were given me, I should not know what to do, as to the existing institution. My first impulse would be to free all the slaves, and send them to Liberia, — to their own native land. But a moment's reflection would convince me, that whatever of high hope, (as I think there is) there may be in this, in the long run, its sudden execution is impossible. If they were all landed there in a day, they would all perish in the next ten days; and there are not surplus shipping and surplus money enough in the world to carry them there in many times ten days. What then? Free them all, and keep them among us as underlings? Is it quite certain that this betters their condition? I think I would not hold one in slavery, at any rate; yet the point is not clear enough for me to denounce people upon. What next? Free them, and make them politically and socially, our equals? My own feelings will not admit of this; and if mine would, we well know that those of the great mass of white people will not. Whether this feeling accords with justice and sound judgment, is not the sole question, if indeed, it is any part of it. A universal feeling, whether well or ill-founded, can not be safely disregarded. We can not, then, make them equals. It does seem to me that systems of gradual emancipation might be adopted; but for their tardiness in this, I will not undertake to judge our brethren of the south.

When they remind us of their constitutional rights, I acknowledge them, not grudgingly, but fully, and fairly; and I would give them any legislation for the reclaiming of their fugitives, which should not, in its stringency, be more likely to carry a free man into slavery, than our ordinary criminal laws are to hang an innocent one.

But all this; to my judgment, furnishes no more excuse for permitting slavery to go into our own free territory, than it would for reviving the African slave trade by law. The law which forbids the bringing of slaves *from* Africa; and that which has so long forbid the taking them *to* Nebraska, can hardly be distinguished on any moral principle; and the repeal of the former could find quite as plausible excuses as that of the latter. . . .

Some men, mostly whigs, who condemn the repeal of the Missouri Compromise, nevertheless hesitate to go for its restoration, lest they be thrown in company with the abolitionist. Will they allow me as an old whig to tell them good humoredly, that I think this is very silly? Stand with anybody that stands RIGHT. Stand with him while he is right and PART with him when he goes wrong. Stand WITH the abolitionist in restoring the Missouri Compromise; and stand AGAINST him when he attempts to repeal the fugitive slave law. In the latter case you stand with the southern disunionist. What of that? you are still right. In both cases you are right. In both cases you oppose the dangerous extremes. In both you stand on middle ground and hold the ship level and steady. In both you are national and nothing less than national. This is good old whig ground. To desert such ground, because of any company, is to be less than a whig—less than a man—less than an American.

I particularly object to the NEW position which the avowed principle of this Nebraska law gives to slavery in the body politic. I object to it because it assumes that there CAN be MORAL RIGHT in the enslaving of one man by another. I object to it as a dangerous dalliance for a free people—a sad evidence that, feeling prosperity we forget right—that liberty, as a principle, we have ceased to revere. I object to it because the fathers of the republic eschewed, and rejected it. The argument of "Necessity" was the only argument they ever admitted in favor of slavery; and so far, and so far only as it carried them, did they ever go. They found the institution existing among us, which they could not help; and they cast blame upon the British King for having permitted its introduction. BEFORE the constitution, they prohibited its introduction into the north-western Territory—the only country we owned, then free from it. AT the framing and adoption of the constitution, they forbore to so much as mention the word "slave" or "slavery" in the whole instrument. In the provision for the recovery of fugitives, the slave is spoken of as a "PERSON HELD TO SERVICE OR LABOR." In that prohibiting the abolition of the African slave trade for twenty years, that trade is spoken of as "The migration or importation of such persons as any of the States NOW EXISTING, shall think proper to admit," &c. These are the only provisions alluding to slavery. Thus, the thing is hid away, in the constitution, just as an afflicted man hides away a wen or a cancer, which he dares not cut out at once, lest he bleed to death; with the promise, nevertheless, that the cutting may begin at the end of a given time. Less than this our fathers COULD not do; and MORE they WOULD not do. Necessity drove them so far, and farther, they would not go. But this is not all. The earliest Congress, under the constitution, took the same view of slavery. They hedged and hemmed it in to the narrowest limits of necessity.

In 1794, they prohibited an out-going slave-trade—that is, the taking of slaves FROM the United States to sell.

In 1798, they prohibited the bringing of slaves from Africa, INTO the Mississippi Territory—this territory then comprising what are now the States of Mississippi and Alabama. This was TEN YEARS before they had the authority to do the same thing as to the States existing at the adoption of the constitution.

In 1800 they prohibited AMERICAN CITIZENS from trading in slaves between foreign countries—as, for instance, from Africa to Brazil.

In 1803 they passed a law in aid of one or two State laws, in restraint of the internal slave trade.

In 1807, in apparent hot haste, they passed the law, nearly a year in advance, to take effect the first day of 1808—the very first day the constitution would permit—prohibiting the African slave trade by heavy pecuniary and corporal penalties.

In 1820, finding these provisions ineffectual, they declared the trade piracy, and annexed to it, the extreme penalty of death. While all this was passing in the general government, five or six of the original slave States had adopted systems of gradual emancipation; and by which the institution was rapidly becoming extinct within these limits.

Thus we see, the plain unmistakable spirit of that age, towards slavery, was hostility to the PRINCIPLE, and toleration, ONLY BY NECESSITY.

But NOW it is to be transformed into a "sacred right." Nebraska brings it forth, places it on the high road to extension and perpetuity; and, with a pat on its back, says to it, "Go, and God speed you." Henceforth it is to be the chief jewel of the nation—the very figure-head of the ship of State. Little by little, but steadily as man's march to the grave, we have been giving up the OLD for the NEW faith. Near eighty years ago we began by declaring that all men are created equal; but now from that beginning we have run down to the other declaration, that for SOME men to enslave OTHERS is a "sacred right of self-government." These principles can not stand together. They are as opposite as God and mammon; and whoever holds to the one, must despise the other. When Pettit,[5] in connection with his support of the Nebraska bill, called the Declaration of Independence "a self-evident lie" he only did what consistency and candor require all other Nebraska men to do. Of the forty odd Nebraska Senators who sat present and heard him, no one rebuked him. Nor am I apprized that any Nebraska newspaper, or any Nebraska orator, in the whole nation, has ever yet rebuked him. If this had been said among Marion's men,[6] Southerners though they were, what would have become of the man who said it? If this had been said to the men who captured André,[7] the man who said it, would probably have been hung sooner than André was. If it had been said in old Independence Hall, seventy-eight years ago, the very door-keeper would have throttled the man, and thrust him into the street.

Let no one be deceived. The spirit of seventy-six and the spirit of Nebraska, are utter antagonisms; and the former is being rapidly displaced by the latter.

[5]John Pettit was a Democratic Senator from Indiana.
[6]Francis Marion, a South Carolina planter who became a hero during the American Revolution, successfully led guerrilla fighters against British troops.
[7]John André, a British spy who served in the colonial army during the American Revolution, cooperated with the traitor Benedict Arnold. He was captured in New York and hanged at George Washington's army headquarters in 1780.

Fellow countrymen—Americans south, as well as north, shall we make no effort to arrest this? Already the liberal party throughout the world, express the apprehension "that the one retrograde institution in America, is undermining the principles of progress, and fatally violating the noblest political system the world ever saw." This is not the taunt of enemies, but the warning of friends. Is it quite safe to disregard it—to despise it? Is there no danger to liberty itself, in discarding the earliest practice, and first precept of our ancient faith? In our greedy chase to make profit of the negro, let us beware, lest we "cancel and tear to pieces" even the white man's charter of freedom.

Our republican robe is soiled, and trailed in the dust. Let us repurify it. Let us turn and wash it white, in the spirit, if not the blood, of the Revolution. Let us turn slavery from its claims of "moral right," back upon its existing legal rights, and its arguments of "necessity." Let us return it to the position our fathers gave it; and there let it rest in peace. Let us re-adopt the Declaration of Independence, and with it, the practices, and policy, which harmonize with it. Let north and south—let all Americans—let all lovers of liberty everywhere—join in the great and good work. If we do this, we shall not only have saved the Union; but we shall have so saved it, as to make, and to keep it, forever worthy of the saving. We shall have so saved it, that the succeeding millions of free happy people, the world over, shall rise up, and call us blessed, to the latest generations. . . .

JUSTIFICATIONS OF SLAVERY

In his speeches, Lincoln explained his opposition to slavery in terms of the nation's commitment, in his view, to the ideals of freedom and equality. In a brief, undated note evidently written to crystallize his thoughts, Lincoln condensed his critique of arguments often used to justify the existence of slavery. The note subverts the conventional racial defense of slavery as the proper place for black people by showing that the same arguments could be employed to defend enslavement of anybody, including whites.

Fragment on Slavery
Possibly 1854

If A. can prove, however conclusively, that he may, of right, enslave B.— why may not B. snatch the same argument, and prove equally, that he may enslave A?—

You say A. is white, and B. is black. It is *color,* then; the lighter, having the right to enslave the darker? Take care. By this rule, you are to be slave to the first man you meet, with a fairer skin than your own.

You do not mean *color* exactly?—You mean the whites are *intellectually* the superiors of the blacks, and, therefore have the right to enslave them? Take care again. By this rule, you are to be slave to the first man you meet, with an intellect superior to your own.

But, say you, it is a question of *interest;* and, if you can make it your *interest,* you have the right to enslave another. Very well. And if he can make it his interest, he has the right to enslave you.

"WHERE I NOW STAND"

The furor over slavery renewed by the Kansas-Nebraska Act strained Lincoln's relationship with Joshua Speed, one of his oldest and best friends. The two men shared a room and even slept in the same bed for several years after Lincoln arrived in Springfield in 1837.[8] As roommates often do today, the two men confided in each other about many subjects, including their courtships of the women they eventually married. Speed grew up in a wealthy Kentucky family that owned some seventy slaves on a plantation near Louisville. In 1841, Speed moved back to Kentucky, and Lincoln visited him there late that summer. In 1855, when their differences about slavery threatened to disrupt their long friendship, Lincoln tried to reassure Speed that, under the Constitution, slaveholders could not be deprived of their slave property. Yet Lincoln's moral opposition to slavery and his insistence that the expansion of slavery was intolerable separated him from both his old friend and his old attachment to the Whig party. Although Lincoln's views threatened—as he said—to "unwhig" him, he affirmed his personal sympathies for Speed and other slaveholders, despite deep political differences. Lincoln's unusual respect for people who held views in conflict with his own, evident in the following letter, continued to characterize his thought and action after he became president.

[8]Crowded housing often required men to share a bed; travelers commonly had to sleep in the same bed with a complete stranger.

Letter to Joshua F. Speed

August 24, 1855

Springfield, [Illinois]

Dear Speed:

You know what a poor correspondent I am. Ever since I received your very agreeable letter of the 22nd. of May I have been intending to write you in answer to it. You suggest that in political action now, you and I would differ. I suppose we would; not quite as much, however, as you may think. You know I dislike slavery; and you fully admit the abstract wrong of it. So far there is no cause of difference. But you say that sooner than yield your legal right to the slave—especially at the bidding of those who are not themselves interested, you would see the Union dissolved. I am not aware that *any one* is bidding you to yield that right; very certainly *I* am not. I leave that matter entirely to yourself. I also acknowledge *your* rights and *my* obligations, under the constitution, in regard to your slaves. I confess I hate to see the poor creatures hunted down, and caught, and carried back to their stripes, and unrewarded toils; but I bite my lip and keep quiet. In 1841 you and I had together a tedious low-water trip, on a Steam Boat from Louisville to St. Louis. You may remember, as I well do, that from Louisville to the mouth of the Ohio there were, on board, ten or a dozen slaves, shackled together with irons. That sight was a continual torment to me; and I see something like it every time I touch the Ohio, or any other slave-border.[9] It is hardly fair for you to assume, that I have no interest in a thing which has, and continually exercises, the power of making me miserable. You ought rather to appreciate how much the great body of the Northern people do crucify their feelings, in order to maintain their loyalty to the constitution and the Union.

---

[9]Back in 1841, Lincoln described the slaves on the steamboat in a letter to Joshua Speed's half sister, Mary, without mentioning that the sight "was a continual torment" to him. Lincoln wrote, "By the way; a fine example was presented on board the boat for contemplating the effect of *condition* upon human happiness. A gentleman had purchased twelve negroes in diferent parts of Kentucky and was taking them to a farm in the South. They were chained six and six together. A small iron clevis was around the left wrist of each, and this fastened to the main chain by a shorter one at a convenient distance from the others; so that the negroes were strung together precisely like so many fish upon a trot-line. In this condition they were being separated forever from the scenes of their childhood, their friends, their fathers and mothers, and brothers and sisters, and many of them, from their wives and children, and go-ing into perpetual slavery where the lash of the master is proverbially more ruthless and unrelenting than any other where; and yet amid all these distressing circumstances, as we would think them, they were the most cheerful and apparantly happy creatures on board. One, whose offence for which he had been sold was an over-fondness for his wife, played the fiddle almost continually; and the others danced, sung, cracked jokes, and played various games with cards from day to day. How true it is that 'God tempers the wind to the shorn lamb,' or in other words, that He renders the worst of human conditions tolerable, while He permits the best, to be nothing better than tolerable." *CW*, I, 259–61.

I do oppose the extension of slavery, because my judgment and feelings so prompt me; and I am under no obligation to the contrary. If for this you and I must differ, differ we must. You say if you were President, you would send an army and hang the leaders of the Missouri outrages upon the Kansas elections;[10] still, if Kansas fairly votes herself a slave state, she must be admitted, or the Union must be dissolved. But how if she votes herself a slave state *unfairly*—that is, by the very means for which you say you would hang men? Must she still be admitted, or the Union be dissolved? That will be the phase of the question when it first becomes a practical one. In your assumption that there may be a *fair* decision of the slavery question in Kansas, I plainly see you and I would differ about the Nebraska-law. I look upon that enactment not as a *law,* but as *violence* from the beginning. It was conceived in violence, passed in violence, is maintained in violence, and is being executed in violence. I say it was *conceived* in violence, because the destruction of the Missouri Compromise, under the circumstances, was nothing less than violence. It was *passed* in violence, because it could not have passed at all but for the votes of many members, in violent disregard of the known will of their constituents. It is *maintained* in violence because the elections since, clearly demand it's repeal, and this demand is openly disregarded. *You* say men ought to be hung for the way they are executing that law; and *I* say the way it is being executed is quite as good as any of its antecedents. It is being executed in the precise way which was intended from the first; else why does no Nebraska man express astonishment or condemnation? Poor Reeder[11] is the only public man who has been silly enough to believe that any thing like fairness was ever intended; and he has been bravely undeceived.

That Kansas will form a Slave constitution, and, with it, will ask to be admitted into the Union, I take to be an already settled question; and so settled by the very means you so pointedly condemn. By every principle of law, ever held by any court, North or South, every negro taken to Kansas is free; yet in utter disregard of this—in the spirit of violence merely—that beautiful Legislature gravely passes a law to hang men who shall venture to inform a negro of his legal rights. This is the substance, and real object of the law. If, like Haman,[12] they should hang upon the gallows of their own building, I shall not be among the mourners for their fate.

[10]Thousands of proslavery Missourians crossed the border into Kansas and voted illegally in the fall of 1854 for a proslavery delegate to Congress and in March 1855 for proslavery members of the territorial legislature, easily defeating free-soil candidates.

[11]Andrew F. Reeder, a Pennsylvania Democrat, was appointed territorial governor of Kansas by President Franklin Pierce, a Democrat from New Hampshire who supported the Kansas-Nebraska bill. The violence and fraudulent voting in Kansas shocked Reeder. But when Reeder urged Pierce to repudiate the elections, Pierce instead replaced Reeder with a more reliably proslavery territorial governor.

[12]The Bible (Esther, 3–9) tells the story of Haman, a high official in the court of the Persian king, who announced that all Jews would be killed. Esther, the king's beautiful Jewish wife, subverted Haman's plan. The king executed Haman, hanging him on the gallows Haman had intended for Jewish victims.

In my humble sphere, I shall advocate the restoration of the Missouri Compromise, so long as Kansas remains a territory;[13] and when, by all these foul means, it seeks to come into the Union as a Slave-state, I shall oppose it. I am very loth, in any case, to withhold my assent to the enjoyment of property *acquired,* or *located,* in good faith; but I do not admit that *good faith,* in taking a negro to Kansas, to be held in slavery, is a *possibility* with any man. Any man who has sense enough to be the controller of his own property, has too much sense to misunderstand the outrageous character of this whole Nebraska business. But I digress. In my opposition to the admission of Kansas I shall have some company; but we may be beaten. If we are, I shall not, on that account, attempt to dissolve the Union. On the contrary, if we succeed, there will be enough of us to take care of the Union. I think it probable, however, we shall be beaten. Standing as a unit among yourselves, you can, directly, and indirectly, bribe enough of our men to carry the day—as you could on an open proposition to establish monarchy. Get hold of some man in the North, whose position and ability is such, that he can make the support of your measure—whatever it may be—a *democratic party necessity,* and the thing is done. *Apropos* of this, let me tell you an anecdote. Douglas introduced the Nebraska bill in January. In February afterwards, there was a call session of the Illinois Legislature. Of the one hundred members composing the two branches of that body, about seventy were democrats. These latter held a caucus, in which the Nebraska bill was talked of, if not formally discussed. It was thereby discovered that just three, and no more, were in favor of the measure. In a day or two Douglas' orders came on to have resolutions passed approving the bill; and they were passed by large majorities!!! The truth of this is vouched for by a bolting democratic member. The masses too, democratic as well as whig, were even, nearer unanamous against it; but as soon as the party necessity of supporting it, became apparent, the way the democracy[14] began to see the *wisdom* and *justice* of it, was perfectly astonishing.

You say if Kansas fairly votes herself a free state, as a christian you will rather rejoice at it. All decent slave-holders *talk* that way; and I do not doubt their candor. But they never *vote* that way. Although in a private letter, or conversation, you will express your preference that Kansas shall be free, you would vote for no man for Congress who would say the same thing publicly. No such man could be elected from any district in any slave-state. You think Stringfellow & Co ought to be hung; and yet, at the next presidential election you will vote for the exact type and representative of Stringfellow.[15] The slave-breeders and slave-traders, are a small, odious and detested class, among you; and yet in politics, they dictate the course of all of you, and are as completely your masters, as you are the masters of your own negroes.

[13]The Missouri Compromise provided that slavery was prohibited from the territory that, by 1854, had become Kansas.

[14]The Democratic party.

[15]John Stringfellow, editor of a rabidly proslavery newspaper in Atchison, Kansas, promised to bring enough Missouri border ruffians into Kansas "to kill every God-damned abolitionist in the Territory." Quoted in Alice Nichols, *Bleeding Kansas* (New York, 1954), 26.

You enquire where I now stand. That is a disputed point. I think I am a whig; but others say there are no whigs, and that I am an abolitionist. When I was at Washington I voted for the Wilmot Proviso[16] as good as forty times, and I never heard of any one attempting to unwhig me for that. I now do no more than oppose the *extension* of slavery.

I am not a Know-Nothing.[17] That is certain. How could I be? How can any one who abhors the oppression of negroes, be in favor of degrading classes of white people? Our progress in degeneracy appears to me to be pretty rapid. As a nation, we began by declaring that *"all men are created equal."* We now practically read it "all men are created equal, *except negroes."* When the Know-Nothings get control, it will read "all men are created equal, except negroes, *and foreigners, and catholics."* When it comes to this I should prefer emigrating to some country where they make no pretence of loving liberty—to Russia, for instance, where despotism can be taken pure, and without the base alloy of hypocracy.

Mary[18] will probably pass a day or two in Louisville in October. My kindest regards to Mrs. Speed. On the leading subject of this letter, I have more of her sympathy than I have of yours.

And yet let me say I am Your friend forever
A. LINCOLN

[16]In August 1846, David Wilmot—a first-term Democratic congressman from Pennsylvania—proposed an amendment providing that slavery and involuntary servitude would never be permitted to exist in any territory acquired as a result of the Mexican war. The Wilmot Proviso became the focal point of heated debate between proslavery and free-soil forces. The Proviso never became law; free-soil majorities in the House of Representatives supported it, but it stalled in the Senate, where slave state senators counterbalanced those from free states.

[17]The Know-Nothing party, organized as a secret society in 1854, was anti-immigrant, anti-Catholic, and—for the most part—anti-Democratic, since many Irish Catholic immigrants who flooded into the nation after 1845 voted for Democrats. Many former Whigs gravitated toward the Know-Nothings after the Kansas-Nebraska Act.

[18]Lincoln's wife, Mary Todd Lincoln.

THE *DRED SCOTT* DECISION

In March 1857, the U.S. Supreme Court announced its decision in the *Dred Scott* case. Scott, a Missouri slave whose master had taken him North where slavery was prohibited, had filed suit to obtain his freedom. Many Americans hoped that the Court's decision would finally settle the slavery controversy. They were disappointed. Chief Justice Roger B. Taney, a Maryland Democrat and former slaveholder who had been appointed to the Court in 1836 by President Andrew Jackson, wrote the majority opinion. Taney held that Congress had no constitutional power to regulate slavery in the territories and that black people—even if they were free—had no rights under the Constitution. Taney's purpose, as Don E. Fehrenbacher, the preeminent historian of the *Dred Scott* case has written, was "to launch a sweeping counterattack on the antislavery movement and to reinforce the bastions of slavery at every rampart and parapet."[19] Taney's opinion effectively declared the Republican party's opposition to the expansion of slavery unconstitutional, putting Lincoln and other Republicans in the uncomfortable position of defending a policy that had been ruled illegal by the highest court in the land.

Late in June, Lincoln spoke out against Taney's decision in Springfield, two weeks after hearing Stephen A. Douglas defend the court's verdict. In his speech, subsequently published in the *Illinois Journal* and other newspapers, Lincoln argued that while he and other Republicans vehemently disagreed with Taney, they did not resist the Court's ruling. Above all, Lincoln attacked Taney's claim that the Declaration of Independence and the Constitution did not apply to blacks. Lincoln affirmed the humanity and political rights of black people and contrasted his Republican convictions with the Democrats' determination to oppress blacks in every way. Since Douglas and other Democrats appealed to the widespread belief in white supremacy among northern voters by accusing Republicans of advocating social equality for blacks, Lincoln took care to explain his view of the limits of racial equality.

Speech on the Dred Scott *Decision*

June 26, 1857

Springfield, Illinois

. . . And now as to the Dred Scott decision. That decision declares two propositions—first, that a negro cannot sue in the U.S. Courts; and secondly, that Congress cannot prohibit slavery in the Territories. It was made by a divided court[20]—dividing differently on the different points. Judge Douglas does not discuss the merits of the decision; and, in that respect, I shall follow his example, believing I could no more improve on McLean[21] and Curtis,[22] than he could on Taney.

[19]Don E. Fehrenbacher, *The Dred Scott Case: Its Significance in American Law and Politics* (New York, 1978), 341.

[20]On the principal issues, the court was divided seven to two.

[21]John McLean, author of one of the dissenting opinions, was from Ohio; originally a Democrat, he had become a Republican by 1857.

[22]Benjamin R. Curtis, another dissenter, was a Massachusetts Whig who, like Lincoln, had moved into Republican ranks.

He denounces all who question the correctness of that decision, as offering violent resistance to it. But who resists it? Who has, in spite of the decision, declared Dred Scott free, and resisted the authority of his master over him?

Judicial decisions have two uses—first, to absolutely determine the case decided, and secondly, to indicate to the public how other similar cases will be decided when they arise. For the latter use, they are called "precedents" and "authorities."

We believe, as much as Judge Douglas, (perhaps more) in obedience to, and respect for the judicial department of government. We think its decisions on Constitutional questions, when fully settled, should control, not only the particular cases decided, but the general policy of the country, subject to be disturbed only by amendments of the Constitution as provided in that instrument itself. More than this would be revolution. But we think the Dred Scott decision is erroneous. We know the court that made it, has often over-ruled its own decisions, and we shall do what we can to have it to over-rule this. We offer no *resistance* to it.

Judicial decisions are of greater or less authority as precedents, according to circumstances. That this should be so, accords both with common sense, and the customary understanding of the legal profession.

If this important decision had been made by the unanimous concurrence of the judges, and without any apparent partisan bias, and in accordance with legal public expectation, and with the steady practice of the departments throughout our history, and had been in no part, based on assumed historical facts which are not really true; or, if wanting in some of these, it had been before the court more than once, and had there been affirmed and re-affirmed through a course of years, it then might be, perhaps would be, factious, nay, even revolutionary, to not acquiesce in it as a precedent.

But when, as it is true we find it wanting in all these claims to the public confidence, it is not resistance, it is not factious, it is not even disrespectful, to treat it as not having yet quite established a settled doctrine for the country.... [T]he Chief Justice does not directly assert, but plainly assumes, as a fact, that the public estimate of the black man is more favorable *now* than it was in the days of the Revolution. This assumption is a mistake. In some trifling particulars, the condition of that race has been ameliorated; but, as a whole, in this country, the change between then and now is decidedly the other way; and their ultimate destiny has never appeared so hopeless as in the last three or four years. In two of the five States—New Jersey and North Carolina—that then gave the free negro the right of voting, the right has since been taken away; and in a third—New York—it has been greatly abridged; while it has not been extended, so far as I know, to a single additional State, though the number of the States has more than doubled. In those days, as I understand, masters could, at their own pleasure, emancipate their slaves; but since then, such legal restraints have been made upon emancipation, as to amount almost to prohibition. In those days, Legislatures held the unquestioned power to abolish slavery in their respective States; but now it is becoming quite fashionable for State Constitutions to withhold that power from the Legislatures. In those days, by common consent, the spread of the black man's bondage to new countries was prohibited; but now, Congress decides that it *will* not continue the prohibition, and the Supreme Court decides that it *could* not if it would. In those days, our Declaration of Independence was held sacred by all, and thought to include all; but now, to aid in making the bondage of the negro universal and eternal, it is assailed, and sneered at, and construed, and hawked at, and torn, till, if its framers could rise from their graves, they could not at all recognize it. All the powers of earth seem rapidly combining against him.[23] Mammon is after him; ambition follows, and philosophy follows, and the Theology of the day is fast joining the cry. They have him in his prison house; they have searched his person, and left no prying instrument with him. One after another they have closed the heavy iron doors upon him, and now they have him, as it were, bolted in with a lock of a hundred keys, which can never be unlocked without the concurrence of every key; the keys in the hands of a hundred different men, and they scattered to a hundred different and distant places; and they stand musing as to what invention, in all the dominions of mind and matter, can be produced to make the impossibility of his escape more complete than it is.

It is grossly incorrect to say or assume, that the public estimate of the negro is more favorable now than it was at the origin of the government. . . .

There is a natural disgust in the minds of nearly all white people, to the idea of an indiscriminate amalgamation of the white and black races; and Judge Douglas evidently is basing his chief hope, upon the chances of being able to appropriate the benefit of this disgust to himself. If he can, by much drumming and repeating, fasten the odium of that idea upon his adversaries, he thinks he can struggle through the storm. He therefore clings to this hope, as a drowning man to the last plank. He makes an occasion for lugging it in from the opposition to the Dred Scott decision. He finds the Republicans insisting that the Declaration of Independence includes ALL men, black as well as white; and forthwith he boldly denies that it includes negroes at all, and proceeds to argue gravely that all who contend it does, do so only because they want to vote, and eat, and sleep, and marry with negroes! He will have it that they cannot be consistent else. Now I protest against that counterfeit logic which concludes that, because I do not want a black woman for a *slave* I must necessarily want her for a *wife*. I need not have her for either, I can just leave her alone. In some respects she certainly is not my equal; but in her natural right to eat the bread she earns with her own hands without asking leave of any one else, she is my equal, and the equal of all others.

---

[23]By *him,* Lincoln means "the Negro."

Chief Justice Taney, in his opinion in the Dred Scott case, admits that the language of the Declaration is broad enough to include the whole human family, but he and Judge Douglas argue that the authors of that instrument did not intend to include negroes, by the fact that they did not at once, actually place them on an equality with the whites. Now this grave argument comes to just nothing at all, by the other fact, that they did not at once, *or ever afterwards,* actually place all white people on an equality with one or another. And this is the staple argument of both the Chief Justice and the Senator, for doing this obvious violence to the plain unmistakable language of the Declaration. I think the authors of that notable instrument intended to include *all* men, but they did not intend to declare all men equal *in all respects.* They did not mean to say all were equal in color, size, intellect, moral developments, or social capacity. They defined with tolerable distinctness, in what respects they did consider all men created equal—equal in "certain inalienable rights, among which are life, liberty, and the pursuit of happiness." This they said, and this meant. They did not mean to assert the obvious untruth, that all were then actually enjoying that equality, nor yet, that they were about to confer it immediately upon them. In fact they had no power to confer such a boon. They meant simply to declare the *right,* so that the *enforcement* of it might follow as fast as circumstances should permit. They meant to set up a standard maxim for free society, which should be familiar to all, and revered by all; constantly looked to, constantly labored for, and even though never perfectly attained, constantly approximated, and thereby constantly spreading and deepening its influence, and augmenting the happiness and value of life to all people of all colors everywhere. The assertion that "all men are created equal" was of no practical use in effecting our separation from Great Britain; and it was placed in the Declaration, not for that, but for future use. Its authors meant it to be, thank God, it is now proving itself, a stumbling block to those who in after times might seek to turn a free people back into the hateful paths of despotism. They knew the proneness of prosperity to breed tyrants, and they meant when such should re-appear in this fair land and commence their vocation they should find left for them at least one hard nut to crack. . . .

I have said that the separation of the races is the only perfect preventive of amalgamation [of the races]. I have no right to say all the members of the Republican party are in favor of this, nor to say that as a party they are in favor of it. There is nothing in their platform directly on the subject. But I can say a very large proportion of its members are for it, and that the chief plank in their platform—opposition to the spread of slavery—is most favorable to that separation.

Such separation, if ever effected at all, must be effected by colonization; and no political party, as such, is now doing anything directly for colonization. Party operations at present only favor or retard colonization incidentally. The enterprise is a difficult one; but "when there is a will there is a way;" and what colonization needs most is a hearty will. Will springs from the two elements of moral sense and self-interest. Let us be brought to believe it is morally right, and, at the same time, favorable to, or, at least, not against, our interest, to transfer the African to his native clime, and we shall find a way to do it, however great the task may be. The children of Israel, to such numbers as to include four hundred thousand fighting men, went out of Egyptian bondage in a body.

How differently the respective courses of the Democratic and Republican parties incidentally bear on the question of forming a will—a public sentiment—for colonization, is easy to see. The Republicans inculcate, with whatever of ability they can, that the negro is a man; that his bondage is cruelly wrong, and that the field of his oppression ought not to be enlarged. The Democrats deny his manhood; deny, or dwarf to insignificance, the wrong of his bondage; so far as possible, crush all sympathy for him, and cultivate and excite hatred and disgust against him; compliment themselves as Union-savers for doing so; and call the indefinite outspreading of his bondage "a sacred right of self-government."

The plainest print cannot be read through a gold eagle;[24] and it will be ever hard to find many men who will send a slave to Liberia, and pay his passage while they can send him to a new country, Kansas for instance, and sell him for fifteen hundred dollars, and the rise.

[24] A gold eagle was a ten-dollar gold coin. In other words, Lincoln is saying that many people are motivated by financial self-interest.

3

Leading the Republican Party

By 1858, Lincoln stood in the front rank of Republicans in Illinois; two years later, he headed the Republican ticket in the campaign for president of the United States. Lincoln's skill in defining doctrines that appealed to the most important constituencies in the emerging Republican coalition contributed to his remarkable ascension as a Republican leader. In speech after speech during his campaign against Stephen A. Douglas for the U.S. Senate and afterward, Lincoln explained his views of how Republicans differed from Democrats, freedom from slavery, and whites from blacks. His insistence on fundamental human equality and the immorality of slavery sharply distinguished Republicans from many Democrats who denied both propositions. His profession of respect for constitutional restraints on federal action against slavery reassured conservative former Whigs in the North that at least this Republican did not intend to translate his moral opposition to slavery into a call for immediate abolition and thereby precipitate a constitutional crisis and possibly disunion. His refusal to scapegoat German and Irish immigrants contrasted with the nativism of the Know-Nothing (or American) party, while his failure to engage in public criticism of Know-Nothings left the door to the Republican party conveniently open to former Whigs who had found a temporary home in the American party. His repeated attacks on Stephen A. Douglas's perversion of the hallowed ideals of the Declaration of Independence also invited anti-Nebraska Democrats to affirm their traditional beliefs—which he claimed Douglas had abandoned—by adopting a new political affiliation.

In June 1858, Lincoln was the unanimous selection of the Illinois Republican convention to run against Douglas for the U.S. Senate. After his "House Divided" speech and his celebrated debates with Douglas, Lincoln began to attract attention in Republican circles throughout the North. Although Lincoln lost the senatorial race, he remained a leading Republican spokesman, and when the party met for its 1860 convention in Chicago,

Figure 2.   Lincoln in 1858
This photograph shows Lincoln as he appeared during the famous Lincoln-Douglas debates, the highlight of the 1858 campaign for the election of U.S. senator from Illinois.

he enjoyed the united support of the Illinois delegation for the presidential nomination. Republicans knew they could win the presidency if they nominated a candidate who maintained their majorities in the states carried by Frémont in 1856 and who added victories in Pennsylvania plus either Indiana or Illinois. On the third ballot, they nominated Lincoln.

Unlike presidential aspirants today, Lincoln did not give speeches to promote his candidacy. In fact, he seldom left home. During and after the presidential campaign, he maintained an active correspondence and met with countless visitors and office-seekers, but he avoided speaking out on the developing crisis. He believed that his previous speeches had thoroughly explained the policies he would pursue as president. The following selections from Lincoln's political speeches between his 1858 nomination for the U.S. Senate and his victory in the 1860 presidential election document both Lincoln's ideas and what any interested person of the era could have known about them.

A HOUSE DIVIDED

Lincoln delivered his famous "House Divided" speech shortly after the Illinois State Republican convention selected him to run for the U.S. Senate in the fall election against Democratic incumbent Stephen A. Douglas. Lincoln did not originate the "house divided" metaphor. It appears several times in the Bible, and it had been used in recent years by both proslavery and antislavery advocates. Lincoln employed the metaphor to emphasize his view that slavery was on the verge of becoming national, rather than remaining confined to the southern states. Lincoln argued that leading Democrats, headed by Douglas, conspired to pass the Kansas-Nebraska Act, to repeal the Missouri Compromise, and most recently to undermine the Constitution with the *Dred Scott* decision, all with the intent to make slavery legal throughout the nation. Although no such conspiracy really existed, it was possible—as Lincoln pointed out—that the Supreme Court would soon declare that the principles of the *Dred Scott* decision applied not just to federal territories but also to states, thereby preventing states like Illinois from excluding slavery.

Lincoln paid special attention to Douglas's indifference to the spread of slavery because of recent events in Kansas. Late in 1857, voters in Kansas had approved the Lecompton constitution, which would make Kansas a slave state. The constitution passed easily because antislavery Kansans boycotted the election, protesting the proslavery dominance of the convention that had drafted the constitution. Early in 1858, President James Buchanan recommended that Congress admit Kansas to the Union, organized as a slave state under the Lecompton constitution. Douglas and other northern Democrats joined Republicans in denouncing the Lecompton constitution as the result of an unfair and unrepresentative election. Douglas's opposition to Lecompton made some Republicans flirt with the possibility of supporting him rather than Lincoln in the Illinois Senate race. In what amounted to the opening salvo in the senatorial campaign, Lincoln tried to end that flirtation by showing that a Republican was a far safer choice than a Democrat in the looming crisis of the house divided. Lincoln's speech was published in the *Illinois State Journal,* reprinted in other papers, and read by many people outside Illinois.

"A House Divided" Speech at Springfield, Illinois[1]
June 16, 1858

Mr. PRESIDENT and Gentlemen of the Convention.

If we could first know *where* we are, and *whither* we are tending, we could then better judge *what* to do, and *how* to do it.

We are now far into the *fifth* year, since a policy was initiated, with the *avowed* object, and *confident* promise, of putting an end to slavery agitation.

Under the operation of that policy, that agitation has not only, *not ceased,* but has *constantly augmented.*

In *my* opinion, it *will* not cease, until a *crisis* shall have been reached, and passed.

"A house divided against itself cannot stand."

I believe this government cannot endure, permanently half *slave* and half *free*.

I do not expect the Union to be *dissolved*—I do not expect the house to *fall*—but I *do* expect it will cease to be divided.

It will become *all* one thing, or *all* the other.

Either the *opponents* of slavery, will arrest the further spread of it, and place it where the public mind shall rest in the belief that it is in course of ultimate extinction; or its *advocates* will push it forward, till it shall become alike lawful in *all* the States, *old* as well as *new*—*North* as well as *South*.

Have we no *tendency* to the latter condition?

Let any one who doubts, carefully contemplate that now almost complete legal combination—piece of *machinery* so to speak—compounded of the Nebraska doctrine, and the Dred Scott decision. Let him consider not only *what work* the machinery is adapted to do, and *how well* adapted; but also, let him study the *history* of its construction, and trace, if he can, or rather *fail,* if he can, to trace the evidences of design, and concert of action, among its chief bosses, from the beginning.

---

[1]The text of this speech follows that in Abraham Lincoln, *Selected Speeches and Writings,* ed. Don E. Fehrenbacher (New York, 1992), 131–32.

The new year of 1854 found slavery excluded from more than half the States by State Constitutions, and from most of the national territory by Congressional prohibition.

Four days later, commenced the struggle, which ended in repealing that Congressional prohibition.

This opened all the national territory to slavery; and was the first point gained.

But, so far, *Congress* only, had acted; and an *indorsement* by the people, *real* or apparent, was indispensable, to *save* the point already gained, and give chance for more.

This necessity had not been overlooked; but had been provided for, as well as might be, in the notable argument of *"squatter sovereignty,"* otherwise called *"sacred right of self government,"* which latter phrase, though expressive of the only rightful basis of any government, was so perverted in this attempted use of it as to amount to just this: That if any *one* man, choose to enslave *another*, no *third* man shall be allowed to object.

That argument was incorporated into the Nebraska bill itself, in the language which follows: *"It being the true intent and meaning of this act not to legislate slavery into any Territory or state, nor to exclude it therefrom; but to leave the people thereof perfectly free to form and regulate their domestic institutions in their own way, subject only to the Constitution of the United States."*

Then opened the roar of loose declamation in favor of "Squatter Sovereignty," and "Sacred right of self government."

"But," said opposition members, "let us be more *specific*—let us *amend* the bill so as to expressly declare that the people of the territory *may* exclude slavery." "Not we," said the friends of the measure; and down they voted the amendment.

While the Nebraska bill was passing through congress, a *law case,* involving the question of a negroe's freedom, by reason of his owner having voluntarily taken him first into a free state and then a territory covered by the congressional prohibition, and held him as a slave, for a long time in each, was passing through the U.S. Circuit Court for the District of Missouri; and both Nebraska bill and law suit were brought to a decision in the same month of May, 1854. The negroe's name was "Dred Scott," which name now designates the decision finally made in the case.

Before the *then* next Presidential election, the law case came *to,* and was argued *in* the Supreme Court of the United States; but the *decision* of it was deferred until *after* the election. Still, *before* the election, Senator Trumbull,[2] on the floor of the Senate, requests the leading advocate[3] of the Nebraska bill to state *his opinion* whether the people of a territory can constitutionally

[2]Lyman Trumbull, senator from Illinois, was an anti-Nebraska Democrat who became a Republican.
[3]Stephen A. Douglas.

exclude slavery from their limits; and the latter answers, "That is a question for the Supreme Court."

The election came. Mr. Buchanan[4] was elected, and the *indorsement,* such as it was, secured. That was the *second* point gained. The indorsement, however, fell short of a clear popular majority by nearly four hundred thousand votes,[5] and so, perhaps, was not overwhelmingly reliable and satisfactory.

The *outgoing* President,[6] in his last annual message, as impressively as possible *echoed back* upon the people the *weight* and *authority* of the indorsement.

The Supreme Court met again; *did not* announce their decision, but ordered a re-argument.

The Presidential inauguration came, and still no decision of the court; but the *incoming* President, in his inaugural address, fervently exhorted the people to abide by the forthcoming decision, *whatever it might be.*

Then, in a few days, came the decision.

The reputed author[7] of the Nebraska bill finds an early occasion to make a speech at this capitol indorsing the Dred Scott Decision, and vehemently denouncing all opposition to it.

The new President,[8] too, seizes the early occasion of the Silliman letter to *indorse* and strongly *construe* that decision, and to express his *astonishment* that any different view had ever been entertained.

At length a squabble springs up between the President and the author of the Nebraska bill, on the *mere* question of *fact,* whether the Lecompton constitution was or was not, in any just sense, made by the people of Kansas; and in that squabble the latter declares that all he wants is a fair vote for the people, and that he *cares* not whether slavery be voted *down* or voted *up.* I do not understand his declaration that he cares not whether slavery be voted down or voted up, to be intended by him other than as an *apt definition* of the *policy* he would impress upon the public mind—the *principle* for which he declares he has suffered much, and is ready to suffer to the end.

And well may he cling to that principle. If he has any parental feeling, well may he cling to it. That principle, is the only *shred* left of his original Nebraska doctrine. Under the Dred Scott decision, "squatter sovereignty" squatted out of existence, tumbled down like temporary scaffolding—like the mould at the foundry served through one blast and fell back into loose sand—helped to carry an election, and then was kicked to the winds. His late *joint* struggle with the Republicans, against the Lecompton Constitution,

[4]James Buchanan, a Democrat from Pennsylvania.

[5]In the 1856 presidential election, Buchanan received 45 percent of the popular vote, almost 379,000 votes less than the combined total of his opponents, the Republican candidate John C. Frémont (33 percent) and the American (Know-Nothing) party candidate Millard Fillmore (22 percent).

[6]Franklin Pierce, a Democrat from New Hampshire.

[7]Stephen A. Douglas.

[8]James Buchanan.

involves nothing of the original Nebraska doctrine. That struggle was made on a point, the right of a people to make their own constitution, upon which he and the Republicans have never differed.

The several points of the Dred Scott decision, in connection with Senator Douglas' "care not" policy, constitute the piece of machinery, in its *present* state of advancement. This was the third point gained.

The *working* points of that machinery are:

First, that no negro slave, imported as such from Africa, and no descendant of such slave can ever be a *citizen* of any State, in the sense of that term as used in the Constitution of the United States.

This point is made in order to deprive the negro, in every possible event, of the benefit of this provision of the United States Constitution, which declares that—

"The citizens of each State shall be entitled to all privileges and immunities of citizens in the several States."

Secondly, that "subject to the Constitution of the United States," neither *Congress* nor a *Territorial Legislature* can exclude slavery from any United States territory.

This point is made in order that individual men may *fill up* the territories with slaves, without danger of losing them as property, and thus to enhance the chances of *permanency* to the institution through all the future.

Thirdly, that whether the holding a negro in actual slavery in a free State, makes him free, as against the holder, the United States courts will not decide, but will leave to be decided by the courts of any slave State the negro may be forced into by the master.

This point is made, not to be pressed *immediately;* but, if acquiesced in for a while, and apparently *indorsed* by the people at an election, *then* to sustain the logical conclusion that what Dred Scott's master might lawfully do with Dred Scott, in the free State of Illinois, every other master may lawfully do with any other *one,* or one *thousand* slaves, in Illinois, or in any other free State.

Auxiliary to all this, and working hand in hand with it, the Nebraska doctrine, or what is left of it, is to *educate* and *mould* public opinion, at least *Northern* public opinion, to not *care* whether slavery is voted *down* or voted *up.*

This shows exactly where we now *are;* and *partially* also, whither we are tending.

It will throw additional light on the latter, to go back, and run the mind over the string of historical facts already stated. Several things will *now* appear less *dark* and *mysterious* than they did *when* they were transpiring. The people were to be left "perfectly free" "subject only to the Constitution." What the *Constitution* had to do with it, outsiders could not *then* see. Plainly enough *now,* it was an exactly fitted *niche,* for the Dred Scott decision to afterwards come in, and declare the *perfect freedom* of the people, to be just no freedom at all. . . .

We can not absolutely *know* that all these exact adaptations are the result of preconcert. But when we see a lot of framed timbers, different portions of which we know have been gotten out at different times and places and by different workmen—Stephen, Franklin, Roger and James,[9] for instance—and when we see these timbers joined together, and see they exactly make the frame of a house or a mill, all the tenons and mortices exactly fitting, and all the lengths and proportions of the different pieces exactly adapted to their respective places, and not a piece too many or too few—not omitting even scaffolding—or, if a single piece be lacking, we can see the place in the frame exactly fitted and prepared to yet bring such piece in—in *such* a case, we find it impossible to not *believe* that Stephen and Franklin and Roger and James all understood one another from the beginning, and all worked upon a common *plan* or *draft* drawn up before the first lick was struck.

It should not be overlooked that, by the Nebraska bill, the people of a *State* as well as *Territory,* were to be left *"perfectly free"* *"subject only to the Constitution."*

Why mention a *State?* They were legislating for *territories,* and not *for* or *about* States. Certainly the people of a State *are* and *ought to be* subject to the Constitution of the United States; but why is mention of this *lugged* into this merely *territorial* law? Why are the people of a *territory* and the people of a *state* therein *lumped* together, and their relation to the Constitution therein treated as being *precisely* the same?

While the opinion of *the Court,* by Chief Justice Taney, in the Dred Scott case, and the separate opinions of all the concurring Judges, expressly declare that the Constitution of the United States neither permits Congress nor a Territorial legislature to exclude slavery from any United States territory, they all *omit* to declare whether or not the same Constitution permits a *state,* or the people of a State, to exclude it.

Possibly, this was a mere *omission;* but who can be *quite* sure. . . .

The nearest approach to the point of declaring the power of a State over slavery, is made by Judge Nelson.[10] He approaches it more than once, using the precise idea, and *almost* the language too, of the Nebraska act. On one occasion his exact language is, "except in cases where the power is restrained by the Constitution of the United States, the law of the State is supreme over the subject of slavery within its jurisdiction."

In what *cases* the power of the *states is* so restrained by the U.S. Constitution, is left an *open* question, precisely as the same question, as to the restraint on the power of the *territories* was left open in the Nebraska act. Put *that* and *that* together, and we have another nice little niche, which we

---

[9]That is, Senator Stephen A. Douglas, President Franklin Pierce, Chief Justice of the Supreme Court Roger B. Taney, and President James Buchanan, all Democrats.

[10]Samuel Nelson was a Supreme Court justice who wrote a separate opinion in the Dred Scott case that Lincoln refers to here.

may, ere long, see filled with another Supreme Court decision, declaring that the Constitution of the United States does not permit a *state* to exclude slavery from its limits.

And this may especially be expected if the doctrine of "care not whether slavery be voted *down* or voted *up*," shall gain upon the public mind sufficiently to give promise that such a decision can be maintained when made.

Such a decision is all that slavery now lacks of being alike lawful in all the States.

Welcome or unwelcome, such decision *is* probably coming, and will soon be upon us, unless the power of the present political dynasty shall be met and overthrown.

We shall *lie down* pleasantly dreaming that the people of *Missouri* are on the verge of making their State *free;* and we shall *awake* to the *reality,* instead, that the *Supreme* Court has made *Illinois* a *slave* State.

To meet and overthrow the power of that dynasty, is the work now before all those who would prevent that consummation.

That is *what* we have to do.

But *how* can we best do it?

There are those who denounce us *openly* to their *own* friends, and yet whisper *us softly,* that *Senator Douglas* is the *aptest* instrument there is, with which to effect that object. *They* do *not* tell us, nor has *he* told us, that he *wishes* any such object to be effected. They wish us to *infer* all, from the facts, that he now has a little quarrel[11] with the present head of the dynasty; and that he[12] has regularly voted with us,[13] on a single point, upon which, he and we, have never differed.

They remind us that *he* is a very *great man,* and that the largest of *us* are very small ones. Let this be granted. But "a *living dog* is better than a *dead lion*." Judge Douglas, if not a *dead* lion *for this work,* is at least a *caged* and *toothless* one. How can he oppose the advances of slavery? He don't *care* anything about it. His avowed *mission is impressing* the "public heart" to *care* nothing about it.

A leading Douglas Democratic newspaper thinks Douglas' superior talent will be needed to resist the revival of the African slave trade.

Does Douglas believe an effort to revive that trade is approaching? He has not said so. Does he *really* think so? But if it is, how can he resist it? For years he has labored to prove it a *sacred right* of white men to take negro slaves into the new territories. Can he possibly show that it is *less* a sacred right to *buy* them where they can be bought cheapest? And, unquestionably they can be bought *cheaper in Africa* than in *Virginia.*

He has done all in his power to reduce the whole question of slavery to one of a mere *right of property;* and as such, how can *he* oppose the foreign

---

[11] That is, Douglas differed with President Buchanan about the admission of Kansas under the Lecompton constitution.

[12] Douglas.

[13] Republicans.

slave trade—how can he refuse that trade in that "property" shall be "perfectly free"—unless he does it as a *protection* to the home production? And as the home *producers* will probably not *ask* the protection, he will be wholly without a ground of opposition.

Senator Douglas holds, we know, that a man may rightfully be *wiser today* than he was *yesterday*—that he may rightfully *change* when he finds himself wrong.

But, can we for that reason, run ahead, and *infer* that he *will* make any particular change, of which he, himself, has given no intimation? Can we *safely* base *our* action upon any such *vague* inference?

Now, as ever, I wish to not *misrepresent* Judge Douglas' *position,* question his *motives,* or do ought that can be personally offensive to him.

Whenever, *if ever,* he and we can come together on *principle* so that *our great cause* may have assistance from *his great ability,* I hope to have interposed no adventitious obstacle.

But clearly, he is not *now* with us—he does not *pretend* to be—he does not *promise* to *ever* be.

Our cause, then, must be intrusted to, and conducted by its own undoubted friends—those whose hands are free, whose hearts are in the work—who *do care* for the result.

Two years ago the Republicans of the nation mustered over thirteen hundred thousand strong.[14]

We did this under the single impulse of resistance to a common danger, with every external circumstance against us.

Of *strange, discordant,* and even, *hostile* elements, we gathered from the four winds, and *formed* and fought the battle through, under the constant hot fire of a disciplined, proud, and pampered enemy.

Did we brave all *then,* to *falter* now?—*now*—when that same enemy is *wavering,* dissevered and belligerent?

The result is not doubtful. We shall not fail—if we stand firm, we shall not fail.

Wise councils may *accelerate* or *mistakes delay* it, but, sooner or later the victory is *sure* to come.

---

[14]John C. Frémont, the Republican candidate, received over 1.3 million votes in the 1856 presidential election.

THE LINCOLN-DOUGLAS DEBATES

The Lincoln-Douglas debates highlighted the 1858 senatorial campaign in Illinois. Both men gave dozens of other speeches during the campaign, crisscrossing the state from village to town to city, each of them traveling thousands of miles. Lincoln, knowing that he faced an uphill battle in a predominantly Democratic state, hoped to improve his prospects by challenging Douglas to face-to-face debates. Douglas, by far the better known and more prominent candidate, reluctantly agreed to seven debates, one in each of Illinois's congressional districts, with the exception of the districts centering on Chicago and Springfield where the candidates had already appeared. Each debate followed a similar format: The candidates alternated speaking first; the leadoff speaker had one hour, the second speaker had an hour and a half, followed by a half-hour rebuttal by the first speaker. These three-hour marathons of political analysis attracted huge crowds. Newspapers sent reporters to describe the scene and transcribe every word. Neither candidate presented strikingly new ideas. Instead, they emphasized the differences between themselves and between their parties.

Douglas argued that Lincoln and the Republicans were in fact abolitionists whose zeal to end slavery would ride roughshod over the property rights of slaveowners, explicitly protected by the Constitution, and would be likely to precipitate disunion, even civil war. Worse, Douglas declared, Lincoln's insistence on the equality of whites and blacks violated the rights and privileges of white citizens of Illinois because it grew out of a misunderstanding of the Declaration of Independence, which was never intended to apply to anyone but whites. Douglas proclaimed that "this Government was made by our fathers on the white basis. It was made by white men for the benefit of white men and their posterity forever."[15] Far more important than any misplaced sympathy for slaves, Douglas repeatedly pointed out, was the sacred principle of democracy. Voters should be able to decide for themselves about slavery, as they did about other fundamental matters. He announced, "I care more for the great principle of self-government, the right of the people to rule, than I do for all the negroes in Christendom."[16]

Lincoln responded to Douglas's assertions by defining clearly what he and other Republicans stood for. While Republicans believed slavery was wrong, Lincoln insisted that they did not intend to harm it where it already existed, only to prevent it from expanding—hardly an abolitionist agenda. Lincoln reiterated that he did not advocate or desire full political or social equality for blacks, although blacks and whites did share the inalienable rights to life, liberty, and the pursuit of happiness posited in the Declaration of Independence. Lincoln took care to detail his views of the limits of

[15]Robert W. Johannsen, ed., *The Lincoln-Douglas Debates of 1858* (New York, 1965), 216.
[16]Ibid., 326.

racial equality, understanding full well that the vast majority of Illinois voters considered black people inferior and wanted nothing to do with them. In 1848, for example, a 70 percent majority of Illinois voters favored prohibiting blacks from entering the state, a plan put into effect by the legislature in 1853. Above all, Lincoln emphasized that Republicans, unlike Democrats, believed slavery was morally wrong.

Lincoln's arguments did not elevate him to the U.S. Senate. Since the Illinois legislature, not the voters at large, elected U.S. senators, neither Lincoln nor Douglas appeared on the ballot. In the November election, Democrats maintained their edge in the legislature and re-elected Douglas to the Senate by a margin of 54 to 46. "I am glad I made the late race," Lincoln wrote an old Whig friend. "It gave me a hearing on the great and durable question of the age, which I could have had in no other way; and though I now sink out of view, and shall be forgotten, I believe I have made some marks which will tell for the cause of civil liberty long after I am gone."[17]

Lincoln did not "sink out of view," of course. Prominent Republicans outside Illinois noticed his speeches and recognized him as an attractive moderate, positioned between the more militant antislavery Republicans and the more conservative old Whigs — notice Lincoln promoted by having the debates published in book form. Lincoln's performance in the senatorial campaign also consolidated his leadership in the Illinois Republican party, a matter of significance when Republicans gathered in Chicago two years later to nominate a candidate for president. The ideas Lincoln expressed on "the great and durable question of the age" in the following selections from his debates with Douglas became even more important when the defeated senatorial candidate became President of the United States and confronted the crisis of the Union.

[17]Lincoln to Anson G. Henry. *CW,* III, 339.

First Lincoln-Douglas Debate

August 21, 1858

Ottawa, Illinois

... This is the true complexion of all I have ever said in regard to the institution of slavery and the black race. This is the whole of it, and anything that argues me into his idea of perfect social and political equality with the negro, is but a specious and fantastic arrangement of words, by which a man can prove a horse chestnut to be a chestnut horse. [Laughter.] I will say here, while upon this subject, that I have no purpose directly or indirectly to interfere with the institution of slavery in the States where it exists. I believe I have no lawful right to do so, and I have no inclination to do so. I have no purpose to introduce political and social equality between the white and the black races. There is a physical difference between the two, which in my judgment will probably forever forbid their living together upon the footing of perfect equality, and inasmuch as it becomes a necessity that there must be a difference, I, as well as Judge Douglas, am in favor of the race to which I belong, having the superior position. I have never said anything to the contrary, but I hold that notwithstanding all this, there is no reason in the world why the negro is not entitled to all the natural rights enumerated in the Declaration of Independence, the right to life, liberty and the pursuit of happiness. [Loud cheers.] I hold that he is as much entitled to these as the white man. I agree with Judge Douglas he is not my equal in many respects—certainly not in color, perhaps not in moral or intellectual endowment. But in the right to eat the bread, without leave of anybody else, which his own hand earns, *he is my equal and the equal of Judge Douglas and the equal of every living man.* [Great applause.] ...

I ask the attention of the people here assembled and elsewhere, to the course that Judge Douglas is pursuing every day as bearing upon this question of making slavery national.... In the first place what is necessary to make the institution national? Not war. There is no danger that the people of Kentucky will shoulder their muskets and with a young nigger stuck on every bayonet march into Illinois and force them upon us. There is no danger of our going over there and making war upon them. Then what is necessary for the nationalization of slavery? It is simply the next Dred Scott decision. It is merely for the Supreme Court to decide that no *State* under the Constitution can exclude it, just as they have already decided that under the Constitution neither Congress nor the Territorial Legislature can do it....

Henry Clay, my beau ideal of a statesman, the man for whom I fought all my humble life—Henry Clay once said of a class of men who would repress all tendencies to liberty and ultimate emancipation, that they must, if they would do this, go back to the era of our Independence, and muzzle the cannon which thunders its annual joyous return; they must blow out the moral lights around us; they must penetrate the human soul, and eradicate there the love of liberty; and then and not till then, could they perpetuate slavery in this country! [Loud cheers.] To my thinking, Judge Douglas is, by his example and vast influence, doing that very thing in this community, [cheers,] when he says that the negro has nothing in the Declaration of Independence. Henry Clay plainly understood the contrary. Judge Douglas is going back to the era of our Revolution, and to the extent of his ability, muzzling the cannon which thunders its annual joyous return. When he invites any people willing to have slavery, to establish it, he is blowing out the moral lights around us. [Cheers.] When he says he "cares not whether slavery is voted down or voted up,"—that it is a sacred right of self government—he is in my judgment penetrating the human soul and eradicating the light of reason and the love of liberty in this American people. [Enthusiastic and continued applause.] And now I will only say that when, by all these means and appliances, Judge Douglas shall succeed in bringing public sentiment to an exact accordance with his own views—when these vast assemblages shall echo back all these sentiments—when they shall come to repeat his views and to avow his principles, and to say all that he says on these mighty questions—then it needs only the formality of the second Dred Scott decision, which he endorses in advance, to make Slavery alike lawful in all the States—old as well as new, North as well as South.

Fourth Lincoln-Douglas Debate

September 18, 1858

Charleston, Illinois

While I was at the hotel to-day an elderly gentleman called upon me to know whether I was really in favor of producing a perfect equality between the negroes and white people. [Great laughter.] . . . I will say then that I am not, nor ever have been in favor of bringing about in any way the social and political equality of the white and black races, [applause]—that I am not nor ever have been in favor of making voters or jurors of negroes, nor of qualifying them to hold office, nor to intermarry with white people; and I will say in addition to this that there is a physical difference between the white and black races which I believe will for ever forbid the two races living together on terms of social and political equality. And inasmuch as they cannot so live, while they do remain together there must be the position of superior and inferior, and I as much as any other man am in favor of having the superior position assigned to the white race. I say upon this occasion I do not perceive that because the white man is to have the superior position the negro should be denied everything. I do not understand that because I do not want a negro woman for a slave I must necessarily want her for a wife. [Cheers and laughter.] My understanding is that I can just let her alone. I am now in my fiftieth year, and I certainly never have had a black woman for either a slave or a wife. So it seems to me quite possible for us to get along without making either slaves or wives of negroes. I will add to this that I have never seen to my knowledge a man, woman or child who was in favor of producing a perfect equality, social and political, between negroes and white men.... I have never had the least apprehension that I or my friends would marry negroes if there was no law to keep them from it, [laughter] but as Judge Douglas and his friends seem to be in great apprehension that they might, if there were no law to keep them from it, [roars of laughter] I give him the most solemn pledge that I will to the very last stand by the law of this State, which forbids the marrying of white people with negroes. [Continued laughter and applause.] I will add one further word, which is this, that I do not understand there is any place where an alteration of the social and political relations of the negro and the white man can be made except in the State Legislature—not in the Congress of the United States—and as I do not really apprehend the approach of any such thing myself, and as Judge Douglas seems to be in constant horror that some such danger is rapidly approaching, I propose as the best means to prevent it that the Judge be kept at home and placed in the State Legislature to fight the measure. [Uproarious laughter and applause.]...

Judge Douglas has said to you that he has not been able to get from me an answer to the question whether I am in favor of negro citizenship. So far as I know, the Judge never asked me the question before. [Applause.] He shall have no occasion to ever ask it again, for I tell him very frankly that I am not in favor of negro citizenship. [Renewed applause.]... Now my opinion is that the different States have the power to make a negro a citizen under the Constitution of the United States if they choose. The Dred Scott decision decides that they have not that power. If the State of Illinois had that power I should be opposed to the exercise of it. [Cries of "good," "good," and applause.] That is all I have to say about it....

Fifth Lincoln-Douglas Debate

October 7, 1858

Galesburg, Illinois

The Judge has alluded to the Declaration of Independence, and insisted that negroes are not included in that Declaration; and that it is a slander upon the framers of that instrument, to suppose that negroes were meant therein; and he asks you: Is it possible to believe that Mr. Jefferson, who penned the immortal paper, could have supposed himself applying the language of that instrument to the negro race, and yet held a portion of that race in slavery?

Would he not at once have freed them? . . . I believe the entire records of the world, from the date of the Declaration of Independence up to within three years ago, may be searched in vain for one single affirmation, from one single man, that the negro was not included in the Declaration of Independence. I think I may defy Judge Douglas to show that he ever said so, that Washington ever said so, that any President ever said so, that any member of Congress ever said so, or that any living man upon the whole earth ever said so, until the necessities of the present policy of the Democratic party, in regard to slavery, had to invent that affirmation. [Tremendous applause.] And I will remind Judge Douglas and this audience, that while Mr. Jefferson was the owner of slaves, as undoubtedly he was, in speaking upon this very subject, he used the strong language that "he trembled for his country when he remembered that God was just;" and I will offer the highest premium in my power to Judge Douglas if he will show that he, in all his life, ever uttered a sentiment at all akin to that of Jefferson. [Great applause and cries of "Hit him again," "good," "good."] . . .

When the Judge says, in speaking on this subject, that I make speeches of one sort for the people of the Northern end of the State, and of a different sort for the Southern people, he assumes that I do not understand that my speeches will be put in print and read North and South. . . . And I have not supposed, and do not now suppose, that there is any conflict whatever between them. ["They are all good speeches!" "Hurrah for Lincoln!"] But the Judge will have it that if we do not confess that there is a sort of inequality between the white and black races, which justifies us in making them slaves, we must, then, insist that there is a degree of equality that requires us to make them our wives. [Loud applause, and cries, "Give it to him;" "Hit him again."] . . . I have all the while maintained, that in so far as it should be insisted that there was an equality between the white and black races that should produce a perfect social and political equality, it was an impossibility. This you have seen in my printed speeches, and with it I have said, that in their right to "life, liberty and the pursuit of happiness," as proclaimed in that old Declaration, the inferior races are our equals. [Long-continued cheering.] And these declarations I have constantly made in reference to the abstract moral question, to contemplate and consider when we are legislating about any new country which is not already cursed with the actual presence of the evil—slavery. I have never manifested any impatience with the necessities that spring from the actual presence of black people amongst us, and the actual existence of slavery amongst us where it does already exist; but I have insisted that, in legislating for new countries, where it does not exist, there is no just rule other than that of moral and abstract right! With reference to those new countries, those maxims as to the right of a people to "life, liberty and the pursuit of happiness," were the just rules to be constantly referred to. . . .

The essence of the Dred Scott case is compressed into the sentence which I will now read: "Now, as we have already said in an earlier part of this opinion, upon a different point, the right of property in a slave is distinctly and expressly affirmed in the Constitution." ... I believe that the right of property in a slave *is not* distinctly and expressly affirmed in the Constitution, and Judge Douglas thinks it *is*. I believe that the Supreme Court and the advocates of that decision may search in vain for the place in the Constitution where the right of property in a slave is distinctly and expressly affirmed.... This is but an opinion, and the opinion of one very humble man; but it is my opinion that the Dred Scott decision, as it is, never would have been made in its present form if the party that made it had not been sustained previously by the elections. My own opinion is, that the new Dred Scott decision, deciding against the right of the people of the States to exclude slavery, will never be made, if that party is not sustained by the elections. [Cries of "Yes, yes."] I believe, further, that it is just as sure to be made as to-morrow is to come, if that party shall be sustained. ["We won't sustain it, never, never."] ...

Sixth Lincoln-Douglas Debate
October 13, 1858

Quincy, Illinois

We have in this nation this element of domestic slavery. It is a matter of absolute certainty that it is a disturbing element. It is the opinion of all the great men who have expressed an opinion upon it, that it is a dangerous element. We keep up a controversy in regard to it. That controversy necessarily springs from difference of opinion, and if we can learn exactly—can reduce to the lowest elements—what that difference of opinion is, we perhaps shall be better prepared for discussing the different systems of policy that we would propose in regard to that disturbing element. I suggest that the difference of opinion, reduced to its lowest terms, is no other than the difference between the men who think slavery a wrong and those who do not think it wrong. The Republican party think it wrong—we think it is a moral, a social and a political wrong. We think it is a wrong not confining itself merely to the persons or the States where it exists, but that it is a wrong in its tendency, to say the least, that extends itself to the existence of the whole nation. Because we think it wrong, we propose a course of policy that shall deal with it as a wrong. We deal with it as with any other wrong, in so far as we can prevent its growing any larger, and so deal with it that in the run of time there may be some promise of an end to it. We have a due regard to the actual presence of it amongst us and the difficulties of getting rid of it in any satisfactory way, and all the constitutional obligations thrown about it. I suppose that in reference both to its actual existence in the nation, and to our constitutional obligations, we have no right at all to disturb it in the States where it exists, and we profess that we have no more inclination to disturb it than we have the right to do it. We go further than that; we don't propose to disturb it where, in one instance, we think the Constitution would permit us. We think the Constitution would permit us to disturb it in the District of Columbia. Still we do not propose to do that, unless it should be in terms which I don't suppose the nation is very likely soon to agree to—the terms of making the emancipation gradual and compensating the unwilling owners. Where we suppose we have the constitutional right, we restrain ourselves in reference to the actual existence of the institution and the difficulties thrown about it. We also oppose it as an evil so far as it seeks to spread itself. We insist on the policy that shall restrict it to its present limits. We don't suppose that in doing this we violate anything due to the actual presence of the institution, or anything due to the constitutional guarantees thrown around it.

We oppose the Dred Scott decision in a certain way, upon which I ought perhaps to address you a few words. We do not propose that when Dred Scott has been decided to be a slave by the court, we, as a mob, will decide him to be free. We do not propose that, when any other one, or one thousand, shall be decided by that court to be slaves, we will in any violent way disturb the rights of property thus settled; but we nevertheless do oppose that decision as a political rule which shall be binding on the voter, to vote for nobody who thinks it wrong, which shall be binding on the members of Congress or the President to favor no measure that does not actually concur with the principles of that decision. We do not propose to be bound by it as a political rule in that way, because we think it lays the foundation not merely of enlarging and spreading out what we consider an evil, but it lays the foundation for spreading that evil into the States themselves. We propose so resisting it as to have it reversed if we can, and a new judicial rule established upon this subject.

I will add this, that if there be any man who does not believe that slavery is wrong in the three aspects which I have mentioned, or in any one of them, that man is misplaced, and ought to leave us. While, on the other hand, if there be any man in the Republican party who is impatient over the necessity springing from its actual presence, and is impatient of the constitutional guarantees thrown around it, and would act in disregard of these, he too is misplaced standing with us. He will find his place somewhere else; for we have a due regard, so far as we are capable of understanding them, for all these things. This, gentlemen, as well as I can give it, is a plain statement of our principles in all their enormity.

I will say now that there is a sentiment in the country contrary to me—a sentiment which holds that slavery is not wrong, and therefore it goes for policy that does not propose dealing with it as a wrong. That policy is the Democratic policy, and that sentiment is the Democratic sentiment. . . . [T]urn it in any way you can, in all the arguments sustaining the Democratic policy, and in that policy itself, there is a careful, studied exclusion of the idea that there is anything wrong in slavery. Let us understand this. I am not, just here, trying to prove that we are right and they are wrong. I have been stating where we and they stand, and trying to show what is the real difference between us; and I now say that whenever we can get the question distinctly stated—can get all these men who believe that slavery is in some of these respects wrong, to stand and act with us in treating it as a wrong—then, and not till then, I think we will in some way come to an end of this slavery agitation. [Prolonged cheers.] . . .

Judge Douglas has sung paeans to his "Popular Sovereignty" doctrine until his Supreme Court cooperating with him has *squatted* his Squatter Sovereignty out. [Uproarious laughter and applause.] But he will keep up this species of humbuggery about Squatter Sovereignty. He has at last invented this sort of *do nothing Sovereignty*—[renewed laughter]—that the people may exclude slavery by a sort of "Sovereignty" that is exercised by doing nothing at all. [Continued laughter.] Is not that running his Popular Sovereignty down awfully? [Laughter.] Has it not got down as thin as the homoeopathic soup that was made by boiling the shadow of a pigeon that had starved to death? [Roars of laughter and cheering.] But at last, when it is brought to the test of close reasoning, there is not even that thin decoction of it left. It is a presumption impossible in the domain of thought. It is precisely no other than the putting of that most unphilosophical proposition, that two bodies may occupy the same space at the same time. The Dred Scott decision covers the whole ground, and while it occupies it, there is no room even for the shadow of a starved pigeon to occupy the same ground. [Great cheering and laughter.] . . .

Seventh Lincoln-Douglas Debate

October 15, 1858

Alton, Illinois

I have stated upon former occasions, and I may as well state again, what I understand to be the real issue in this controversy between Judge Douglas and myself. On the point of my wanting to make war between the free and the slave States, there has been no issue between us. So, too, when he assumes that I am in favor of introducing a perfect social and political equality between the white and black races. These are false issues, upon which Judge Douglas has tried to force the controversy. There is no foundation in truth for the charge that I maintain either of these propositions. The real issue in this controversy—the one pressing upon every mind—is the sentiment on the part of one class that looks upon the institution of slavery *as a wrong,* and of another class that *does not* look upon it as a wrong. The sentiment that contemplates the institution of slavery in this country as a wrong is the sentiment of the Republican party. It is the sentiment around which all their actions—all their arguments circle—from which all their propositions radiate. They look upon it as being a moral, social and political wrong; and while they contemplate it as such, they nevertheless have due regard for its actual existence among us, and the difficulties of getting rid of it in any satisfactory way and to all the constitutional obligations thrown about it. Yet having a due regard for these, they desire a policy in regard to it that looks to its not creating any more danger. They insist that it should as far as may be, *be treated* as a wrong, and one of the methods of treating it as a wrong is to *make provision that it shall grow no larger.* [Loud applause.] They also desire a policy that looks to a peaceful end of slavery at sometime, as being wrong. These are the views they entertain in regard to it as I understand them; and all their sentiments—all their arguments and propositions are brought within this range. . . .

On this subject of treating it as a wrong, and limiting its spread, let me say a word. Has any thing ever threatened the existence of this Union save and except this very institution of Slavery? What is it that we hold most dear amongst us? Our own liberty and prosperity. What has ever threatened our liberty and prosperity save and except this institution of Slavery? If this is true, how do you propose to improve the condition of things by enlarging Slavery—by spreading it out and making it bigger? You may have a wen or a cancer upon your person and not be able to cut it out lest you bleed to death; but surely it is no way to cure it, to engraft it and spread it over your whole body. That is no proper way of treating what you regard a wrong. You see this peaceful way of dealing with it as a wrong—restricting the spread of it, and not allowing it to go into new countries where it has not already existed. That is the peaceful way, the old-fashioned way, the way in which the fathers themselves set us the example.

On the other hand, I have said there is a sentiment which treats it as *not* being wrong. That is the Democratic sentiment of this day. I do not mean to say that every man who stands within that range positively asserts that it is right. That class will include all who positively assert that it is right, and all who like Judge Douglas treat it as indifferent and do not say it is either right or wrong. . . . You may turn over everything in the Democratic policy from beginning to end, whether in the shape it takes on the statute book, in the shape it takes in the Dred Scott decision, in the shape it takes in conversation or the shape it takes in short maxim-like arguments—it everywhere carefully excludes the idea that there is anything wrong in it.

That is the real issue. That is the issue that will continue in this country when these poor tongues of Judge Douglas and myself shall be silent. It is the eternal struggle between these two principles—right and wrong—throughout the world. They are the two principles that have stood face to face from the beginning of time; and will ever continue to struggle. The one is the common right of humanity and the other the divine right of kings. It is the same principle in whatever shape it develops itself. It is the same spirit that says, "You work and toil and earn bread, and I'll eat it." [Loud applause.] No matter in what shape it comes, whether from the mouth of a king who seeks to bestride the people of his own nation and live by the fruit of their labor, or from one race of men as an apology for enslaving another race, it is the same tyrannical principle.... Whenever the issue can be distinctly made, and all extraneous matter thrown out so that men can fairly see the real difference between the parties, this controversy will soon be settled, and it will be done peaceably too. There will be no war, no violence. It will be placed again where the wisest and best men of the world, placed it....

PARTISAN TACTICS

A cagey politician, Lincoln did not rely on ideas alone to sway voters. The following letter illustrates that Lincoln was willing to try to manipulate Irish immigrant voters who, he feared, were controlled by Democratic power brokers. The letter demonstrates that Lincoln was not immune to the anti-Irish prejudices common among members of the Know-Nothing party. A measure of his strong desire to win the election, the letter also reveals Lincoln's careful study of the balance of voters in each locale, a theme found throughout Lincoln's political correspondence.

Letter to Norman B. Judd
October 20, 1858

Rushville, [Illinois]

Hon. N. B. Judd[18]
My dear Sir:
I now have a high degree of confidence that we shall succeed, if we are not over-run with fraudulent votes to a greater extent than usual. On alighting from the cars[19] and walking three squares at Naples, [Illinois,] on Monday, I met fifteen Celtic gentlemen, with black carpet-sacks in their hands.

I learned that they had crossed over the Rail-road in Brown county, but where they were going no one could tell. They dropped in about the doggeries,[20] and were still hanging about when I left. At Brown County yesterday I was told that about four hundred of the same sort were to be brought

[18]Judd, a political ally of Lincoln, was a Chicago lawyer.
[19]That is, the passenger cars of a train.
[20]That is, the cheap saloons.

into Schuyler, before the election, to work on some new Railroad; but on reaching here I find Bagby[21] thinks that is not so.

What I most dread is that they will introduce into the doubtful districts numbers of men who are legal voters in all respects except *residence* and who will swear to residence and thus put it beyond our power to exclude them [from voting]. They can & I fear will swear falsely on that point, because they know it is next to impossible to convict them of Perjury upon it.

Now the great remaining part of the campaign, is finding a way to head this thing off. Can it be done at all?

I have a bare suggestion. When there is a known body of these voters, could not a true man, of the *"detective"* class, be introduced among them in disguise, who could, at the nick of time, control their votes.[22] Think this over. It would be a great thing, when this trick is attempted upon us, to have the saddle come up on the other horse. . . .

If we can head off the fraudulent votes we shall carry the day.

Yours as ever
A. LINCOLN

[21]John B. Bagby, one of Lincoln's political allies.
[22]That is, influence them to vote Republican.

THE 1860 CAMPAIGN FOR PRESIDENT

After losing to Douglas in the fall election, Lincoln traveled throughout the Midwest addressing Republican groups and stressing themes he had developed in his speeches since 1854. When his name began to be mentioned as a possible presidential candidate, he was "flattered, and gratified," he wrote an Illinois newspaper editor in the spring of 1859, but he added, "I must, in candor, say I do not think myself fit for the Presidency."[23] In truth, Lincoln did not have an auspicious record for a presidential aspirant: His national political experience was limited to one term in Congress ten years earlier, he had never served as governor of Illinois or mayor of Springfield, and he had been defeated twice in races for the U.S. Senate.

Lincoln's strongest political qualifications for the presidency were his ideas outlining a moderate Republicanism that had wide appeal among northern voters. Other Republican candidates were ostensibly better qualified than Lincoln, especially William H. Seward, U.S. senator and former

[23]Lincoln to Thomas J. Pickett. *CW,* III, 377.

governor of New York, and Salmon P. Chase, governor of Ohio. But both Seward and Chase were more fervently antislavery and more closely associated with abolitionism than Lincoln. In a presidential election, their ideas threatened to alienate centrist voters who, like Lincoln, tended to view both abolitionists and proslavery militants as extremists who jeopardized the Union.

When Lincoln received an invitation to speak to a gathering of Republicans in New York in February 1860, he jumped at the chance to present his ideas to an audience of sophisticated easterners right in Seward's backyard. Knowing the importance of the occasion, Lincoln crafted his speech with care. His address contrasted Republican doctrines with the distorted and misleading convictions of white southerners and Democrats, as the following selection illustrates. The enthusiastic response to the speech, which was published in the *New York Tribune* and reprinted as a pamphlet, elevated Lincoln to many Republicans' second choice for the presidential nomination, behind the front-runners Seward and Chase. The excitement caused Lincoln to confess to a Republican friend who asked if he intended to compete for the nomination, "I will be entirely frank. The taste is in my mouth a little."[24]

[24]Lincoln to Lyman Trumbull. *CW,* IV, 45.

Address at Cooper Institute
February 27, 1860

New York City
. . . It is surely safe to assume that the thirty-nine framers of the original Constitution, and the seventy-six members of the Congress which framed the amendments thereto, taken together, do certainly include those who may be fairly called "our fathers who framed the Government under which we live." And so assuming, I defy any man to show that any one of them ever, in his whole life, declared that, in his understanding, any proper division of local from federal authority, or any part of the Constitution, forbade the Federal Government to control as to slavery in the federal territories. . . . To those who now so declare, I give, not only "our fathers who framed the Government under which we live," but with them all other living men within the century in which it was framed, among whom to search, and they shall not be able to find the evidence of a single man agreeing with them.

Now, and here, let me guard a little against being misunderstood. I do not mean to say we are bound to follow implicitly in whatever our fathers did. To do so, would be to discard all the lights of current experience—to reject all progress—all improvement. What I do say is, that if we would supplant the opinions and policy of our fathers in any case, we should do so upon evidence so conclusive, and argument so clear, that even their great authority, fairly considered and weighed, cannot stand; and most surely not in a case whereof we ourselves declare they understood the question better than we. . . .

Let all who believe that "our fathers, who framed the Government under which we live, understood this question just as well, and even better, than we do now," speak as they spoke, and act as they acted upon it. This is all Republicans ask—all Republicans desire—in relation to slavery. As those fathers marked it, so let it be again marked, as an evil not to be extended, but to be tolerated and protected only because of and so far as its actual presence among us makes that toleration and protection a necessity. Let all the guaranties those fathers gave it, be, not grudgingly, but fully and fairly maintained. For this Republicans contend, and with this, so far as I know or believe, they will be content.

And now, if they would listen—as I suppose they will not—I would address a few words to the Southern people.

I would say to them: —You consider yourselves a reasonable and a just people; and I consider that in the general qualities of reason and justice you are not inferior to any other people. Still, when you speak of us Republicans, you do so only to denounce us as reptiles, or, at the best, as no better than outlaws. You will grant a hearing to pirates or murderers, but nothing like it to "Black Republicans." In all your contentions with one another, each of you deems an unconditional condemnation of "Black Republicanism" as the first thing to be attended to. Indeed, such condemnation of us seems to be an indispensable prerequisite—license, so to speak—among you to be admitted or permitted to speak at all. Now, can you, or not, be prevailed upon to pause and to consider whether this is quite just to us, or even to yourselves? Bring forward your charges and specifications, and then be patient long enough to hear us deny or justify.

You say we are sectional. We deny it. That makes an issue; and the burden of proof is upon you. You produce your proof; and what is it? Why, that our party has no existence in your section—gets no votes in your section. The fact is substantially true; but does it prove the issue? If it does, then in case we should, without change of principle, begin to get votes in your section, we should thereby cease to be sectional. You cannot escape this conclusion; and yet, are you willing to abide by it? If you are, you will probably soon find that we have ceased to be sectional, for we shall get votes in your section this very year. You will then begin to discover, as the truth plainly is, that your proof does not touch the issue. The fact that we get no votes in your section, is a fact of your making, and not of ours. And if there be fault in that fact, that fault is primarily yours, and remains so until you show that we repel you by some wrong principle or practice. If we do repel you by any wrong principle or practice, the fault is ours; but this brings you to where you ought to have started—to a discussion of the right or wrong of our principle. If our principle, put in practice, would wrong your section for the benefit of ours, or for any other object, then our principle, and we with it, are sectional, and are justly opposed and denounced as such. Meet us, then, on the question of whether our principle, put in practice, would wrong your section; and so meet us as if it were possible that something may be said on our side. Do you accept the challenge? No! Then you really believe that the principle which "our fathers who framed the Government under which we live" thought so clearly right as to adopt it, and indorse it again and again, upon their official oaths, is in fact so clearly wrong as to demand your condemnation without a moment's consideration.

Some of you delight to flaunt in our faces the warning against sectional parties given by Washington in his Farewell Address. Less than eight years before Washington gave that warning, he had, as President of the United States, approved and signed an act of Congress, enforcing the prohibition of slavery in the Northwestern Territory, which act embodied the policy of the Government upon that subject up to and at the very moment he penned that warning; and about one year after he penned it, he wrote La Fayette that he considered that prohibition a wise measure, expressing in the same connection his hope that we should at some time have a confederacy of free States.

Bearing this in mind, and seeing that sectionalism has since arisen upon this same subject, is that warning a weapon in your hands against us, or in our hands against you? Could Washington himself speak, would he cast the blame of that sectionalism upon us, who sustain his policy, or upon you who repudiate it? We respect that warning of Washington, and we commend it to you, together with his example pointing to the right application of it.

But you say you are conservative—eminently conservative—while we are revolutionary, destructive, or something of the sort. What is conservatism? Is it not adherence to the old and tried, against the new and untried? We stick to, contend for, the identical old policy on the point in controversy which was adopted by "our fathers who framed the Government under which we live;" while you with one accord reject, and scout, and spit upon that old policy, and insist upon substituting something new. True, you disagree among yourselves as to what that substitute shall be. You are divided on new propositions and plans, but you are unanimous in rejecting and denouncing the old policy of the fathers. Some of you are for reviving the foreign slave trade; some for a Congressional Slave-Code for the Territories; some for Congress forbidding the Territories to prohibit Slavery within their limits; some for maintaining Slavery in the Territories through the judiciary; some for the "gur-reat pur-rinciple" that "if one man would enslave another, no third man should object," fantastically called "Popular Sovereignty;" but never a man among you in favor of federal prohibition of slavery in federal territories, according to the practice of "our fathers who framed the Government under which we live." Not one of all your various plans can show a precedent or an advocate in the century within which our Government originated. Consider, then, whether your claim of conservatism for yourselves, and your charge of destructiveness against us, are based on the most clear and stable foundations.

Again, you say we have made the slavery question more prominent than it formerly was. We deny it. We admit that it is more prominent, but we deny that we made it so. It was not we, but you, who discarded the old policy of the fathers. We resisted, and still resist, your innovation; and thence comes the greater prominence of the question. Would you have that question reduced to its former proportions? Go back to that old policy. What has been will be again, under the same conditions. If you would have the peace of the old times, readopt the precepts and policy of the old times.

You charge that we stir up insurrections among your slaves. We deny it; and what is your proof? Harper's Ferry! John Brown!! John Brown[25] was no Republican; and you have failed to implicate a single Republican in his Harper's Ferry enterprise. If any member of our party is guilty in that matter, you know it or you do not know it. If you do know it, you are inexcusable for not designating the man and proving the fact. If you do not know it, you are inexcusable for asserting it, and especially for persisting in the assertion after you have tried and failed to make the proof. You need not be told that persisting in a charge which one does not know to be true, is simply malicious slander.

Some of you admit that no Republican designedly aided or encouraged the Harper's Ferry affair; but still insist that our doctrines and declarations necessarily lead to such results. We do not believe it. We know we hold to no doctrine, and make no declaration, which were not held to and made by "our fathers who framed the Government under which we live." You never dealt fairly by us in relation to this affair. When it occurred, some important State elections were near at hand, and you were in evident glee with the belief that, by charging the blame upon us, you could get an advantage of us in those elections. The elections came, and your expectations were not quite fulfilled. Every Republican man knew that, as to himself at least, your charge was a slander, and he was not much inclined by it to cast his vote in your favor. Republican doctrines and declarations are accompanied with a continual protest against any interference whatever with your slaves, or with you about your slaves. Surely, this does not encourage them to revolt. True, we do, in common with "our fathers, who framed the Government under which

[25]John Brown, intending to incite a slave insurrection, led a group of five black and seventeen white abolitionists in an attack on the federal armory at Harpers Ferry, Virginia, on October 16, 1859. The attack was quickly suppressed, and Brown was captured, tried for treason, and executed by the state of Virginia.

we live," declare our belief that slavery is wrong; but the slaves do not hear us declare even this. For anything we say or do, the slaves would scarcely know there is a Republican party. I believe they would not, in fact, generally know it but for your misrepresentations of us, in their hearing. In your political contests among yourselves, each faction charges the other with sympathy with Black Republicanism; and then, to give point to the charge, defines Black Republicanism to simply be insurrection, blood and thunder among the slaves.

Slave insurrections are no more common now than they were before the Republican party was organized. What induced the Southampton insurrection,[26] twenty-eight years ago, in which, at least, three times as many lives were lost as at Harper's Ferry? You can scarcely stretch your very elastic fancy to the conclusion that Southampton was "got up by Black Republicanism." In the present state of things in the United States, I do not think a general, or even a very extensive slave insurrection, is possible. The indispensable concert of action cannot be attained. The slaves have no means of rapid communication; nor can incendiary freemen, black or white, supply it. The explosive materials are everywhere in parcels; but there neither are, nor can be supplied, the indispensable connecting trains.

Much is said by Southern people about the affection of slaves for their masters and mistresses; and a part of it, at least, is true. A plot for an uprising could scarcely be devised and communicated to twenty individuals before some one of them, to save the life of a favorite master or mistress, would divulge it. This is the rule; and the slave revolution in Hayti[27] was not an exception to it, but a case occurring under peculiar circumstances. The gunpowder plot of British history,[28] though not connected with slaves, was more in point. In that case, only about twenty were admitted to the secret; and yet one of them, in his anxiety to save a friend, betrayed the plot to that friend, and, by consequence, averted the calamity. Occasional poisonings from the kitchen, and open or stealthy assassinations in the field, and local revolts extending to a score or so, will continue to occur as the natural results of slavery; but no general insurrection of slaves, as I think, can happen in this country for a long time. Whoever much fears, or much hopes for such an event, will be alike disappointed.

[26]In 1831, in Southhampton County, Virginia, a group of about sixty slaves led by Nat Turner initiated a slave insurrection that killed more than seventy white men, women, and children. White officials wasted no time capturing, trying, and executing the rebels, while suspicious whites tortured and killed hundreds of other slaves.

[27]In 1791, in the midst of revolutionary turmoil in France, slaves in Haiti, France's most important colony, rebelled against both their owners and their colonial overlords. Under the leadership of former slave Toussaint L'Ouverture, the rebels ultimately abolished slavery and created an independent nation.

[28]The Gunpowder Plot, a conspiracy among a small group of English Catholics to blow up Parliament and King James I in 1605, was foiled when the conspirators' secret plans were leaked to leaders loyal to the king.

In the language of Mr. Jefferson, uttered many years ago, "It is still in our power to direct the process of emancipation, and deportation, peaceably, and in such slow degrees, as that the evil will wear off insensibly; and their places be ... filled up by free white laborers. If, on the contrary, it is left to force itself on, human nature must shudder at the prospect held up."

Mr. Jefferson did not mean to say, nor do I, that the power of emancipation is in the Federal Government. He spoke of Virginia; and, as to the power of emancipation, I speak of the slaveholding States only. The Federal Government, however, as we insist, has the power of restraining the extension of the institution—the power to insure that a slave insurrection shall never occur on any American soil which is now free from slavery.

John Brown's effort was peculiar. It was not a slave insurrection. It was an attempt by white men to get up a revolt among slaves, in which the slaves refused to participate. In fact, it was so absurd that the slaves, with all their ignorance, saw plainly enough it could not succeed. That affair, in its philosophy, corresponds with the many attempts, related in history, at the assassination of kings and emperors. An enthusiast broods over the oppression of a people till he fancies himself commissioned by Heaven to liberate them. He ventures the attempt, which ends in little else than his own execution. Orsini's attempt on Louis Napoleon,[29] and John Brown's attempt at Harper's Ferry were, in their philosophy, precisely the same. The eagerness to cast blame on old England in the one case, and on New England in the other, does not disprove the sameness of the two things.

And how much would it avail you, if you could, by the use of John Brown, Helper's Book,[30] and the like, break up the Republican organization? Human action can be modified to some extent, but human nature cannot be changed. There is a judgment and a feeling against slavery in this nation, which cast at least a million and a half of votes. You cannot destroy that judgment and feeling—that sentiment—by breaking up the political organization which rallies around it. You can scarcely scatter and disperse an army which has been formed into order in the face of your heaviest fire; but if you could, how much would you gain by forcing the sentiment which created it out of the peaceful channel of the ballot-box, into some other channel? What would that other channel probably be? Would the number of John Browns be lessened or enlarged by the operation?

But you will break up the Union rather than submit to a denial of your Constitutional rights.

---

[29]Felice Orsini was an Italian nationalist who attempted to assassinate the French Emperor, Louis Napoleon III, in 1858. Some people in France blamed Orsini's action on England, France's traditional enemy.

[30]In 1857, Hinton Rowan Helper, a white North Carolinian, published *The Impending Crisis of the South,* a vehement attack on slavery and slaveholders for impoverishing slaveless southern whites and the South in general. Republicans distributed thousands of copies of Helper's book during the 1860 presidential campaign.

That has a somewhat reckless sound; but it would be palliated, if not fully justified, were we proposing, by the mere force of numbers, to deprive you of some right, plainly written down in the Constitution. But we are proposing no such thing.

When you make these declarations, you have a specific and well-understood allusion to an assumed Constitutional right of yours, to take slaves into the federal territories, and to hold them there as property. But no such right is specifically written in the Constitution. That instrument is literally silent about any such right. We, on the contrary, deny that such a right has any existence in the Constitution, even by implication.

Your purpose, then, plainly stated, is, that you will destroy the Government, unless you be allowed to construe and enforce the Constitution as you please, on all points in dispute between you and us. You will rule or ruin in all events.

This, plainly stated, is your language. Perhaps you will say the Supreme Court has decided the disputed Constitutional question in your favor. Not quite so. But waiving the lawyer's distinction between dictum and decision, the Court have decided the question for you in a sort of way. The Court have substantially said, it is your Constitutional right to take slaves into the federal territories, and to hold them there as property. When I say the decision was made in a sort of way, I mean it was made in a divided Court, by a bare majority of the Judges, and they not quite agreeing with one another in the reasons for making it; that it is so made as that its avowed supporters disagree with one another about its meaning, and that it was mainly based upon a mistaken statement of fact—the statement in the opinion that "the right of property in a slave is distinctly and expressly affirmed in the Constitution."

An inspection of the Constitution will show that the right of property in a slave is not "*distinctly*" and "*expressly* affirmed" in it. Bear in mind, the Judges do not pledge their judicial opinion that such right is *impliedly* affirmed in the Constitution; but they pledge their veracity that it is "*distinctly* and *expressly*" affirmed there—"distinctly," that is, not mingled with anything else—"expressly," that is, in words meaning just that, without the aid of any inference, and susceptible of no other meaning.

If they had only pledged their judicial opinion that such right is affirmed in the instrument by implication, it would be open to others to show that neither the word "slave" nor "slavery" is to be found in the Constitution, nor the word "property" even, in any connection with language alluding to the things slave, or slavery, and that wherever in that instrument the slave is alluded to, he is called a "person;"—and wherever his master's legal right in relation to him is alluded to, it is spoken of as "service or labor which may be due,"—as a debt payable in service or labor. Also, it would be open to show, by contemporaneous history, that this mode of alluding to slaves and slavery, instead of speaking of them, was employed on purpose to exclude from the Constitution the idea that there could be property in man.

To show all this, is easy and certain.

When this obvious mistake of the Judges shall be brought to their notice, is it not reasonable to expect that they will withdraw the mistaken statement, and reconsider the conclusion based upon it?

And then it is to be remembered that "our fathers, who framed the Government under which we live"—the men who made the Constitution—decided this same Constitutional question in our favor, long ago—decided it without division among themselves, when making the decision; without division among themselves about the meaning of it after it was made, and, so far as any evidence is left, without basing it upon any mistaken statement of facts.

Under all these circumstances, do you really feel yourselves justified to break up this Government, unless such a court decision as yours is, shall be at once submitted to as a conclusive and final rule of political action? But you will not abide the election of a Republican President! In that supposed event, you say, you will destroy the Union; and then, you say, the great crime of having destroyed it will be upon us! That is cool. A highwayman holds a pistol to my ear, and mutters through his teeth, "Stand and deliver, or I shall kill you, and then you will be a murderer!"

To be sure, what the robber demanded of me—my money—was my own; and I had a clear right to keep it; but it was no more my own than my vote is my own; and the threat of death to me, to extort my money, and the threat of destruction to the Union, to extort my vote, can scarcely be distinguished in principle.

A few words now to Republicans. *It is exceedingly desirable that all parts of this great Confederacy shall be at peace, and in harmony, one with another. Let us Republicans do our part to have it so. Even though much provoked, let us do nothing through passion and ill temper. Even though the southern people will not so much as listen to us, let us calmly consider their demands, and yield to them if, in our deliberate view of our duty, we possibly can.* Judging by all they say and do, and by the subject and nature of their controversy with us, let us determine, if we can, what will satisfy them.

Will they be satisfied if the Territories be unconditionally surrendered to them? We know they will not. In all their present complaints against us, the Territories are scarcely mentioned. Invasions and insurrections are the rage now. Will it satisfy them, if, in the future, we have nothing to do with invasions and insurrections? We know it will not. We so know, because we know we never had anything to do with invasions and insurrections; and yet this total abstaining does not exempt us from the charge and the denunciation.

The question recurs, what will satisfy them? Simply this: We must not only let them alone, but we must, somehow, convince them that we do let them alone. This, we know by experience, is no easy task. We have been so trying to convince them from the very beginning of our organization, but with no success. In all our platforms and speeches we have constantly protested our purpose to let them alone; but this has had no tendency to convince them. Alike unavailing to convince them, is the fact that they have never detected a man of us in any attempt to disturb them.

These natural, and apparently adequate means all failing, what will convince them? This, and this only: cease to call slavery *wrong,* and join them in calling it *right.* And this must be done thoroughly—done in *acts* as well as in *words.* Silence will not be tolerated—we must place ourselves avowedly with them. Senator Douglas's new sedition law[31] must be enacted and enforced, suppressing all declarations that slavery is wrong, whether made in politics, in presses, in pulpits, or in private. We must arrest and return their fugitive slaves with greedy pleasure. We must pull down our Free State constitutions. The whole atmosphere must be disinfected from all taint of opposition to slavery, before they will cease to believe that all their troubles proceed from us.

I am quite aware they do not state their case precisely in this way. Most of them would probably say to us, "Let us alone, *do* nothing to us, and *say* what you please about slavery." But we do let them alone—have never disturbed them—so that, after all, it is what we say, which dissatisfies them. They will continue to accuse us of doing, until we cease saying.

I am also aware they have not, as yet, in terms, demanded the overthrow of our Free-State Constitutions. Yet those Constitutions declare the wrong of slavery, with more solemn emphasis, than do all other sayings against it; and when all these other sayings shall have been silenced, the overthrow of these Constitutions will be demanded, and nothing be left to resist the demand. It is nothing to the contrary, that they do not demand the whole of this just now. Demanding what they do, and for the reason they do, they can voluntarily stop nowhere short of this consummation. Holding, as they do, that slavery is morally right, and socially elevating, they cannot cease to demand a full national recognition of it, as a legal right, and a social blessing.

Nor can we justifiably withhold this, on any ground save our conviction that slavery is wrong. If slavery is right, all words, acts, laws, and constitutions against it, are themselves wrong, and should be silenced, and swept away. If it is right, we cannot justly object to its nationality—its universality; if it is wrong, they cannot justly insist upon its extension—its enlargement. All they ask, we could readily grant, if we thought slavery right; all we ask, they could as readily grant, if they thought it wrong. Their thinking it right, and our thinking it wrong, is the precise fact upon which depends the whole controversy. Thinking it right, as they do, they are not to blame for desiring its full recognition, as being right; but, thinking it wrong, as we do, can we yield to them? Can we cast our votes with their view, and against our own? In view of our moral, social, and political responsibilities, can we do this?

Wrong as we think slavery is, we can yet afford to let it alone where it is, because that much is due to the necessity arising from its actual presence in the nation; but can we, while our votes will prevent it, allow it to spread into the National Territories, and to overrun us here in these Free States? If our

---

[31] In mid-January, Douglas proposed a law that prohibited conspiracies to "invade, assail, or molest the government, inhabitants, property, or institutions" of states and territories. The proposal was eventually tabled and never passed. Robert W. Johannsen, *Stephen A. Douglas* (New York, 1973), 723–25.

sense of duty forbids this, then let us stand by our duty, fearlessly and effectively. Let us be diverted by none of those sophistical contrivances wherewith we are so industriously plied and belabored—contrivances such as groping for some middle ground between the right and the wrong, vain as the search for a man who should be neither a living man nor a dead man—such as a policy of "don't care" on a question about which all true men do care—such as Union appeals beseeching true Union men to yield to Disunionists, reversing the divine rule, and calling, not the sinners, but the righteous to repentance—such as invocations to Washington, imploring men to unsay what Washington said, and undo what Washington did.

Neither let us be slandered from our duty by false accusations against us, nor frightened from it by menaces of destruction to the Government nor of dungeons to ourselves. LET US HAVE FAITH THAT RIGHT MAKES MIGHT, AND IN THAT FAITH, LET US, TO THE END, DARE TO DO OUR DUTY AS WE UNDERSTAND IT.

Lincoln did not attend the Republican convention in Chicago that nominated him for the presidency. Even after he had received the nomination, Lincoln stayed in Springfield, corresponding with scores of Americans about matters large and small, but saying as little as possible in public, as was customary in presidential campaigns. Throughout the North, however, Republicans staged rallies, organized parades, and waved banners proclaiming enthusiasm for Honest Abe the Rail-Splitter.

Remarks at a Republican Rally during the Presidential Campaign

August 8, 1860

Springfield, Illinois

My Fellow Citizens:—I appear among you upon this occasion with no intention of making a speech.

It has been my purpose, since I have been placed in my present position, to make no speeches. This assemblage having been drawn together at the place of my residence, it appeared to be the wish of those constituting this vast assembly[32] to see me; and it is certainly my wish to see all of you. I

---

[32]The rally attracted hundreds of Republican enthusiasts to the Springfield fairgrounds. When Lincoln arrived in his carriage, he was lifted above the heads of the crowd and carried to one of the speaking stands, where he delivered these remarks, later published in the *Illinois State Journal*.

appear upon the ground here at this time only for the purpose of affording myself the best opportunity of seeing you, and enabling you to see me.

I confess with gratitude, be it understood, that I did not suppose my appearance among you would create the tumult which I now witness. I am profoundly gratified for this manifestation of your feelings. I am gratified, because it is a tribute such as can be paid to no man as a man. It is the evidence that four years from this time you will give a like manifestation to the next man who is the representative of the truth on the questions that now agitate the public. And it is because you will then fight for this cause as you do now, or with even greater ardor than now, though I be dead and gone. I most profoundly and sincerely thank you.

Having said this much, allow me now to say that it is my wish that you will hear this public discussion by others of our friends who are present for the purpose of addressing you, and that you will kindly let me be silent.

Letter to Grace Bedell

October 19, 1860

Private

Springfield, Ills.

Miss. Grace Bedell
My dear little Miss.
Your very agreeable letter[33] of the 15th. is received.

I regret the necessity of saying I have no daughters. I have three sons—one seventeen, one nine, and one seven, years of age. They, with their mother, constitute my whole family.

As to the whiskers, having never worn any, do you not think people would call it a piece of silly affection if I were to begin it now?

Your very sincere well-wisher
A. LINCOLN.

[33]In her letter of October 15, 1860, Grace Bedell, who lived in Westfield, New York, wrote Lincoln, "My father has just home from the fair and brought home your picture and Mr. Hamlin's [Lincoln's Republican running mate]. I am a little girl only eleven years old, but want you should be President of the United States very much so I hope you wont think me very bold to write such a great man as you are. Have you any little girls about as large as I am. . . . I have got 4 brother's and part of them will vote for you any way and if you will let your whiskers grow I will try and get the rest of them to vote for you you would look a great deal better for your face is so thin. All the ladies like whiskers and they would tease their husband's to vote for you and then you would be President. My father is a going to vote for you and if I was a man I would vote for you to but I will try and get every one to vote for you that I can. . . ." Of course, Lincoln did grow a beard. On the way to Washington for his inauguration, the bewhiskered Lincoln met Grace Bedell when his train stopped in her hometown. *CW,* IV, 130, 219.

Letter to George T. M. Davis

October 27, 1860

Private & confidential.

Springfield, Ills.

Geo. T. M. Davis,[34] Esq.

My dear Sir:

Mr. Dubois[35] has shown me your letter of the 20th.; and I promised him to write you. What is it I could say which would quiet alarm? Is it that no interference by the government, with slaves or slavery within the states, is intended? I have said this so often already, that a repetition of it is but mockery, bearing an appearance of weakness, and cowardice, which perhaps should be avoided. Why do not uneasy men *read* what I have already said? and what our *platform* says? If they will not read, or heed, then, would they read, or heed, a repetition of them? Of course the declaration that there is no intention to interfere with slaves or slavery, in the states, with all that is fairly implied in such declaration, is true; and I should have no objection to make, and repeat the declaration a thousand times, if there were no danger of encouraging bold bad men to believe they are dealing with one who can be scared into anything. . . .

Yours very truly
A. LINCOLN.

[34]Davis was a New York businessman and had been an old friend of Lincoln's since the 1830s when he lived in Illinois.

[35]Davis's letter to Jesse K. Dubois reported that rumors were circulating in New York that a plan was afoot to create a financial panic if Lincoln was elected. He hoped Lincoln would make an announcement that would scotch the rumors and prevent a panic.

Lincoln's public reticence and Republican electioneering proved successful. Although Lincoln won just under 40 percent of the popular vote, he carried every northern state except New Jersey (where he split the electoral vote with Douglas), easily compiling an electoral vote majority of 180. The nominee of the National Democratic Party, Lincoln's old rival Douglas, polled nearly 30 percent of the popular vote, but only won in Missouri, accounting for just 12 electoral votes in all. John Bell, the nominee of the Constitutional Union Party, carried the border states of Virginia, Kentucky, and Tennessee for 39 electoral votes with 13 percent of the popular vote. Every other southern state voted for John C. Breckinridge, nominee of the Southern

Figure 3. 1860 Presidential Campaign

This photograph, taken in August 1860, shows Lincoln (standing at the right of the doorway) at his home in Springfield — where he and his family had lived since 1844 — being serenaded by a group of Republican enthusiasts, including both men and women.

Democratic Party, who amassed 72 electoral votes from 18 percent of the popular vote. Never before had a presidential election created such deep sectional fissures.

Remarks after Victory in the Presidential Election, Springfield, Illinois

November 20, 1860

FRIENDS AND FELLOW-CITIZENS:—Please excuse me, on this occasion, from making a speech. I thank you for the kindness and compliment of this call.[36] I thank you, in common with all others, who have thought fit, by their votes, to indorse the Republican cause. I rejoice with you in the success which has, so far, attended that cause. Yet in all our rejoicing let us neither express, nor cherish, any harsh feeling towards any citizen who, by his vote, has differed with us. Let us at all times remember that all American citizens are brothers of a common country, and should dwell together in the bonds of fraternal feeling.

Let me again beg you to accept my thanks, and to excuse me from further speaking at this time.

[36] A parade of Republican Wide-Awakes, celebrating Lincoln's victory in the presidential election, passed his house and called him out to address them.

4

The Secession Crisis

Lincoln's victory in the November presidential election provoked secessionists to launch a campaign to lead southern states out of the Union. Four months later when Lincoln took the oath of office, seven Deep South states—South Carolina, Mississippi, Florida, Alabama, Georgia, Louisiana, and Texas—had seceded and seized many federal facilities, including forts, arsenals, and customs houses. As president-elect, Lincoln had no official power. He could do little more than watch as outgoing President James Buchanan declared that although secession was illegal, he could do nothing about it.

While the nation drifted toward dissolution, Lincoln used his influence as the leader of the Republican party, writing privately to political leaders to demand that his own party hold firm to its opposition to the extension of slavery and to reassure southerners that a Republican administration posed no threat. In February 1861, Lincoln broke his public silence, speaking at nearly every whistle-stop on his long train journey from Springfield to Washington. The ideas Lincoln outlined in these public speeches and private letters structured his inaugural address on March 4 and defined the basic assumptions that guided his subsequent responses to the secession crisis, as the documents in this chapter illustrate.

THE LIMITS OF COMPROMISE

While voters across the South chose delegates to state conventions that would decide whether to secede, President-Elect Lincoln remained in Springfield, deluged with the requests of office-seekers and the advice of friends and foes. In Washington, House and Senate committees considered compromise proposals that might forestall disunion. In a series of private letters, from which the following selections are drawn, Lincoln made it clear that he was willing to conciliate the slave states but that no compromise was acceptable that permitted the expansion of territory open to slavery. After South Carolina officially seceded on December 20, followed by six other Deep South states by February 1, Lincoln began to formulate his views on secession.

Letter to Lyman Trumbull

December 10, 1860

Private, & confidential

Springfield, Ills.

Hon. L. Trumbull.[1]

My dear Sir: Let there be no compromise on the question of *extending* slavery. If there be, all our labor is lost, and, ere long, must be done again. The dangerous ground—that into which some of our friends have a hankering to run—is Pop[ular] Sov[ereignty]. Have none of it. Stand firm. The tug has to come, & better now, than any time hereafter.

Yours as ever
A. LINCOLN.

[1]Trumbull, a U.S. senator from Illinois and a Republican, was in Washington, where committees in both the House and the Senate were considering proposals to reach a compromise on sectional differences.

Letter to John A. Gilmer

December 15, 1860

Strictly confidential.

Springfield, Ill.

Hon. John A. Gilmer:[2]

My dear Sir—Yours of the 10th is received.[3] I am greatly disinclined to write a letter on the subject embraced in yours; and I would not do so, even privately as I do, were it not that I fear you might misconstrue my silence. Is it desired that I shall shift the ground upon which I have been elected? I can not do it. You need only to acquaint yourself with that ground, and press it on the attention of the South. It is all in print and easy of access. May I be pardoned if I ask whether even you have ever attempted to procure the reading

[2]Gilmer, a congressman from North Carolina, was an old Whig who opposed secession.
[3]Gilmer's letter asked Lincoln to answer a series of questions about his position by issuing a public announcement.

of the Republican platform, or my speeches, by the Southern people? If not, what reason have I to expect that any additional production of mine would meet a better fate? It would make me appear as if I repented for the crime of having been elected, and was anxious to apologize and beg forgiveness. To so represent me, would be the principal use made of any letter I might now thrust upon the public. My old record cannot be so used; and that is precisely the reason that some new declaration is so much sought.

Now, my dear sir, be assured, that I am not questioning *your* candor; I am only pointing out, that, while a new letter would hurt the cause which I think a just one, you can quite as well effect every patriotic object with the old record. Carefully read . . . the volume of Joint Debates between Senator Douglas and myself, with the Republican Platform adopted at Chicago, and all your questions will be substantially answered. I have no thought of recommending the abolition of slavery in the District of Columbia, nor the slave trade among the slave states, even on the conditions indicated; and if I were to make such recommendation, it is quite clear Congress would not follow it.

As to employing slaves in Arsenals and Dockyards,[4] it is a thing I never thought of in my life, to my recollection, till I saw your letter; and I may say of it, precisely as I have said of the two points above.

As to the use of patronage in the slave states, where there are few or no Republicans, I do not expect to inquire for the politics of the appointee, or whether he does or not own slaves. I intend in that matter to accommodate the people in the several localities, if they themselves will allow me to accommodate them. In one word, I never have been, am not now, and probably never shall be, in a mood of harassing the people, either North or South.

On the territorial question, I am inflexible, as you see my position in the book. On that, there is a difference between you and us; and it is the only substantial difference. You think slavery is right and ought to be extended; we think it is wrong and ought to be restricted. For this, neither has any just occasion to be angry with the other.

As to the state laws,[5] mentioned in your sixth question, I really know very little of them. I never have read one. If any of them are in conflict with the fugitive slave clause, or any other part of the constitution, I certainly should be glad of their repeal; but I could hardly be justified, as a citizen of Illinois, or as President of the United States, to recommend the repeal of a statute of Vermont, or South Carolina.

With the assurance of my highest regards I subscribe myself

Your obt. Servt.,

A. LINCOLN

[4]That is, Lincoln had no plan to replace white workingmen in federal arsenals or dockyards by employing slaves.

[5]Southern leaders demanded that northern states repeal laws—often called "personal liberty laws"—intended to impede enforcement of the federal fugitive slave law.

Letter to Alexander H. Stephens

December 22, 1860

For your own eye only.

Springfield, Ills.

Hon. A. H. Stephens[6]—
My dear Sir
Your obliging answer[7] to my short note is just received, and for which please accept my thanks. I fully appreciate the present peril the country is in, and the weight of responsibility on me.

Do the people of the South really entertain fears that a Republican administration would, *directly,* or *indirectly,* interfere with their slaves, or with them, about their slaves? If they do, I wish to assure you, as once a friend, and still, I hope, not an enemy, that there is no cause for such fears.

The South would be in no more danger in this respect, than it was in the days of Washington. I suppose, however, this does not meet the case. You think slavery is *right* and ought to be extended; while we think it is *wrong* and ought to be restricted. That I suppose is the rub. It certainly is the only substantial difference between us.

Yours very truly
A. LINCOLN

[6]Stephens, a former Whig from Georgia who had served in Congress with Lincoln, opposed secession. After Georgia seceded, he supported the decision and was chosen vice president of the Confederacy in February 1861.
[7]Stephens's letter urged Lincoln to "do what you can to save our common country" by declaring publicly that he did not intend to harm slavery. *CW,* IV, 161.

Letter to Duff Green

December 28, 1860

Springfield, Ill.

Gen. Duff Green.[8]
My dear Sir—I do not desire any amendment of the Constitution. Recognizing, however, that questions of such amendment rightfully belong to the American People, I should not feel justified, nor inclined, to withhold from

[8]Green, an old Democratic partisan, had come to Springfield as an emissary of President Buchanan, seeking Lincoln's support for a constitutional amendment that guaranteed federal power would never be used to abolish slavery in the states. Just such an amendment, among others, was proposed by the U.S. Senate's Committee of Thirteen, which concluded its deliberations on the day Lincoln wrote this letter.

them, if I could, a fair opportunity of expressing their will thereon, through either of the modes prescribed in the instrument.

In addition I declare that the maintainance inviolate of the rights of the States, and especially the right of each state to order and control its own domestic institutions according to its own judgment exclusively, is essential to that balance of powers on which the perfection, and endurance of our political fabric depends—and I denounce the lawless invasion, by armed force, of the soil of any State or Territory, no matter under what pretext, as the gravest of crimes.

I am greatly averse to writing anything for the public at this time; and I consent to the publication of this, only upon the condition that six of the twelve United States Senators for the States of Georgia, Alabama, Mississippi, Louisiana, Florida, and Texas shall sign their names to what is written on this sheet below my name, and allow the whole to be published together.

Yours truly
A. LINCOLN.

We recommend to the people of the States we represent respectively, to suspend all action for dismemberment of the Union, at least, until some act, deemed to be violative of our rights, shall be done by the incoming administration.[9]

[9]The southern senators never signed this statement, and therefore Lincoln's letter never became public.

Letter to James W. Webb
December 29, 1860

Private

Springfield, Ills.

Col. J. W. Webb[10]
My dear Sir:
Yours kindly seeking my view as to the proper mode of dealing with secession, was received several days ago, but, for want of time I could not answer it till now. I think we should hold the forts, or retake them, as the case may be, and collect the revenue. *We* shall have to forego the use of the federal courts, and *they* that of the mails, for a while. We can not fight them in to holding courts, or receiving the mails.

This is an outline of my view; and perhaps suggests sufficiently, the whole of it.

Yours very truly
A. LINCOLN

[10]Webb was the editor of the *New York Courier and Enquirer*.

Letter to James T. Hale

January 11, 1861

Confidential.

Springfield, Ill.

Hon. J. T. Hale[11]

My dear Sir—Yours of the 6th is received.[12] I answer it only because I fear you would misconstrue my silence. What is our present condition? We have just carried an election on principles fairly stated to the people. Now we are told in advance, the government shall be broken up, unless we surrender to those we have beaten, before we take the offices. In this they are either attempting to play upon us, or they are in dead earnest. Either way, if we surrender, it is the end of us, and of the government. They will repeat the experiment upon us *ad libitum.*[13] A year will not pass, till we shall have to take Cuba as a condition upon which they will stay in the Union. They now have the Constitution, under which we have lived over seventy years, and acts of Congress of their own framing, with no prospect of their being changed; and they can never have a more shallow pretext for breaking up the government, or extorting a compromise, than now. There is, in my judgment, but one compromise which would really settle the slavery question, and that would be a prohibition against acquiring any more territory.

Yours very truly,
A. LINCOLN.

[11] Hale was a Republican congressman from Pennsylvania.
[12] Hale's letter sought Lincoln's endorsement for a congressional compromise proposal similar to that of the Senate's Committee of Thirteen.
[13] A Latin term meaning "at their pleasure."

Letter to William H. Seward

February 1, 1861

Private & confidential.

Springfield, Ills.

Hon. W. H. Seward[14]

My dear Sir ... I say now, however, as I have all the while said, that on the territorial question—that is, the question of extending slavery under the national auspices,—I am inflexible. I am for no compromise which *assists* or

[14] Seward had agreed late in December 1860 to accept Lincoln's invitation to become secretary of state.

permits the extension of the institution on soil owned by the nation. And any trick by which the nation is to acquire territory, and then allow some local authority to spread slavery over it, is as obnoxious as any other.

I take it that to effect some such result as this, and to put us again on the high-road to a slave empire is the object of all these proposed compromises. I am against it.

As to fugitive slaves, District of Columbia, slave trade among the slave states, and whatever springs of necessity from the fact that the institution is amongst us, I care but little, so that what is done be comely, and not altogether outrageous. Nor do I care much about New-Mexico, if further extension were hedged against.

Yours very truly
A. LINCOLN

RALLYING THE UNION

On February 11, Lincoln and his family boarded a special train for the trip to Washington. Instead of making a beeline for the capital, the train proceeded slowly across Indiana into southern Ohio, jogged north to Pittsburgh and Cleveland, then moved east and south through New York, New Jersey, and Pennsylvania before finally arriving in Washington on February 23. At every stop, huge crowds turned out to catch a glimpse of the new president, the first to be born west of the Appalachian Mountains. Lincoln took advantage of these brief public encounters. In speech after speech, from which the following selections were drawn, Lincoln proclaimed his devotion to the Union and his determination to preserve it. He ridiculed secession and sought to rally support for the Union among all citizens, regardless of how they had voted in the presidential election. Newspapers avidly reported Lincoln's speeches, spreading his views to a national audience for the first time since his election. The same newspapers also carried dispatches from Montgomery, Alabama, where the newly organized Confederacy selected Jefferson Davis as its president on February 18, while Lincoln was midway on his journey to Washington.

Farewell Address at Springfield, Illinois

February 11, 1861

My friends—No one, not in my situation, can appreciate my feeling of sadness at this parting. To this place, and the kindness of these people, I owe every thing. Here I have lived a quarter of a century, and have passed from a young to an old man. Here my children have been born, and one is buried. I now leave, not knowing when, or whether ever, I may return, with a task before me greater than that which rested upon Washington. Without the assistance of that Divine Being, who ever attended him, I cannot succeed. With that assistance I cannot fail. Trusting in Him, who can go with me, and remain with you and be every where for good, let us confidently hope that all will yet be well. To His care commending you, as I hope in your prayers you will commend me, I bid you an affectionate farewell

Speech from the Balcony of the Bates House at Indianapolis, Indiana

February 11, 1861

It is not possible, in my journey to the national capital, to address assemblies like this which may do me the great honor to meet me as you have done, but very briefly. I should be entirely worn out if I were to attempt it. I appear before you now to thank you for this very magnificent welcome which you have given me, and still more for the very generous support which your State recently gave to the political cause of the whole country, and the whole world. [Applause.] Solomon has said, that there is a time to keep silence. [Renewed and deafening applause.]* * * * * [15] . . .

The words "coercion" and "invasion" are in great use about these days. Suppose we were simply to try if we can, and ascertain what, is the meaning of these words. Let us get, if we can, the exact definitions of these words—not from dictionaries, but from the men who constantly repeat them—what things they mean to express by the words. What, then, is "coercion"? What is "invasion"? Would the marching of an army into South Carolina, for instance, without the consent of her people, and in hostility against them, be coercion or invasion? I very frankly say, I think it would be invasion, and it would be coercion too, if the people of that country were forced to submit.

[15] These asterisks appear in the original report of the speech published in the *Indianapolis Daily Sentinel*. They evidently indicate that loud applause prevented the reporter from hearing what Lincoln said.

But if the Government, for instance, but simply insists upon holding its own forts, or retaking those forts which belong to it,—[cheers,]—or the enforcement of the laws of the United States in the collection of duties upon foreign importations,—[renewed cheers,]—or even the withdrawal of the mails from those portions of the country where the mails themselves are habitually violated; would any or all of these things be coercion? Do the lovers of the Union contend that they will resist coercion or invasion of any State, understanding that any or all of these would be coercing or invading a State? If they do, then it occurs to me that the means for the preservation of the Union they so greatly love, in their own estimation, is of a very thin and airy character. [Applause.] If sick, they would consider the little pills of the homoepathist as already too large for them to swallow. In their view, the Union, as a family relation, would not be anything like a regular marriage at all, but only as a sort of free-love arrangement,—[laughter,]—to be maintained on what that sect calls passionate attraction. [Continued laughter.] But, my friends, enough of this.

What is the particular sacredness of a State? I speak not of that position which is given to a State in and by the Constitution of the United States, for that all of us agree to—we abide by; but that position assumed, that a State can carry with it out of the Union that which it holds in sacredness by virtue of its connection with the Union. I am speaking of that assumed right of a State, as a primary principle, that the Constitution should rule all that is less than itself, and ruin all that is bigger than itself. [Laughter.] But, I ask, wherein does consist that right? If a State, in one instance, and a county in another, should be equal in extent of territory, and equal in the number of people, wherein is that State any better than the county? Can a change of name change the right? By what principle of original right is it that one-fiftieth or one-ninetieth of a great nation, by calling themselves a State, have the right to break up and ruin that nation as a matter of original principle? Now, I ask the question—I am not deciding anything—[laughter,]—and with the request that you will think somewhat upon that subject and decide for yourselves, if you choose, when you get ready,—where is the mysterious, original right, from principle, for a certain district of country with inhabitants, by merely being called a State, to play tyrant over all its own citizens, and deny the authority of everything greater than itself. [Laughter.] I say I am deciding nothing, but simply giving something for you to reflect upon; and, with having said this much, and having declared, in the start, that I will make no long speeches, I thank you again for this magnificent welcome, and bid you an affectionate farewell. [Cheers.]

Speech to Germans at Cincinnati, Ohio

February 12, 1861

MR. CHAIRMAN: I thank you and those whom you represent,[16] for the compliment you have paid me, by tendering me this address. In so far as there is an allusion to our present national difficulties, which expresses, as you have said, the views of the gentlemen present, I shall have to beg pardon for not entering fully upon the questions, which the address you have now read, suggests.

I deem it my duty—a duty which I owe to my constituents—to you, gentlemen, that I should wait until the last moment, for a development of the present national difficulties, before I express myself decidedly what course I shall pursue. I hope, then, not to be false to anything that you have to expect of me.

I agree with you, Mr. Chairman, that the working men are the basis of all governments, for the plain reason that they are the most numerous, and as you added that those were the sentiments of the gentlemen present, representing not only the working class, but citizens of other callings than those of the mechanic, I am happy to concur with you in these sentiments, not only of the native born citizens, but also of the Germans and foreigners from other countries.

Mr. Chairman, I hold that while man exists, it is his duty to improve not only his own condition, but to assist in ameliorating mankind; and therefore, without entering upon the details of the question, I will simply say, that I am for those means which will give the greatest good to the greatest number.

In regard to the Homestead Law,[17] I have to say that in so far as the Government lands can be disposed of, I am in favor of cutting up the wild lands into parcels, so that every poor man may have a home.

In regard to the Germans and foreigners, I esteem them no better than other people, nor any worse. [Cries of good.] It is not my nature, when I see a people borne down by the weight of their shackles—the oppression of tyranny—to make their life more bitter by heaping upon them greater burdens; but rather would I do all in my power to raise the yoke, than to add anything that would tend to crush them.

Inasmuch as our country is extensive and new, and the countries of Europe are densely populated, if there are any abroad who desire to make this the land of their adoption, it is not in my heart to throw aught in their way, to prevent them from coming to the United States.

Mr. Chairman, and Gentlemen, I will bid you an affectionate farewell.

[16]Lincoln responded to a speech by Frederick Oberkline, the chairman of a committee representing eighteen organizations of German workingmen.

[17]Congress had recently approved a homestead bill allowing settlers to obtain farm-sized allotments of government land for free, but President Buchanan vetoed the bill. A new homestead law was passed in 1862 by the Republican-dominated Congress and signed by Lincoln.

Speech at Cleveland, Ohio

February 15, 1861

MR. CHAIRMAN AND FELLOW CITIZENS OF CLEVELAND:—We have been marching about two miles through snow, rain and deep mud. The large numbers that have turned out under these circumstances testify that you are in earnest about something or other. But do I think so meanly of you as to suppose that that earnestness is about me personally? I would be doing you injustice to suppose you did. You have assembled to testify your respect to the Union, the constitution and the laws, and here let me say that it is with you, the people, to advance the great cause of the Union and the constitution, and not with any one man. It rests with you alone. This fact is strongly impressed on my mind at present. In a community like this, whose appearance testifies to their intelligence, I am convinced that the cause of liberty and the Union can never be in danger. Frequent allusion is made to the excitement at present existing in our national politics, and it is as well that I should also allude to it here. I think that there is no occasion for any excitement. The crisis, as it is called, is altogether an artificial crisis. In all parts of the nation there are differences of opinion and politics. There are differences of opinion even here. You did not all vote for the person who now addresses you. What is happening now will not hurt those who are farther away from here. Have they not all their rights now as they ever have had? Do they not have their fugitive slaves returned now as ever? Have they not the same constitution that they have lived under for seventy odd years? Have they not a position as citizens of this common country, and have we any power to change that position? (Cries of "No.") What then is the matter with them? Why all this excitement? Why all these complaints? As I said before, this crisis is all artificial. It has no foundation in facts. It was not argued up, as the saying is, and cannot, therefore, be argued down. Let it alone and it will go down of itself (Laughter.) . . . [T]his reception was . . . [given] by men of all parties. This is as it should be. If Judge Douglas had been elected and had been here on his way to Washington, as I am to-night, the republicans should have joined his supporters in welcoming him, just as his friends have joined with mine to-night. If all do not join now to save the good old ship of the Union this voyage nobody will have a chance to pilot her on another voyage. . . .

Speech in Independence Hall, Philadelphia, Pennsylvania

February 22, 1861

MR. CUYLER[18]—I am filled with deep emotion at finding myself standing here in the place where were collected together the wisdom, the patriotism, the devotion to principle, from which sprang the institutions under which we live. You have kindly suggested to me that in my hands is the task of restoring peace to our distracted country. I can say in return, sir, that all the political sentiments I entertain have been drawn, so far as I have been able to draw them, from the sentiments which originated, and were given to the world from this hall in which we stand. I have never had a feeling politically that did not spring from the sentiments embodied in the Declaration of Independence. (Great cheering.) I have often pondered over the dangers which were incurred by the men who assembled here and adopted that Declaration of Independence—I have pondered over the toils that were endured by the officers and soldiers of the army, who achieved that Independence. (Applause.) I have often inquired of myself, what great principle or idea it was that kept this Confederacy so long together. It was not the mere matter of the separation of the colonies from the mother land; but something in that Declaration giving liberty, not alone to the people of this country, but hope to the world for all future time. (Great applause.) It was that which gave promise that in due time the weights should be lifted from the shoulders of all men, and that *all* should have an equal chance. (Cheers.) This is the sentiment embodied in that Declaration of Independence.

Now, my friends, can this country be saved upon that basis? If it can, I will consider myself one of the happiest men in the world if I can help to save it. If it can't be saved upon that principle, it will be truly awful. But, if this country cannot be saved without giving up that principle—I was about to say I would rather be assassinated[19] on this spot than to surrender it. (Applause.)

Now, in my view of the present aspect of affairs, there is no need of bloodshed and war. There is no necessity for it. I am not in favor of such a course, and I may say in advance, there will be no blood shed unless it be forced upon the Government. The Government will not use force unless force is used against it. (Prolonged applause and cries of "That's the proper sentiment.")

My friends, this is a wholly unprepared speech. I did not expect to be called upon to say a word when I came here—I supposed I was merely to do

---

[18]Theodore L. Cuyler, president of the Select Council of Philadelphia, gave a welcoming address.

[19]Lincoln had recently received word of a threat to assassinate him when he passed through Baltimore.

something towards raising a flag. I may, therefore, have said something indiscreet, (cries of "no, no"), but I have said nothing but what I am willing to live by, and, in the pleasure of Almighty God, die by.

FIRST INAUGURAL ADDRESS

When Lincoln took the oath of office—administered by Chief Justice Roger B. Taney, whose *Dred Scott* decision Lincoln had denounced repeatedly—the controversy over the extension of slavery had been eclipsed by secession and the formation of the Confederacy. In his inaugural address, Lincoln explained that he would govern according to the Constitution. Attempting to reassure unionists in the slave states, he explained that he did not intend to interfere with slavery where it existed, protected by the federal Constitution and state laws. He contrasted his devotion to the Constitution with secession, which he believed violated the Constitution's assumption of a perpetual union. Secession was anarchy, he declared. Safety, peace, and democratic order lay within the Union, Lincoln argued, while secession offered danger, bloodshed, and lawlessness. In sum, Lincoln coupled an intransigent defense of the Union with a promise of benign government under the Constitution for all Americans, South and North. Lincoln's insistence that the Union was unbroken and unbreakable remained the bedrock principle of his presidency.

First Inaugural Address
March 4, 1861

Fellow citizens of the United States:
In compliance with a custom as old as the government itself, I appear before you to address you briefly, and to take, in your presence, the oath prescribed by the Constitution of the United States, to be taken by the President "before he enters on the execution of his office."

I do not consider it necessary, at present, for me to discuss those matters of administration about which there is no special anxiety, or excitement.

Apprehension seems to exist among the people of the Southern States, that by the accession of a Republican Administration, their property, and their peace, and personal security, are to be endangered. There has never been any reasonable cause for such apprehension. Indeed, the most ample evidence to the contrary has all the while existed, and been open to their inspection. It is found in nearly all the published speeches of him who now addresses you. I do but quote from one of those speeches when I declare that "I have no purpose, directly or indirectly, to interfere with the institution of slavery in the States where it exists. I believe I have no lawful right to do so, and I have no inclination to do so." Those who nominated and elected me did so with full knowledge that I had made this, and many similar declarations, and had never recanted them. And more than this, they placed in the platform, for my acceptance, and as a law to themselves, and to me, the clear and emphatic resolution which I now read:

"*Resolved,* That the maintenance inviolate of the rights of the States, and especially the right of each State to order and control its own domestic institutions according to its own judgment exclusively, is essential to that balance of power on which the perfection and endurance of our political fabric depend; and we denounce the lawless invasion by armed force of the soil of any State or Territory, no matter under what pretext, as among the gravest of crimes."

I now reiterate these sentiments: and in doing so, I only press upon the public attention the most conclusive evidence of which the case is susceptible, that the property, peace and security of no section are to be in anywise endangered by the now incoming Administration. I add too, that all the protection which, consistently with the Constitution and the laws, can be given, will be cheerfully given to all the States when lawfully demanded, for whatever cause—as cheerfully to one section, as to another.

There is much controversy about the delivering up of fugitives from service or labor. The clause I now read is as plainly written in the Constitution as any other of its provisions:

"No person held to Service or labor in one State, under the laws thereof, escaping into another, shall, in consequence of any law or regulation therein, be discharged from such service or labor, but shall be delivered up on claim of the party to whom such service or labor may be due."

It is scarcely questioned that this provision was intended by those who made it, for the reclaiming of what we call fugitive slaves; and the intention of the law-giver is the law. All members of Congress swear their support to the whole Constitution—to this provision as much as to any other. To the proposition, then, that slaves whose cases come within the terms of this clause, "shall be delivered up," their oaths are unanimous. Now, if they would make the effort in good temper, could they not, with nearly equal unanimity, frame and pass a law, by means of which to keep good that unanimous oath?

There is some difference of opinion whether this clause should be enforced by national or by state authority; but surely that difference is not a very material one. If the slave is to be surrendered, it can be of but little consequence to him, or to others, by which authority it is done. And should any one, in any case, be content that his oath shall go unkept, on a merely unsubstantial controversy as to *how* it shall be kept?

Again, in any law upon this subject, ought not all the safeguards of liberty known in civilized and humane jurisprudence to be introduced, so that a free man be not, in any case, surrendered as a slave? And might it not be well, at the same time, to provide by law for the enforcement of that clause in the Constitution which guarranties that "The citizens of each State shall be entitled to all previleges and immunities of citizens in the several States?"

I take the official oath to-day, with no mental reservations, and with no purpose to construe the Constitution or laws, by any hypercritical rules. And while I do not choose now to specify particular acts of Congress as proper to be enforced, I do suggest, that it will be much safer for all, both in official and private stations, to conform to, and abide by, all those acts which stand unrepealed, than to violate any of them, trusting to find impunity in having them held to be unconstitutional.

It is seventy-two years since the first inauguration of a President under our national Constitution. During that period fifteen different and greatly distinguished citizens, have, in succession, administered the executive branch of the government. They have conducted it through many perils; and, generally, with great success. Yet, with all this scope for precedent, I now enter upon the same task for the brief constitutional term of four years, under great and peculiar difficulty. A disruption of the Federal Union heretofore only menaced, is now formidably attempted.

I hold, that in contemplation of universal law, and of the Constitution, the Union of these States is perpetual. Perpetuity is implied, if not expressed, in the fundamental law of all national governments. It is safe to assert that no government proper, ever had a provision in its organic law for its own termination. Continue to execute all the express provisions of our national Constitution, and the Union will endure forever—it being impossible to destroy it, except by some action not provided for in the instrument itself.

Again, if the United States be not a government proper, but an association of States in the nature of contract merely, can it, as a contract, be peaceably unmade, by less than all the parties who made it? One party to a contract may violate it—break it, so to speak; but does it not require all to lawfully rescind it?

Descending from these general principles, we find the proposition that, in legal contemplation, the Union is perpetual, confirmed by the history of the Union itself. The Union is much older than the Constitution. It was formed in fact, by the Articles of Association in 1774. It was matured and continued by the Declaration of Independence in 1776. It was further matured and the faith of all the then thirteen States expressly plighted and engaged that it should be perpetual, by the Articles of Confederation in 1778. And finally, in 1787, one of the declared objects for ordaining and establishing the Constitution, was *"to form a more perfect union."*

But if destruction of the Union, by one, or by a part only, of the States, be lawfully possible, the Union is *less* perfect than before the Constitution, having lost the vital element of perpetuity.

It follows from these views that no State, upon its own mere motion, can lawfully get out of the Union,—that *resolves* and *ordinances* to that effect are legally void; and that acts of violence, within any State or States, against the authority of the United States, are insurrectionary or revolutionary, according to circumstances.

I therefore consider that, in view of the Constitution and the laws, the Union is unbroken; and, to the extent of my ability, I shall take care, as the Constitution itself expressly enjoins upon me, that the laws of the Union be faithfully executed in all the States. Doing this I deem to be only a simple duty on my part; and I shall perform it, so far as practicable, unless my rightful masters, the American people, shall withhold the requisite means, or, in some authoritative manner, direct the contrary. I trust this will not be regarded as a menace, but only as the declared purpose of the Union that it *will* constitutionally defend, and maintain itself.

In doing this there needs to be no bloodshed or violence; and there shall be none, unless it be forced upon the national authority. The power confided to me, will be used to hold, occupy, and possess the property, and places belonging to the government, and to collect the duties and imposts; but beyond what may be necessary for these objects, there will be no invasion— no using of force against, or among the people anywhere. Where hostility to the United States, in any interior locality, shall be so great and so universal, as to prevent competent resident citizens from holding the Federal offices, there will be no attempt to force obnoxious strangers among the people for that object. While the strict legal right may exist in the government to enforce the exercise of these offices, the attempt to do so would be so irritating, and so nearly impracticable with all, that I deem it better to forego, for the time, the uses of such offices.

The mails, unless repelled, will continue to be furnished in all parts of the Union. So far as possible, the people everywhere shall have that sense of perfect security which is most favorable to calm thought and reflection. The course here indicated will be followed, unless current events, and experience, shall show a modification, or change, to be proper; and in every case and exigency, my best discretion will be exercised, according to circumstances actually existing, and with a view and a hope of a peaceful solution of the national troubles, and the restoration of fraternal sympathies and affections.

That there are persons in one section, or another who seek to destroy the Union at all events, and are glad of any pretext to do it, I will neither affirm or deny; but if there be such, I need address no word to them. To those, however, who really love the Union, may I not speak?

Before entering upon so grave a matter as the destruction of our national fabric, with all its benefits, its memories, and its hopes, would it not be wise to ascertain precisely why we do it? Will you hazard so desperate a step, while there is any possibility that any portion of the ills you fly from, have no real existence? Will you, while the certain ills you fly to, are greater than all the real ones you fly from? Will you risk the commission of so fearful a mistake?

All profess to be content in the Union, if all constitutional rights can be maintained. Is it true, then, that any right, plainly written in the Constitution, has been denied? I think not. Happily the human mind is so constituted, that no party can reach to the audacity of doing this. Think, if you can, of a single instance in which a plainly written provision of the Constitution has ever been denied. If, by the mere force of numbers, a majority should deprive a minority of any clearly written constitutional right, it might, in a moral point of view, justify revolution—certainly would, if such right were a vital one. But such is not our case. All the vital rights of minorities, and of individuals, are so plainly assured to them, by affirmations and negations, guarranties and prohibitions, in the Constitution, that controversies never arise concerning them. But no organic law can ever be framed with a provision specifically applicable to every question which may occur in practical administration. No foresight can anticipate, nor any document of reasonable length contain express provisions for all possible questions. Shall fugitives from labor be surrendered by national or by State authority? The Constitution does not expressly say. *May* Congress prohibit slavery in the territories? The Constitution does not expressly say. *Must* Congress protect slavery in the territories? The Constitution does not expressly say.

From questions of this class spring all our constitutional controversies, and we divide upon them into majorities and minorities. If the minority will not acquiesce, the majority must, or the government must cease. There is no other alternative; for continuing the government, is acquiescence on one side or the other. If a minority, in such case, will secede rather than acquiesce, they make a precedent which, in turn, will divide and ruin them; for a minority of their own will secede from them, whenever a majority refuses to be controlled by such minority. For instance, why may not any portion of a new confederacy, a year or two hence, arbitrarily secede again, precisely as portions of the present Union now claim to secede from it. All who cherish disunion sentiments, are now being educated to the exact temper of doing this. Is there such perfect identity of interests among the States to compose a new Union, as to produce harmony only, and prevent renewed secession?

Plainly, the central idea of secession, is the essence of anarchy. A majority, held in restraint by constitutional checks, and limitations, and always changing easily, with deliberate changes of popular opinions and sentiments, is the only true sovereign of a free people. Whoever rejects it, does, of necessity, fly to anarchy or to despotism. Unanimity is impossible; the rule of a minority, as a permanent arrangement, is wholly inadmissable; so that, rejecting the majority principle, anarchy, or despotism in some form, is all that is left.

I do not forget the position assumed by some, that constitutional questions are to be decided by the Supreme Court; nor do I deny that such decisions must be binding in any case, upon the parties to a suit, as to the object of that suit, while they are also entitled to very high respect and consideration, in all paralel cases, by all other departments of the government. And while it is obviously possible that such decision may be erroneous in any given case, still the evil effect following it, being limited to that particular case, with the chance that it may be over-ruled, and never become a precedent for other cases, can better be borne than could the evils of a different practice. At the same time the candid citizen must confess that if the policy of the government, upon vital questions, affecting the whole people, is to be irrevocably fixed by decisions of the Supreme Court, the instant they are made, in ordinary litigation between parties, in personal actions, the people will have ceased, to be their own rulers, having, to that extent, practically resigned their government, into the hands of that eminent tribunal. Nor is there, in this view, any assault upon the court, or the judges. It is a duty, from which they may not shrink, to decide cases properly brought before them; and it is no fault of theirs, if others seek to turn their decisions to political purposes.

One section of our country believes slavery is *right,* and ought to be extended, while the other believes it is *wrong,* and ought not to be extended. This is the only substantial dispute. The fugitive slave clause of the Constitution, and the law for the suppression of the foreign slave trade, are each as well enforced, perhaps, as any law can ever be in a community where the moral sense of the people imperfectly supports the law itself. The great body of the people abide by the dry legal obligation in both cases, and a few break over in each. This, I think, cannot be perfectly cured; and it would be worse in both cases *after* the separation of the sections, than before. The foreign slave trade, now imperfectly suppressed, would be ultimately revived without restriction, in one section; while fugitive slaves, now only partially surrendered, would not be surrendered at all, by the other.

Physically speaking, we cannot separate. We cannot remove our respective sections from each other, nor build an impassable wall between them. A husband and wife may be divorced, and go out of the presence, and beyond the reach of each other; but the different parts of our country cannot do this. They cannot but remain face to face; and intercourse, either amicable or hostile, must continue between them. Is it possible then to make that intercourse more advantageous, or more satisfactory, *after* separation than *before?* Can aliens make treaties easier than friends can make laws? Can treaties be more faithfully enforced between aliens, than laws can among friends? Suppose you go to war, you cannot fight always; and when, after much loss on both sides, and no gain on either, you cease fighting, the identical old questions, as to terms of intercourse, are again upon you.

This country, with its institutions, belongs to the people who inhabit it. Whenever they shall grow weary of the existing government, they can exercise their *constitutional* right of amending it, or their *revolutionary* right to dismember, or overthrow it. I can not be ignorant of the fact that many worthy, and patriotic citizens are desirous of having the national constitution amended. While I make no recommendation of amendments, I fully recognize the rightful authority of the people over the whole subject, to be exercised in either of the modes prescribed in the instrument itself; and I should, under existing circumstances, favor, rather than oppose, a fair oppertunity being afforded the people to act upon it.

I will venture to add that, to me, the convention mode seems preferable, in that it allows amendments to originate with the people themselves, instead of only permitting them to take, or reject, propositions, originated by others, not especially chosen for the purpose, and which might not be precisely such, as they would wish to either accept or refuse. I understand a proposed amendment to the Constitution—which amendment, however, I have not seen, has passed Congress, to the effect that the federal government, shall never interfere with the domestic institutions of the States, including that of persons held to service.[20] To avoid misconstruction of what I have said, I depart from my purpose not to speak of particular amendments, so far as to say that, holding such a provision to now be implied constitutional law, I have no objection to its being made express, and irrevocable.

The Chief Magistrate derives all his authority from the people, and they have conferred none upon him to fix terms for the separation of the States. The people themselves can do this also if they choose; but the executive, as such, has nothing to do with it. His duty is to administer the present government, as it came to his hands, and to transmit it, unimpaired by him, to his successor.

Why should there not be a patient confidence in the ultimate justice of the people? Is there any better, or equal hope, in the world? In our present differences, is either party without faith of being in the right? If the Almighty Ruler of nations, with his eternal truth and justice, be on your side of the North, or on yours of the South, that truth, and that justice, will surely prevail, by the judgment of this great tribunal, the American people.

By the frame of the government under which we live, this same people have wisely given their public servants but little power for mischief; and have, with equal wisdom, provided for the return of that little to their own hands at very short intervals.

While the people retain their virtue, and vigilence, no administration, by any extreme of wickedness or folly, can very seriously injure the government, in the short space of four years.

My countrymen, one and all, think calmly and *well,* upon this whole subject. Nothing valuable can be lost by taking time. If there be an object to *hurry* any of you, in hot haste, to a step which you would never take *deliber-*

---

[20]Shortly before Lincoln's inauguration, two-thirds majorities of the House and the Senate approved and sent to the states for ratification a proposed Thirteenth Amendment to the Constitution that guaranteed that the federal government would never interfere with slavery in the states. When the war began, the states ignored ratification. After four years of war, a very different Thirteenth Amendment, abolishing slavery, was ratified.

ately, that object will be frustrated by taking time; but no good object can be frustrated by it. Such of you as are now dissatisfied, still have the old Constitution unimpaired, and, on the sensitive point, the laws of your own framing under it; while the new administration will have no immediate power, if it would, to change either. If it were admitted that you who are dissatisfied, hold the right side in the dispute, there still is no single good reason for precipitate action. Intelligence, patriotism, Christianity, and a firm reliance on Him, who has never yet forsaken this favored land, are still competent to adjust, in the best way, all our present difficulty.

In *your* hands, my dissatisfied fellow countrymen, and not in *mine,* is the momentous issue of civil war. The government will not assail *you.* You can have no conflict, without being yourselves the aggressors. *You* have no oath registered in Heaven to destroy the government, while *I* shall have the most solemn one to "preserve, protect and defend" it.

I am loth to close. We are not enemies, but friends. We must not be enemies. Though passion may have strained, it must not break our bonds of affection. The mystic chords of memory, stretching from every battle-field, and patriot grave, to every living heart and hearthstone, all over this broad land, will yet swell the chorus of the Union, when again touched, as surely they will be, by the better angels of our nature.

5

A War to Save the Union

Lincoln encountered the military consequences of secession at Fort Sumter in the harbor of Charleston, South Carolina. When Confederate batteries opened fire on the fort in the predawn darkness of April 12, 1861, the political controversies of secession became inextricably entangled in the military realities of civil war. After April 15, when Lincoln called for volunteers to suppress the secessionist rebels, four more slave states seceded—Tennessee, Arkansas, North Carolina, and Virginia. While Lincoln anxiously oversaw the organization of Union armies, he just as anxiously sought to prevent the slave states still in the Union—Maryland, Kentucky, Missouri, and Delaware—from joining the secession stampede. During his first year in office, Lincoln fashioned his military policies according to his views of the politics of secession, views he summarized in his addresses to Congress in July and December 1861.

Lincoln considered himself to be the president of the entire United States, including the states that claimed to have seceded. He consistently refused to acknowledge that secession was an accomplished fact or that the Confederacy was a political entity separate from the Union. Instead, he declared secession an internal rebellion, an insurrection against the laws and Constitution of the United States. After the firing on Fort Sumter, Lincoln believed that war was necessary to suppress the insurrection and to prevent the Confederacy from achieving its goal of independence. In his view, the goal of the war was to prevent disunion, rather than to reunite two separate sovereignties.

Lincoln's concept of an indestructible Union shaped his military strategy. He believed secessionists were political insurgents—somewhat akin to an extremist political party—who had won elections in the slave states and had created governments and armies to pursue their separatist ambitions. But Lincoln suspected that secessionists did not command the loyalty of many southern citizens. Within the Confederacy, Lincoln claimed, hun-

116

dreds of thousands of white southerners remained loyal to the Union. From the outset of the war, Lincoln sought to avoid offending these unionists within the seceding states by repeatedly affirming that their constitutional rights to property, including their slaves, would continue to be protected. By insisting on the distinction between disloyal southerners—who staffed and supported Confederate armies—and loyal southerners—who did neither—Lincoln hoped to awaken the sleeping giant of southern unionism, which would then cooperate with the federal government and work to defeat secessionists both militarily and politically. He also hoped that a war carefully targeted against disloyal secessionists would prevent the border slave states of Maryland, Kentucky, and Missouri from joining the Confederacy by reassuring their residents that the goal of the war was to prevent disunion, not to undermine their right to own slaves. Lincoln's appeal to southern unionists in the Confederacy and in the loyal border states was the chief political component of his military strategy between the assault on Fort Sumter and his proclamation of emancipation on January 1, 1863.

THE FORT SUMTER CRISIS

The day after his inauguration, Lincoln learned that the garrison at Fort Sumter had supplies for only six more weeks before starvation would force the fort to be evacuated and surrendered to the Confederacy. Major Robert Anderson, the commander at Fort Sumter, had moved his men there from an indefensible position on the shore during the night of December 26, causing consternation among Confederates who believed that President Buchanan had agreed not to make any military changes while they negotiated with him about assuming control of federal facilities. In the North, however, Anderson's occupation of Fort Sumter made him a hero, a popular symbol of federal resistance to rebellion. Early in January, when Buchanan attempted to send supplies and reinforcements to Anderson on the *Star of the West,* an unarmed merchant ship, Confederate artillery opened fire and chased the ship away. Isolated and under siege in the heart of the Confederacy, Fort Sumter presented Lincoln with the first major crisis of his presidency.

Although Fort Sumter had no vital military or strategic value, its political significance was incalculable, as the following documents show. If Lincoln allowed the fort to be abandoned, he would be violating his inaugural pledge to hold and occupy federal property. He would also appear to be caving in to Confederate demands, arousing the ire of the many northerners who applauded Anderson and whose support Lincoln desperately needed. On the other hand, if Lincoln tried to reinforce and resupply the fort, he was likely to ignite a conflagration that could strengthen the Confederacy by prompting other slave states to secede. In addition, precipitating a battle in defense of Fort Sumter would place on Lincoln the onus for starting the war, making him appear to be just the sort of aggressive president secessionists had predicted. Furthermore, Lincoln soon learned from Winfield Scott, general in chief of the army, that a military mission to defend Fort Sumter would require more ships and soldiers than the government could muster.

While Lincoln struggled to find a way to support the beleagured soldiers at Fort Sumter and to avoid causing war, he faced all the problems of organizing his administration. Lincoln's cabinet and military advisers could not agree on a plan to defuse the Fort Sumter crisis, while Lincoln himself spent hours every day greeting visitors who thronged the White House to request favors large and small. When Secretary of State William Seward planned to initiate a foreign war in order to unify the nation and thereby project himself into the role of premier policymaker, relegating the president to a figurehead, Lincoln made it clear that he alone had presidential power and that he intended to exercise it.

Unable to delay longer, Lincoln resolved in early April to send an expedition to resupply Fort Sumter, taking care to inform Francis W. Pickens, the governor of South Carolina, that no reinforcements or military provisions would be brought into the fort. Confederate president Jefferson Davis quickly learned of Lincoln's plan and ordered Confederate forces to attack and capture Fort Sumter before it was resupplied. At 4:30 in the morning of April 12, Confederate batteries began to bombard the fort, finally forcing Anderson and his men to surrender on April 14.

Letter to Winfield Scott

March 9, 1861

Executive Mansion

Lieutenant General Scott:

My dear Sir:

On the 5th inst. I received from the Hon. Joseph Holt, the then faithful and vigilant Secretary of War, a letter of that date, inclosing a letter and accompanying documents received by him on the 4th inst. from Major Robert Anderson commanding at Fort Sumpter South Carolina; and copies of all which I now transmit. Immediately on the receipt of them by me, I transmitted the whole to you for your consideration; and the same day you returned the package to me with your opinion endorsed upon it, a copy of which opinion I now also transmit to you.[1] Learning from you verbally that since then you have given the subject a more full and thorough consideration, you will much oblige me by giving answers, in writing, to the following interrogatories:

1st To what point of time can Major Anderson maintain his position at Fort Sumpter, without fresh supplies or reinforcement?

2d. Can you, with all the means now in your control, supply or re-inforce Fort Sumpter within that time?

3d If not, what amount of means and of what description, in addition to that already at your control, would enable you to supply and reinforce that fortress within the time?

Please answer these, adding such statements, information, and counsel as your great skill and experience may suggest.[2]

Your obedient Servant

A. LINCOLN.

[1] Both Holt and Scott endorsed surrendering Fort Sumter since the army did not have sufficient men to hold it.

[2] Scott answered Lincoln on March 11, explaining that Anderson had food for about four to six weeks, that the men and equipment to reinforce him could not be assembled for months, and that it would require a fleet of ships and about 25,000 soldiers to reinforce the garrison.

Letter to William H. Seward

April 1, 1861

Executive Mansion

Hon: W. H. Seward:

My dear Sir:

Since parting with you I have been considering your paper dated this day, and entitled "Some thoughts for the President's consideration." The first proposition in it is, "1st. We are at the end of a month's administration, and yet without a policy, either domestic or foreign."

At the *beginning* of that month, in the inaugeral, I said "The power confided to me will be used to hold, occupy and possess the property and places belonging to the government, and to collect the duties, and imposts." This had your distinct approval at the time; and, taken in connection with the order I immediately gave General Scott, directing him to employ every means in his power to strengthen and hold the forts, comprises the exact domestic policy you now urge, with the single exception, that it does not propose to abandon Fort Sumpter.

Again, I do not perceive how the re-inforcement of Fort Sumpter would be done on a slavery, or party issue, while that of Fort Pickens[3] would be on a more national, and patriotic one.

The news received yesterday in regard to St. Domingo,[4] certainly brings a new item within the range of our foreign policy; but up to that time we have been preparing circulars, and instructions to ministers, and the like, all in perfect harmony, without even a suggestion that we had no foreign policy.

Upon your closing propositions, that "whatever policy we adopt, there must be an energetic prossecution of it"

"For this purpose it must be somebody's business to pursue and direct it incessantly"

"Either the President must do it himself, and be all the while active in it, or"

"Devolve it on some member of his cabinet"

---

[3]Fort Pickens, in the Florida panhandle on an island at the mouth of Pensacola Bay, was still under federal control. In his letter, Seward argued that surrendering Fort Sumter and reinforcing Fort Pickens would *"Change the question before the Public from one . . . about Slavery"* for a question upon *Union or Disunion." CW,* IV, 317.

[4]Spain had recently sent troops from Cuba to aid rebellious Spanish colonists in Santo Domingo. In his letter, Seward proposed that the United States "demand explanations from Spain and France," which might intervene in Mexico, and also from Britain and Russia, which might send agents to the Western Hemisphere. These foreign policy initiatives would unite the country in a *"spirit of independence* . . . against European intervention," Seward argued, and if "satisfactory explanations are not received," it would be necessary to "declare war." *CW,* IV, 318.

"Once adopted, debates on it must end, and all agree and abide"[5] I remark that if this must be done, *I* must do it. When a general line of policy is adopted, I apprehend there is no danger of its being changed without good reason, or continuing to be a subject of unnecessary debate; still, upon points arising in its progress, I wish, and suppose I am entitled to have the advice of all the cabinet.

Your Obt. Servt.
A. LINCOLN

[5]Seward's letter concluded, "It is not in my especial province [as secretary of state]. But I neither seek to evade nor assume responsibility," in effect volunteering "to pursue and direct" the administration's policies. *CW,* IV, 318.

Letter to Robert Anderson
April 4, 1861

[War Department], Washington

Sir: Your letter[6] of the 1st. inst. occasions some anxiety to the President.

On the information of Capt. Fox,[7] he had supposed you could hold out till the 15th. inst. without any great inconvenience; and had prepared an expedition to relieve you before that period.

Hoping still that you will be able to sustain yourself till the 11th. or 12th. inst. the expedition will go forward; and, finding your flag flying, will attempt to provision you, and, in case the effort is resisted, will endeavor also to reinforce you.[8]

You will therefore hold out if possible till the arrival of the expedition.

It is not, however, the intention of the President to subject your command to any danger or hardship beyond what, in your judgment, would be usual in military life; and he has entire confidence that you will act as becomes a patriot and a soldier, under all circumstances.

Whenever, if at all, in your judgment, to save yourself and command, a capitulation becomes a necessity, you are authorized to make it.

[6]Anderson's letter reported that his rations would last about a week at most.

[7]Gustavus V. Fox, a former naval officer from Massachusetts, advised Lincoln that Fort Sumter could be reinforced. Lincoln appointed him assistant secretary of the navy and put him in charge of the Sumter expedition.

[8]The Sumter relief expedition included men and materials to reinforce the fort that were ordered to be used only if the Confederates attacked. As it turned out, stormy seas prevented the relief fleet from providing any help to Anderson and his men when the shelling began on April 12.

ORGANIZING FOR WAR

By ordering the Confederate attack on Fort Sumter, Jefferson Davis inadvertently unified the North and aided Lincoln. The attack outraged almost all northerners and generated a tidal wave of patriotic fervor that swept through the free states, propelling men to volunteer to defend the nation and fight the rebels. Lincoln immediately called for 75,000 militia, and as the massive scale of the conflict began to come into focus, he soon asked for an additional 42,000 volunteers to serve for three years. By calling for troops, Lincoln exercised presidential powers explicitly authorized by the Constitution. He insisted that the Confederacy represented a domestic insurrection, not a foreign enemy. Although Lincoln needed and sought congressional support for the war, he directed the Union war effort with his constitutional powers as president and commander in chief.

While thousands of northern men hurriedly donned uniforms, organized companies and regiments, and said good-bye to friends and families, Lincoln declared a blockade of southern ports. Designed to strangle the Confederacy, the blockade was the centerpiece of what General Scott termed the Anaconda strategy. Although it never eliminated Confederate maritime trade, it greatly reduced the Confederacy's access to supplies from abroad and its ability to raise funds by selling cotton in foreign markets. The blockade contradicted Lincoln's concept of the war as a domestic rebellion. As critics pointed out, the blockade represented a de facto recognition by Lincoln that the Confederacy was a separate sovereignty. Lincoln, however, shrugged off this contradiction and kept the blockade in place throughout the war.

Proclamation Calling Militia and Convening Congress

April 15, 1861

BY THE PRESIDENT OF THE UNITED STATES
A PROCLAMATION.

Whereas the laws of the United States have been for some time past, and now are opposed, and the execution thereof obstructed, in the States of South Carolina, Georgia, Alabama, Florida, Mississippi, Louisiana and Texas, by combinations too powerful to be suppressed by the ordinary course of judicial proceedings, or by the powers vested in the Marshals by law,

Now therefore, I, Abraham Lincoln, President of the United States, in virtue of the power in me vested by the Constitution, and the laws, have thought fit to call forth, and hereby do call forth, the militia of the several States of the Union, to the aggregate number of seventy-five thousand, in order to suppress said combinations, and to cause the laws to be duly executed. The details, for this object, will be immediately communicated to the State authorities through the War Department.

I appeal to all loyal citizens to favor, facilitate and aid this effort to maintain the honor, the integrity, and the existence of our National Union, and the perpetuity of popular government; and to redress wrongs already long enough endured.

I deem it proper to say that the first service assigned to the forces hereby called forth will probably be to re-possess the forts, places, and property which have been seized from the Union; and in every event, the utmost care will be observed, consistently with the objects aforesaid, to avoid any devastation, any destruction of, or interference with, property, or any disturbance of peaceful citizens in any part of the country.

And I hereby command the persons composing the combinations aforesaid to disperse, and retire peaceably to their respective abodes within twenty days from this date.

Deeming that the present condition of public affairs presents an extraordinary occasion, I do hereby, in virtue of the power in me vested by the Constitution, convene both Houses of Congress. Senators and Representatives are therefore summoned to assemble at their respective chambers, at 12 o'clock, noon, on Thursday, the fourth day of July,[9] next, then and there to consider and determine, such measures, as, in their wisdom, the public safety, and interest may seem to demand. . . .

ABRAHAM LINCOLN

[9] A 1795 law limited the service of militia called up by the president to no more than thirty days after the assembly of Congress. Therefore, the service of the men who responded to this proclamation officially ended on August 4.

Lincoln's most immediate concern following the attack on Fort Sumter was to secure the defense of Washington, D.C., which was surrounded by the slave states of Maryland and Virginia. Maryland secessionists quickly destroyed the bridges and cut the telegraph lines that connected Washington with the North. By April 25, enough soldiers had arrived in Washington to defend the capital, but the possibility still existed that Maryland would secede along with the rest of the slave states, a possibility both militarily and politically unacceptable to Lincoln. The president watched developments in Maryland closely. Although Maryland remained in the Union,

Lincoln authorized the suspension of the writ of habeas corpus, an action that allowed military officers to arrest and hold without a judicial hearing any person they believed to be aiding the Confederacy. Revoking the constitutional guarantee of habeas corpus—which requires release of any person a court determines to be unlawfully arrested—signaled Lincoln's willingness to resort to extraordinary measures to protect Washington, the headquarters of the Union.

Reply to a Baltimore Committee
April 22, 1861

[Washington]

You, gentlemen,[10] come here to me and ask for peace on any terms, and yet have no word of condemnation for those who are making war on us. You express great horror of bloodshed, and yet would not lay a straw in the way of those who are organizing in Virginia and elsewhere to capture this city. The rebels attack Fort Sumter, and your citizens attack troops sent to the defense of the Government,[11] and the lives and property in Washington, and yet you would have me break my oath and surrender the Government without a blow. There is no Washington in that—no Jackson in that—no manhood nor honor in that. I have no desire to invade the South; but I must have troops to defend this Capital. Geographically it lies surrounded by the soil of Maryland; and mathematically the necessity exists that they [the troops] should come over her territory. Our men are not moles, and can't dig under the earth; they are not birds, and can't fly through the air. There is no way but to march across [Maryland], and that they must do. But in doing this there is no need of collision. Keep your rowdies in Baltimore, and there will be no bloodshed. Go home and tell your people that if they will not attack us, we will not attack them; but if they do attack us, we will return it, and that severely.[12]

[10]The committee from Baltimore was made up of fifty men who represented the Young Men's Christian Association.
[11]On April 19, a Baltimore mob attacked a Massachusetts regiment passing through the city on the way to defend Washington. Four soldiers and twelve civilians died in the melee, and dozens of others suffered wounds.
[12]Reports of this meeting appeared in Baltimore, Philadelphia, and New York newspapers.

Letter to Reverdy Johnson

April 24, 1861

Confidential.

Executive Mansion

Hon. Reverdy Johnson[13]

My dear Sir: Your note of this morning is just received. I forebore to answer yours of the 22d[14] because of my aversion (which I thought you understood,) to getting on paper, and furnishing new grounds for misunderstanding.

I *do* say the sole purpose of bringing troops *here* is to defend this capital.

I *do* say I have no purpose to *invade* Virginia, with them or any other troops, as I understand the word *invasion.* But suppose Virginia[15] sends her troops, or admits others through her borders, to assail this capital, am I not to repel them, even to the crossing of the Potomac if I can?

Suppose Virginia erects, or permits to be erected, batteries on the opposite shore, to bombard the city, are we to stand still and see it done? In a word, if Virginia strikes us, are we not to strike back, and as effectively as we can?

Again, are we not to hold Fort Monroe[16] (for instance) if we can? I have no objection to declare a thousand times that I have no purpose to *invade* Virginia or any other State, but I do not mean to let them invade us without striking back.

Yours truly
A. LINCOLN

[13]Johnson was a Democratic leader and a former U.S. senator from Maryland.

[14]Johnson's letter reported the widespread fear in Maryland and Virginia that Lincoln intended to invade those states with the troops assembling in Washington.

[15]On April 17, the Virginia convention had resolved to secede. Virginia voters subsequently ratified the secession ordinance on May 23.

[16]Fort Monroe was located on the southern coast of Virginia, at the mouth of the James River across from Norfolk, where Confederates had seized the federal naval yard on April 20.

By July 4 when Congress assembled, Lincoln had not only exercised his authority as president and commander in chief, but he had also authorized the expenditure of vast sums to equip and supply the armed forces, a constitutional prerogative granted to Congress, not the president. In his message to the legislators, Lincoln reviewed the unprecedented crisis he confronted when he became president, explaining what he had done and why.

Message to Congress in Special Session

July 4, 1861

Fellow-citizens of the Senate and House of Representatives: Having been convened on an extraordinary occasion, as authorized by the Constitution, your attention is not called to any ordinary subject of legislation.

At the beginning of the present Presidential term, four months ago, the functions of the Federal Government were found to be generally suspended within the several States of South Carolina, Georgia, Alabama, Mississippi, Louisiana, and Florida, excepting only those of the Post Office Department.

Within these States, all the Forts, Arsenals, Dock-yards, Custom-houses, and the like, including the movable and stationary property in, and about them, had been seized, and were held in open hostility to this Government, excepting only Forts Pickens, Taylor, and Jefferson, on, and near the Florida coast, and Fort Sumter, in Charleston harbor, South Carolina. The Forts thus seized had been put in improved condition; new ones had been built; and armed forces had been organized, and were organizing, all avowedly with the same hostile purpose.

The Forts remaining in the possession of the Federal government, in, and near, these States, were either besieged or menaced by warlike preparations; and especially Fort Sumter was nearly surrounded by well-protected hostile batteries, with guns equal in quality to the best of its own, and outnumbering the latter as perhaps ten to one. A disproportionate share, of the Federal muskets and rifles, had somehow found their way into these States, and had been seized, to be used against the government. Accumulations of the public revenue, lying within them, had been seized for the same object. The Navy was scattered in distant seas; leaving but a very small part of it within the immediate reach of the government. Officers of the Federal Army and Navy, had resigned in great numbers; and, of those resigning, a large proportion had taken up arms against the government. Simultaneously, and in connection, with all this, the purpose to sever the Federal Union, was openly avowed. In accordance with this purpose, an ordinance had been adopted in each of these States, declaring the States, respectively, to be separated from the National Union. A formula for instituting a combined government of these states had been promulgated; and this illegal organization, in the character of confederate States was already invoking recognition, aid, and intervention, from Foreign Powers.

Finding this condition of things, and believing it to be an imperative duty upon the incoming Executive, to prevent, if possible, the consummation of such attempt to destroy the Federal Union, a choice of means to that end became indispensable. This choice was made; and was declared in the Inaugural address. The policy chosen looked to the exhaustion of all peaceful measures, before a resort to any stronger ones. It sought only to hold the public places and property, not already wrested from the Government, and to collect the revenue; relying for the rest, on time, discussion, and the ballot-box. It promised a continuance of the mails, at government expense, to the very people who were resisting the government; and it gave repeated pledges against any disturbance to any of the people, or any of their rights. Of all that which a president might constitutionally, and justifiably, do in such a case, everything was foreborne, without which, it was believed possible to keep the government on foot.

On the 5th of March, (the present incumbent's first full day in office) a letter of Major Anderson, commanding at Fort Sumter, written on the 28th of February, and received at the War Department on the 4th of March, was, by that Department, placed in his hands. This letter expressed the professional opinion of the writer, that reinforcements could not be thrown into that Fort within the time for his relief, rendered necessary by the limited supply of provisions, and with a view of holding possession of the same, with a force of less than twenty thousand good, and well-disciplined men. This opinion was concurred in by all the officers of his command; and their *memoranda* on the subject, were made enclosures of Major Anderson's letter. The whole was immediately laid before Lieutenant General Scott, who at once concurred with Major Anderson in opinion. On reflection, however, he took full time, consulting with other officers, both of the Army and the Navy; and, at the end of four days, came reluctantly, but decidedly, to the same conclusion as before. He also stated at the same time that no such sufficient force was then at the control of the Government, or could be raised, and brought to the ground, within the time when the provisions in the Fort would be exhausted. In a purely military point of view, this reduced the duty of the administration, in the case, to the mere matter of getting the garrison safely out of the Fort.

It was believed, however, that to so abandon that position, under the circumstances, would be utterly ruinous; that the *necessity* under which it was to be done, would not be fully understood—that, by many, it would be construed as a part of a *voluntary* policy—that, at home, it would discourage the friends of the Union, embolden its adversaries, and go far to insure to the latter, a recognition abroad—that, in fact, it would be our national destruction consummated. This could not be allowed. Starvation was not yet upon the garrison; and ere it would be reached, *Fort Pickens* might be reinforced. This last, would be a clear indication of *policy,* and would better enable the country to accept the evacuation of Fort Sumter, as a military *necessity.* An order was at once directed to be sent for the landing of the troops from the Steam-ship Brooklyn, into Fort Pickens. This order could not go by land, but must take the longer, and slower route by sea. The first return news from the order was received just one week before the fall of Fort Sumter. The news itself was, that the officer commanding the Sabine, to which vessel the troops had been transferred from the Brooklyn, acting upon some *quasi* armistice of the late administration, (and of the existence of which, the present administration, up to the time the order was despatched, had only too vague and uncertain rumors, to fix attention) had refused to land the troops. To now re-inforce Fort Pickens, before a crisis would be reached at Fort Sumter was impossible—rendered so by the near exhaustion of provisions in the latter-named Fort. In precaution against such a conjuncture, the government had, a few days before, commenced preparing an expedition, as well adapted as might be, to relieve Fort Sumter; which expedition was intended to be ultimately used, or not, according to circumstances. The strongest anticipated case, for using it, was now presented; and it was resolved to send it forward. As had been intended, in this contingency, it was also resolved to notify the Governor of South Carolina, that he might expect an attempt would be made to provision the Fort; and that, if the attempt should not be resisted, there would be no effort to throw in men, arms, or ammunition, without further notice, or in case of an attack upon the Fort. This notice was accordingly given; whereupon the Fort was attacked, and bombarded to its fall, without even awaiting the arrival of the provisioning expedition.

It is thus seen that the assault upon, and reduction of, Fort Sumter, was, in no sense, a matter of self defence on the part of the assailants. They well knew that the garrison in the Fort could, by no possibility, commit aggression upon them. They knew—they were expressly notified—that the giving of bread to the few brave and hungry men of the garrison, was all which would on that occasion be attempted, unless themselves, by resisting so much, should provoke more. They knew that this Government desired to keep the garrison in the Fort, not to assail them, but merely to maintain visible possession, and thus to preserve the Union from actual, and immediate dissolution—trusting, as herein-before stated, to time, discussion, and the ballot-box, for final adjustment; and they assailed, and reduced the Fort, for precisely the reverse object—to drive out the visible authority of the Federal Union, and thus force it to immediate dissolution.

That this was their object, the Executive well understood; and having said to them in the inaugural address, "You can have no conflict without being yourselves the aggressors," he took pains, not only to keep this declaration good, but also to keep the case so free from the power of ingenious sophistry, as that the world should not be able to misunderstand it. By the affair at Fort Sumter, with its surrounding circumstances, that point was reached. Then, and thereby, the assailants of the Government, began the conflict of arms, without a gun in sight, or in expectancy, to return their fire, save only the few in the Fort, sent to that harbor, years before, for their own protection, and still ready to give that protection, in whatever was lawful. In this act, discarding all else, they have forced upon the country, the distinct issue: "Immediate dissolution, or blood."

And this issue embraces more than the fate of these United States. It presents to the whole family of man, the question, whether a constitutional republic, or a democracy—a government of the people, by the same people—can, or cannot, maintain its territorial integrity, against its own domestic foes. It presents the question, whether discontented individuals, too few in numbers to control administration, according to organic law, in any case, can always, upon the pretences made in this case, or on any other pretences, or arbitrarily, without any pretence, break up their Government, and thus practically put an end to free government upon the earth. It forces us to ask: "Is there, in all republics, this inherent, and fatal weakness?" "Must a government, of necessity, be too *strong* for the liberties of its own people, or too *weak* to maintain its own existence?"

So viewing the issue, no choice was left but to call out the war power of the Government; and so to resist force, employed for its destruction, by force, for its preservation.

The call was made; and the response of the country was most gratifying; surpassing, in unanimity and spirit, the most sanguine expectation. Yet none of the States commonly called Slave-States, except Delaware, gave a Regiment through regular State organization. A few regiments have been organized within some others of those States, by individual enterprise, and received into the government service. Of course the seceded States, so called, (and to which Texas had been joined about the time of the inauguration,) gave no troops to the cause of the Union. The border States, so called, were not uniform in their actions; some of them being almost *for* the Union, while in others—as Virginia, North Carolina, Tennessee, and Arkansas—the Union sentiment was nearly repressed, and silenced. The course taken in Virginia was the most remarkable—perhaps the most important. A convention, elected by the people of that State, to consider this very question of disrupting the Federal Union, was in session at the capital of Virginia when Fort Sumter fell. To this body the people had chosen a large majority of *professed* Union men. Almost immediately after the fall of Sumter, many members of that majority went over to the original disunion minority, and, with them, adopted an ordinance for withdrawing the State from the Union. Whether this change was wrought by their great approval of the assault upon Sumter, or their great resentment at the government's resistance to that assault, is not definitely known. Although they submitted the ordinance, for ratification, to a vote of the people, to be taken on a day then somewhat more than a month distant, the convention, and the Legislature, (which was also in session at the same time and place) with leading men of the State, not members of either, immediately commenced acting, as if the State were already out of the Union. They pushed military preparations vigorously forward all over the state. They seized the United States Armory at Harper's Ferry, and the Navy-yard at Gosport, near Norfolk. They received—perhaps invited—into their state, large bodies of troops, with their warlike appointments, from the so-called seceded States. They formally entered into a treaty of temporary alliance, and co-operation with the so-called "Confederate States," and sent members to their Congress at Montgomery. And, finally, they permitted the insurrectionary government to be transferred to their capital at Richmond.[17]

The people of Virginia have thus allowed this giant insurrection to make

[17]The Confederate Congress agreed on May 21 to move its capital from Montgomery, Alabama, to Richmond, Virginia.

its nest within her borders; and this government has no choice left but to deal with it, *where* it finds it. And it has the less regret, as the loyal citizens have, in due form, claimed its protection. Those loyal citizens, this government is bound to recognize, and protect, as being Virginia.

In the border States, so called—in fact, the middle states—there are those who favor a policy which they call "armed neutrality"—that is, an arming of those states to prevent the Union forces passing one way, or the disunion, the other, over their soil. This would be disunion completed. Figuratively speaking, it would be the building of an impassable wall along the line of separation. And yet, not quite an impassable one; for, under the guise of neutrality, it would tie the hands of the Union men, and freely pass supplies from among them, to the insurrectionists, which it could not do as an open enemy. At a stroke, it would take all the trouble off the hands of secession, except only what proceeds from the external blockade. It would do for the disunionists that which, of all things, they most desire—feed them well, and give them disunion without a struggle of their own. It recognizes no fidelity to the Constitution, no obligation to maintain the Union; and while very many who have favored it are, doubtless, loyal citizens, it is, nevertheless, treason in effect.

Recurring to the action of the government, it may be stated that, at first, a call was made for seventy-five thousand militia; and rapidly following this, a proclamation was issued for closing the ports of the insurrectionary districts by proceedings in the nature of Blockade. So far all was believed to be strictly legal. At this point the insurrectionists announced their purpose to enter upon the practice of privateering.

Other calls were made for volunteers, to serve three years, unless sooner discharged; and also for large additions to the regular Army and Navy. These measures, whether strictly legal or not, were ventured upon, under what appeared to be a popular demand, and a public necessity; trusting, then as now, that Congress would readily ratify them. It is believed that nothing has been done beyond the constitutional competency of Congress.

Soon after the first call for militia, it was considered a duty to authorize the Commanding General, in proper cases, according to his discretion, to suspend the privilege of the writ of habeas corpus; or, in other words, to arrest, and detain, without resort to the ordinary processes and forms of law, such individuals as he might deem dangerous to the public safety. This authority has purposely been exercised but very sparingly. Nevertheless, the legality and propriety of what has been done under it are questioned; and the attention of the country has been called to the proposition that one who is sworn to "take care that the laws be faithfully executed," should not himself violate them.[18] Of

[18]Lincoln is referring to the case of John Merryman, a rabid secessionist from Baltimore who was arrested and jailed at Fort McHenry. Merryman petitioned to be released under a writ of habeas corpus, and his plea was ultimately decided by Supreme Court Justice Roger B. Taney on May 28. In *Ex parte Merryman,* Taney ruled that Lincoln had no constitutional power to suspend the writ of habeas corpus. Lincoln ignored Taney's decision and defended his actions in his address to Congress.

course some consideration was given to the questions of power, and propriety, before this matter was acted upon. The whole of the laws which were required to be faithfully executed, were being resisted, and failing of execution, in nearly one-third of the States. Must they be allowed to finally fail of execution, even had it been perfectly clear, that by the use of the means necessary to their execution, some single law, made in such extreme tenderness of the citizen's liberty, that practically, it relieves more of the guilty, than of the innocent, should, to a very limited extent, be violated? To state the question more directly, are all the laws, *but one,* to go unexecuted, and the government itself go to pieces, lest that one be violated? Even in such a case, would not the official oath be broken, if the government should be overthrown, when it was believed that disregarding the single law, would tend to preserve it? But it was not believed that this question was presented. It was not believed that any law was violated. The provision of the Constitution that "The privilege of the writ of habeas corpus, shall not be suspended unless when, in cases of rebellion or invasion, the public safety may require it," is equivalent to a provision—is a provision—that such privilege may be suspended when, in cases of rebellion, or invasion, the public safety *does* require it. It was decided that we have a case of rebellion, and that the public safety does require the qualified suspension of the privilege of the writ which was authorized to be made. Now it is insisted that Congress, and not the Executive, is vested with this power. But the Constitution itself, is silent as to which, or who, is to exercise the power; and as the provision was plainly made for a dangerous emergency, it cannot be believed the framers of the instrument intended, that in every case, the danger should run its course, until Congress could be called together; the very assembling of which might be prevented, as was intended in this case, by the rebellion.

No more extended argument is now offered; as an opinion, at some length, will probably be presented by the Attorney General. Whether there shall be any legislation upon the subject, and if any, what, is submitted entirely to the better judgment of Congress.

The forbearance of this government had been so extraordinary, and so long continued, as to lead some foreign nations to shape their action as if they supposed the early destruction of our national Union was probable. While this, on discovery, gave the Executive some concern, he is now happy to say that the sovereignty, and rights of the United States, are now everywhere practically respected by foreign powers; and a general sympathy with the country is manifested throughout the world.

The reports of the Secretaries of the Treasury, War, and the Navy, will give the information in detail deemed necessary, and convenient for your deliberation, and action; while the Executive, and all the Departments, will stand ready to supply omissions, or to communicate new facts, considered important for you to know.

It is now recommended that you give the legal means for making this contest a short, and a decisive one; that you place at the control of the government, for the work, at least four hundred thousand men, and four hundred millions of dollars. That number of men is about one tenth of those of proper ages within the regions where, apparently, *all* are willing to engage; and the sum is less than a twentythird part of the money value owned by the men who seem ready to devote the whole. A debt of six hundred millions of dollars *now,* is a less sum per head, than was the debt of our revolution, when we came out of that struggle; and the money value in the country now, bears even a greater proportion to what it was *then,* than does the population. Surely each man has as strong a motive *now,* to *preserve* our liberties, as each had *then,* to *establish* them.

A right result, at this time, will be worth more to the world, than ten times the men, and ten times the money. The evidence reaching us from the country, leaves no doubt, that the material for the work is abundant; and that it needs only the hand of legislation to give it legal sanction, and the hand of the Executive to give it practical shape and efficiency. One of the greatest perplexities of the government, is to avoid receiving troops faster than it can provide for them. In a word, the people will save their government, if the government itself, will do its part, only indifferently well.

It might seem, at first thought, to be of little difference whether the present movement at the South be called "secession" or "rebellion." The movers, however, well understand the difference. At the beginning, they knew they could never raise their treason to any respectable magnitude, by any name which implies *violation* of law. They knew their people possessed as much of moral sense, as much of devotion to law and order, and as much pride in, and reverence for, the history, and government, of their common country, as any other civilized, and patriotic people. They knew they could make no advancement directly in the teeth of these strong and noble sentiments. Accordingly they commenced by an insidious debauching of the public mind. They invented an ingenious sophism, which, if conceded, was followed by perfectly logical steps, through all the incidents, to the complete destruction of the Union. The sophism itself is, that any state of the Union may, *consistently* with the national Constitution, and therefore *lawfully,* and *peacefully,* withdraw from the Union, without the consent of the Union, or of any other state. The little disguise that the supposed right is to be exercised only for just cause, themselves to be the sole judge of its justice, is too thin to merit any notice.

With rebellion thus sugar-coated, they have been drugging the public mind of their section for more than thirty years; and, until at length, they have brought many good men to a willingness to take up arms against the government the day *after* some assemblage of men have enacted the farcical pretence of taking their State out of the Union, who could have been brought to no such thing the day *before.*

This sophism derives much—perhaps the whole—of its currency, from the assumption, that there is some omnipotent, and sacred supremacy, pertaining to a *State*—to each State of our Federal Union. Our States have neither more, nor less power, than that reserved to them, in the Union, by the

Constitution—no one of them ever having been a State *out* of the Union. The original ones passed into the Union even *before* they cast off their British colonial dependence; and the new ones each came into the Union directly from a condition of dependence, excepting Texas. And even Texas, in its temporary independence, was never designated a State. The new ones only took the designation of States, on coming into the Union, while that name was first adopted for the old ones, in, and by, the Declaration of Independence. Therein the "United Colonies" were declared to be "Free and Independent States"; but, even then, the object plainly was not to declare their independence of *one another,* or of the *Union;* but directly the contrary, as their mutual pledge, and their mutual action, before, at the time, and afterwards, abundantly show. The express plighting of faith, by each and all of the original thirteen, in the Articles of Confederation, two years later, that the Union shall be perpetual, is most conclusive. Having never been States, either in substance, or in name, *outside* of the Union, whence this magical omnipotence of "State rights," asserting a claim of power to lawfully destroy the Union itself? Much is said about the "sovereignty" of the States; but the word, even, is not in the national Constitution; nor, as is believed, in any of the State constitutions. What is a "sovereignty," in the political sense of the term? Would it be far wrong to define it "A political community, without a political superior"? Tested by this, no one of our States, except Texas, ever was a sovereignty. And even Texas gave up the character on coming into the Union; by which act, she acknowledged the Constitution of the United States, and the laws and treaties of the United States made in pursuance of the Constitution, to be, for her, the supreme law of the land. The States have their *status* IN the Union, and they have no other *legal status.* If they break from this, they can only do so against law, and by revolution. The Union, and not themselves separately, procured their independence, and their liberty. By conquest, or purchase, the Union gave each of them, whatever of independence, and liberty, it has. The Union is older than any of the States; and, in fact, it created them as States. Originally, some dependent colonies made the Union; and, in turn, the Union threw off their old dependence, for them, and made them States, such as they are. Not one of them ever had a State constitution, independent of the Union. Of course, it is not forgotten that all the new States framed their constitutions, before they entered the Union; nevertheless, dependent upon, and preparatory to, coming into the Union.

Unquestionably the States have the powers, and rights, reserved to them in, and by the National Constitution; but among these, surely, are not included all conceivable powers, however mischievous, or destructive; but, at most, such only, as were known in the world, at the time, as governmental powers; and certainly, a power to destroy the government itself, had never been known as a governmental—as a merely administrative power. This relative matter of National power, and State rights, as a principle, is no other than the principle of *generality,* and *locality.* Whatever concerns the whole, should be confided to the whole—to the general government; while, whatever concerns *only* the State, should be left exclusively, to the State. This is all there is of original principle about it. Whether the National Constitution, in defining boundaries between the two, has applied the principle with exact accuracy, is not to be questioned. We are all bound by that defining, without question.

What is now combatted, is the position that secession is *consistent* with the Constitution—is *lawful,* and *peaceful.* It is not contended that there is any express law for it; and nothing should ever be implied as law, which leads to unjust, or absurd consequences. The nation purchased, with money, the countries out of which several of these States were formed. Is it just that they shall go off without leave, and without refunding? The nation paid very large sums, (in the aggregate, I believe, nearly a hundred millions) to relieve Florida of the aboriginal tribes. Is it just that she shall now be off without consent, or without making any return? The nation is now in debt for money applied to the benefit of these so-called seceding States, in common with the rest. Is it just, either that creditors shall go unpaid, or the remaining States pay the whole? A part of the present national debt was contracted to pay the old debts of Texas. Is it just that she shall leave, and pay no part of this herself?

Again, if one State may secede, so may another; and when all shall have seceded, none is left to pay the debts. Is this quite just to creditors? Did we notify them of this sage view of ours, when we borrowed their money? If we now recognize this doctrine, by allowing the seceders to go in peace, it is difficult to see what we can do, if others choose to go, or to extort terms upon which they will promise to remain.

The seceders insist that our Constitution admits of secession. They have assumed to make a National Constitution of their own, in which, of necessity, they have either *discarded,* or *retained,* the right of secession, as they insist, it exists in ours. If they have discarded it, they thereby admit that, on principle, it ought not to be in ours. If they have retained it, by their own construction of ours they show that to be consistent they must secede from one another, whenever they shall find it the easiest way of settling their debts, or effecting any other selfish, or unjust object. The principle itself is one of disintegration, and upon which no government can possibly endure.

If all the States, save one, should assert the power to *drive* that one out of the Union, it is presumed the whole class of seceder politicians would at once deny the power, and denounce the act as the greatest outrage upon State rights. But suppose that precisely the same act, instead of being called "driving the one out," should be called "the seceding of the others from that one," it would be exactly what the seceders claim to do; unless, indeed, they make the point, that the one, because it is a minority, may rightfully do, what the others, because they are a majority, may not rightfully do. These politicians are subtle, and profound, on the rights of minorities. They are not partial to that power which made the Constitution, and speaks from the preamble, calling itself "We, the People."

It may well be questioned whether there is, to-day, a majority of the legally qualified voters of any State, except perhaps South Carolina, in favor of disunion. There is much reason to believe that the Union men are the majority in many, if not in every other one, of the so-called seceded States. The contrary has not been demonstrated in any one of them. It is ventured to affirm this, even of Virginia and Tennessee; for the result of an election, held in military camps, where the bayonets are all on one side of the question voted upon, can scarcely be considered as demonstrating popular sentiment.[19] At such an election, all that large class who are, at once, *for* the Union, and *against* coercion, would be coerced to vote against the Union.

It may be affirmed, without extravagance, that the free institutions we enjoy, have developed the powers, and improved the condition, of our whole people, beyond any example in the world. Of this we now have a striking, and an impressive illustration. So large an army as the government has now on foot, was never before known, without a soldier in it, but who had taken his place there, of his own free choice. But more than this: there are many single Regiments whose members, one and another, possess full practical knowledge of all the arts, sciences, professions, and whatever else, whether useful or elegant, is known in the world; and there is scarcely one, from which there could not be selected, a President, a Cabinet, a Congress, and perhaps a Court, abundantly competent to administer the government itself. Nor do I say this is not true, also, in the army of our late friends, now adversaries, in this contest; but if it is, so much better the reason why the government, which has conferred such benefits on both them and us, should not be broken up. Whoever, in any section, proposes to abandon such a government, would do well to consider, in deference to what principle it is, that he does it—what better he is likely to get in its stead—whether the substitute will give, or be intended to give, so much of good to the people. There are some foreshadowings on this subject. Our adversaries have adopted some Declarations of Independence; in which, unlike the good old one, penned by Jefferson, they omit the words "all men are created equal." Why? They have adopted a temporary national constitution, in the preamble of which, unlike our good old one, signed by Washington, they omit "We, the People," and substitute "We, the deputies of the sovereign and independent States." Why? Why this deliberate pressing out of view, the rights of men, and the authority of the people?

This is essentially a People's contest. On the side of the Union, it is a struggle for maintaining in the world, that form, and substance of government, whose leading object is, to elevate the condition of men—to lift artificial weights from all shoulders—to clear the paths of laudable pursuit for all—to afford all, an unfettered start, and a fair chance, in the race of life. Yielding to partial, and temporary departures, from necessity, this is the leading object of the government for whose existence we contend.

[19]Lincoln is referring to the popular vote for secession in Virginia that took place on May 23, weeks after Virginians had organized military units to support the Confederacy.

I am most happy to believe that the plain people understand, and appreciate this. It is worthy of note, that while in this, the government's hour of trial, large numbers of those in the Army and Navy, who have been favored with the offices, have resigned, and proved false to the hand which had pampered them, not one common soldier, or common sailor is known to have deserted his flag.

Great honor is due to those officers who remain true, despite the example of their treacherous associates; but the greatest honor, and most important fact of all, is the unanimous firmness of the common soldiers, and common sailors. To the last man, so far as known, they have successfully resisted the traitorous efforts of those, whose commands, but an hour before, they obeyed as absolute law. This is the patriotic instinct of the plain people. They understand, without an argument, that destroying the government, which was made by Washington, means no good to them.

Our popular government has often been called an experiment. Two points in it, our people have already settled—the successful *establishing,* and the successful *administering* of it. One still remains—its successful *maintenance* against a formidable internal attempt to overthrow it. It is now for them to demonstrate to the world, that those who can fairly carry an election, can also suppress a rebellion—that ballots are the rightful, and peaceful, successors of bullets; and that when ballots have fairly, and constitutionally, decided, there can be no successful appeal, back to bullets; that there can be no successful appeal, except to ballots themselves, at succeeding elections. Such will be a great lesson of peace; teaching men that what they cannot take by an election, neither can they take it by a war—teaching all, the folly of being the beginners of a war.

Lest there be some uneasiness in the minds of candid men, as to what is to be the course of the government, towards the Southern States, *after* the rebellion shall have been suppressed, the Executive deems it proper to say, it will be his purpose then, as ever, to be guided by the Constitution, and the laws; and that he probably will have no different understanding of the powers, and duties of the Federal government, relatively to the rights of the States, and the people, under the Constitution, than that expressed in the inaugural address.

He desires to preserve the government, that it may be administered for all, as it was administered by the men who made it. Loyal citizens everywhere, have the right to claim this of their government; and the government has no right to withhold, or neglect it. It is not perceived that, in giving it, there is any coercion, any conquest, or any subjugation, in any just sense of those terms.

The Constitution provides, and all the States have accepted the provision, that "The United States shall guarantee to every State in this Union a republican form of government." But, if a State may lawfully go out of the Union, having done so, it may also discard the republican form of government; so that to prevent its going out, is an indispensable *means,* to the *end,* of maintaining the guaranty mentioned; and when an end is lawful and obligatory, the indispensable means to it, are also lawful, and obligatory.

It was with the deepest regret that the Executive found the duty of employing the war-power, in defence of the government, forced upon him. He could but perform this duty, or surrender the existence of the government. No compromise, by public servants, could, in this case, be a cure; not that compromises are not often proper, but that no popular government can long survive a marked precedent, that those who carry an election, can only save the government from immediate destruction, by giving up the main point, upon which the people gave the election. The people themselves, and not their servants, can safely reverse their own deliberate decisions. As a private citizen, the Executive could not have consented that these institutions shall perish; much less could he, in betrayal of so vast, and so sacred a trust, as these free people had confided to him. He felt that he had no moral right to shrink; nor even to count the chances of his own life, in what might follow. In full view of his great responsibility, he has, so far, done what he has deemed his duty. You will now, according to your own judgment, perform yours. He sincerely hopes that your views, and your action, may so accord with his, as to assure all faithful citizens, who have been disturbed in their rights, of a certain, and speedy restoration to them, under the Constitution, and the laws.

And having thus chosen our course, without guile, and with pure purpose, let us renew our trust in God, and go forward without fear, and with manly hearts.

Abraham Lincoln

THE AFTERMATH OF DEFEAT AT BULL RUN

The first major collision of Union and Confederate armies occurred about twenty-five miles from Washington at Bull Run, a small river just north of Manassas, the junction of rail lines stretching west to the Shenandoah Valley and south toward Richmond. Under pressure from Lincoln to advance toward Richmond, General Irwin McDowell attacked Confederate forces commanded by General Pierre G. T. Beauregard on July 21. After a long day of fighting, a Confederate counterattack forced Union soldiers to retreat. The retreat turned into a rout as officers lost control of their men, many of them near the end of their ninety-day enlistments, and the disorganized army rushed pell-mell back to Washington. The humiliating defeat at Bull Run convinced Lincoln and his advisers that the rapidly growing

Union army needed to be much better trained, organized, and disciplined before undertaking a major campaign. The defeat also made clear that the war would require more soldiers and more time than anyone, including Lincoln, had anticipated. Within days, Lincoln authorized the recruitment of an additional one million men for three-year terms, and he replaced General McDowell with General George B. McClellan, whom he charged to organize the newly formed Army of the Potomac into fighting trim.

As the following documents illustrate, Lincoln began to think about the larger strategy for defeating the Confederacy. While Union armies formed, drilled, and positioned themselves more rapidly than they could be fully supplied, Lincoln continued to suspend the writ of habeas corpus to prevent rebel sympathizers from subverting federal mobilization.

Memoranda of Military Policy Suggested by the Bull Run Defeat

July 23, 1861

1 Let the plan for making the Blockade effective be pushed forward with all possible despatch.
2 Let the volunteer forces at Fort-Monroe & vicinity—under Genl. Butler[20]—be constantly drilled, disciplined, and instructed without more for the present.
3. Let Baltimore be held, as now, with a gentle, but firm, and certain hand.
4 Let the force now under Patterson,[21] or Banks,[22] be strengthened, and made secure in it's possition.
5. Let the forces in Western Virginia act, till further orders, according to instructions, or orders from Gen. McClellan.[23]
6. Let Gen. Fremont[24] push forward his organization, and opperations

[20]General Benjamin F. Butler had been a Democratic politician in Massachusetts before the war.

[21]General Robert Patterson, who commanded a federal contingent near Harper's Ferry, Virginia, had failed to prevent Confederate forces in his theater from sending reinforcements to Manassas.

[22]General Nathaniel P. Banks, who replaced Patterson, had served as governor of Massachusetts and Speaker of the House of Representatives, but he had no military experience.

[23]General George B. McClellan, a highly respected graduate of West Point, commanded the Department of the Ohio.

[24]General John C. Frémont, the Republican candidate for president in 1856, commanded the Department of the West, headquartered in St. Louis.

in the West as rapidly as possible, giving rather special attention to Missouri.

7 Let the forces late before Manassas, except the three months men, be reorganized as rapidly as possible, in their camps here and about Arlington.[25]

8. Let the three months forces, who decline to enter the longer service, be discharged as rapidly as circumstances will permit.

9 Let the new volunteer forces be brought forward as fast as possible; and especially into the camps on the two sides of the river here.

[25]Arlington, Virginia, lies just across the Potomac River from Washington.

July 27, 1861

When the foregoing shall have been substantially attended to—

1. Let Manassas junction, (or some point on one or other of the railroads near it;); and Strasburg,[26] be seized, and permanently held, with an open line from Washington to Manassas; and and [*sic*] open line from Harper's Ferry to Strasburg—the military men to find the way of doing these.

2. This done, a joint movement from Cairo[27] on Memphis; and from Cincinnati on East Tennessee.

[26]Strasburg was a small town in western Virginia, west of Harper's Ferry on the railroad line that connected Harper's Ferry to Manassas.

[27]Cairo, Illinois, lies at the confluence of the Ohio and Mississippi rivers, about 150 miles upstream from Memphis, Tennessee. An invasion down the Mississippi was the second part of General Scott's Anaconda strategy.

Letter to John A. McClernand

November 10, 1861

Washington.

Brigadier General McClernand[28]

My Dear Sir

This is not an official but a social letter. You have had a battle,[29] and without being able to judge as to the precise measure of its value, I think it is safe to say that you, and all with you have done honor to yourselves and the flag

[28]General John A. McClernand was a Democrat and former congressman from Illinois.

[29]McClernand, under the command of General Ulysses S. Grant, had fought at Belmont, Missouri, on November 7. During the indecisive battle, both sides suffered numerous casualties.

and service to the country. Most gratefully do I thank you and them. In my present position, I must care for the whole nation; but I hope it will be no injustice to any other state, for me to indulge a little home pride, that Illinois does not disappoint us.

I have just closed a long interview with Mr. Washburne[30] in which he has detailed the many difficulties you, and those with you labor under. Be assured, we do not forget or neglect you. Much, very much, goes undone: but it is because we have not the power to do it faster than we do. Some of your forces are without arms, but the same is true here, and at every other place where we have considerable bodies of troops. The plain matter-of-fact is, our good people have rushed to the rescue of the Government, faster than the government can find arms to put into their hands.

It would be agreeable to each division of the army to know its own precise destination: but the Government cannot immediately, nor inflexibly at any time, determine as to all; nor if determined, can it tell its *friends* without at the same time telling its *enemies.*

We know you do all as wisely and well as you can; and you will not be deceived if you conclude the same is true of us. Please give my respects and thanks to all.

Yours very truly
A LINCOLN.

[30]Elihu B. Washburne, a Republican congressman from Illinois and a member of a committee investigating government contracts, had just returned from two weeks in Saint Louis.

In his first annual message to Congress, Lincoln summarized the few encouraging military developments of the year, reiterated his intent to protect the property—including slaves—of loyal citizens throughout the nation, and declared that the struggle to maintain the Union represented a defense of democratic government and free labor.

Annual Message to Congress
December 3, 1861

Fellow Citizens of the Senate and House of Representatives:
In the midst of unprecedented political troubles, we have cause of great gratitude to God for unusual good health, and most abundant harvests.

You will not be surprised to learn that, in the peculiar exigencies of the times, our intercourse with foreign nations has been attended with profound solicitude, chiefly turning upon our own domestic affairs.

A disloyal portion of the American people have, during the whole year, been engaged in an attempt to divide and destroy the Union. A nation which endures factious domestic division, is exposed to disrespect abroad; and one party, if not both, is sure, sooner or later, to invoke foreign intervention.

Nations, thus tempted to interfere, are not always able to resist the counsels of seeming expediency, and ungenerous ambition, although measures adopted under such influences seldom fail to be unfortunate and injurious to those adopting them.

The disloyal citizens of the United States who have offered the ruin of our country, in return for the aid and comfort which they have invoked abroad, have received less patronage and encouragement than they probably expected. If it were just to suppose, as the insurgents have seemed to assume, that foreign nations, in this case, discarding all moral, social, and treaty obligations, would act solely, and selfishly, for the most speedy restoration of commerce, including, especially, the acquisition of cotton, those nations appear, as yet, not to have seen their way to their object more directly, or clearly, through the destruction, than through the preservation, of the Union. If we could dare to believe that foreign nations are actuated by no higher principle than this, I am quite sure a sound argument could be made to show them that they can reach their aim more readily, and easily, by aiding to crush this rebellion, than by giving encouragement to it.

The principal lever relied on by the insurgents for exciting foreign nations to hostility against us, as already intimated, is the embarrassment of commerce. Those nations, however, not improbably, saw from the first, that it was the Union which made as well our foreign, as our domestic, commerce. They can scarcely have failed to perceive that the effort for disunion produces the existing difficulty; and that one strong nation promises more durable peace, and a more extensive, valuable and reliable commerce, than can the same nation broken into hostile fragments.

It is not my purpose to review our discussions with foreign states, because whatever might be their wishes, or dispositions, the integrity of our country, and the stability of our government, mainly depend, not upon them, but on the loyalty, virtue, patriotism, and intelligence of the American people. . . .

Under and by virtue of the act of Congress entitled "An act to confiscate property used for insurrectionary purposes," approved August, 6, 1861, the legal claims of certain persons to the labor and service of certain other persons have become forfeited;[31] and numbers of the latter, thus liberated, are

---

[31]This first confiscation act provided that owners relinquished their claims to all property used in support of the rebellion, including slaves "employed in or upon any fort, navy yard, dock, armory, ship, entrenchment, or in the military or naval service." *The Statutes at Large, Treaties, and Proclamations of the United States . . . ,* XII, ed., George P. Sanger (Boston, 1863), 389.

already dependent on the United States,[32] and must be provided for in some way. Besides this, it is not impossible that some of the States will pass similar enactments for their own benefit respectively, and by operation of which persons of the same class[33] will be thrown upon them for disposal. In such case I recommend that Congress provide for accepting such persons from such States, according to some mode of valuation, in lieu . . . of direct taxes, or upon some other plan to be agreed on with such States respectively; that such persons, on such acceptance by the general government, be at once deemed free; and that, in any event, steps be taken for colonizing both classes, (or the one first mentioned, if the other shall not be brought into existence,) at some place, or places, in a climate congenial to them.[34] It might be well to consider, too,—whether the free colored people already in the United States could not, so far as individuals may desire, be included in such colonization.

To carry out the plan of colonization may involve the acquiring of territory, and also the appropriation of money beyond that to be expended in the territorial acquisition. Having practiced the acquisition of territory for nearly sixty years, the question of constitutional power to do so is no longer an open one with us. The power was questioned at first by Mr. Jefferson, who, however, in the purchase of Louisiana, yielded his scruples on the plea of great expediency. If it be said that the only legitimate object of acquiring territory is to furnish homes for white men, this measure effects that object; for the emigration of colored men leaves additional room for white men remaining or coming here. Mr. Jefferson, however, placed the importance of procuring Louisiana more on political and commercial grounds than on providing room for population.

On this whole proposition,—including the appropriation of money with the acquisition of territory, does not the expediency amount to absolute necessity—that, without which the government itself cannot be perpetuated? The war continues. In considering the policy to be adopted for suppressing the insurrection, I have been anxious and careful that the inevitable conflict for this purpose shall not degenerate into a violent and remorseless revolutionary struggle. I have, therefore, in every case, thought it proper to keep the integrity of the Union prominent as the primary object of the contest on our part, leaving all questions which are not of vital military importance to the more deliberate action of the legislature.

[32]Slaves ran away from their owners and into Union lines almost from the beginning of the war. Northern soldiers were under orders to return fugitive slaves to loyal owners, unless the slaves had been employed to support the rebellion, in which case—under the terms of the first confiscation act—they no longer had owners and should not be returned. Hundreds, and later thousands, of such slaves were employed by the Union army, at first without official authorization. The evolution of Lincoln's policies about slavery is documented in chapter 7.

[33]That is, slaves.

[34]Lincoln's plans for colonization are documented in detail in chapter 7.

In the exercise of my best discretion I have adhered to the blockade of the ports held by the insurgents, instead of putting in force, by proclamation, the law of Congress enacted at the late session, for closing those ports.[35]

So, also, obeying the dictates of prudence, as well as the obligations of law, instead of transcending, I have adhered to the act of Congress to confiscate property used for insurrectionary purposes. If a new law upon the same subject shall be proposed, its propriety will be duly considered.

The Union must be preserved, and hence, all indispensable means must be employed. We should not be in haste to determine that radical and extreme measures, which may reach the loyal as well as the disloyal, are indispensable.

The inaugural address at the beginning of the Administration, and the message to Congress at the late special session, were both mainly devoted to the domestic controversy out of which the insurrection and consequent war have sprung. Nothing now occurs to add or subtract, to or from, the principles or general purposes stated and expressed in those documents.

The last ray of hope for preserving the Union peaceably, expired at the assault upon Fort Sumter; and a general review of what has occurred since may not be unprofitable. What was painfully uncertain then, is much better defined and more distinct now; and the progress of events is plainly in the right direction. The insurgents confidently claimed a strong support from north of Mason and Dixon's line; and the friends of the Union were not free from apprehension on the point. This, however, was soon settled definitely and on the right side. South of the line, noble little Delaware led off right from the first. Maryland was made to *seem* against the Union. Our soldiers were assaulted, bridges were burned, and railroads torn up, within her limits; and we were many days, at one time, without the ability to bring a single regiment over her soil to the capital. Now, her bridges and railroads are repaired and open to the government; she already gives seven regiments to the cause of the Union and none to the enemy; and her people, at a regular election, have sustained the Union, by a larger majority, and a larger aggregate vote than they ever before gave to any candidate, or any question. Kentucky, too, for some time in doubt, is now decidedly, and, I think, unchangeably, ranged on the side of the Union. Missouri is comparatively quiet; and I believe cannot again be overrun by the insurrectionists. These three States of Maryland, Kentucky, and Missouri, neither of which would promise a single soldier at first, have now an aggregate of not less than forty thousand in the field, for the Union; while, of their citizens, certainly not more than a third of that number, and they of doubtful whereabouts, and

[35]Lincoln believed that foreign governments were far less likely to contest a blockade than a closure of southern ports to commerce. The distinction between a blockade and a closure of ports is a legal technicality; a nation imposed a blockade on an enemy power; it could order a closure of its own ports. Lincoln was not troubled by this distinction.

doubtful existence, are in arms against it. After a somewhat bloody struggle of months, winter closes on the Union people of western Virginia, leaving them masters of their own country.[36]

An insurgent force of about fifteen hundred, for months dominating the narrow peninsular region, constituting the counties of Accomac and Northampton, and known as eastern shore of Virginia, together with some contiguous parts of Maryland, have laid down their arms; and the people there have renewed their allegiance to, and accepted the protection of, the old flag. This leaves no armed insurrectionist north of the Potomac, or east of the Chesapeake.

Also we have obtained a footing at each of the isolated points, on the southern coast, of Hatteras,[37] Port Royal,[38] Tybee Island, near Savannah, and Ship Island;[39] and we likewise have some general accounts of popular movements, in behalf of the Union, in North Carolina and Tennessee.

These things demonstrate that the cause of the Union is advancing steadily and certainly southward.

Since your last adjournment, Lieutenant General Scott has retired from the head of the army. During his long life, the nation has not been unmindful of his merit; yet, on calling to mind how faithfully, ably and brilliantly he has served the country, from a time far back in our history, when few of the now living had been born, and thenceforward continually, I cannot but think we are still his debtors. I submit, therefore, for your consideration, what further mark of recognition is due to him, and to ourselves, as a grateful people.

With the retirement of General Scott came the executive duty of appointing, in his stead, a general-in-chief of the army. It is a fortunate circumstance that neither in council nor country was there, so far as I know, any difference of opinion as to the proper person to be selected. The retiring chief repeatedly expressed his judgment in favor of General McClellan for the position; and in this the nation seemed to give a unanimous concurrence.[40] The designation of General McClellan is therefore in considerable degree, the selection of the Country as well as of the Executive; and hence there is better reason to hope there will be given him, the confidence, and cordial support thus, by

[36]Western Virginia overwhelmingly opposed secession. A provisional government in Wheeling declared the secession government in Richmond illegal, proclaimed that they were the true, loyal state of Virginia, and sent senators and representatives to Congress. A prolonged federal military campaign finally pushed Confederate forces from the region by mid-November 1861. The new state of West Virginia was admitted to the Union on June 20, 1863.

[37]On August 29, Union forces defeated the Confederate garrison at Hatteras Inlet, an opening through the barrier islands off the coast of North Carolina.

[38]On November 7, a federal fleet captured the Confederate stronghold at Port Royal, South Carolina, securing federal control of the best Atlantic harbor in Confederate territory. The Union navy subsequently captured Tybee Island near the mouth of the Savannah River.

[39]After the Confederates abandoned Ship Island in September 1861, federal forces used it to supply ships enforcing the blockade along the Gulf Coast and to organize an assault on New Orleans.

[40]General McClellan became general in chief of the army on November 1, 1861.

fair implication, promised, and without which, he cannot, with so full efficiency, serve the country.

It has been said that one bad general is better than two good ones; and the saying is true, if taken to mean no more than that an army is better directed by a single mind, though inferior, than by two superior ones, at variance, and cross-purposes with each other.

And the same is true, in all joint operations wherein those engaged, *can* have none but a common end in view, and *can* differ only as to the choice of means. In a storm at sea, no one on board *can* wish the ship to sink; and yet, not unfrequently, all go down together, because too many will direct, and no single mind can be allowed to control.

It continues to develop that the insurrection is largely, if not exclusively, a war upon the first principle of popular government—the rights of the people. Conclusive evidence of this is found in the most grave and maturely considered public documents, as well as in the general tone of the insurgents. In those documents we find the abridgement of the existing right of suffrage and the denial to the people of all right to participate in the selection of public officers, except the legislative boldly advocated, with labored arguments to prove that large control of the people in government, is the source of all political evil. Monarchy itself is sometimes hinted at as a possible refuge from the power of the people.

In my present position, I could scarcely be justified were I to omit raising a warning voice against this approach of returning despotism.

It is not needed, nor fitting here, that a general argument should be made in favor of popular institutions; but there is one point, with its connexions, not so hackneyed as most others, to which I ask a brief attention. It is the effort to place *capital* on an equal footing with, if not above *labor,* in the structure of government. It is assumed that labor is available only in connexion with capital; that nobody labors unless somebody else, owning capital, somehow by the use of it, induces him to labor. This assumed, it is next considered whether it is best that capital shall *hire* laborers, and thus induce them to work by their own consent, or *buy* them, and drive them to it without their consent. Having proceeded so far, it is naturally concluded that all laborers are either *hired* laborers, or what we call slaves. And further it is assumed that whoever is once a hired laborer, is fixed in that condition for life.

Now, there is no such relation between capital and labor as assumed; nor is there any such thing as a free man being fixed for life in the condition of a hired laborer. Both these assumptions are false, and all inferences from them are groundless.

Labor is prior to, and independent of, capital. Capital is only the fruit of labor, and could never have existed if labor had not first existed. Labor is the superior of capital, and deserves much the higher consideration. Capital has its rights, which are as worthy of protection as any other rights. Nor is it denied that there is, and probably always will be, a relation between labor and capital, producing mutual benefits. The error is in assuming that the whole labor of community exists within that relation. A few men own capital, and that few avoid labor themselves, and, with their capital, hire or buy another few to labor for them. A large majority belong to neither class—neither work for others, nor have others working for them. In most of the southern States, a majority of the whole people of all colors are neither slaves nor masters; while in the northern a large majority are neither hirers nor hired. Men with their families—wives, sons, and daughters—work for themselves, on their farms, in their houses, and in their shops, taking the whole product to themselves, and asking no favors of capital on the one hand, nor of hired laborers or slaves on the other. It is not forgotten that a considerable number of persons mingle their own labor with capital—that is, they labor with their own hands, and also buy or hire others to labor for them; but this is only a mixed, and not a distinct class. No principle stated is disturbed by the existence of this mixed class.

Again: as has already been said, there is not, of necessity, any such thing as the free hired laborer being fixed to that condition for life. Many independent men everywhere in these States, a few years back in their lives, were hired laborers. The prudent, penniless beginner in the world, labors for wages awhile, saves a surplus with which to buy tools or land for himself; then labors on his own account another while, and at length hires another new beginner to help him. This is the just, and generous, and prosperous system, which opens the way to all—gives hope to all, and consequent energy, and progress, and improvement of condition to all. No men living are more worthy to be trusted than those who toil up from poverty—none less inclined to take, or touch, aught which they have not honestly earned. Let them beware of surrendering a political power which they already possess, and which, if surrendered, will surely be used to close the door of advancement against such as they, and to fix new disabilities and burdens upon them, till all of liberty shall be lost.

From the first taking of our national census to the last are seventy years; and we find our population at the end of the period eight times as great as it was at the beginning. The increase of those other things which men deem desirable has been even greater. We thus have at one view, what the popular principle applied to government, through the machinery of the States and the Union, has produced in a given time; and also what, if firmly maintained, it promises for the future. There are already among us those, who, if the Union be preserved, will live to see it contain two hundred and fifty millions. The struggle of today, is not altogether for today—it is for a vast future also. With a reliance on Providence, all the more firm and earnest, let us proceed in the great task which events have devolved upon us.

ABRAHAM LINCOLN

6

Marching South

By the end of 1861, Lincoln had made little progress on his pledge to save the Union. Huge armies costing millions of dollars camped along the Mason-Dixon line from Washington to Illinois, but they did not march forward to fight Confederates. Jefferson Davis and his leading generals understood that their goal was to defend the Confederacy. They won if the Confederacy maintained its independence. Lincoln could not afford such a strategy. Defending the Union required attacking the Confederacy. But the humiliating defeat at Bull Run in July 1861 made most Union commanders cautious. They were reluctant to attack until they believed their soldiers were sufficiently numerous, trained, and supplied. Eight months after the surrender of Fort Sumter, the Union Army had yet to mount a significant invasion of Confederate territory, with the exception of the coastal forts Lincoln mentioned in his December 1861 congressional address.

Republicans throughout the North criticized Lincoln and his generals and clamored for action. On December 20, 1861, Congress organized the Joint Committee on the Conduct of the War, providing a forum for Lincoln's critics and a powerful impetus for the military to do something, and soon. But few agreed on what the army should do. Antislavery leaders urged Lincoln to add freedom for slaves to the war aim of union, but he resisted for reasons that are documented in the next chapter. Lincoln himself could not even learn the plans of his general in chief, General George B. McClellan. McClellan had little regard for Lincoln—referring to him privately as an "idiot" and a "well meaning baboon"[1]—and simply refused to tell the president what he intended to do with his army. Lincoln was so discouraged in early January that he asked the army quartermaster-general Montgomery

---

[1] Stephen W. Sears, ed., *The Civil War Papers of George B. McClellan* (New York, 1989), 85, 106.

C. Meigs, "General, what shall I do? The people are impatient.... The bottom is out of the tub. What shall I do?"[2]

Lincoln, in effect, answered his own question. Since his generals showed so little initiative, he assumed responsibility for the overall direction of military strategy. His own military experience was limited, as he said, to "charges upon the wild onions" and "a good many bloody struggles with the musquetoes" during the Black Hawk War thirty years earlier.[3] He tried to educate himself by checking out several books on military strategy from the Library of Congress early in January 1862. He began to outline a three-part offensive strategy. First, to boost morale and preserve political support for the war in the North, Union commanders must start to fight. Second, Union generals should coordinate their attacks to put maximum pressure on Confederate defenders and to prevent them from shifting reinforcements from one front to another. Third, Union officers should seek to punish and defeat Confederate armies. The Union would not be saved until the Confederacy could no longer field an effective army.

Lincoln advised, cajoled, and ordered his generals to follow his strategy, as the documents in this chapter illustrate. By the end of 1862, Union armies had won important victories and advanced deep into Confederate territory. Though bloodied, the Confederacy was far from defeated. The Union, too, was bloodied and seemingly stalled, making some in the North question whether the war should continue. Lincoln defended his leadership and refused to consider any peace that involved disunion. But he finally concluded that his military strategy could not succeed without a major new objective: emancipation, the subject of the next chapter.

"DELAY IS RUINING US"

Lincoln peppered his commanders with questions and demanded that they take action. The following documents illustrate his efforts to direct military strategy. As commander in chief, Lincoln continually reminded his generals that their action—or inaction—had political as well as military conse-

[2]"General M. C. Meigs on the Conduct of the Civil War," *American Historical Review*, 26 (1920–21), 292.

[3]Lincoln described his military service during the Black Hawk War in a speech to the House of Representatives, July 27, 1848. *CW*, I, 510.

quences. In the West, Union armies achieved notable victories in the first half of 1862, while in the East, Lincoln became increasingly frustrated by General McClellan, who—Lincoln told a friend—"has got the 'slows.'"[4]

[4]William E. Smith, *The Francis Preston Blair Family in Politics* (2 vols.; New York, 1933), II, 144–45.

Letter to Ambrose E. Burnside
December 26, 1861

Executive Mansion,
Washington, D.C.

Brig. Genl. Burnside
My Dear Sir:

It is of great importance you should move as soon as possible.[5] Are you ready? Gen. McClellan (who is sick[6]) tells me you are. Is he or not mistaken? Is Goldsborough[7] ready? If you both are, be off at once. If not, get ready, and be off. Consumption of time is killing us. Please answer by return mail.[8]

Yours truly,
A. LINCOLN

[5]General Ambrose E. Burnside, a West Point graduate from Rhode Island, was poised to launch an attack on Roanoke Island with the intention of eventually controlling all ports in North Carolina.

[6]McClellan came down with typhoid fever in mid-December and was unable to carry out his duties for several weeks.

[7]Captain Louis M. Goldsborough commanded the naval force supporting Burnside's soldiers.

[8]Storms delayed Burnside's attack, but he succeeded in taking Roanoke Island on February 8; Newbern, North Carolina, on March 14; and Beaufort, North Carolina, on April 26, giving the Union control of the North Carolina coast.

Letter to Don C. Buell

January 4, 1862

Washington, D.C.

Brig. Gen. Buell[9]
Louisville, Ky.

Have arms gone forward for East-Tennessee?[10] Please tell me the progress and condition of the movement, in that direction. Answer.

A. LINCOLN

[9]General Don Carlos Buell, a West Point graduate from Ohio, was given command of the Department of Ohio on November 9, 1861.

[10]Lincoln was eager to provide protection for the numerous unionists in mountainous eastern Tennessee, where Confederates had declared martial law, executed several unionists, and imprisoned hundreds of others.

Letter to Don C. Buell

January 6, 1862

Executive Mansion,
Washington

Brig. Gen. Buell
My dear Sir

Your despatch[11] of yesterday has been received, and it disappoints and distresses me. I have shown it to Gen. McClellan, who says he will write you to-day. I am not competent to criticise your views; and therefore what I offer is merely in justification of myself. Of the two, I would rather have a point on the Railroad south of Cumberland Gap,[12] than Nashville, first, because it cuts a great artery of the enemies' communication, which Nashville does not, and secondly because it is in the midst of loyal people, who would rally around it, while Nashville is not. Again, I cannot see why the movement on East Tennessee would not be a diversion in your favor, rather than a disadvantage, assuming that a movement towards Nashville is the main object.

But my distress is that our friends in East Tennessee are being hanged and driven to despair, and even now I fear, are thinking of taking rebel arms

[11]Buell's testy answer to Lincoln's January 4 telegram read, "Arms can only go forward for East Tennessee under the protection of an army." Buell explained that he doubted the "wisdom" of such a move, preferring instead to attack Nashville. *CW,* V, 90.

[12]The Cumberland Gap in the Allegheny Mountains is near the Kentucky-Tennessee border, about sixty miles north of Knoxville.

for the sake of personal protection. In this we lose the most valuable stake we have in the South. My despatch, to which yours is an answer, was sent with the knowledge of Senator Johnson[13] and Representative Maynard[14] of East Tennessee, and they will be upon me to know the answer, which I cannot safely show them. They would despair—possibly resign to go and save their families somehow, or die with them.

I do not intend this to be an order in any sense, but merely, as intimated before, to show you the grounds of my anxiety.

Yours very Truly
A. LINCOLN

[13] Andrew Johnson, an eastern Tennessee Democrat, strongly supported Lincoln. He remained in the Senate after Tennessee seceded, where he was the only senator from a Confederate state.
[14] Horace Maynard was a unionist Tennessee congressman who strongly supported Lincoln.

Letter to Don C. Buell
January 7, 1862

Washington, D.C.

Brigr. General Buell
Louisville, Ky.
Please name as early a day as you safely can, on, or before which you can be ready to move Southward in concert with Gen. Halleck. Delay is ruining us; and it is indispensable for me to have something definite. I send a like despatch to Halleck.

A. LINCOLN.

Letter to George B. McClellan
January 9, 1862

I send the within copy of dispatch from Gen. Buell, with the remark that neither he nor Halleck meets my request to name the DAY when they can be ready to move.[15]

[15] Buell's telegram reported that he would "work with what I have, and as soon as possible." *CW,* V, 94.

Lincoln outlined his thinking about the necessity of coordinated, simultaneous attacks in the following letter to Generals Buell and Halleck. In the abstract, Lincoln's plan made sense, but it was difficult to put into practice because of the complications of battles involving tens of thousands of men and animals on different battlefields, often separated by hundreds of miles. Lincoln acknowledged these practical difficulties, but as the following selections show, he continued to insist that the general plan was sound.

Letter to Don C. Buell

January 13, 1862

COPY—one also sent to Gen. Halleck.

Executive Mansion,
Washington

Brig Genl. Buell
My dear Sir:
Your despatch of yesterday is received, in which you say "I have received your letter and Gen. McClellan's; and will, at once devote all my efforts to your views, and his." In the midst of my many cares, I have not seen, or asked to see, Gen. McClellan's letter to you. For my own views, I have not offered, and do not now offer them as orders; and while I am glad to have them respectfully considered, I would blame you to follow them contrary to your own clear judgment—unless I should put them in the form of orders. As to Gen. McClellan's views, you understand your duty in regard to them better than I do. With this preliminary, I state my general idea of this war to be that we have the *greater* numbers, and the enemy has the *greater* facility of concentrating forces upon points of collision; that we must fail, unless we can find some way of making *our* advantage an over-match for *his;* and that this can only be done by menacing him with superior forces at *different* points, at the *same* time; so that we can safely attack, one, or both, if he makes no change; and if he *weakens* one to *strengthen* the other, forbear to attack the strengthened one, but seize, and hold the weakened one, gaining so much. To illustrate, suppose last summer, when Winchester[16] ran away to re-inforce Mannassas, we had forborne to attack Mannassas, but had seized and held Winchester. I mention this to illustrate, and not to criticise. I did not

---

[16]Just before the battle of Bull Run in mid-July 1861, Confederate General Joseph E. Johnston pulled his army out of Winchester, Virginia, in the Shenandoah Valley, and took it to reinforce Confederate positions at Manassas, making a crucial contribution to that Confederate victory.

lose confidence in McDowell,[17] and I think less harshly of Patterson[18] than some others seem to. In application of the general rule I am suggesting, every particular case will have its modifying circumstances, among which the most constantly present, and most difficult to meet, will be the want of perfect knowledge of the enemies' movements. This had it's part in the Bull-Run case; but worse, in that case, was the expiration of the terms of the three months men.[19] Applying the principle to your case, my idea is that Halleck shall menace Columbus,[20] and "down river" generally; while you menace Bowling-Green,[21] and East Tennessee. If the enemy shall concentrate at Bowling-Green, do not retire from his front; yet do not fight him there, either, but seize Columbus and East Tennessee, one or both, left exposed by the concentration at Bowling Green. It is matter of no small anxiety to me and one which I am sure you will not over-look, that the East Tennessee line,[22] is so long, and over so bad a road.

Yours very truly
A. LINCOLN.

[17]General Irvin McDowell was the commander of the Union forces at the battle of Bull Run.

[18]General Robert Patterson, commander of the Union army near Winchester, Virginia, failed to pin down Johnston and prevent him from reinforcing Confederates at Manassas.

[19]General Patterson, fearing that the many ninety-day recruits in his army could not be relied on in a hard fight, tried to hold Johnston's army by maneuver rather than by attacking it. General McDowell's army at Bull Run was also largely made up of three-month men, many of whom abandoned their positions near the end of the battle when counterattacked by Confederates.

[20]Columbus, a town on the Mississippi River in far western Kentucky, was the terminus of a railroad that ran south all the way to Mobile, Alabama, on the Gulf of Mexico.

[21]Bowling Green, a town in central Kentucky about 150 miles east of Columbus, was the junction of railroads that branched southwest to Memphis and south to Nashville and on into Alabama.

[22]General George H. Thomas, a West Point graduate from Virginia who remained loyal to the Union, launched a drive toward eastern Tennessee and defeated a Confederate force at Mill Springs in southeastern Kentucky on January 19. But the mountainous terrain, execrable roads, and harsh winter weather stalled his invasion of Tennessee.

Impatient with the inaction of Union forces, Lincoln issued a series of orders demanding that his commanders delay no longer. His principal objective for the simultaneous attacks was action.

President's General War Order No. 1

January 27, 1862

Executive Mansion,
Washington

President's general War Order No. 1

Ordered that the 22nd. day of February 1862, be the day for a general movement of the Land and Naval forces of the United States against the insurgent forces. That especially—

The Army at & about, Fortress Monroe.[23]

The Army of the Potomac.[24]

The Army of Western Virginia[25]

The Army near Munfordsville, Ky.[26]

The Army and Flotilla at Cairo.[27]

And a Naval force in the Gulf of Mexico,[28] be ready for a movement on that day.

That all other forces, both Land and Naval, with their respective commanders, obey existing orders, for the time, and be ready to obey additional orders when duly given.

That the Heads of Departments, and especially the Secretaries of War and of the Navy, with all their subordinates; and the General-in-Chief,[29] with all other commanders and subordinates, of Land and Naval forces, will severally be held to their strict and full responsibilities, for the prompt execution of this order.

ABRAHAM LINCOLN

[23]Commanded by General John E. Wool.
[24]Commanded by General George B. McClellan.
[25]Commanded by General William S. Rosecrans.
[26]Commanded by General Don Carlos Buell.
[27]Commanded by General Ulysses S. Grant and Flag Officer Andrew H. Foote.
[28]Commanded by Flag Officer David G. Farragut.
[29]General George B. McClellan.

THE PENINSULA CAMPAIGN

Lincoln was especially eager to get General McClellan's Army of the Potomac in motion. Stationed in and around Washington, McClellan's army drilled in the spotlight of public scrutiny. Lincoln firmly believed that McClellan should attack the Confederate forces closest to Washington, at Manassas. Three months earlier, McClellan had ventured an attack on Leesburg, Virginia, about thirty miles north of Manassas, and had suffered

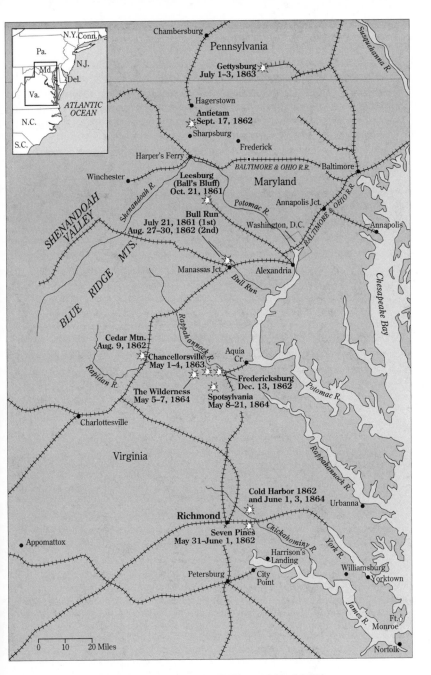

Map 3. Eastern Theater of the Civil War, 1861–1865

The proximity of Washington, the Union capital, and Richmond, the Confederate capital, concentrated armies, battles, and attention on killing fields within a 150-mile radius of Lincoln's office.

an embarrassing defeat at Ball's Bluff on October 21, 1861. McClellan now had different plans about how best to deploy his army. Instead of attacking rebel positions near Washington, he proposed to take his men down the Potomac River and south on the Chesapeake Bay to the peninsula between the James and York rivers, southeast of Richmond. Lincoln expressed doubts about this peninsula campaign.

Letter to George B. McClellan
February 3, 1862

Executive Mansion,
Washington

Major General McClellan
My dear Sir:
You and I have distinct, and different plans for a movement of the Army of the Potomac—yours to be down the Chesapeake, up the Rappahannock to Urbana, and across land to the terminus of the Railroad[30] on the York River—, mine to move directly to a point on the Railroad South West of Manassas.

If you will give me satisfactory answers to the following questions, I shall gladly yield my plan to yours.

1st. Does not your plan involve a greatly larger expenditure of *time,* and *money* than mine?

2nd. Wherein is a victory *more certain* by your plan than mine?

3rd. Wherein is a victory *more valuable* by your plan than mine?

4th. In fact, would it not be *less* valuable, in this, that it would break no great line of the enemie's communications, while mine would?

5th. In case of disaster, would not a safe retreat be more difficult by your plan than by mine?[31]

Yours truly
A. LINCOLN

[30]The railroad ran to Richmond.

[31]McClellan wrote a long letter to Secretary of War Edwin Stanton in response to Lincoln's questions. McClellan argued that his plan "affords the shortest possible land routes to Richmond, & strikes directly at the enemy's power in the East.... This movement if successful gives us the capital, the communications, the supplies of the rebels; Norfolk would fall; all the waters of the Chesapeake would be ours; all Virginia would be in our power; & the enemy forced to abandon Tennessee & North Carolina.... *In conclusion I would respectfully, but firmly, advise that I may be authorized to undertake at once the movement by Urbana[.] I believe that it can be carried into execution so nearly simultaneously with the final advance of Buell & Halleck that the columns will support each other[.] I will stake my life, my reputation on the result—more than that, I will stake upon it the success of our cause. I hope but little from the attack on Manassas;—my judgment is against it.*" CW, V, 122, 124.

Letter to George B. McClellan

February 8, 1862

Executive Mansion,
Washington

Major Genl. McClellan
My dear Sir—
Have you any farther news from the West?[32]
Have you heard from the Canal-boats?[33]
Have you determined, as yet, upon the contemplated movement we last talked of?

Yours truly
A. LINCOLN

[32]The news from the West was good. On February 6, General Ulysses S. Grant and Flag Officer Andrew H. Foote cooperated to capture Fort Henry on the Tennessee River, opening a waterway through Tennessee to northern Alabama. Ten days later, Grant and Foote defeated the Confederate garrison at Fort Donelson on the Cumberland River, opening a waterway to Nashville, which General Buell captured on February 25.

[33]McClellan built special boats to be used as a pontoon bridge to permit his soldiers to cross the Potomac River and attack Confederate forces at Harper's Ferry, astride the Baltimore and Ohio Railroad. The boats turned out to be about six inches too wide to fit into the locks of the canal, and the proposed attack had to be abandoned. When McClellan's chief of staff, General Randolph B. Marcy, informed Lincoln about this fiasco on February 27, Lincoln expressed his growing frustration with McClellan: "Why in the [tar]nation, General Marcy, couldn't the General have known whether a boat would go through that lock before he spent a million dollars getting them there? I am no engineer, but it seems to me that if I wished to know whether a boat would go through a hole, or a lock, common sense would teach me to go and measure it. I am almost despairing at these results. Everything seems to fail. The general impression is daily growing that the General [McClellan] does not intend to do anything. . . . I am grievously disappointed and almost in despair." Don E. Fehrenbacher and Virginia Fehrenbacher, eds., *Recollected Words of Abraham Lincoln* (Stanford, 1996), 345–46.

Letter to George B. McClellan

March 13, 1862

War Department

The President having considered the plan of operations agreed upon by yourself and the commanders of army corps, makes no objection to the same, but gives the following directions as to its execution:

1st. Leave such force at Manassas Junction as shall make it entirely certain that the enemy shall not repossess himself of that position and line of communication.[34]

2d. Leave Washington secure.

3d. Move the remainder of the force down the Potomac, choosing a new base at Fortress Monroe,[35] or anywhere between here and there; or, at all events, move such remainder of the army at once in pursuit of the enemy by some route.

[34]In early March, the Confederate forces near Manassas commanded by General Joseph E. Johnston withdrew to strengthen the defenses of Richmond. Learning of the withdrawal, McClellan led his entire army out to inspect Johnston's abandoned fortifications. To his embarrassment, he discovered that the Confederates had numbered only about half as many as he had claimed and that most of their artillery were in fact "Quaker guns," logs painted to resemble cannons.

[35]Johnston's withdrawal from Manassas forced McClellan to change his plans about where to land his army for the assault on Richmond. Instead of going up the Rappahannock River, now defended by Johnston's troops, McClellan set out for Fort Monroe on the peninsula between the James and York rivers.

Letter to George B. McClellan

April 9, 1862

Washington

Major General McClellan
My dear Sir.

Your despatches[36] complaining that you are not properly sustained, while they do not offend me, do pain me very much.

Blencker's Division was withdrawn from you before you left here;[37] and

[36]In the last few days, Lincoln had received several telegrams from McClellan complaining that he was being deprived of soldiers and supplies. On April 5, McClellan had begun a siege of Yorktown, Virginia, about twenty miles up the peninsula from Fort Monroe, where he had landed his army.

[37]On March 31, Lincoln had transferred General Louis Blenker's division of about ten thousand men to the Mountain Department of General Frémont, who agreed to use the reinforcements to attack the railroad near Knoxville, Tennessee.

you knew the pressure under which I did it, and, as I thought, acquiesced in it—certainly not without reluctance.

After you left, I ascertained that less than twenty thousand unorganized men, without a single field battery, were all you designed to be left for the defence of Washington, and Manassas Junction;[38] and part of this even, was to go to Gen. Hooker's old position. Gen Banks' corps, once designed for Manassas Junction, was diverted, and tied up on the line of Winchester and Strausburg, and could not leave it without again exposing the upper Potomac, and the Baltimore and Ohio Railroad.[39] This presented, (or would present, when McDowell and Sumner should be gone[40]) a great temptation to the enemy to turn back from the Rappahanock, and sack Washington. My explicit order that Washington should, by the judgment of *all* the commanders of Army corps, be left entirely secure, had been neglected. It was precisely this that drove me to detain McDowell.[41]

I do not forget that I was satisfied with your arrangement to leave Banks at Mannassas Junction; but when that arrangement was broken up, and *nothing* was substituted for it, of course I was not satisfied. I was constrained to substitute something for it myself. And now allow me to ask "Do you really think I should permit the line[42] from Richmond, *via* Mannassas Junction, to this city to be entirely open, except what resistance could be presented by less than twenty thousand unorganized troops?" This is a question which the country will not allow me to evade.

There is a curious mystery about the *number* of the troops now with you. When I telegraphed you on the 6th. saying you had over a hundred thousand with you, I had just obtained from the Secretary of War, a statement, taken as he said, from your own returns, making 108,000 then with you, and *en route* to you. You now say you will have but 85,000, when all *en route* to you shall have reached you. How can the discrepancy of 23,000 be accounted for?

As to Gen. Wool's command,[43] I understand it is doing for you precisely what a like number of your own would have to do, if that command was away.

I suppose the whole force which has gone forward for you, is with you by this time; and if so, I think it is the precise time for you to strike a blow. By delay the enemy will relatively gain upon you—that is, he will gain faster, by *fortifications* and *re-inforcements,* than you can by re-inforcements alone.

[38]On April 2, the War Department reported to Lincoln that his order to leave Washington "entirely secure" (General War Order Number 3) had not been obeyed by McClellan.

[39]General Nathaniel P. Banks was ordered to defend against a Confederate attack up the Shenandoah Valley by holding the Virginia towns of Winchester and Strasburg, both of them on important railroads.

[40]That is, McClellan had ordered the corps commanded by Generals Irvin McDowell and Edwin V. Sumner to leave Washington and accompany him.

[41]Lincoln ordered McDowell's corps to defend Washington.

[42]That is, the rail line.

[43]In a telegram of April 7, McClellan complained that General John E. Wool's command had been removed from his control to protect his rear lines of communication.

And, once more let me tell you, it is indispensable to *you* that you strike a blow. *I* am powerless to help this. You will do me the justice to remember I always insisted, that going down the Bay in search of a field, instead of fighting at or near Mannassas, was only shifting, and not surmounting, a difficulty—that we would find the same enemy, and the same, or equal, intrenchments, at either place. The country will not fail to note—is now noting—that the present hesitation to move upon an intrenched enemy, is but the story of Manassas repeated.

I beg to assure you that I have never written you, or spoken to you, in greater kindness of feeling than now, nor with a fuller purpose to sustain you, so far as in my most anxious judgment, I consistently can. *But you must act.*

Yours very truly

A. LINCOLN

By early May, Lincoln's plan of simultaneous, coordinated attacks seemed to be working. After having been bogged down for a month in a siege, McClellan finally took Yorktown on May 4 and began his long delayed advance toward Richmond. While McClellan's main force marched up the peninsula, another contingent captured Norfolk on May 9, forcing the rebels to evacuate, but not before they destroyed the *Merrimac*—the ironclad ship the Confederates had captured and renamed the *Virginia*—and other ships, weapons, and supplies about to fall into the hands of the Yankees.

McClellan's movement came on the heels of Union successes in the West. General Grant, under Halleck's command, had moved south along the Tennessee River heading for Corinth, Mississippi, the junction point of the Confederacy's major north-south and east-west railroads in the lower Mississippi Valley. Grant suffered a ferocious surprise attack near Shiloh, Tennessee, on April 6 but regrouped his men and, with reinforcements from General Buell, counterattacked the next day and forced the rebel army to retreat to Corinth. About twenty thousand men were killed or wounded at Shiloh, an omen of the brutal, remorseless fighting that lay ahead. While Halleck's army licked its wounds and began to inch toward Corinth, Flag Officer David G. Farragut captured New Orleans on April 25, securing federal control of the mouth of the Mississippi.

Letter to George B. McClellan

May 25, 1862

United States Military Telegraph
War Department, Washington, D.C.

To/
General McClellan: The enemy[44] is moving North in sufficient force to drive Banks before him in precisely what force we can not tell. He is also threatening Leesburgh and Geary on the Manassas Gap Rail Road from both north and south in precisely what force we can not tell. I think the movement is a general and concerted one, such as could not be if he was acting upon the purpose of a very desperate defence of Richmond. I think the time is near when you must either attack Richmond or give up the job and come to the defence of Washington. Let me hear from you instantly.

A. LINCOLN.

[44]In early May, Confederate General Thomas J. "Stonewall" Jackson launched a surprise campaign up the Shenandoah Valley to menace Union forces under General Nathaniel Banks and to prevent them from being sent to reinforce McClellan's attack on Richmond. On May 23, Jackson overwhelmed Union defenders at Front Royal, Virginia, and marched rapidly toward Winchester and Harper's Ferry, while Banks retreated across the Potomac River into Maryland.

Letter to George B. McClellan

June 26, 1862

Washington
Major-General McClellan: Your three dispatches of yesterday[45] in relation to the affair, ending with the statement that you completely succeeded in making your point, are very gratifying. The later one of 6:15 p.m., suggesting the probability of your being overwhelmed by 200,000, and talking of where the responsibility will belong, pains me very much.[46] I give you all I can, and act on the presumption that you will do the best you can with what you have,

[45]On June 25, McClellan had attacked Confederate forces at Oak Grove, Virginia, initiating what became known as the Seven Days' Battles.
[46]McClellan had written Lincoln, "I regret my great inferiority in numbers, but feel that I am in no way responsible for it. . . . I will do all that a general can do with the splendid army I have the honor to command, and if it is destroyed by overwhelming numbers, can at least die with it and share its fate. But if the result of the action, which will probably occur tomorrow . . . , is a disaster, the responsibility cannot be thrown on my shoulders; it must rest where it belongs." In fact, the Confederate force defending Richmond numbered no more than ninety thousand. *CW,* V, 286–87.

while you continue, ungenerously I think, to assume that I could give you more if I would. I have omitted and shall omit no opportunity to send you reenforcements whenever I possibly can.

A. LINCOLN

Letter to George B. McClellan
June 28, 1862

Washington City, D.C.

Major Gen. McClellan

Save your Army at all events.[47] Will send re-inforcements as fast as we can. Of course they can not reach you to-day, to-morrow, or next day. I have not said you were ungenerous for saying you needed re-inforcement. I thought you were ungenerous in assuming that I did not send them as fast as I could. I feel any misfortune to you and your Army quite as keenly as you feel it yourself. If you have had a drawn battle, or a repulse, it is the price we pay for the enemy not being in Washington. We protected Washington, and the enemy concentrated on you; had we stripped Washington, he would have been upon us before the troops sent could have got to you. Less than a week ago you notified us that re-inforcements were leaving Richmond to come in front of us. It is the nature of the case, and neither you or the government that is to blame. Please tell at once the present condition and aspect of things. . . .

A. LINCOLN

[47]On June 26, General Robert E. Lee attacked McClellan at Mechanicsville, just north of the Chickahominy River on the outskirts of Richmond. McClellan reported, "I have lost this battle because my force was too small. . . . I know that a few thousand more men would have changed this battle from a defeat to a victory." McClellan concluded his message with two inflammatory sentences that the telegraph officer simply deleted from the text sent to Secretary of War Stanton and to Lincoln: "If I save this army now, I tell you plainly that I owe no thanks to you or to any other persons in Washington. You have done your best to sacrifice this army." *CW,* V, 290.

Lee's attack and McClellan's retreat down the peninsula convinced Lincoln that the war was taking a disastrous turn and that the Union urgently needed more soldiers.

Letter to William H. Seward

June 28, 1862

Executive Mansion

Hon. W. H. Seward

My dear Sir

My view of the present condition of the War is about as follows:

The evacuation of Corinth,[48] and our delay by the flood in the Chicahominy,[49] has enabled the enemy to concentrate too much force in Richmond for McClellan to successfully attack. In fact there soon will be no substantial rebel force any where else. But if we send all the force from here to McClellan, the enemy will, before we can know of it, send a force from Richmond and take Washington. Or, if a large part of the Western Army be brought here to McClellan, they will let us have Richmond, and retake Tennessee, Kentucky, Missouri &c. What should be done is to hold what we have in the West, open the Mississippi,[50] and, take Chatanooga[51] & East Tennessee, without more—a reasonable force should, in every event, be kept about Washington for it's protection. Then let the country give us a hundred thousand new troops in the shortest possible time, which added to McClellan, directly or indirectly, will take Richmond, without endangering any other place which we now hold—and will substantially end the war. I expect to maintain this contest until successful, or till I die, or am conquered, or my term expires, or Congress or the country forsakes me; and I would publicly appeal to the country for this new force, were it not that I fear a general panic and stampede would follow—so hard is it to have a thing understood as it really is. I think the new force should be all, or nearly all infantry, principally because such can be raised most cheaply and quickly.

Yours very truly

A. Lincoln

[48]Corinth, Mississippi, had been evacuated by its Confederate defenders on May 30.

[49]The flooded Chickahominy River delayed McClellan's attack on Richmond.

[50]Union forces had captured Baton Rouge, Louisiana, on May 12, and Memphis on June 6. But the Mississippi River remained under Confederate control from Port Hudson, Louisiana—about twenty-five miles upriver from Baton Rouge—to Vicksburg, Mississippi—about two hundred miles upriver from Port Hudson.

[51]Chattanooga, in the mountains of southeastern Tennessee, was an important railroad center with lines stretching north into the Carolinas, south into Georgia, and west into Alabama.

Letter to George B. McClellan

July 1, 1862

Executive Mansion,
Washington

Major Genl. McClellan—

It is impossible to re-inforce you for your present emergency. If we had a million of men we could not get them to you in time. We have not the men to send. If you are not strong enough to face the enemy you must find a place of security, and wait, rest, and repair. Maintain your ground if you can, but save the Army at all events, even if you fall back to Fortress-Monroe.[52] We still have strength enough in the country, and will bring it out.[53]

A. LINCOLN

[52]On July 1, McClellan fought Lee's soldiers at Malvern Hill, the last of the Seven Days' Battles, and the next day retreated to entrenchments at Harrison's Landing on the James River.

[53]On July 1, Lincoln called for 300,000 additional three-year volunteers.

On July 7, Lincoln left Washington to speak directly with McClellan and his subordinate officers at Harrison's Landing, Virginia. Lincoln conferred with the generals and visited with other soldiers before returning to Washington on July 10. The next day, Lincoln signaled his loss of confidence in McClellan by naming Halleck—whose western armies had enjoyed such success in the last five months—general in chief, the position McClellan held before beginning the peninsula campaign. But McClellan still commanded the Army of the Potomac, and Lincoln had not yet given up hope that something might be salvaged from McClellan's campaign.

Lincoln told General Halleck that "he was satisfied McClellan would not fight [and] . . . that if by magic he could reinforce McClellan with 100,000 men today, he [McClellan] would be in ecstasy over it, thank him [Lincoln] for it, and tell him he would go to Richmond tomorrow; but that when tomorrow came, he would telegraph that he had certain information that the enemy had 400,000 men and that he could not advance without reinforcements."[54] Lincoln urged McClellan to use the soldiers he had, but

[54]Theodore Calvin Pease and James G. Randall, eds., *The Diary of Orville Browning* (2 vols.; Springfield, 1925–33), I, 563.

McClellan did not renew his attack on Richmond. Instead, his failed Peninsula campaign came to an end quietly on August 14, when, under orders from Halleck, he began to withdraw his army from Harrison's Landing for redeployment in northern Virginia.

Lincoln reflected on McClellan's campaign in a letter to Count Agénor-Etienne de Gasparin, the author of a book about America and an admirer of Lincoln's. In mid-July, Gasparin had written to encourage Lincoln. "The check sustained by the federal army before Richmond was certainly a situation of difficulty for the United States." But, he added, "learn that your friends in Europe do not lose courage, and that they pray for you. This, besides, is not a Bull Run. There is nothing in it like defeat." Gasparin could not resist asking a question and offering some military advice that did not come as news to Lincoln. "Why is it that the north with her great armies, so often is found, with inferiority in numbers, face to face with the armies of the South?" Gasparin inquired. "You know that battles are won by the feet! and that the great principle of war is to concentrate forces in place of scattering them. It is necessary that at important points the national troops should always outnumber those of the rebel forces. It seems that the contrary has too often taken place."[55]

[55]Gasparin's letter was translated and given to Lincoln on August 1. *CW,* V, 356.

Letter to Agénor-Etienne de Gasparin
August 4, 1862

Executive Mansion,
Washington

Dear Sir: Your very acceptable letter dated Orbe Canton de Vaud, Switzerland 18th of July 1862 is received. The moral effect was the worst of the affair before Richmond; and that has run its course downward: we are now at a stand, and shall soon be rising again, as we hope. I believe it is true that in men and material, the enemy suffered more than we, in that series of conflicts; while it is certain he is less able to bear it.

With us every soldier is a man of character and must be treated with more consideration than is customary in Europe. Hence our great army for slighter causes than could have prevailed there has dwindled rapidly, bringing the necessity for a new call, earlier than was anticipated. We shall easily obtain the new levy, however. Be not alarmed if you shall learn that we shall have resorted to a draft[56] for part of this. It seems strange, even to me, but it is true, that the Government is now pressed to this course by a popular demand. Thousands who wish not to personally enter the service are nevertheless anxious to pay and send substitutes,[57] provided they can have assurance that unwilling persons similarly situated will be compelled to do likewise. Besides this, volunteers mostly choose to enter newly forming regiments, while drafted men can be sent to fill up the old ones, wherein, man for man, they are quite doubly as valuable.

You ask "why is it that the North with her great armies, so often is found, with inferiority of numbers, face to face with the armies of the South?" While I painfully know the fact, a military man, which I am not, would better answer the question. The fact I know, has not been overlooked; and I suppose the cause of its continuance lies mainly in the other facts that the enemy holds the interior, and we the exterior lines; and that we operate where the people convey information to the enemy, while he operates where they convey none to us. . . .

You are quite right, as to the importance to us, for its bearing upon Europe, that we should achieve military successes;[58] and the same is true for us at home as well as abroad. Yet it seems unreasonable that a series of successes, extending through half-a-year, and clearing more than a hundred thousand square miles of country, should help us so little, while a single half-defeat should hurt us so much. But let us be patient.

I am very happy to know that my course has not conflicted with your judgement, of propriety and policy.

I can only say that I have acted upon my best convictions without selfishness or malice, and that by the help of God, I shall continue to do so.

Please be assured of my highest respect and esteem.

[56]In mid-July, Congress passed a new militia law that applied to all able-bodied men between eighteen and forty-five and that authorized the president to call these militia into service for nine months. On August 4, Lincoln issued a call for three hundred thousand militia in addition to the three hundred thousand volunteers he had called for in July. States could avoid *drafting* men into the militia if they recruited sufficient nine-month and three-year volunteers, as most did.

[57]Men could avoid going into the army by hiring substitutes to serve in their place.

[58]In his letter, Gasparin had declared that "the greatest peril of America is to be found" in Europe; "without the chances of European intervention [on the side of the Confederacy], or mediation, the revolt . . . would have been at an end long since." Gasparin counseled Lincoln, "That ideas of intervention may be counteracted in our old world, there is need not only of military successes achieved by you, but more than that, a continuation of your wise policy; avoid, I entreat you . . . revolutionary measures—confiscations—capital punishments—appeals to negroes—precipitate emancipation. . . . On the day when it can be said in Europe that your Government is, either indifferent to abolition, or carried away by the extreme abolitionists, the partizans of intervention, in favor of the South, will succeed in effecting it." *CW,* V, 356.

THE SECOND BATTLE OF BULL RUN AND ANTIETAM

While the peninsula campaign was coming to an end, Union General John Pope led the Army of Virginia south of Manassas, along the route to Richmond that Lincoln had long advocated. About fifty miles south of Manassas, Pope encountered Stonewall Jackson's army at Cedar Mountain, Virginia, on August 9 and was driven back. Pope slowly retreated northward along the rail line back to Manassas, awaiting reinforcement by McClellan. Before McClellan's men arrived, General Robert E. Lee reinforced Jackson, and the Confederates mauled Pope's army at the second battle of Bull Run between August 28 and 30. Once again, defeated federal soldiers streamed into Washington, and victorious rebel armies camped within twenty miles of the White House.

Pope's defeat alarmed Lincoln. He confided to his cabinet that "he felt almost ready to hang himself."[59] Victory over the Confederacy, which had seemed within reach in June, now seemed to verge on outright defeat. Profoundly demoralized, Lincoln brooded about God's purpose in permitting the war to continue. Fearing an imminent attack on Washington, he removed Pope from command on September 2 and replaced him with McClellan. Somebody was needed to organize the dispirited troops, and, Lincoln told his secretary, "If he [McClellan] can't fight, he excels in making others ready to fight."[60] But McClellan had little time to organize.

Rather than marching methodically from Manassas to attack Washington, General Lee set out to invade the North, crossing the Potomac River on September 5 and soon reaching Frederick, Maryland—about fifty miles northwest of Washington. Lincoln's frequent requests for news from McClellan reflected his awareness of the depth of the crisis. For once, McClellan moved quickly. In battles east of Frederick at Crampton's Gap and South Mountain on September 14, he pushed Lee back to Sharpsburg, Maryland, between the Potomac River and Antietam Creek, about ten miles north of Harper's Ferry. In the battle of Antietam on September 17, McClellan attacked Lee repeatedly in fighting that left twenty-three thousand killed and wounded, more casualties than any other single day in the war. The next day the two battered armies remained in place without fighting. That night Lee quietly retreated across the Potomac into Virginia.

[59] *CW,* V, 486.
[60] Tyler Dennet, ed., *Lincoln and the Civil War in the Diaries and Letters of John Hay* (New York, 1939), 47.

McClellan had succeeded in turning back Lee's invasion of the North, but Lincoln and many other northerners were far from satisfied, for reasons the following documents make clear.

Meditation on Divine Will

September 2, 1862?[61]

The will of God prevails. In great contests each party claims to act in accordance with the will of God. Both *may* be, and one *must* be wrong. God can not be *for,* and *against* the same thing at the same time. In the present civil war it is quite possible that God's purpose is something different from the purpose of either party—and yet the human instrumentalities, working just as they do, are of the best adaptation to effect His purpose. I am almost ready to say this is probably true—that God wills this contest, and wills that it shall not end yet. By his mere quiet power, on the minds of the now contestants, He could have either *saved* or *destroyed* the Union without a human contest. Yet the contest began. And having begun He could give the final victory to either side any day. Yet the contest proceeds.

[61] Although the original is not dated, the editors of Lincoln's papers agree that it was written sometime in September 1862 and conjecture that it probably was written soon after the second battle of Bull Run, when Lincoln "seemed wrung by the bitterest anguish," according to one of his cabinet members. It is also possible the fragment was written in late October when Lincoln met with Eliza P. Gurney, an English Quaker. *CW,* V, 404, 478.

Letter to George B. McClellan

September 8, 1862

Washington, D.C.

Major General McClellan
Rockville, Md.
How does it look now?

A. LINCOLN

Letter to George B. McClellan

September 10, 1862

Washington City,
10/15 AM.

Major Genl. McClellan.
Rockville, Md.
How does it look now?

A. LINCOLN

Letter to George B. McClellan

September 12, 1862

Washington City, D.C.
4.A.M.

Major General McClellan
Clarksburg, Md.
How does it look now?

A. LINCOLN

Letter to George B. McClellan

September 15, 1862

Washington, D.C.,
2/45

Major General McClellan.
Your despatches of to-day received.[62] God bless you, and all with you.
Destroy the rebel army, if possible.

A. LINCOLN

[62]McClellan's telegrams reported the victories at South Mountain and Crampton's Gap.

McClellan's success at Antietam on September 17 pleased Lincoln, but he was deeply discouraged by Lee's escape with his army intact. McClellan "did not follow up his advantages after Antietam," Lincoln told a friend. "The army of the enemy should have been annihilated, but it was permitted

Figure 4. Lincoln and McClellan at Antietam

Taken on October 3, 1862, shortly after the battle of Antietam and Lincoln's announcement of the Preliminary Emancipation Proclamation, this photograph shows Lincoln on his visit to the army and General McClellan (the second man to the right of Lincoln).

to recross the Potomac without the loss of a man, and McClellan would not follow." Lincoln pointed out that he "coaxed, urged, and ordered" McClellan to pursue Lee, but to no avail. "At the expiration of two weeks after a peremptory order [to go after Lee, McClellan] ... had only three-fourths of his army across the [Potomac] river and was six days doing that, whereas the rebel army ... effected a crossing in one day."[63]

    Lincoln continued to press McClellan to pursue Lee, who positioned his army south of Harper's Ferry near Winchester, Virginia. Confederate Gen-

---

[63]Pease and Randall, eds., *Diary of Orville Browning,* I, 589–90.

eral J. E. B. Stuart dramatized McClellan's passivity by leading a cavalry raid around McClellan's whole army between October 10 and 12, reaching as far north as Chambersburg, Pennsylvania, and returning almost entirely unscathed.

Letter to George B. McClellan
October 13, 1862

Executive Mansion,
Washington

Major General McClellan
My dear Sir

You remember my speaking to you of what I called your over-cautiousness. Are you not over-cautious when you assume that you can not do what the enemy is constantly doing? Should you not claim to be at least his equal in prowess, and act upon the claim?

As I understand, you telegraph Gen. Halleck that you can not subsist your army at Winchester unless the Railroad from Harper's Ferry to that point be put in working order. But the enemy does now subsist his army at Winchester at a distance nearly twice as great from railroad transportation as you would have to do without the railroad last named. He now wagons from Culpepper C.H.[64] which is just about twice as far as you would have to do from Harper's Ferry. He is certainly not more than half as well provided with wagons as you are. I certainly should be pleased for you to have the advantage of the Railroad from Harper's Ferry to Winchester, but it wastes all the remainder of autumn to give it to you; and, in fact ignores the question of *time,* which can not, and must not be ignored.

Again, one of the standard maxims of war, as you know, is "to operate upon the enemy's communications as much as possible without exposing your own." You seem to act as if this applies *against* you, but can not apply in your *favor.* Change positions with the enemy, and think you not he would break your communication with Richmond within the next twentyfour hours? You dread his going into Pennsylvania. But if he does so in full force, he gives up his communications to you absolutely, and you have nothing to do but to follow, and ruin him; if he does so with less than full force, fall upon, and beat what is left behind all the easier.

Exclusive of the water line, you are now nearer Richmond than the enemy is by the route that you *can,* and he *must* take. Why can you not

[64]Culpepper Courthouse stood about fifty miles south of Winchester.

reach there before him, unless you admit that he is more than your equal on a march. His route is the arc of a circle, while yours is the chord. The roads are as good on yours as on his.

You know I desired, but did not order, you to cross the Potomac below, instead of above the Shenandoah and Blue Ridge.[65] My idea was that this would at once menace the enemies' communications, which I would seize if he would permit. If he should move Northward I would follow him closely, holding his communications. If he should prevent our seizing his communications, and move towards Richmond, I would press closely to him, fight him if a favorable opportunity should present, and, at least, try to beat him to Richmond on the inside track. I say "try"; if we never try, we shall never succeed. If he make a stand at Winchester, moving neither North or South, I would fight him there, on the idea that if we can not beat him when he bears the wastage of coming to us, we never can when we bear the wastage of going to him. This proposition is a simple truth, and is too important to be lost sight of for a moment. In coming to us, he tenders us an advantage which we should not waive. We should not so operate as to merely drive him away. As we must beat him somewhere, or fail finally, we can do it, if at all, easier near to us, than far away. If we can not beat the enemy where he now is, we never can, he again being within the entrenchments of Richmond.

Recurring to the idea of going to Richmond on the inside track, the facility of supplying from the side away from the enemy is remarkable—as it were, by the different spokes of a wheel extending from the hub towards the rim—and this whether you move directly by the chord, or on the inside arc, hugging the Blue Ridge more closely.... I should think it preferable to take the route nearest the enemy, disabling him to make an important move without your knowledge, and compelling him to keep his forces together, for dread of you. The gaps [through the Blue Ridge] would enable you to attack if you should wish. For a great part of the way, you would be practically between the enemy and both Washington and Richmond, enabling us to spare you the greatest number of troops from here. When at length, running for Richmond ahead of him enables him to move this way; if he does so, turn and attack him in rear. But I think he should be engaged long before such point is reached. It is all easy if our troops march as well as the enemy; and it is unmanly to say they can not do it.

This letter is in no sense an order.

Yours truly
A. LINCOLN.

[65] That is, Lincoln desired McClellan to cross the Potomac south of Harper's Ferry in order to be positioned between Lee's army and Richmond.

Less than two weeks later, Lincoln became exasperated when he received a report that about half the horses in one of McClellan's cavalry units were "positively and absolutely unable to leave camp, from the following causes, viz, sore-tongue, grease, and consequent lameness, and sore backs [and] . . . the horses, which are still sound, are absolutely broken down from fatigue and want of flesh."[66]

[66]*CW,* V, 474.

Letter to George B. McClellan
October 24 [25], 1862

Washington City, D.C.

Majr. Genl. McClellan
I have just read your despatch about sore tongued and fatiegued horses. Will you pardon me for asking what the horses of your army have done since the battle of Antietam that fatigue anything?

A. Lincoln

Lincoln expressed his utter frustration with the caution of McClellan and other generals in a brief note that contrasted their views about what it would take to end the war with his. Early in November, Lincoln finally removed McClellan from his command and replaced him with General Ambrose E. Burnside.

Memorandum on Furloughs
November 1862

The Army is constantly depleted by company officers who give their men leave of absence in the very face of the enemy, and on the eve of an engagement, which is almost as bad as desertion. At this very moment there are between seventy and one hundred thousand men absent on furlough from the Army of the Potomac. The army, like the nation, has become demoralized by the idea that the war is to be ended, the nation united, and peace restored, by *strategy,* and not by hard desperate fighting. Why, then, should not the soldiers have furloughs?

HOME-FRONT POLITICS

The long lists of casualties published by every newspaper across the North brought the costs of the war home to every family with a man in uniform. Lincoln's call for another six hundred thousand recruits in July and August 1862 made even more northern families scan those lists and wonder why Lincoln had a nearly insatiable need for soldiers. Although Lee's invasion of the North had been repulsed at the battle of Antietam in September, the Union army had made little progress toward defeating the Confederacy since the victories in the West in May and June. Many northern citizens criticized Lincoln's leadership and questioned his policies, especially after he announced the Preliminary Emancipation Proclamation on September 22, 1862 (discussed in the next chapter). Resistance to fighting for black freedom coupled with resistance to fighting at all required Lincoln to send soldiers into Pennsylvania, Ohio, Indiana, and Wisconsin to enforce the recruitment of militia. Lincoln suspended the writ of habeas corpus throughout the nation, and hundreds of northerners were arrested and jailed, accused of resisting the militia draft or giving aid and comfort to the Confederacy. Many of the arrested dissidents were Democrats, an issue the party used in the fall elections—along with opposition to emancipation—with impressive success, boosting their congressional representation from forty-four to seventy-two.

Although Republicans retained a majority in both houses of Congress, they, too, criticized Lincoln. On December 13, General Burnside initiated yet another drive toward Richmond by attacking General Lee's army at Fredericksburg, Virginia. In a deadly frontal assault on Confederate defenses, Burnside sustained a crushing defeat. A few days later, after Republican senators met with Lincoln and condemned the disastrous course of the war, Lincoln confessed to a friend, "They wish to get rid of me, and I am sometimes half disposed to gratify them.... We are now on the brink of destruction. It appears to me the Almighty is against us, and I can hardly see a ray of hope."[67]

Profoundly discouraged, Lincoln refused to give in to despair. He deflected peace overtures, congratulated the Army of the Potomac for its courage at Fredericksburg and expressed confidence in ultimate victory, and acknowledged the grief felt by families throughout the nation. In these dark days, the ray of hope Lincoln could glimpse came from emancipation.

[67]Pease and Randall, eds., *Diary of Orville Browning,* I, 600.

Proclamation Suspending the Writ of Habeas Corpus

September 24, 1862

BY THE PRESIDENT OF THE UNITED STATES OF AMERICA: A PROCLAMATION.

Whereas, it has become necessary to call into service not only volunteers but also portions of the militia of the States by draft in order to suppress the insurrection existing in the United States, and disloyal persons are not adequately restrained by the ordinary processes of law from hindering this measure and from giving aid and comfort in various ways to the insurrection;

Now, therefore, be it ordered, first, that during the existing insurrection and as a necessary measure for suppressing the same, all Rebels and Insurgents, their aiders and abettors within the United States, and all persons discouraging volunteer enlistments, resisting militia drafts, or guilty of any disloyal practice, affording aid and comfort to Rebels against the authority of the United States, shall be subject to martial law and liable to trial and punishment by Courts Martial or Military Commission:

Second. That the Writ of Habeas Corpus is suspended in respect to all persons arrested, or who are now, or hereafter during the rebellion shall be, imprisoned in any fort, camp, arsenal, military prison, or other place of confinement by any military authority or by the sentence of any Court Martial or Military Commission.[68] . . .

ABRAHAM LINCOLN.

[68]The arrest of so many northern citizens engendered such a public opposition that most of them were released by late November, under orders from the War Department.

Letter to Carl Schurz

November 24, 1862

Executive Mansion,
Washington

Gen. Carl Schurz[69]

My dear Sir

I have just received, and read, your letter of the 20th.[70] The purport of it is that we lost the late elections, and the administration is failing, because the war is unsuccessful; and that I must not flatter myself that I am not justly to blame for it. I certainly know that if the war fails, the administration fails, and that I *will* be blamed for it, whether I deserve it or not. And I ought to be blamed, if I could do better. You think I could do better; therefore you blame me already. I think I could not do better; therefore I blame you for blaming me. I understand you *now* to be willing to accept the help of men, who are not republicans, provided they have "heart in it." Agreed. I want no others. But who is to be the judge of hearts, or of "heart in it"? If I must discard my own judgment, and take yours, I must also take that of others; and by the time I should reject all I should be advised to reject, I should have none left, republicans, or others—not even yourself. For, be assured, my dear sir, there are men who have "heart in it" that think you are performing your part as poorly as you think I am performing mine.[71] I certainly have been dissatisfied with the slowness of Buell and McClellan; but before I relieved them[72] I had great fears I should not find successors to them, who would do better; and I am sorry to add, that I have seen little since to relieve those fears. I do not clearly see the prospect of any more rapid movements. I fear we shall at last find out that the difficulty is in our case, rather than in particular generals. I wish to disparage no one—certainly not those who sympathize with me; but I must say I need success more than I need sympathy, and that I have not seen the so much greater evidence of getting success from my sympathizers, than from those who are denounced as the contrary. It does seem to me that in the field the two classes have been very much alike, in what they have done, and what they have failed to do. In sealing their faith with

---

[69]General Carl Schurz, a German immigrant from Wisconsin, was an ardent Republican.

[70]In his letter, Schurz urged Lincoln to "indulge in no delusions as to the true causes of our defeat in the elections.... The people had sown confidence and reaped disaster and disappointment.... *The result of the elections was a most serious and severe reproof administered to the administration.*" Schurz accused Lincoln of putting "old democrats into high military positions" and continuing to support them "after they had been found failing ... not only in a political but also in a military sense." *CW,* V, 511.

[71]General Schurz commanded a division in the Union defeat at the second battle of Bull Run.

[72]Lincoln had removed General Buell from command of the Army of the Cumberland on October 30 and had replaced him with General William S. Rosecrans.

their blood, Baker,[73] an[d] Lyon,[74] and Bohlen,[75] and Richardson,[76] republicans, did all that men could do; but did they any more than Kearney,[77] and Stevens,[78] and Reno,[79] and Mansfield,[80] none of whom were republicans, and some, at least of whom, have been bitterly, and repeatedly, denounced to me as secession sympathizers? I will not perform the ungrateful task of comparing cases of failure.

In answer to your question "Has it not been publicly stated in the newspapers, and apparantly proved as a fact, that from the commencement of the war, the enemy was continually supplied with information by some of the confidential subordinates of as important an officer as Adjutant General Thomas?"[81] I must say "no" so far as my knowledge extends. And I add that if you can give any tangible evidence upon that subject, I will thank you to come to the City and do so.

Very truly Your friend
A. LINCOLN

[73]Colonel Edward D. Baker, a friend of Lincoln's, was killed at Balls Bluff, Virginia, October 21, 1861.

[74]General Nathaniel Lyon, a strong supporter of Lincoln, was killed at Wilson's Creek, Missouri, August 10, 1861.

[75]General Henry Bohlen was killed at Freeman's Ford, Virginia, August 22, 1862.

[76]General Israel B. Richardson was wounded at South Mountain, September 17, and died of the wounds at Antietam, November 3, 1862.

[77]General Philip Kearney was killed at Chantilly, Virginia, September 1, 1862.

[78]General Isaac I. Stevens was killed at Chantilly, Virginia, September 1, 1862.

[79]General Jesse L. Reno was killed at South Mountain, September 14, 1862.

[80]General Joseph F. K. Mansfield was mortally wounded at Antietam, September 17, 1862, and died the next day.

[81]Adjutant General Lorenzo Thomas served on the military staff of Secretary of War Edwin Stanton, who disliked him and suspected—incorrectly—that he was disloyal.

Congratulations to the Army of the Potomac

December 22, 1862

Executive Mansion,
Washington

To the Army of the Potomac:[82] I have just read your Commanding General's preliminary report of the battle of Fredericksburg. Although you were not successful, the attempt was not an error, nor the failure other than an accident. The courage with which you, in an open field, maintained the contest against an entrenched foe, and the consummate skill and success with which you crossed and re-crossed the river, in face of the enemy, show that you possess all the qualities of a great army, which will yet give victory to the cause

[82]This letter was printed as a leaflet and was distributed to the Army of the Potomac.

of the country and of popular government. Condoling with the mourners for the dead, and sympathizing with the severely wounded, I congratulate you that the number of both is comparatively so small.[83]

I tender to you, officers and soldiers, the thanks of the nation.

ABRAHAM LINCOLN.

[83]In fact, the Union casualties at Fredericksburg were nearly as great as at Antietam: about thirteen thousand killed and wounded.

Letter to Fanny McCullough
December 23, 1862

Executive Mansion,
Washington

Dear Fanny[84]

It is with deep grief that I learn of the death of your kind and brave Father; and, especially, that it is affecting your young heart beyond what is common in such cases. In this sad world of ours, sorrow comes to all; and, to the young, it comes with bitterest agony, because it takes them unawares. The older have learned to ever expect it. I am anxious to afford some alleviation of your present distress. Perfect relief is not possible, except with time. You can not now realize that you will ever feel better. Is not this so? And yet it is a mistake. You are sure to be happy again. To know this, which is certainly true, will make you some less miserable now. I have had experience enough to know what I say; and you need only to believe it, to feel better at once. The memory of your dear Father, instead of an agony, will yet be a sad sweet feeling in your heart, of a purer, and holier sort than you have known before.

Please present my kind regards to your afflicted mother.

Your sincere friend
A. LINCOLN.

[84]Fanny McCullough was the young daughter of Lieutenant Colonel William McCullough, commander of an Illinois cavalry unit who was killed in battle near Coffeeville, Mississippi, December 5, 1862. McCullough had been a court official in Bloomington, Illinois, where Lincoln came to know him well.

7

Toward Emancipation

Before Lincoln became president, he pledged to protect slavery where it existed and to prevent its expansion into federal territories. As he had explained in speech after speech since 1854, he believed that slavery was morally wrong but that the Constitution gave the federal government no power to abolish it. Legally, slaves were a form of property protected by the federal Constitution. Only states had the power to decide whether they would permit or prohibit slavery.

Lincoln's prepresidential speeches also made clear that widespread belief in white supremacy throughout the North limited the popular appeal of eliminating slavery because it immediately raised the question of whether free blacks should be equal to whites—a question to which most white northerners unhesitatingly answered no. Lincoln himself did not fully share these white supremacist views. As he had outlined in his speeches, he did not believe whites and blacks were equal in all ways, but he insisted that they had equal claims to the fruits of their labor and to the basic human right of liberty. Lincoln knew that many white citizens did not agree with him and that, in a representative democracy of white men, their views mattered, even though he thought they were wrong.

In sum, Lincoln's ideas about the immorality of slavery were constrained by his overriding faith in the morality of democracy. When he became president, he believed that what he could do about slavery was limited legally by the Constitution and socially and politically by the ideology of white supremacy. The war changed his thinking about slavery in three fundamental ways, as the documents in this chapter demonstrate.

First, as commander in chief in wartime, he possessed the constitutional authority to undertake otherwise unconstitutional actions—including against slavery—if demanded by military necessity. Second, his strategy to end disunion and win the war determined how he exercised his powers as commander in chief. From the beginning of the war through the middle

179

of 1862, Lincoln believed that protecting slavery would appeal to loyal unionists within the Confederacy and would cement the loyalty of the border slave states of Maryland, Delaware, Kentucky, and Missouri. Discouraging news from the battlefield during the last half of 1862, the certainty that the border states would not join the Confederacy, and the failure of unionists in the seceded states to assert themselves to oppose the rebels— all of these developments brought Lincoln to believe that ending, rather than protecting, slavery was the way to win the war.

Third, Lincoln perceived that the war changed northern public opinion about slavery. Union soldiers who carried out Lincoln's policies while fighting in the South came to believe that by protecting slavery they were aiding the enemy, who benefited from slave labor. When slaves began to flee from their masters and flock toward Union lines, many soldiers concluded that the army should protect slaves, not slaveholders. Most white northerners began to agree, especially after the military reverses of 1862. The war created political momentum in the North in favor of ending slavery as a way to defeat the rebellion.

Lincoln's movement toward emancipation reflected a shift in his thinking about the most important parts of his political constituency. In the North, he became less focused on loyal slaveholders in the border states and more concerned about maintaining support for the war, especially among Republicans. In the South, his search for potential allies against the rebels shifted away from loyal unionists and toward slaves. By January 1863, both shifts identified Lincoln and the Republican party with war and black freedom to a degree unthinkable when Lincoln became president— unthinkable, that is, except by the secessionists whose actions ultimately propelled Lincoln to become the Great Emancipator. In the final analysis, secessionist slaveholders were their own worst enemies.

REASSURING LOYAL SOUTHERNERS

During the first year of war, Lincoln tried to end disunion by combating secessionist rebels and reassuring loyal southerners that their rights as U.S. citizens, including their right to own slaves, would not be impaired. This conciliatory appeal to southern unionists aroused the ire of antislavery Republicans who believed the war should be against slavery as well as against secession.

When slaves escaped to Union lines, Lincoln's promise to protect loyal slaveholders' rights to slave property turned many Union soldiers into

Figure 5.   Virginia Contraband
This carefully posed photograph—taken in the spring of 1862 near Yorktown, Virginia, during McClellan's peninsula campaign—portrays four Virginia slaves, perhaps members of one family, doing laundry and chopping wood for Union soldiers from the large encampment in the background.

slave catchers, an experience few soldiers liked and many abhorred. In May 1861, General Benjamin F. Butler declared the slaves who came to his garrison at Fortress Monroe, Virginia, "contraband of war," and he put them to work for his army. *Contraband* became a synonym for fugitive slaves throughout the North. Lincoln acceded to Butler's contraband policy, but he did not adopt it as general practice for the Union army. Instead, Lincoln insisted that soldiers return slaves who belonged to loyal masters. The First Confiscation Act, passed by Congress on August 6, 1861, provided that any slaves who worked to support the Confederate military effort could not be claimed by their masters. But the Confiscation Act did not otherwise alter the distinction Lincoln maintained between loyal and disloyal slaveholders. In September 1861, General John C. Frémont, commander of federal forces in Missouri, unilaterally declared that the slaves of disloyal owners were free, prompting Lincoln to assert his primacy to determine policies about slavery.

Letter to John C. Frémont

September 2, 1861

Private and confidential.

Washington D.C.

Major General Fremont:

My dear Sir:

Two points in your proclamation of August 30th[1] give me some anxiety. First, should you shoot a man, according to the proclamation,[2] the Confederates would very certainly shoot our best man in their hands in retaliation; and so, man for man, indefinitely. It is therefore my order that you allow no man to be shot, under the proclamation, without first having my approbation or consent.

Secondly, I think there is great danger that the closing paragraph,[3] in relation to the confiscation of property, and the liberating slaves of traiterous owners, will alarm our Southern Union friends, and turn them against us—perhaps ruin our rather fair prospect for Kentucky. Allow me therefore to ask, that you will as of your own motion, modify that paragraph so as to

[1]General Frémont's proclamation declared that, as commanding general, he had to "assume the administrative powers of the State" of Missouri because its "disorganized condition, the helplessness of civil authority, the total insecurity of life, and the devastation of property by bands of murderers and marauders, who infest nearly every county of the State, and avail themselves of the public misfortunes and the vicinity of a hostile force to gratify private and neighborhood vengeance, and who find an enemy wherever they find plunder . . . demand the severest measures." Ira Berlin et al., eds., *Freedom: A Documentary History of Emancipation, 1861–1867,* Series I, Volume I, *The Destruction of Slavery* (New York, 1985), 415.

[2]Frémont's proclamation specified that "all persons who shall be taken with arms in their hands within these lines shall be tried by court-martial, and if found guilty will be shot." *CW,* IV, 507.

[3]The proclamation stated, "The property, real and personal, of all persons in the state of Missouri who shall take up arms against the United States, or who shall be directly proven to have taken an active part with their enemies in the field, is declared to be confiscated to the public use, and their slaves, if any they have, are hereby declared freemen." Berlin et al., eds., *The Destruction of Slavery,* 415.

conform to the *first* and *fourth* sections of the act of Congress, entitled, "An act to confiscate property used for insurrectionary purposes," approved August, 6th, 1861, and a copy of which act I herewith send you.[4] This letter is written in a spirit of caution and not of censure.

I send it by a special messenger, in order that it may certainly and speedily reach you.

Yours very truly
A. LINCOLN

[4]The first section of the Confiscation Act provided that the property of rebels could be seized by the army. The fourth section stated that if a slave was "employed in hostile service against the government," the slave's owner "shall forfeit his claim" to the slave. *The Statutes at Large, Treaties, and Proclamations of the United States . . . ,* ed. George P. Sanger (Boston, 1863), XII, 389.

Letter to John C. Frémont

September 11, 1861

Washington, D.C.

Major General John C. Fremont.
Sir: Yours of the 8th. in answer to mine of 2nd. Inst. is just received.[5] Assuming that you, upon the ground, could better judge of the necessities of your position than I could at this distance, on seeing your proclamation of August 30th. I perceived no general objection to it. The particular clause, however, in relation to the confiscation of property and the liberation of slaves, appeared to me to be objectionable, in it's non-conformity to the Act of Congress passed the 6th. of last August upon the same subjects; and hence I wrote you expressing my wish that that clause should be modified accordingly. Your answer, just received, expresses the preference on your part, that I should make an open order for the modification, which I very cheerfully do. It is therefore ordered that the said clause of said proclamation be so modified, held, and construed, as to conform to, and not to transcend, the provisions on the same subject contained in the act of Congress entitled "An Act to confiscate property used for insurrectionary purposes" Approved, August 6. 1861; and that said act be published at length with this order.

Your Obt. Servt.
A. LINCOLN.

[5]Frémont's letter stated, in part, "If . . . your better judgment still decides that I am wrong in the article respecting the liberation of slaves, I have to ask that you will openly direct me to make the correction. . . . I acted with full deliberation and . . . the conviction that it was . . . right and necessary. I still think so." *CW,* IV, 507.

Letter to Orville H. Browning

September 22, 1861

Private & confidential.

Executive Mansion,
Washington

Hon. O. H. Browning[6]
My dear Sir

Yours of the 17th is just received; and coming from you, I confess it astonishes me. That you should object to my adhering to a law, which you had assisted in making, and presenting to me, less than a month before, is odd enough. But this is a very small part. Genl. Fremont's proclamation, as to confiscation of property, and the liberation of slaves, is *purely political,* and not within the range of *military* law, or necessity. If a commanding General finds a necessity to seize the farm of a private owner, for a pasture, an encampment, or a fortification, he has the right to do so, and to so hold it, as long as the necessity lasts; and this is within military law, because within military necessity. But to say the farm shall no longer belong to the owner, or his heirs forever; and this as well when the farm is not needed for military purposes as when it is, is purely political, without the savor of military law about it. And the same is true of slaves. If the General needs them, he can seize them, and use them; but when the need is past, it is not for him to fix their permanent future condition. That must be settled according to laws made by law-makers, and not by military proclamations. The proclamation in the point in question, is simply "dictatorship." It assumes that the general may do *anything* he pleases—confiscate the lands and free the slaves of *loyal* people, as well as of disloyal ones. And going the whole figure I have no doubt would be more popular with some thoughtless people, than that which has been done! But I cannot assume this reckless position; nor allow others to assume it on my responsibility. You speak of it as being the only means of *saving* the government. On the contrary it is itself the surrender of the government. Can it be pretended that it is any longer the government of the U.S.—any government of Constitution and laws,—wherein a General, or a President, may make permanent rules of property by proclamation?

I do not say Congress might not with propriety pass a law, on the point, just such as General Fremont proclaimed. I do not say I might not, as a member of Congress, vote for it. What I object to, is, that I as President, shall expressly or impliedly seize and exercise the permanent legislative functions of the government.

So much as to principle. Now as to policy. No doubt the thing was popu-

---

[6]Orville H. Browning, a Republican, was a U.S. senator from Illinois and a friend of Lincoln's.

lar in some quarters, and would have been more so if it had been a general declaration of emancipation. The Kentucky Legislature would not budge till that proclamation was modified;[7] and Gen. Anderson[8] telegraphed me that on the news of Gen. Fremont having actually issued deeds of manumission, a whole company of our Volunteers threw down their arms and disbanded. I was so assured, as to think it probable, that the very arms we had furnished Kentucky would be turned against us. I think to lose Kentucky is nearly the same as to lose the whole game. Kentucky gone, we can not hold Missouri, nor, as I think, Maryland. These all against us, and the job on our hands is too large for us. We would as well consent to separation at once, including the surrender of this capitol. On the contrary, if you will give up your restlessness for new positions, and back me manfully on the grounds upon which you and other kind friends gave me the election, and have approved in my public documents, we shall go through triumphantly.

You must not understand I took my course on the proclamation *because* of Kentucky. I took the same ground in a private letter to General Fremont before I heard from Kentucky.

You think I am inconsistent because I did not also forbid Gen. Fremont to shoot men under the proclamation. I understand that part to be within military law; but I also think, and so privately wrote Gen. Fremont, that it is impolitic in this, that our adversaries have the power, and will certainly exercise it, to shoot as many of our men as we shoot of theirs. I did not say this in the public letter, because it is a subject I prefer not to discuss in the hearing of our enemies.

There has been no thought of removing Gen. Fremont on any ground connected with his proclamation. . . .

Your friend as ever
A. LINCOLN

[7]In other words, the Kentucky legislature insisted that Frémont's proclamation be nullified. Lincoln's old Kentucky friend, Joshua Speed, wrote him that "so fixed is public sentiment in this state against freeing negroes . . . that you had as well attack the freedom of worship in the North or the right of a parent to teach his child to read, as to wage war in a slave state on such a principle." Quoted in Victor B. Howard, *Black Liberation in Kentucky: Emancipation and Freedom, 1862–1884* (Lexington, 1983), 6.

[8]General Robert Anderson, of Fort Sumter fame, now commanded the Department of Kentucky.

Instead of threatening the rights of slaveholders, Lincoln asked Congress to approve his plan for gradual, compensated emancipation. Such a plan, he argued, honored the constitutional limits of federal power while strengthening the Union. Lincoln's plan also included a threat, only partially veiled, that emancipation could come about in a way that slaveholders and other Americans would find less palatable.

Message to Congress

March 6, 1862

Fellow-citizens of the Senate, and House of Representatives,

I recommend the adoption of a Joint Resolution by your honorable bodies which shall be substantially as follows:

"Resolved that the United States ought to co-operate with any state which may adopt gradual abolishment of slavery, giving to such state pecuniary aid, to be used by such state in it's discretion, to compensate for the inconveniences public and private, produced by such change of system"

If the proposition contained in the resolution does not meet the approval of Congress and the country, there is the end; but if it does command such approval, I deem it of importance that the states and people immediately interested, should be at once distinctly notified of the fact, so that they may begin to consider whether to accept or reject it. The federal government would find it's highest interest in such a measure, as one of the most efficient means of self-preservation. The leaders of the existing insurrection entertain the hope that this government will ultimately be forced to acknowledge the independence of some part of the disaffected region, and that all the slave states North of such part will then say "the Union, for which we have struggled, being already gone, we now choose to go with the Southern section." To deprive them of this hope, substantially ends the rebellion; and the initiation of emancipation completely deprives them of it, as to all the states initiating it. The point is not that *all* the states tolerating slavery would very soon, if at all, initiate emancipation; but that, while the offer is equally made to all, the more Northern shall, by such initiation, make it certain to the more Southern, that in no event, will the former ever join the latter, in their proposed confederacy. I say "initiation" because, in my judgment, gradual, and not sudden emancipation, is better for all. In the mere financial, or pecuniary view, any member of Congress, with the census-tables and Treasury-reports before him, can readily see for himself how very soon the current expenditures of this war would purchase, at fair valuation, all the slaves in any named State. Such a proposition, on the part of the general government, sets up no claim of a right, by federal authority, to interfere with slavery within state limits, referring, as it does, the absolute control of the subject, in each case, to the state and it's people, immediately interested. It is proposed as a matter of perfectly free choice with them.

In the annual message last December, I thought fit to say "The Union must be preserved; and hence all indispensable means must be employed." I said this, not hastily, but deliberately. War has been made, and continues to be, an indispensable means to this end. A practical re-acknowledgment of the national authority would render the war unnecessary, and it would at once cease. If, however, resistance continues, the war must also continue; and it is impossible to foresee all the incidents, which may attend and all the ruin which may follow it. Such as may seem indispensable, or may obviously promise great efficiency towards ending the struggle, must and will come.

The proposition now made, though an offer only, I hope it may be esteemed no offence to ask whether the pecuniary consideration tendered would not be of more value to the States and private persons concerned, than are the institution, and property in it, in the present aspect of affairs.

While it is true that the adoption of the proposed resolution would be merely initiatory, and not within itself a practical measure, it is recommended in the hope that it would soon lead to important practical results. In full view of my great responsibility to my God, and to my country, I earnestly beg the attention of Congress and the people to the subject.

ABRAHAM LINCOLN

Letter to Henry J. Raymond

March 9, 1862

Private

Executive Mansion,
Washington

Hon. Henry J. Raymond:[9]

My dear Sir: I am grateful to the New-York Journals, and not less so to the Times than to others, for their kind notices of the late special Message to Congress. Your paper, however, intimates that the proposition, though well-intentioned, must fail on the score of expense. I do hope you will reconsider this. Have you noticed the facts that less than one half-day's cost of this war would pay for all the slaves in Delaware, at four hundred dollars per head?—that eighty-seven days cost of this war would pay for all in Delaware, Maryland, District of Columbia, Kentucky, and Missouri at the same price? Were those states to take the step, do you doubt that it would shorten the war more than eighty seven days, and thus be an actual saving of expense. Please look at these things, and consider whether there should not be another article in the Times?

Yours very truly,
A. LINCOLN

[9]Henry J. Raymond was the founder and editor of the *New York Times.*

On March 10, Lincoln met with a delegation of border-state congressmen to encourage them to support his plan. According to Maryland congressman John W. Crisfield, Lincoln said that "we were engaged in a terrible, wasting, and tedious war; immense armies were in the field, and must continue on the field as long as the war lasts; that these armies must, of necessity, be brought into contact with slaves in the [border] states we represented and in other states as they advanced; that slaves would come to the camps and continual irritation was kept up; that he was constantly annoyed by conflicting and antagonistic complaints; on the one side, a certain class complained if the slave was not protected by the army; persons were frequently found who, participating in these views, acted in a way unfriendly to the slaveholder; on the other hand, slaveholders complained that their rights were interfered with, their slaves induced to abscond and protected within the lines; these complaints were numerous, loud, and deep, were a serious annoyance to him and embarrassing to the progress of the war; that it kept alive a spirit hostile to the government in the states we represented; strengthened the hopes of the Confederates that at some day the border states would unite with them and thus tend to prolong the war; and he was of the opinion, if this resolution should be adopted by Congress and accepted by our [border] states, these causes of irritation and these hopes would be removed and more would be accomplished towards shortening the war than could be hoped from the greatest victory achieved by the Union armies."[10]

While Congress deliberated on Lincoln's proposal, it adopted an article of war on March 13 that prohibited any Union soldier or sailor from returning fugitive slaves to their masters. Slaveowners who claimed to be loyal could still come within Union lines to retrieve their slaves, but military personnel were forbidden to aid them.

---

[10]Quoted in Edward McPherson, *The Political History of the United States of America, During the Great Rebellion* (Washington, D.C., 1864), 210.

Letter to Horace Greeley

March 24, 1862

Private

Executive Mansion,
Washington

Hon. Horace Greeley[11] —
My dear Sir:
.... I am grateful for the generous sentiments and purposes expressed towards the administration. Of course I am anxious to see the policy proposed in the late special message, go forward; but you have advocated it from the first, so that I need to say little to you on the subject. If I were to suggest anything it would be that as the North are already for the measure, we should urge it *persuasively,* and not *menacingly,* upon the South. I am a little uneasy about the abolishment in this District, not but I would be glad to see it abolished, but as to the time and manner of doing it. If some one or more of the border-states would move fast, I should greatly prefer it; but if this can not be in a reasonable time, I would like the bill to have three main features — gradual — compensation — and vote of the people — I do not talk to members of congress on the subject, except when they ask me. I am not prepared to make any suggestion about compensation. . . .

Yours truly
A. LINCOLN

[11]Horace Greeley, a staunch Republican, was the editor of the *New York Tribune.*

A few weeks later, on April 10, Congress adopted Lincoln's plan for gradual, compensated emancipation. The congressional vote was an omen of the limited appeal of the plan to border-state slaveholders. Almost all Democrats and border-state unionists voted against the plan; Republicans united in its support.

Soon afterward, on April 16, Congress took the lead and abolished slavery in the District of Columbia, providing funds to compensate slaveowners and to colonize freed slaves someplace outside the United States. Lincoln told a friend that "he regretted the bill had been passed in its present form; that it should have been for gradual emancipation; that now families would at once be deprived of cooks, stable boys, etc., and they of their protectors without any provision for them."[12] Nonetheless, Lincoln approved the bill, announcing, "I have never doubted the constitutional authority of congress to abolish slavery in this District; and I have ever desired to see the national capital freed from the institution in some satisfactory way. Hence there has never been, in my mind, any question upon the subject, except the one of expediency, arising in view of all the circumstances."[13]

In the South, the circumstances did not favor emancipation, Lincoln believed. In early May, General David Hunter, commander of Union forces occupying coastal enclaves along the South Carolina and Georgia coast, decided to declare that the tens of thousands of slaves in his region were free. Claiming military necessity, Hunter issued his declaration without consulting or informing Lincoln. Lincoln responded quickly, appealing again for border states to adopt a plan for gradual, compensated emancipation.

---

[12]Theodore Calvin Pease and James G. Randall, eds., *The Diary of Orville Hickman Browning* (2 vols., Springfield, 1925–53), I, 541.
    [13]"Message to Congress," April 16, 1862, *CW,* V, 192.

Proclamation Revoking General Hunter's Order of Military Emancipation

May 19, 1862

BY THE PRESIDENT OF THE
UNITED STATES OF AMERICA.
A PROCLAMATION.

Whereas there appears in the public prints,[14] what purports to be a proclamation, of Major General Hunter, in the words and figures following, towit:

> *Headquarters Department of the South,*
> Hilton Head, S.C., May 9, 1862
> General Orders No. 11.—The three States of Georgia, Florida and South Carolina, comprising the military department of the south, having deliberately declared themselves no longer under the protection of the United States of America, and having taken up arms against the said United States, it becomes a military necessity to declare them

---

[14]That is, Lincoln learned about General Hunter's proclamation when it was printed in the newspapers.

under martial law. This was accordingly done on the 25th day of April, 1862. Slavery and martial law in a free country are altogether incompatible; the persons in these three States—Georgia, Florida and South Carolina—heretofore held as slaves, are therefore declared forever free.

DAVID HUNTER,

(Official)   Major General Commanding. . . .

And whereas the same is producing some excitement, and misunderstanding: therefore

I, Abraham Lincoln, president of the United States, proclaim and declare, that the government of the United States, had no knowledge, information, or belief, of an intention on the part of General Hunter to issue such a proclamation; nor has it yet, any authentic information that the document is genuine. And further, that neither General Hunter, nor any other commander, or person, has been authorized by the Government of the United States, to make proclamations declaring the slaves of any State free; and that the supposed proclamation, now in question, whether genuine or false, is altogether void, so far as respects such declaration.

I further make known that whether it be competent for me, as Commander-in-Chief of the Army and Navy, to declare the Slaves of any state or states, free, and whether at any time, in any case, it shall have become a necessity indispensable to the maintainance of the government, to exercise such supposed power, are questions which, under my responsibility, I reserve to myself, and which I can not feel justified in leaving to the decision of commanders in the field. These are totally different questions from those of police regulations in armies and camps.

On the sixth day of March last, by a special message, I recommended to Congress the adoption of a joint resolution to be substantially as follows:

Resolved, That the United States ought to co-operate with any State which may adopt a gradual abolishment of slavery, giving to such State pecuniary aid, to be used by such State in its discretion to compensate for the inconveniences, public and private, produced by such change of system.

The resolution, in the language above quoted, was adopted by large majorities in both branches of Congress, and now stands an authentic, definite, and solemn proposal of the nation to the States and people most immediately interested in the subject matter. To the people of those states I now earnestly appeal. I do not argue. I beseech you to make the arguments for yourselves. You can not if you would, be blind to the signs of the times. I beg of you a calm and enlarged consideration of them, ranging, if it may be, far above personal and partizan politics. This proposal makes common cause for a common object, casting no reproaches upon any. It acts not the pharisee.[15] The change it contemplates would come gently as the dews of heaven, not rending or wrecking anything. Will you not embrace it? So much good has not been done, by one effort, in all past time, as, in the providence of God, it is now your high previlege to do. May the vast future not have to lament that you have neglected it.

In witness whereof, I have hereunto set my hand, and caused the seal of the United States to be affixed. . . .

ABRAHAM LINCOLN.

[15]That is, it does not adopt a self-righteous, sanctimonious, holier-than-thou stance toward slavery. As Lincoln told border-state congressmen back in March, "Slavery existed . . . as well by the act of the North as of the South; and in any scheme to get rid of it, the North, as well as the South, was morally bound to do its full and equal share." Quoted in McPherson, *Political History of the United States,* 11.

After the failure of General McClellan's peninsula campaign, Lincoln invited senators and representatives from the loyal slave states to meet with him. He appealed again for their support for gradual compensated emancipation.

Appeal to Border State Representatives to Favor Compensated Emancipation
July 12, 1862

Gentlemen. After the adjournment of Congress, now very near, I shall have no opportunity of seeing you for several months. Believing that you of the border-states hold more power for good than any other equal number of members, I feel it a duty which I can not justifiably waive, to make this appeal to you. I intend no reproach or complaint when I assure you that in my opinion, if you all had voted for the resolution in the gradual emancipation message of last March, the war would now be substantially ended. And the plan therein proposed is yet one of the most potent, and swift means of ending it. Let the states which are in rebellion see, definitely and certainly, that, in no event, will the states you represent ever join their proposed Confederacy, and they can not, much longer maintain the contest. But you can not divest them of their hope to ultimately have you with them so long as you show a determination to perpetuate the institution within your own states. Beat them at elections, as you have overwhelmingly done, and, nothing daunted, they still claim you as their own. You and I know what the lever of their power is. Break that lever before their faces, and they can shake you no more forever.

Most of you have treated me with kindness and consideration; and I trust you will not now think I improperly touch what is exclusively your own, when, for the sake of the whole country I ask "Can you, for your states, do better than to take the course I urge?" Discarding *punctillio,*[16] and maxims adapted to more manageable times, and looking only to the unprecedentedly stern facts of our case, can you do better in any possible event? You prefer that the constitutional relation of the states to the nation shall be practically restored, without disturbance of the institution; and if this were done, my whole duty, in this respect, under the constitution, and my oath of office, would be performed. But it is not done, and we are trying to accomplish it by war. The incidents of the war can not be avoided. If the war continue long, as it must, if the object be not sooner attained, the institution in your states will be extinguished by mere friction and abrasion—by the mere incidents of the war. It will be gone, and you will have nothing valuable in lieu of it. Much of it's value is gone already. How much better for you, and for your people, to take the step which, at once, shortens the war, and secures substantial compensation for that which is sure to be wholly lost in any other event. How much better to thus save the money which else we sink forever in the war. How much better to do it while we can, lest the war ere long render us pecuniarily unable to do it. How much better for you, as seller, and the nation as buyer, to sell out, and buy out, that without which the war could never have been, than to sink both the thing to be sold, and the price of it, in cutting one another's throats.

I do not speak of emancipation *at once,* but of a *decision* at once to emancipate *gradually.* Room in South America for colonization can be obtained cheaply, and in abundance; and when numbers shall be large enough to be company and encouragement for one another, the freed people will not be so reluctant to go.

I am pressed with a difficulty not yet mentioned—one which threatens division among those who, united are none too strong. An instance of it is known to you. Gen. Hunter is an honest man. He was, and I hope, still is, my friend. I valued him none the less for his agreeing with me in the general wish that all men everywhere, could be free. He proclaimed all men free within certain states, and I repudiated the proclamation. He expected more good, and less harm from the measure, than I could believe would follow. Yet in repudiating it, I gave dissatisfaction, if not offence, to many whose support the country can not afford to lose. And this is not the end of it. The pressure, in this direction, is still upon me, and is increasing. By conceding what I now ask, you can relieve me, and much more, can relieve the country, in this important point. Upon these considerations I have again begged your attention to the message of March last. Before leaving the Capital, consider and discuss it among yourselves. You are patriots and statesmen; and, as

---

[16]That is, setting aside fine points of formal doctrines, such as states' rights to govern slavery.

such, I pray you, consider this proposition; and, at the least, commend it to the consideration of your states and people. As you would perpetuate popular government for the best people in the world, I beseech you that you do in no wise omit this. Our common country is in great peril, demanding the loftiest views, and boldest action to bring it speedy relief. Once relieved, it's form of government is saved to the world; it's beloved history, and cherished memories, are vindicated; and it's happy future fully assured, and rendered inconceivably grand. To you, more than to any others, the previlege is given, to assure that happiness, and swell that grandeur, and to link your own names therewith forever.

Lincoln's arguments failed to persuade most of the border-state representatives. Eight of them agreed with Lincoln, but a majority of twenty replied that the federal government could not afford to compensate slaveholders and that in any case Lincoln's plan would strengthen rebellion in the Confederacy and in the loyal border states while not reducing the political pressure to take the unconstitutional step of emancipating slaves by proclamation.

Disappointed by border-state recalcitrance and demoralized by Union military reverses, Lincoln concluded, as he told two of his cabinet members privately on June 13, 1862, "We must free the slaves or be ourselves subdued."[17] While Lincoln contemplated emancipation, Congress passed the Second Confiscation Act on July 17, 1862. This law reflected the desire of Congress to move beyond Lincoln's policy of conciliation toward the South. The act declared the slaves of disloyal masters to be free and delegated to federal courts the task of determining the loyalty of slaveowners. Since federal courts, after all, were not operating in the Confederacy, the act provided that slaves who came to Union lines were captives of war and that no federal official could surrender them to any person who claimed them. In effect, the Second Confiscation Act made Union army lines a haven of freedom for fugitive slaves. Once within federal lines, slaves were protected from the ownership claims of any master, and if the master was disloyal, slaves had congressional sanction for their freedom. The act also authorized Lincoln to employ "persons of African descent" in "any war service for which they may be found competent."[18] Lincoln signed the Second Confiscation Act but took the unusual step of explaining his objections to Congress.

[17]Howard K. Beale, ed., *Diary of Gideon Welles, Secretary of the Navy under Lincoln and Johnson* (3 vols., New York, 1960), I, 70.
[18]*Statutes at Large,* XII, 589–92.

Message to the Senate and House of Representatives

July 17, 1862

Fellow-Citizens of the Senate, and House of Representatives,
Considering the bill for "An act to suppress insurrection, to punish treason, and rebellion, to seize and confiscate the property of rebels...."

There is much in the bill to which I perceive no objection. It is wholly prospective; and it touches neither person or property, of any loyal citizen; in which particulars, it is just and proper. The first and second section provide for the conviction and punishment of persons who shall be guilty of treason, and persons who shall "incite, set on foot, assist, or engage in any rebellion, or insurrection, against the authority of the United States, or the laws thereof, or shall give aid and comfort thereto...." By fair construction, persons within these sections are not to be punished without regular trials, in duly constituted courts, under the forms, and all the substantial provisions of law, and of the constitution, applicable to their several cases. To this I perceive no objection.... It is also provided, that the slaves of persons convicted under these sections shall be free. I think there is an unfortunate form of expression, rather than a substantial objection, in this. It is startling to say that congress can free a slave within a state; and yet if it were said the ownership of the slave had first been transferred to the nation, and that congress had then liberated, him, the difficulty would at once vanish. And this is the real case. The traitor against the general government forfets his slave, at least as justly as he does any other property; and he forfeits both to the government against which he offends. The government, so far as there can be ownership, thus owns the the [*sic*] forfeited slaves; and the question for Congress, in regard to them is, "Shall they be made free, or be sold to new masters?" I perceive no objection to Congress deciding in advance that they shall be free.... Indeed, I do not believe it would be physically possible, for the General government, to return persons, so circumstanced, to actual slavery. I believe there would be physical resistance to it, which could neither be turned aside by argument, nor driven away by force....

That those who make a causeless war should be compelled to pay the cost of it, is too obviously just, to be called in question. To give governmental protection to the property of persons who have abandoned it, and gone on a crusade to overthrow that same government, is absurd, if considered in the mere light of justice. The severest justice may not always be the best policy.... And would it not be wise to ... [let such persons] know they have something to lose by persisting [in their rebellion], and something to save by desisting? ...

Without any special act of congress, I think our military commanders, when, in military phrase, "they are within the enemies country" should in an orderly manner, seize and use whatever of real or personal property may be necessary or convenient for their commands; at the same time, preserving, in some way, the evidence of what they do. . . .

I am ready to say now I think it is proper for our military commanders to employ, as laborers, as many persons of African de[s]cent, as can be used to advantage. . . .

That to which I chiefly object, pervades most of the act. . . . It . . . results in the divesting of title forever. For the causes of treason, and the ingredients of treason, not amounting to the full crime, it declares forfeiture, extending beyond the lives of the guilty parties; whereas the Constitution of the United States declares that "no attainder of treason shall work corruption of blood, or forfeiture, except during the life of the person attainted."[19] . . . With great respect, I am constrained to say I think this feature of the act is unconstitutional. . . .

[19]Lincoln is quoting Article III, Section III, of the Constitution, which prohibits Congress from imposing the penalties of treason (i.e., attainder, loss of all rights as a citizen) on anyone (including family members and descendants) not convicted of treason in court.

The failure of southern unionists to respond to Lincoln's overtures also undermined his willingness to continue his conciliatory policy toward loyal slaveholders. Lincoln expressed his frustration with southern unionists— and indirectly with his own attempts to conciliate them—in letters prompted by complaints of loyal citizens of New Orleans, which had been occupied by Union forces since May 1, 1862. To a large extent, Lincoln considered Louisiana a testing ground for reconstruction policies that would restore rebel states to their prewar relation to the Union.

Letter to Cuthbert Bullitt

July 28, 1862

Private

Washington D.C.

Cuthbert Bullitt Esq.[20]
New Orleans La.
Sir: The copy of a letter addressed to yourself by Mr. Thomas J. Durant,[21] has been shown to me. The writer appears to be an able, a dispassionate, and an entirely sincere man. The first part of the letter is devoted to an effort to

[20]Cuthbert Bullitt was a loyal unionist in New Orleans.
[21]Thomas J. Durant was also a New Orleans unionist.

show that the Secession Ordinance of Louisiana was adopted against the will of a majority of the people. This is probably true; and in that fact may be found some instruction. Why did they allow the Ordinance to go into effect? Why did they not assert themselves? Why stand passive and allow themselves to be trodden down by a minority? Why did they not hold popular meetings, and have a convention of their own, to express and enforce the true sentiment of the state? If preorganization was against them *then,* why not do this *now,* that the United States Army is present to protect them? The paralysis—the dead palsy—of the government in this whole struggle is, that this class of men will do nothing for the government, nothing for themselves, except demanding that the government shall not strike its open enemies, lest they be struck by accident!

Mr. Durant complains that in various ways the relation of master and slave is disturbed by the presence of our Army; and he considers it particularly vexatious that this, in part, is done under cover of an act of Congress, while constitutional guaranties are suspended on the plea of military necessity. The truth is, that what is done, and omitted, about slaves, is done and omitted on the same military necessity. It is a military necessity to have men and money; and we can get neither, in sufficient numbers, or amounts, if we keep from, or drive from, our lines, slaves coming to them. Mr. Durant cannot be ignorant of the pressure in this direction; nor of my efforts to hold it within bounds till he, and such as he shall have time to help themselves.

I am not posted to speak understandingly on all the police regulations of which Mr. Durant complains. If experience shows any one of them to be wrong, let them be set right. I think I can perceive, in the freedom of trade, which Mr. Durant urges, that he would relieve both friends and enemies from the pressure of the blockade. By this he would serve the enemy more effectively than the enemy is able to serve himself. I do not say or believe that to serve the enemy is the purpose of Mr. Durant; or that he is conscious of any purpose, other than national and patriotic ones. Still, if there were a class of men who, having no choice of sides in the contest, were anxious only to have quiet and comfort for themselves while it rages, and to fall in with the victorious side at the end of it, without loss to themselves, their advice as to the mode of conducting the contest would be precisely such as his is. He speaks of no duty—apparently thinks of none—resting upon Union men. He even thinks it injurious to the Union cause that they should be restrained in trade and passage without taking sides. They are to touch neither a sail nor a pump, but to be merely passengers,—dead-heads at that—to be carried snug and dry, throughout the storm, and safely landed right side up. Nay, more; even a mutineer is to go untouched lest these sacred passengers receive an accidental wound.

Of course the rebellion will never be suppressed in Louisiana, if the professed Union men there will neither help to do it, nor permit the government to do it without their help.

Now, I think the true remedy is very different from what is suggested by Mr. Durant. It does not lie in rounding the rough angles of the war, but in removing the necessity for the war. The people of Louisiana who wish protection to person and property, have but to reach forth their hands and take it. Let them, in good faith, reinaugurate the national authority, and set up a State Government conforming thereto under the constitution. They know how to do it, and can have the protection of the Army while doing it. The Army will be withdrawn so soon as such State government can dispense with its presence; and the people of the State can then upon the old Constitutional terms, govern themselves to their own liking. This is very simple and easy.

If they will not do this, if they prefer to hazard all for the sake of destroying the government, it is for them to consider whether it is probable I will surrender the government to save them from losing all. If they decline what I suggest, you scarcely need to ask what I will do. What would you do in my position? Would you drop the war where it is? Or, would you prosecute it in future, with elder-stalk squirts, charged with rose water?[22] Would you deal lighter blows rather than heavier ones? Would you give up the contest, leaving any available means unapplied.

I am in no boastful mood. I shall not do *more* than I can, and I shall do *all* I can to save the government, which is my sworn duty as well as my personal inclination. I shall do nothing in malice. What I deal with is too vast for malicious dealing.

Yours truly
A. LINCOLN.

[22]To collect sap from maple trees to make sugar, farmers often crafted a homemade tube by cutting a finger-length branch from an elder bush, making it hollow by removing the soft pith, and inserting it into a gash in the maple. Mischievous children used elder stalk tubes to squirt fluids at their playmates, a practice not unknown today among children equipped with a drinking straw. Rose water is scented with rose petals. In other words, Lincoln is ridiculing unionists who seem to believe war is child's play.

Letter to August Belmont
July 31, 1862

Dear Sir:[23]

You send to Mr. W[eed] an extract from a letter written at New Orleans the 9th instant, which is shown to me. You do not give the writer's name; but plainly he is a man of ability, and probably of some note. He says: "The time has arrived when Mr. Lincoln must take a decisive course. Trying to please

[23]August Belmont, a New York financier, had received a letter from a man he identified as "a very wealthy and influential planter" in Louisiana, and forwarded a passage from the letter to Thurlow Weed, the prominent New York Republican.

everybody, he will satisfy nobody. A vacillating policy in matters of importance is the very worst. Now is the time, if ever, for honest men who love
their country to rally to its support. Why will not the North say officially
that it wishes for the restoration of the Union as it was?"

And so, it seems, this is the point on which the writer thinks I have no
policy. Why will he not read and understand what I have said?

The substance of the very declaration he desires is in the inaugural, in
each of the two regular messages to Congress, and in many, if not all, the
minor documents issued by the Executive since the inauguration.

Broken eggs cannot be mended; but Louisiana has nothing to do now but
to take her place in the Union as it was, barring the already broken eggs. The
sooner she does so, the smaller will be the amount of that which will be past
mending. This government cannot much longer play a game in which it
stakes all, and its enemies stake nothing. Those enemies must understand
that they cannot experiment for ten years trying to destroy the government,
and if they fail still come back into the Union unhurt. If they expect in any
contingency to ever have the Union as it was, I join with the writer in saying,
"Now is the time."

How much better it would have been for the writer to have gone at this,
under the protection of the army at New Orleans, than to have sat down in a
closet writing complaining letters northward!

Yours truly,
A. LINCOLN

After discussing his plan to issue a proclamation of emancipation with his
cabinet on July 22, Lincoln accepted the advice of Secretary of State
Seward to delay a public announcement. Seward pointed out, Lincoln
recalled later, that "the depression of the public mind, consequent upon our
repeated [military] reverses, is so great I fear the effect of so important a
step. It may be viewed as the last measure of an exhausted government—
a cry for help—the government stretching forth its hands to Ethiopia,
instead of Ethiopia stretching forth her hands to the government." Seward
suggested, according to Lincoln, that "you postpone its issue until you can
give it to the country supported by military success, instead of issuing it,
as would be the case now, upon the greatest disasters of the war," namely
the failure of McClellan's peninsula campaign.[24]

While Lincoln awaited a victory on the battlefield, he invited a delegation of African Americans to the White House to hear his arguments in

---

[24]Lincoln quoted in Francis B. Carpenter, *Six Months at the White House with Abraham
Lincoln: The Story of a Picture* (New York, 1866), 20–24.

favor of colonization, that is, of sending black Americans to Africa, the Caribbean, or South America. Lincoln not only hoped black Americans would see what he believed was the wisdom of colonization, which—following Henry Clay—he had long supported. He also sought to make clear to white Americans that, in his view, emancipation did not need to increase the number of free black people in American society; instead, blacks could be sent away to some foreign land. The following transcript of Lincoln's meeting was published in the *New York Tribune* and other newspapers.

Address on Colonization to a Delegation of Black Americans

August 14, 1862

This afternoon the President of the United States gave audience to a Committee of colored men at the White House. They were introduced by the Rev. J. Mitchell, Commissioner of Emigration.[25] E. M. Thomas,[26] the Chairman, remarked that they were there by invitation to hear what the Executive had to say to them. Having all been seated, the President, after a few preliminary observations, informed them that a sum of money had been appropriated by Congress, and placed at his disposition for the purpose of aiding the colonization in some country of the people, or a portion of them, of African descent, thereby making it his duty, as it had for a long time been his inclination, to favor that cause; and why, he asked, should the people of your race be colonized, and where? Why should they leave this country? This is, perhaps, the first question for proper consideration. You and we are different races. We have between us a broader difference than exists between almost any other two races. Whether it is right or wrong I need not discuss, but this physical difference is a great disadvantage to us both, as I think your race suffer very greatly, many of them by living among us, while ours suffer from your presence. In a word we suffer on each side. If this is admitted, it affords a reason at least why we should be separated. You here are freemen I suppose.

A VOICE: Yes, sir.

The President—Perhaps you have long been free, or all your lives. Your race are suffering, in my judgment, the greatest wrong inflicted on any

---

[25]Reverend James Mitchell of Indiana worked as an emigration agent in support of congressional authorization of $100,000 for colonization in the bill abolishing slavery in the District of Columbia and another $500,000 in an act that granted funds to colonize freed slaves who were in the custody of the federal army.

[26]Edward M. Thomas was the president of the Anglo-African Institute for the Encouragement of Industry and Art.

people. But even when you cease to be slaves, you are yet far removed from being placed on an equality with the white race. You are cut off from many of the advantages which the other race enjoy. The aspiration of men is to enjoy equality with the best when free, but on this broad continent, not a single man of your race is made the equal of a single man of ours. Go where you are treated the best, and the ban is still upon you.

I do not propose to discuss this, but to present it as a fact with which we have to deal. I cannot alter it if I would. It is a fact, about which we all think and feel alike, I and you. We look to our condition, owing to the existence of the two races on this continent. I need not recount to you the effects upon white men, growing out of the institution of Slavery. I believe in its general evil effects on the white race. See our present condition—the country engaged in war!—our white men cutting one another's throats, none knowing how far it will extend; and then consider what we know to be the truth. But for your race among us there could not be war, although many men engaged on either side do not care for you one way or the other. Nevertheless, I repeat, without the institution of Slavery and the colored race as a basis, the war could not have an existence.

It is better for us both, therefore, to be separated. I know that there are free men among you, who even if they could better their condition are not as much inclined to go out of the country as those, who being slaves could obtain their freedom on this condition. I suppose one of the principal difficulties in the way of colonization is that the free colored man cannot see that his comfort would be advanced by it. You may believe you can live in Washington or elsewhere in the United States the remainder of your life [as easily], perhaps more so than you can in any foreign country, and hence you may come to the conclusion that you have nothing to do with the idea of going to a foreign country. This is (I speak in no unkind sense) an extremely selfish view of the case.

But you ought to do something to help those who are not so fortunate as yourselves. There is an unwillingness on the part of our people, harsh as it may be, for you free colored people to remain with us. Now, if you could give a start to white people, you would open a wide door for many to be made free. If we deal with those who are not free at the beginning, and whose intellects are clouded by Slavery, we have very poor materials to start with. If intelligent colored men, such as are before me, would move in this matter, much might be accomplished. It is exceedingly important that we have men at the beginning capable of thinking as white men, and not those who have been systematically oppressed.

There is much to encourage you. For the sake of your race you should sacrifice something of your present comfort for the purpose of being as grand in that respect as the white people. It is a cheering thought throughout life that something can be done to ameliorate the condition of those who have been subject to the hard usage of the world. It is difficult to make a man miserable while he feels he is worthy of himself, and claims kindred to the great God who made him. In the American Revolutionary war sacrifices were made by men engaged in it; but they were cheered by the future. Gen. Washington himself endured greater physical hardships than if he had remained a British subject. Yet he was a happy man, because he was engaged in benefiting his race—something for the children of his neighbors, having none of his own.

The colony of Liberia has been in existence a long time. In a certain sense it is a success. The old President of Liberia, Roberts,[27] has just been with me—the first time I ever saw him. He says they have within the bounds of that colony between 300,000 and 400,000 people, or more than in some of our old States, such as Rhode Island or Delaware, or in some of our newer States, and less than in some of our larger ones. They are not all American colonists, or their descendants. Something less than 12,000 have been sent thither from this country. Many of the original settlers have died, yet, like people elsewhere, their offspring outnumber those deceased.

The question is if the colored people are persuaded to go anywhere, why not there? One reason for an unwillingness to do so is that some of you would rather remain within reach of the country of your nativity. I do not know how much attachment you may have toward our race. It does not strike me that you have the greatest reason to love them. But still you are attached to them at all events.

The place I am thinking about having for a colony is in Central America.[28] It is nearer to us than Liberia—not much more than one-fourth as far as Liberia, and within seven days' run by steamers. Unlike Liberia it is on a great line of travel—it is a highway. The country is a very excellent one for any people, and with great natural resources and advantages, and especially because of the similarity of climate with your native land—thus being suited to your physical condition.

The particular place I have in view is to be a great highway from the Atlantic or Caribbean Sea to the Pacific Ocean, and this particular place has all the advantages for a colony. On both sides there are harbors among the finest in the world. Again, there is evidence of very rich coal mines. A certain amount of coal is valuable in any country, and there may be more than enough for the wants of the country. Why I attach so much importance to coal is, it will afford an opportunity to the inhabitants for immediate employment till they get ready to settle permanently in their homes.[29]

If you take colonists where there is no good landing, there is a bad show; and so where there is nothing to cultivate, and of which to make a farm. But

[27]Joseph Jenkins Roberts served as president of Liberia from 1847 to 1856. Born in Norfolk, Virginia, in 1809, he emigrated to Liberia in 1829.

[28]Lincoln had in mind land in northern Panama on the Chiriquí Lagoon. The Chiriqui Improvement Company, owned by Ambrose W. Thompson—a Philadelphian—purchased hundreds of thousands of acres of land in the region in 1855 and proposed in August 1861 to sell coal to the U.S. Navy at Chiriquí Lagoon for about half the prevailing price.

[29]In other words, Lincoln proposed that black colonists mine and load coal for the Chiriqui Improvement Company, from which they would purchase land, and the navy would buy the coal. A provisional contract to this effect between the U.S. government and the Chiriqui Improvement Company was signed on September 12, 1862. *CW,* IV, 561; V, 2–3, 371, 414, 418–19.

if something is started so that you can get your daily bread as soon as you reach there, it is a great advantage. Coal land is the best thing I know of with which to commence an enterprise.

To return, you have been talked to upon this subject, and told that a speculation is intended by gentlemen, who have an interest in the country, including the coal mines.[30] We have been mistaken all our lives if we do not know whites as well as blacks look to their self-interest. Unless among those deficient of intellect everybody you trade with makes something. You meet with these things here as elsewhere.

If such persons have what will be an advantage to them, the question is whether it cannot be made of advantage to you. You are intelligent, and know that success does not as much depend on external help as on self-reliance. Much, therefore, depends upon yourselves. As to the coal mines, I think I see the means available for your self-reliance.

I shall, if I get a sufficient number of you engaged, have provisions made that you shall not be wronged. If you will engage in the enterprise I will spend some of the money intrusted to me. I am not sure you will succeed. The Government may lose the money, but we cannot succeed unless we try; but we think, with care, we can succeed.

The political affairs in Central America are not in quite as satisfactory condition as I wish. There are contending factions in that quarter; but it is true all the factions are agreed alike on the subject of colonization, and want it, and are more generous than we are here. To your colored race they have no objection. Besides, I would endeavor to have you made equals, and have the best assurance that you should be the equals of the best.

The practical thing I want to ascertain is whether I can get a number of able-bodied men, with their wives and children, who are willing to go, when I present evidence of encouragement and protection. Could I get a hundred tolerably intelligent men, with their wives and children, to "cut their own fodder," so to speak? Can I have fifty? If I could find twenty-five able-bodied men, with a mixture of women and children, good things in the family relation, I think I could make a successful commencement.

I want you to let me know whether this can be done or not. This is the practical part of my wish to see you. These are subjects of very great importance, worthy of a month's study, [instead] of a speech delivered in an hour. I ask you then to consider seriously not pertaining to yourselves merely, nor for your race, and ours, for the present time, but as one of the things, if successfully managed, for the good of mankind—not confined to the present generation, but as

"From age to age descends the lay,
To millions yet to be,
Till far its echoes roll away,
Into eternity."

[30]Lincoln is referring to Ambrose W. Thompson of the Chiriqui Improvement Company.

The above is merely given as the substance of the President's remarks.

The Chairman of the delegation briefly replied that "they would hold a consultation and in a short time give an answer."[31] The President said. "Take your full time—no hurry at all."

The delegation then withdrew.

[31]Most black Americans remained hostile to colonization.

Although Lincoln had resolved privately to issue an emancipation proclamation, in public he continued to insist that his goal was to save the Union without necessarily doing anything about slavery. In a letter published August 19, 1862, in the *New York Tribune,* the prominent Republican editor Horace Greeley criticized Lincoln for "the policy you seem to be pursuing with regard to the slaves of Rebels," raising nine objections, including, "We think you are strangely and disastrously remiss ... with regard to the emancipating provisions of the new Confiscation Act."[32] Lincoln responded to Greeley with the following public letter, quickly reprinted in newspapers across the North, which announced that his policy toward slavery would depend on what was necessary to save the Union, a public hint of his private decision.

Letter to Horace Greeley
August 22, 1862

Executive Mansion,
Washington

Hon. Horace Greely:

Dear Sir

I have just read yours of the 19th. addressed to myself through the New-York Tribune. If there be in it any statements, or assumptions of fact, which I may know to be erroneous, I do not, now and here, controvert them. If there be in it any inferences which I may believe to be falsely drawn, I do not now and here, argue against them. If there be perceptable in it an impatient and dictatorial tone, I waive it in deference to an old friend, whose heart I have always supposed to be right.

As to the policy I "seem to be pursuing" as you say, I have not meant to leave any one in doubt.

[32]*CW,* V, 389.

I would save the Union. I would save it the shortest way under the Constitution. The sooner the national authority can be restored; the nearer the Union will be "the Union as it was." If there be those who would not save the Union, unless they could at the same time *save* slavery, I do not agree with them. If there be those who would not save the Union unless they could at the same time *destroy* slavery, I do not agree with them. My paramount object in this struggle *is* to save the Union, and is *not* either to save or to destroy slavery. If I could save the Union without freeing *any* slave I would do it, and if I could save it by freeing *all* the slaves I would do it; and if I could save it by freeing some and leaving others alone I would also do that. What I do about slavery, and the colored race, I do because I believe it helps to save the Union; and what I forbear, I forbear because I do *not* believe it would help to save the Union. I shall do *less* whenever I shall believe what I am doing hurts the cause, and I shall do *more* whenever I shall believe doing more will help the cause. I shall try to correct errors when shown to be errors; and I shall adopt new views so fast as they shall appear to be true views.

I have here stated my purpose according to my view of *official* duty; and I intend no modification of my oft-expressed *personal* wish that all men every where could be free.

Yours,
A. LINCOLN

ANNOUNCING EMANCIPATION

Union success in the battle of Antietam gave Lincoln enough of a victory to make his emancipation plan public. On September 22, 1862, he convened his cabinet and told them what he had decided to do. Before reading the proclamation to them, Lincoln explained, as Treasury Secretary Salmon P. Chase recorded in his diary, "I have, as you are aware, thought a great deal about the relation of this war to slavery; and you all remember that, several weeks ago, I read to you an order I had prepared on this subject, which, on account of objections made by some of you, was not issued. Ever since then, my mind has been much occupied with this subject, and I have thought all along that the time for acting on it might very probably come. I think the time has come now. I wish it were a better time. I wish that we were in a better condition. The action of the army against the rebels has not been quite what I should have best liked. But they have been driven out of Maryland, and Pennsylvania is no longer in danger of invasion. When the rebel army was at Frederick, I determined, as soon as it should be driven out of Maryland, to issue a proclamation of emancipation such as I thought most likely to be useful. I said nothing to anyone; but I made the promise to myself and [hesitating a little] to my Maker. The rebel army is now driven out, and I am going to fulfill that promise. I have got you together to hear what I have written down. I do not wish your advice about the main matter; for that I have determined for myself."[33]

[33]John Niven et al., eds, *The Salmon P. Chase Papers,* Volume I, *Journals, 1829–1872* (Kent, Ohio, 1993), 393–94.

Preliminary Emancipation Proclamation
September 22, 1862

BY THE PRESIDENT OF THE
UNITED STATES OF AMERICA
A PROCLAMATION.

I, Abraham Lincoln, President of the United States of America, and Commander-in-chief of the Army and Navy thereof, do hereby proclaim and declare that hereafter, as heretofore, the war will be prossecuted for the object of practically restoring the constitutional relation between the United States, and each of the states, and the people thereof, in which states that relation is, or may be suspended, or disturbed.

That it is my purpose, upon the next meeting of Congress to again recommend the adoption of a practical measure tendering pecuniary aid to the free acceptance or rejection of all slave-states, so called, the people whereof may not then be in rebellion against the United States, and which states, may then have voluntarily adopted, or thereafter may voluntarily adopt, immediate, or gradual abolishment of slavery within their respective limits; and that the effort to colonize persons of African descent, with their consent, upon this continent, or elsewhere, with the previously obtained consent of the Governments existing there, will be continued.

That on the first day of January in the year of our Lord, one thousand eight hundred and sixty-three, all persons held as slaves within any state, or designated part of a state, the people whereof shall then be in rebellion against the United States shall be then, thenceforward, and forever free; and the executive government of the United States, including the military and naval authority thereof, will recognize and maintain the freedom of such persons, and will do no act or acts to repress such persons, or any of them, in any efforts they may make for their actual freedom.

That the executive will, on the first day of January aforesaid, by proclamation, designate the States, and parts of states, if any, in which the people thereof respectively, shall then be in rebellion against the United States; and the fact that any state, or the people thereof shall, on that day be, in good faith represented in the Congress of the United States, by members chosen thereto, at elections wherein a majority of the qualified voters of such state shall have participated, shall, in the absence of strong countervailing testimony, be deemed conclusive evidence that such state and the people thereof, are not then in rebellion against the United States.

That attention is hereby called to an act of Congress entitled "An act to make an additional Article of War" approved March 13, 1862, and which act is in the words and figure following:

Be it enacted by the Senate and House of Representatives of the United States of America in Congress assembled, That hereafter the following shall be promulgated as an additional article of war for the government of the army of the United States, and shall be obeyed and observed as such:

Article ——. All officers or persons in the military or naval service of the United States are prohibited from employing any of the forces under their respective commands for the purpose of returning fugitives from service or labor, who may have escaped from any persons to whom such service or labor is claimed to be due, and any officer who shall be found guilty by a court-martial of violating this article shall be dismissed from the service.

SEC. 2. *And be it further enacted,* That this act shall take effect from and after its passage.

Also to the ninth and tenth sections of an act entitled "An Act to suppress Insurrection, to punish Treason and Rebellion, to seize and confiscate property of rebels, and for other purposes," approved July 17, 1862, and which sections are in the words and figures following:

SEC. 9. *And be it further enacted,* That all slaves of persons who shall hereafter be engaged in rebellion against the government of the United States, or who shall in any way give aid or comfort thereto, escaping from such persons and taking refuge within the lines of the army; and all slaves captured from such persons or deserted by them and coming under the control of the government of the United States; and all slaves of such persons found *on* (or) being within any place occupied by rebel forces and afterwards occupied by the forces of the United States, shall be deemed captives of war, and shall be forever free of their servitude and not again held as slaves.

SEC. 10. *And be it further enacted,* That no slave escaping into any State, Territory, or the District of Columbia, from any other State, shall be delivered up, or in any way impeded or hindered of his liberty, except for crime, or some offence against the laws, unless the person claiming said fugitive shall first make oath that the person to whom the labor or service of such fugitive is alleged to be due is his lawful owner, and has not borne arms against the United States in the present rebellion, nor in any way given aid and comfort thereto; and no person engaged in the military or naval service of the United States shall, under any pretence whatever, assume to decide on the validity of the claim of any person to the service or labor of any other person, or surrender up any such person to the claimant, on pain of being dismissed from the service.

And I do hereby enjoin upon and order all persons engaged in the military and naval service of the United States to observe, obey, and enforce, within their respective spheres of service, the act, and sections above recited.

And the executive will in due time recommend that all citizens of the United States who shall have remained loyal thereto throughout the rebellion, shall (upon the restoration of the constitutional relation between the United States, and their respective states, and people, if that relation shall have been suspended or disturbed) be compensated for all losses by acts of the United States, including the loss of slaves....

ABRAHAM LINCOLN

Letter to Hannibal Hamlin

September 28, 1862

(Strictly private.)

Executive Mansion,
Washington

My Dear Sir:[34] Your kind letter of the 25th[35] is just received. It is known to some that while I hope something from the proclamation, my expectations are not as sanguine as are those of some friends. The time for its effect southward has not come; but northward the effect should be instantaneous.

It is six days old, and while commendation in newspapers and by distinguished individuals is all that a vain man could wish, the stocks have declined, and troops come forward more slowly than ever. This, looked soberly in the face, is not very satisfactory. We have fewer troops in the field

[34]Hannibal Hamlin was Lincoln's running mate and vice president. He wrote from his home in Bangor, Maine.

[35]Hamlin's letter praised the Emancipation Proclamation as "the great act of the age" and predicted that "it will be enthusiastically approved and sustained, and future generations will, as I do, say God bless you for this great and noble act." *CW,* V, 444.

at the end of six days than we had at the beginning—the attrition among the old outnumbering the addition by the new. The North responds to the proclamation sufficiently in breath; but breath alone kills no rebels.

I wish I could write more cheerfully; nor do I thank you the less for the kindness of your letter.

Yours very truly,
A. LINCOLN.

One month before the Emancipation Proclamation was to take effect, Lincoln presented to Congress a detailed proposal for the form of gradual, compensated emancipation he preferred. Unlike the Emancipation Proclamation, which applied only to the states in rebellion, Lincoln's proposed scheme for gradual emancipation was designed to eliminate slavery—eventually—throughout the United States.

Annual Message to Congress
December 1, 1862

Fellow-citizens of the Senate and House of Representatives:
Since your last annual assembling another year of health and bountiful harvests has passed. And while it has not pleased the Almighty to bless us with a return of peace, we can but press on, guided by the best light He gives us, trusting that in His own good time, and wise way, all will yet be well. . . .

Applications have been made to me by many free Americans of African descent to favor their emigration, with a view to such colonization as was contemplated in recent acts of Congress. Other parties, at home and abroad—some from interested motives, others upon patriotic considerations, and still others influenced by philanthropic sentiments—have suggested similar measures; while, on the other hand, several of the Spanish-American republics have protested against the sending of such colonies to their respective territories.[36] Under these circumstances, I have declined to move any such colony to any state, without first obtaining the consent of its government, with an agreement on its part to receive and protect such emigrants in all the rights of freemen; and I have, at the same time, offered to the several states situated within the tropics, or having colonies there, to negotiate with them, subject to the advice and consent of the Senate, to favor the voluntary emigration of persons of that class to their respective territories, upon conditions which

---

[36]The governments of Honduras, Nicaragua, and Costa Rica objected to Lincoln's colonization plan for Chiriquí Lagoon, and it was ultimately abandoned.

shall be equal, just, and humane. Liberia and Hayti are, as yet, the only countries to which colonists of African descent from here, could go with certainty of being received and adopted as citizens; and I regret to say such persons, contemplating colonization, do not seem so willing to migrate to those countries, as to some others, nor so willing as I think their interest demands. I believe, however, opinion among them, in this respect, is improving; and that, ere long, there will be an augmented, and considerable migration to both these countries, from the United States. . . .

On the twenty-second day of September last a proclamation was issued by the Executive, a copy of which is herewith submitted.

In accordance with the purpose expressed in the second paragraph of that paper, I now respectfully recall your attention to what may be called "compensated emancipation."

A nation may be said to consist of its territory, its people, and its laws. The territory is the only part which is of certain durability. "One generation passeth away, and another generation cometh, but the earth abideth forever." It is of the first importance to duly consider, and estimate, this ever-enduring part. That portion of the earth's surface which is owned and inhabited by the people of the United States, is well adapted to be the home of one national family; and it is not well adapted for two, or more. Its vast extent, and its variety of climate and productions, are of advantage, in this age, for one people, whatever they might have been in former ages. Steam, telegraphs, and intelligence, have brought these, to be an advantageous combination, for one united people.

In the inaugural address I briefly pointed out the total inadequacy of disunion, as a remedy for the differences between the people of the two sections. . . .

There is no line, straight or crooked, suitable for a national boundary, upon which to divide. Trace through, from east to west, upon the line between the free and slave country, and we shall find a little more than one-third of its length are rivers, easy to be crossed, and populated, or soon to be populated, thickly upon both sides; while nearly all its remaining length, are merely surveyor's lines, over which people may walk back and forth without any consciousness of their presence. No part of this line can be made any more difficult to pass, by writing it down on paper, or parchment, as a national boundary. The fact of separation, if it comes, gives up, on the part of the seceding section, the fugitive slave clause, along with all other constitutional obligations upon the section seceded from, while I should expect no treaty stipulation would ever be made to take its place.

But there is another difficulty. The great interior region, bounded east by the Alleghanies, north by the British dominions, west by the Rocky mountains, and south by the line along which the culture of corn and cotton meets, and which includes part of Virginia, part of Tennessee, all of Kentucky, Ohio, Indiana, Michigan, Wisconsin, Illinois, Missouri, Kansas, Iowa, Minnesota and the Territories of Dakota, Nebraska, and part of Colorado, already has above ten millions of people, and will have fifty millions within fifty years, if not prevented by any political folly or mistake. It contains more than one-third of the country owned by the United States—certainly more than one million of square miles. Once half as populous as Massachusetts already is, it would have more than seventy-five millions of people. A glance at the map shows that, territorially speaking, it is the great body of the republic. The other parts are but marginal borders to it, the magnificent region sloping west from the rocky mountains to the Pacific, being the deepest, and also the richest, in undeveloped resources. In the production of provisions, grains, grasses, and all which proceed from them, this great interior region is naturally one of the most important in the world. Ascertain from the statistics the small proportion of the region which has, as yet, been brought into cultivation, and also the large and rapidly increasing amount of its products, and we shall be overwhelmed with the magnitude of the prospect presented. And yet this region has no sea-coast, touches no ocean anywhere. As part of one nation, its people now find, and may forever find, their way to Europe by New York, to South America and Africa by New Orleans, and to Asia by San Francisco. But separate our common country into two nations, as designed by the present rebellion, and every man of this great interior region is thereby cut off from some one or more of these outlets, not, perhaps, by a physical barrier, but by embarrassing and onerous trade regulations.

And this is true, *wherever* a dividing, or boundary line, may be fixed. Place it between the now free and slave country, or place it south of Kentucky, or north of Ohio, and still the truth remains, that none south of it, can trade to any port or place north of it, and none north of it, can trade to any port or place south of it, except upon terms dictated by a government foreign to them. These outlets, east, west, and south, are indispensable to the well-being of the people inhabiting, and to inhabit, this vast interior region. *Which* of the three may be the best, is no proper question. All, are better than either, and all, of right, belong to that people, and to their successors forever. True to themselves, they will not ask *where* a line of separation shall be, but will vow, rather, that there shall be no such line. Nor are the marginal regions less interested in these communications to, and through them, to the great outside world. They too, and each of them, must have access to this Egypt of the West, without paying toll at the crossing of any national boundary.

Our national strife springs not from our permanent part; not from the land we inhabit; not from our national homestead. There is no possible severing of this, but would multiply, and not mitigate, evils among us. In all its adaptations and aptitudes, it demands union, and abhors separation. In fact, it would, ere long, force reunion, however much of blood and treasure the separation might have cost.

Our strife pertains to ourselves—to the passing generations of men; and it can, without convulsion, be hushed forever with the passing of one generation.

In this view, I recommend the adoption of the following resolution and articles amendatory to the Constitution of the United States:

"*Resolved by the Senate and House of Representatives of the United States of America in Congress assembled,* (two thirds of both houses concurring,) That the following articles be proposed to the legislatures (or conventions) of the several States as amendments to the Constitution of the United States, all or any of which articles when ratified by three-fourths of the said legislatures (or conventions) to be valid as part or parts of the said Constitution, viz:

"Article ———.

"Every State, wherein slavery now exists, which shall abolish the same therein, at any time, or times, before the first day of January, in the year of our Lord one thousand and nine hundred, shall receive compensation from the United States as follows, to wit:

"The President of the United States shall deliver to every such State, bonds of the United States, bearing interest at the rate of _____ per cent, per annum, to an amount equal to the aggregate sum of   for each slave shown to have been therein, by the eighth census of the United States, said bonds to be delivered to such State by instalments, or in one parcel, at the completion of the abolishment, accordingly as the same shall have been gradual, or at one time, within such State; and interest shall begin to run upon any such bond, only from the proper time of its delivery as aforesaid. Any State having received bonds as aforesaid, and afterwards reintroducing or tolerating slavery therein, shall refund to the United States the bonds so received, or the value thereof, and all interest paid thereon.

"Article ———.

"All slaves who shall have enjoyed actual freedom by the chances of the war, at any time before the end of the rebellion, shall be forever free; but all owners of such, who shall not have been disloyal, shall be compensated for them, at the same rates as is provided for States adopting abolishment of slavery, but in such way, that no slave shall be twice accounted for.

"Article ———.

"Congress may appropriate money, and otherwise provide, for colonizing free colored persons, with their own consent, at any place or places without the United States."

I beg indulgence to discuss these proposed articles at some length. Without slavery the rebellion could never have existed; without slavery it could not continue.

Among the friends of the Union there is great diversity, of sentiment, and of policy, in regard to slavery, and the African race amongst us. Some would perpetuate slavery; some would abolish it suddenly, and without compensation; some would abolish it gradually, and with compensation; some would remove the freed people from us, and some would retain them with us; and there are yet other minor diversities. Because of these diversities, we waste much strength in struggles among ourselves. By mutual concession we should harmonize, and act together. This would be compromise; but it would be compromise among the friends, and not with the enemies of the Union. These articles are intended to embody a plan of such mutual concessions. If the plan shall be adopted, it is assumed that emancipation will follow, at least, in several of the States.

As to the first article, the main points are: first, the emancipation; secondly, the length of time for consummating it—thirty-seven years; and thirdly, the compensation.

The emancipation will be unsatisfactory to the advocates of perpetual slavery; but the length of time should greatly mitigate their dissatisfaction. The time spares both races from the evils of sudden derangement—in fact, from the necessity of any derangement—while most of those whose habitual course of thought will be disturbed by the measure will have passed away before its consummation. They will never see it. Another class will hail the prospect of emancipation, but will deprecate the length of time. They will feel that it gives too little to the now living slaves. But it really gives them much. It saves them from the vagrant destitution which must largely attend immediate emancipation in localities where their numbers are very great; and it gives the inspiring assurance that their posterity shall be free forever. The plan leaves to each State, choosing to act under it, to abolish slavery now, or at the end of the century, or at any intermediate time, or by degrees, extending over the whole or any part of the period; and it obliges no two states to proceed alike. It also provides for compensation, and generally the mode of making it. This, it would seem, must further mitigate the dissatisfaction of those who favor perpetual slavery, and especially of those who are to receive the compensation. Doubtless some of those who are to pay, and not to receive will object. Yet the measure is both just and economical. In a certain sense the liberation of slaves is the destruction of property—property acquired by descent, or by purchase, the same as any other property. It is no less true for having been often said, that the people of the south are not more responsible for the original introduction of this property, than are the people of the north; and when it is remembered how unhesitatingly we all use cotton and sugar, and share the profits of dealing in them, it may not be quite safe to say, that the south has been more responsible than the north for its continuance. If then, for a common object, this property is to be sacrificed is it not just that it be done at a common charge?

And if, with less money, or money more easily paid, we can preserve the benefits of the Union by this means, than we can by the war alone, is it not also economical to do it? Let us consider it then. Let us ascertain the sum we have expended in the war since compensated emancipation was proposed last March, and consider whether, if that measure had been promptly accepted, by even some of the slave States, the same sum would not have done more to close the war, than has been otherwise done. If so the measure would save money, and, in that view, would be a prudent and economical measure. Certainly it is not so easy to pay *something* as it is to pay *nothing;*

but it is easier to pay a *large* sum than it is to pay a larger one. And it is easier to pay any sum *when* we are able, than it is to pay it *before* we are able. The war requires large sums, and requires them at once. The aggregate sum necessary for compensated emancipation, of course, would be large. But it would require no ready cash; nor the bonds even, any faster than the emancipation progresses. This might not, and probably would not, close before the end of the thirty-seven years. At that time we shall probably have a hundred millions of people to share the burden, instead of thirty one millions, as now. And not only so, but the increase of our population may be expected to continue for a long time after that period, as rapidly as before; because our territory will not have become full. I do not state this inconsiderately. At the same ratio of increase which we have maintained, on an average, from our first national census, in 1790, until that of 1860, we should, in 1900, have a population of 103,208,415. And why may we not continue that ratio far beyond that period? Our abundant room—our broad national homestead—is our ample resource. Were our territory as limited as are the British Isles, very certainly our population could not expand as stated. Instead of receiving the foreign born, as now, we should be compelled to send part of the native born away. But such is not our condition. We have two millions nine hundred and sixty-three thousand square miles. Europe has three millions and eight hundred thousand, with a population averaging seventy-three and one-third persons to the square mile. Why may not our country, at some time, average as many? Is it less fertile? Has it more waste surface, by mountains, rivers, lakes, deserts, or other causes? Is it inferior to Europe in any natural advantage? If, then, we are, at some time, to be as populous as Europe, how soon? . . .

These figures show that our country *may* be as populous as Europe now is, at some point between 1920 and 1930—say about 1925—our territory, at seventy-three and a third persons to the square mile, being of capacity to contain 217,186,000.

And we *will* reach this, too, if we do not ourselves relinquish the chance, by the folly and evils of disunion, or by long and exhausting war springing from the only great element of national discord among us. While it cannot be foreseen exactly how much one huge example of secession, breeding lesser ones indefinitely, would retard population, civilization, and prosperity, no one can doubt that the extent of it would be very great and injurious.

The proposed emancipation would shorten the war, perpetuate peace, insure this increase of population, and proportionately the wealth of the country. With these, we should pay all the emancipation would cost, together with our other debt, easier than we should pay our other debt, without it. If we had allowed our old national debt to run at six per cent. per annum, simple interest, from the end of our revolutionary struggle until to day, without paying anything on either principal or interest, each man of us would owe less upon that debt now, than each man owed upon it then; and this because our increase of men, through the whole period, has been greater than six per cent.; has run faster than the interest upon the debt. Thus, time alone relieves a debtor nation, so long as its population increases faster than unpaid interest accumulates on its debt.

This fact would be no excuse for delaying payment of what is justly due; but it shows the great importance of time in this connexion—the great advantage of a policy by which we shall not have to pay until we number a hundred millions, what, by a different policy, we would have to pay now, when we number but thirty one millions. In a word, it shows that a dollar will be much harder to pay for the war, than will be a dollar for emancipation on the proposed plan. And then the latter will cost no blood, no precious life. It will be a saving of both.

As to the second article, I think it would be impracticable to return to bondage the class of persons therein contemplated. Some of them, doubtless, in the property sense, belong to loyal owners; and hence, provision is made in this article for compensating such.

The third article relates to the future of the freed people. It does not oblige, but merely authorizes, Congress to aid in colonizing such as may consent. This ought not to be regarded as objectionable, on the one hand, or on the other, in so much as it comes to nothing, unless by the mutual consent of the people to be deported, and the American voters, through their representatives in Congress.

I cannot make it better known than it already is, that I strongly favor colonization. And yet I wish to say there is an objection urged against free colored persons remaining in the country, which is largely imaginary, if not sometimes malicious.

It is insisted that their presence would injure, and displace white labor and white laborers. If there ever could be a proper time for mere catch arguments, that time surely is not now. In times like the present, men should utter nothing for which they would not willingly be responsible through time and in eternity. Is it true, then, that colored people can displace any more white labor, by being free, than by remaining slaves? If they stay in their old places, they jostle no white laborers; if they leave their old places, they leave them open to white laborers. Logically, there is neither more nor less of it. Emancipation, even without deportation, would probably enhance the wages of white labor, and, very surely, would not reduce them. Thus, the customary amount of labor would still have to be performed; the freed people would surely not do more than their old proportion of it, and very probably, for a time, would do less, leaving an increased part to white laborers, bringing their labor into greater demand, and, consequently, enhancing the wages of it. With deportation, even to a limited extent, enhanced wages to white labor is mathematically certain. Labor is like any other commodity in the market—increase the demand for it, and you increase the price of it. Reduce the supply of black labor, by colonizing the black laborer out of the country, and, by precisely so much, you increase the demand for, and wages of, white labor.

But it is dreaded that the freed people will swarm forth, and cover the whole land? Are they not already in the land? Will liberation make them any more numerous? Equally distributed among the whites of the whole country, and there would be but one colored to seven whites. Could the one, in any way, greatly disturb the seven? There are many communities now, having more than one free colored person, to seven whites; and this, without any apparent consciousness of evil from it. The District of Columbia, and the States of Maryland and Delaware, are all in this condition. The District has more than one free colored to six whites; and yet, in its frequent petitions to Congress, I believe it has never presented the presence of free colored persons as one of its grievances. But why should emancipation south, send the free people north? People, of any color, seldom run, unless there be something to run from. *Heretofore* colored people, to some extent, have fled north from bondage; and *now,* perhaps, from both bondage and destitution. But if gradual emancipation and deportation be adopted, they will have neither to flee from. Their old masters will give them wages at least until new laborers can be procured; and the freed men, in turn, will gladly give their labor for the wages, till new homes can be found for them, in congenial climes, and with people of their own blood and race. This proposition can be trusted on the mutual interests involved. And, in any event, cannot the north decide for itself, whether to receive them?

Again, as practice proves more than theory, in any case, has there been any irruption of colored people northward, because of the abolishment of slavery in this District last spring?

What I have said of the proportion of free colored persons to the whites, in the District, is from the census of 1860, having no reference to persons called contrabands, nor to those made free by the act of Congress abolishing slavery here.

The plan consisting of these articles is recommended, not but that a restoration of the national authority would be accepted without its adoption.

Nor will the war, nor proceedings under the proclamation of September 22, 1862, be stayed because of the *recommendation* of this plan. Its timely *adoption,* I doubt not, would bring restoration and thereby stay both.

And, notwithstanding this plan, the recommendation that Congress provide by law for compensating any State which may adopt emancipation, before this plan shall have been acted upon, is hereby earnestly renewed. Such would be only an advance part of the plan, and the same arguments apply to both.

This plan is recommended as a means, not in exclusion of, but additional to, all others for restoring and preserving the national authority throughout the Union. The subject is presented exclusively in its economical aspect. The plan would, I am confident, secure peace more speedily, and maintain it more permanently, than can be done by force alone; while all it would cost, considering amounts, and manner of payment, and times of payment, would be easier paid than will be the additional cost of the war, if we rely solely upon force. It is much—very much—that it would cost no blood at all.

The plan is proposed as permanent constitutional law. It cannot become such without the concurrence of, first, two-thirds of Congress, and, afterwards, three-fourths of the States. The requisite three-fourths of the States will necessarily include seven of the Slave states. Their concurrence, if obtained, will give assurance of their severally adopting emancipation, at no very distant day, upon the new constitutional terms. This assurance would end the struggle now, and save the Union forever.

I do not forget the gravity which should characterize a paper addressed to the Congress of the nation by the Chief Magistrate of the nation. Nor do I forget that some of you are my seniors, nor that many of you have more experience than I, in the conduct of public affairs. Yet I trust that in view of the great responsibility resting upon me, you will perceive no want of respect to yourselves, in any undue earnestness I may seem to display.

Is it doubted, then, that the plan I propose, if adopted, would shorten the war, and thus lessen its expenditure of money and of blood? Is it doubted that it would restore the national authority and national prosperity, and perpetuate both indefinitely? Is it doubted that we here—Congress and Executive—can secure its adoption? Will not the good people respond to a united, and earnest appeal from us? Can we, can they, by any other means, so certainly, or so speedily, assure these vital objects? We can succeed only by concert. It is not "can *any* of us *imagine* better?" but "can we *all* do better?" Object whatsoever is possible, still the question recurs "can we do better?" The dogmas of the quiet past, are inadequate to the stormy present. The occasion is piled high with difficulty, and we must rise with the occasion. As our case is new, so we must think anew, and act anew. We must disenthrall our selves, and then we shall save our country.

Fellow-citizens, *we* cannot escape history. We of this Congress and this administration, will be remembered in spite of ourselves. No personal significance, or insignificance, can spare one or another of us. The fiery trial through which we pass, will light us down, in honor or dishonor, to the latest generation. We *say* we are for the Union. The world will not forget that we say this. We know how to save the Union. The world knows we do know how to save it. We—even *we here* —hold the power, and bear the responsibility. In *giving* freedom to the *slave,* we *assure* freedom to the *free*—honorable alike in what we give, and what we preserve. We shall nobly save, or meanly lose, the last best, hope of earth. Other means may succeed; this could not fail. The way is plain, peaceful, generous, just—a way which, if followed, the world will forever applaud, and God must forever bless.

ABRAHAM LINCOLN

On January 1, 1863, after shaking hands with hundreds of well-wishers at the White House New Year's Day reception, Lincoln signed the Emancipation Proclamation, remarking, "I never in my life felt more certain that I was doing right than I do in signing this paper."[37] Carefully crafted to exert his limited constitutional authority as commander in chief, the proclamation did not emancipate slaves in areas under federal control, where conventional constitutional restraints remained in force. In other words, Lincoln emancipated slaves in rebel states where he claimed constitutional authority as commander in chief, but he did not emancipate slaves in regions where he lacked constitutional authority as commander in chief. More than a decree of emancipation, the proclamation also announced that blacks would now be allowed to serve in Union armed forces.

[37]Frederick W. Seward, *Seward at Washington, as Senator and Secretary of State: A Memoir of His Life with Selections from His Letters, 1861–1872* (New York, 1891), 151.

Emancipation Proclamation
January 1, 1863

BY THE PRESIDENT OF THE UNITED STATES OF AMERICA: A PROCLAMATION.

Whereas, on the twentysecond day of September, in the year of our Lord one thousand eight hundred and sixty two, a proclamation was issued by the President of the United States, containing, among other things, the following, towit:

"That on the first day of January, in the year of our Lord one thousand eight hundred and sixty-three, all persons held as slaves within any State or designated part of a State, the people whereof shall then be in rebellion against the United States, shall be then, thenceforward, and forever free; and the Executive Government of the United States, including the military and naval authority thereof, will recognize and maintain the freedom of such persons, and will do no act or acts to repress such persons, or any of them, in any efforts they may make for their actual freedom.

"That the Executive will, on the first day of January aforesaid, by proclamation, designate the States and parts of States, if any, in which the people thereof, respectively, shall then be in rebellion against the United States; and the fact that any State, or the people thereof, shall on that day be, in good faith, represented in the Congress of the United States by members chosen thereto at elections wherein a majority of the qualified voters of such State shall have participated, shall, in the absence of strong countervailing testimony, be deemed conclusive evidence that such State, and the people thereof, are not then in rebellion against the United States."

Now, therefore I, Abraham Lincoln, President of the United States, by virtue of the power in me vested as Commander-in-Chief, of the Army and Navy of the United States in time of actual armed rebellion against authority and government of the United States, and as a fit and necessary war measure for suppressing said rebellion, do, on this first day of January, in the year of our Lord one thousand eight hundred and sixty three, and in accordance with my purpose so to do publicly proclaimed for the full period of one hundred days, from the day first above mentioned, order and designate as the States and parts of States wherein the people thereof respectively, are this day in rebellion against the United States, the following, towit:

Arkansas, Texas, Louisiana, (except the Parishes of St. Bernard, Plaquemines, Jefferson, St. Johns, St. Charles, St. James[,] Ascension, Assumption, Terrebonne, Lafourche, St. Mary, St. Martin, and Orleans, including the City of New-Orleans) Mississippi, Alabama, Florida, Georgia, South-Carolina, North-Carolina, and Virginia, (except the fortyeight counties designated as West Virginia, and also the counties of Berkley, Accomac, Northampton, Elizabeth-City, York, Princess Ann, and Norfolk, including the cities of Norfolk & Portsmouth[)]; and which excepted parts are, for the present, left precisely as if this proclamation were not issued.

And by virtue of the power, and for the purpose aforesaid, I do order and declare that all persons held as slaves within said designated States, and parts of States, are, and henceforward shall be free; and that the Executive government of the United States, including the military and naval authorities thereof, will recognize and maintain the freedom of said persons.

And I hereby enjoin upon the people so declared to be free to abstain from all violence, unless in necessary self-defence; and I recommend to them that, in all cases when allowed, they labor faithfully for reasonable wages.

And I further declare and make known, that such persons of suitable condition, will be received into the armed service of the United States to garrison forts, positions, stations, and other places, and to man vessels of all sorts in said service.

And upon this act, sincerely believed to be an act of justice, warranted by the Constitution, upon military necessity, I invoke the considerate judgment of mankind, and the gracious favor of Almighty God....

ABRAHAM LINCOLN

8

A War for Freedom and Union

The Emancipation Proclamation signaled Lincoln's conclusion that a war to save the Union could not be won without ending slavery in the Confederacy. In addition to announcing a new war aim, the Emancipation Proclamation declared a new meaning for the Union, a meaning Lincoln explained in his Gettysburg Address.

Without Union victories on the battlefield, the Emancipation Proclamation remained just words on paper. Unless Confederate armies could be defeated, northern superiority in manpower and other military resources would do nothing to free the slaves or to save the Union. Only hard, relentless fighting could prevent the Confederacy from maintaining its independence. Lincoln understood better than any other northern leader the enormous sacrifice required for military success.

In December 1862, after Union attackers in the gruesome defeat at Fredericksburg suffered more than twice as many casualties as Confederate defenders, Lincoln explained to William O. Stoddard, one of his clerks, why the loss was not as bad as it seemed. Stoddard wrote later that Lincoln proposed an "awful arithmetic" that would turn costly losses like Fredericksburg into ultimate victory. According to Stoddard, Lincoln said that if the battle of Fredericksburg "were to be fought over again, every day, through a week of days, with the same relative results, the army under Lee would be wiped out to its last man, the Army of the Potomac would still be a mighty host, the war would be over, the Confederacy gone, and peace would be won at a smaller cost of life than it will be if the week of lost battles must be dragged out through yet another year of camps, marches, and of deaths in hospitals, rather than upon the field. No general yet found can face the arithmetic, but the end of the war will be at hand when he shall be discovered."[1]

During 1863, Lincoln continued to search for a general who grasped this

[1] William O. Stoddard, *Inside the White House in War Times* (New York, 1890), 179.

awful arithmetic. He had difficulty finding generals who fully realized that victory required the destruction of Confederate armies. As commander in chief, he constantly urged his generals not just to win battles but to destroy the enemy. Even after the exhilarating victory at Gettysburg, Pennsylvania, early in July 1863, the defeated Confederates slipped away to regroup and fight again. But the thrilling capture of Vicksburg, Mississippi, in July, followed by the occupation of Chattanooga and Knoxville, Tennessee, later in the year, made clear that General Grant shared Lincoln's vision of victory and how to achieve it. By the end of the year, Lincoln had found his general.

Lincoln's determination to fight an aggressive war for freedom and Union engendered intense political controversy in the North. It also prompted initiatives to take greater advantage of African Americans' contributions to the military effort.

EMANCIPATION AND BLACK SOLDIERS

The Emancipation Proclamation authorized African American men to serve in the armed forces. Aware of the army's pressing need for manpower, Lincoln encouraged army officials to recruit black regiments from the thousands of contrabands streaming into Union camps. Black recruitment went slowly, partly because of doubts among army commanders about whether former slaves would make good soldiers. Lincoln refused to retreat from the new war aim of freedom, but he was well aware that many white northerners—both soldiers and civilians—considered his policy unwise, or worse.

Letter to John A. McClernand
January 8, 1863

Executive Mansion,
Washington

Major General McClernand[2]
My dear Sir
Your interesting communication ... is received.[3] I never did ask more, nor

[2]General McClernand, a staunch Democrat from Illinois, served under General Grant in the Mississippi Valley.
[3]McClernand's letter reported that he had been approached by "warm personal and political friends" from the Confederate army who desired peace, in part because of the commercial ties between the Midwest and the lower Mississippi Valley. *CW,* VI, 49.

ever was willing to accept less, than for all the States, and the people thereof, to take and hold their places, and their rights, in the Union, under the Constitution of the United States. For this alone have I felt authorized to struggle; and I seek neither more nor less now. Still, to use a coarse, but an expressive figure, broken eggs can not be mended. I have issued the emancipation proclamation, and I can not retract it.

After the commencement of hostilities I struggled nearly a year and a half to get along without touching the "institution"; and when finally I conditionally determined to touch it, I gave a hundred days fair notice of my purpose, to all the States and people, within which time they[4] could have turned it wholly aside, by simply again becoming good citizens of the United States. They chose to disregard it, and I made the peremptory proclamation on what appeared to me to be a military necessity. And being made, it must stand. As to the States not included in it, of course they can have their rights in the Union as of old. Even the people of the states included [in the Emancipation Proclamation], if they choose, need not to be hurt by it. Let them adopt systems of apprenticeship for the colored people, conforming substantially to the most approved plans of gradual emancipation; and, with the aid they can have from the general government, they may be nearly as well off, in this respect, as if the present trouble had not occurred, and much better off than they can possibly be if the contest continues persistently.

As to any dread of my having a "purpose to enslave, or exterminate, the whites of the South" [as claimed in McClernand's letter], I can scarcely believe that such dread exists. It is too absurd. I believe you can be my personal witness that no man is less to be dreaded for undue severity, in any case.

If the friends you mention really wish to have peace upon the old terms, they should act at once. Every day makes the case more difficult. They can so act, with entire safety, so far as I am concerned.

I think you would better not make this letter public; but you may rely confidently on my standing by whatever I have said in it. Please write me if any thing more comes to light.

Yours very truly
A. LINCOLN.

[4] *They* refers to the people in the Confederacy.

Letter to John A. Dix

January 14, 1863

Private & confidential

Executive Mansion,
Washington

Major General Dix[5]
My dear Sir:
The [emancipation] proclamation has been issued. We were not succeeding—at best, were progressing too slowly—without it. Now, that we have it, and bear all the disadvantage of it, (as we do bear some in certain quarters) we must also take some benefit from it, if practicable. I therefore will thank you for your well considered opinion whether Fortress-Monroe, and York-Town, one or both, could not, in whole or in part, be garrisoned by colored troops, leaving the white forces now necessary at those places, to be employed elsewhere.[6]

Yours very truly
A. LINCOLN

[5]General Dix commanded the Department of Virginia, including Fort Monroe, situated at the mouth of the James River.
[6]General Dix replied that he could readily use two thousand black soldiers at Fort Monroe but insisted that the other two thousand men in the garrison "should be white troops." *CW,* VI, 56.

Letter to Andrew Johnson

March 26, 1863

Private

Executive Mansion,
Washington

Hon. Andrew Johnson[7]
My dear Sir:
I am told you have at least *thought* of raising a negro military force.[8] In my opinion the country now needs no specific thing so much as some man of your ability, and position, to go to this work. When I speak of your position, I mean that of an eminent citizen of a slave-state, and himself a slave-holder. The colored population is the great *available* and yet *unavailed* of, force for

[7]A loyal Democrat, Andrew Johnson was appointed military governor of Tennessee by Lincoln in April 1863.
[8]Johnson had proposed to incorporate former slaves into the Tennessee militia.

restoring the Union. The bare sight of fifty thousand armed, and drilled black soldiers on the banks of the Mississippi, would end the rebellion at once. And who doubts that we can present that sight, if we but take hold in earnest? If you *have* been thinking of it please do not dismiss the thought.[9]

Yours truly
A. LINCOLN

[9]Johnson, as it turned out, was more interested in using former slaves as laborers than as soldiers, and black recruitment in Tennessee languished until late in 1863.

Letter to David Hunter

April 1, 1863

Private

Executive Mansion
Washington D.C.

Major General Hunter[10]
My dear Sir:
I am glad to see the accounts of your colored force at Jacksonville, Florida.[11] I see the enemy are driving at them fiercely, as is to be expected. It is important to the enemy that such a force shall *not* take shape, and grow, and thrive, in the South; and in precisely the same proportion, it is important to us that it *shall.* Hence the utmost caution and vigilance is necessary on our part. The enemy will make extra efforts to destroy them; and we should do the same to preserve and increase them.

Yours truly
A. LINCOLN

[10]General Hunter, whose emancipation order Lincoln had countermanded a year earlier, commanded Union forces along the southeastern coast.
[11]During the last week of March, Union forces including the First and Second South Carolina Volunteers, both black regiments, captured and occupied Jacksonville.

Letter to Edwin M. Stanton

July 21, 1863

Executive Mansion,
Washington

Hon. Sec. of War
My dear Sir:
I desire that a renewed and vigorous effort be made to raise colored forces along the shores of the Missispi.

Please consult the General-in-Chief;[12] and if it is perceived that any acceleration of the matter can be effected, let it be done.

I think the evidence is nearly conclusive that Gen. Thomas[13] is one of the best, if not the very best, instruments for this service.

Yours truly
A. LINCOLN.

[12]General Henry W. Halleck.
[13]General Lorenzo Thomas was put in charge of the recruitment of African American soldiers in the Mississippi Valley and, by the end of 1863, had enlisted nearly twenty thousand black men.

Letter to Ulysses S. Grant

August 9, 1863

Executive Mansion,
Washington

My dear General Grant:[14]
... Gen. Thomas has gone again to the Mississippi Valley, with the view of raising colored troops. I have no reason to doubt that you are doing what you reasonably can upon the same subject. I believe it is a resource which, if vigorously applied now, will soon close the contest. It works doubly, weakening the enemy and strengthening us. We were not fully ripe for it until the river was opened.[15] Now, I think at least a hundred thousand can, and ought to be rapidly organized along it's shores, relieving all the white troops to serve elsewhere.

[14]Just a month earlier, General Grant had captured Vicksburg, Mississippi. When he received this letter, Grant was in Cairo, Illinois.
[15]That is, the Union did not control the entire length of the Mississippi River until July 1863, with the capture of Vicksburg, Mississippi, and Port Hudson, Louisiana.

Mr. Dana[16] understands you as believing that the emancipation proclamation has helped some in your military operations. I am very glad if this is so.[17] . . .

Yours very truly
A. LINCOLN.

[16]Charles A. Dana, an assistant secretary of war and a former editor of the *New York Tribune,* was with Grant's army during the Vicksburg campaign.

[17]Grant replied to Lincoln that "I have given the subject of arming the negro my hearty support. This, with emancipation . . . is the heavyest blow yet given the Confederacy. . . . Gen. Thomas is now with me and you may rely on it I will give him all the aid in my power." *CW,* VI, 375.

Black soldiers fought valiantly in a number of engagements — including battles at Port Hudson, Louisiana, in May 1863, at Milliken's Bend near Vicksburg, Mississippi, in June 1863, and at Fort Wagner near Charleston, South Carolina, in July 1863. The Confederacy considered black soldiers to be insurrectionists and refused to treat them as prisoners of war when they were captured. Instead, rebel soldiers often summarily executed black captives or sold them into slavery. Lincoln proclaimed that the Union would retaliate against such outrages.

Order of Retaliation
July 30, 1863

Executive Mansion,
Washington D.C.

It is the duty of every government to give protection to its citizens, of whatever class, color, or condition, and especially to those who are duly organized as soldiers in the public service. The law of nations and the usages and customs of war as carried on by civilized powers, permit no distinction as to color in the treatment of prisoners of war as public enemies. To sell or enslave any captured person, on account of his color, and for no offence against the laws of war, is a relapse into barbarism and a crime against the civilization of the age.

The government of the United States will give the same protection to all its soldiers, and if the enemy shall sell or enslave anyone because of his color, the offense shall be punished by retaliation upon the enemy's prisoners in our possession.

It is therefore ordered that for every soldier of the United States killed in violation of the laws of war, a rebel soldier shall be executed; and for every one enslaved by the enemy or sold into slavery, a rebel soldier shall be placed at hard labor on the public works and continued at such labor until the other shall be released and receive the treatment due to a prisoner of war.[18]

ABRAHAM LINCOLN

[18]In practice, the Union enforced this policy haphazardly, fearing that the Confederacy would counter by punishing white Union prisoners similarly. For the remainder of the war, black soldiers captured by the Confederacy were summarily executed, routinely returned to their masters, or sold into slavery. When the Confederacy refused to exchange black prisoners of war for captured Confederates, the Union stopped all prisoner exchanges.

Thousands of slaves liberated by the Emancipation Proclamation—especially women, children, and elderly men—crowded into contraband camps near Union lines in the Mississippi Valley. Lincoln proposed that they be put to work on abandoned plantations.

Draft of a Communication to Stephen A. Hurlbut

Circa August 15, 1863

Executive Mansion,
Washington

[To General Hurlbut[19]]

The within discusses a difficult subject—the most difficult with which we have to deal. The able bodied male contrabands are already employed by the Army. But the rest are in confusion and destitution. They better be set to digging their subsistence out of the ground. If there are plantations near you, on either side of the river, which are abandoned by their owners, first put as many contrabands on such, as they will hold—that is, as can draw subsistence from them. If some still remain, get loyal men,[20] of character in the vicinity, to take them temporarily on wages, to be paid to the contrabands themselves—such men obliging themselves to not let the contrabands be kidnapped, or forcibly carried away. Of course, if any [contrabands] voluntarily make arrangements to work for their living, you will not hinder them. It is thought best to leave details to your discretion subject to the provisions of the acts of Congress & the orders of the War Department.

By direction of the President.

[19]A Republican lawyer from Illinois, General Hurlbut served in commands in the Mississippi Valley throughout the war. Although Lincoln evidently did not send this letter to General Hurlbut, the letter expressed Lincoln's views and described the policy actually adopted by Union forces along the Mississippi and elsewhere.

[20]That is, white unionists.

The Emancipation Proclamation did not apply to the loyal slave states of Maryland, Delaware, Kentucky, or Missouri. Although Lincoln continued to hope these border states would adopt some plan for gradual emancipation, he believed that the Constitution still protected slavery within the Union. In those regions of the Confederacy covered by the Emancipation Proclamation, Lincoln refused to retreat from the promise of freedom for slaves.

Letter to John M. Schofield

June 22, 1863

Executive Mansion,
Washington

Gen. John M. Schofield.[21]
My dear Sir:
Your despatch, asking in substance, whether, in case Missouri shall adopt gradual emancipation,[22] the general government will protect slave owners in that species of property during the short time it shall be permitted by the State to exist within it, has been received. Desirous as I am, that emancipation shall be adopted by Missouri, and believing as I do, that *gradual* can be made better than *immediate* for both black and white, except when military necessity changes the case, my impulse is to say that such protection would be given. I can not know exactly what shape an act of emancipation may take. If the period from the initiation to the final end, should be comparatively short, and the act should prevent persons being sold, during that period, into more lasting slavery, the whole would be easier. I do not wish to pledge the general government to the affirmative support of even temporary slavery, beyond what can be fairly claimed under the constitution. I suppose, however, this is not desired; but that it is desired for the Military force of the United States, while in Missouri, to not be used in subverting the temporarily reserved legal rights in slaves during the progress of emancipation. This I would desire also. I have very earnestly urged the slave-states to adopt eman-

[21] A West Point graduate, General Schofield had commanded troops in Missouri, Arkansas, and Tennessee since the beginning of the war. In May 1863, Lincoln had appointed him commander of the Department of Missouri.
[22] On July 1, 1863, the Missouri constitutional convention adopted a gradual emancipation plan that would take effect in 1870. The plan promised masters continued control over their former slaves until 1876. Slaves who were more than forty years old in 1870 would remain in bondage for life and slaves who were under twelve years old in 1870 would continue their servitude until they were twenty-three. Another Missouri constitutional convention finally abolished slavery unconditionally on January 11, 1865.

cipation; and it ought to be, and is an object with me not to overthrow, or thwart what any of them may in good faith do, to that end.

You are therefore authorized to act in the spirit of this letter, in conjunction with what may appear to be the military necessities of your Department.

Although this letter will become public at some time, it is not intended to be made so now.

Yours truly
A. LINCOLN

Letter to Stephen A. Hurlbut

July 31, 1863

Executive Mansion,
Washington

My dear General Hurlbut:

... The emancipation proclamation applies to Arkansas. I think it is valid in law, and will be so held by the courts. I think I shall not retract or repudiate it. Those who shall have tasted actual freedom I believe can never be slaves, or quasi slaves again. For the rest, I believe some plan, substantially being gradual emancipation, would be better for both white and black. The Missouri plan, recently adopted, I do not object to on account of the time for *ending* the institution; but I am sorry the *beginning* should have been postponed for seven years, leaving all that time to agitate for the repeal of the whole thing. It should begin at once, giving at least the new-born, a vested interest in freedom, which could not be taken away. ...

Yours very truly.
A. LINCOLN

Lincoln resisted pressure to extend the Emancipation Proclamation to regions of the Confederacy exempted because they were under federal control. Since he believed that the Constitution permitted emancipation only as a military necessity, he held that federal initiatives based on any other considerations violated the Constitution and created grave political risks for both the Republican party and the eventual abolition of slavery.

Figure 6.   Wartime President

This photograph taken in 1863, unlike the many formal presidential portraits, captured Lincoln in a more casual pose that may better reflect the canny, shrewd, confident, and cordial man visitors encountered when they met the president.

Letter to Salmon P. Chase
September 2, 1863

Executive Mansion,
Washington

Hon. S. P. Chase.[23]

My dear Sir:

Knowing your great anxiety that the emancipation proclamation shall now be applied to certain parts of Virginia and Louisiana which were exempted from it last January, I state briefly what appear to me to be difficulties in the way of such a step. The original proclamation has no constitutional or legal justification, except as a military measure. The exemptions were made because the military necessity did not apply to the exempted localities. Nor does that necessity apply to them now any more than it did then. If I take the step[24] must I not do so, without the argument of military necessity, and so, without any argument, except the one that I think the measure politically expedient, and morally right? Would I not thus give up all footing upon constitution or law? Would I not thus be in the boundless field of absolutism? Could this pass unnoticed, or unresisted? Could it fail to be perceived that without any further stretch, I might do the same in Delaware, Maryland, Kentucky, Tennessee, and Missouri; and even change any law in any state? Would not many of our own friends shrink away appalled? Would it not lose us the elections, and with them, the very cause we seek to advance?

---

[23] An ambitious antislavery Republican from Ohio, Salmon P. Chase served as Lincoln's Secretary of the Treasury until he was appointed Chief Justice of the Supreme Court in October 1864.

[24] That is, the step of applying the Emancipation Proclamation to the exempted areas.

THE DECISIVE SUMMER OF 1863

The lack of military progress in the Virginia theater by January 1863 caused Lincoln to appoint a new commander, General Joseph Hooker. A West Point graduate, Hooker had gained a reputation as a fighting general in the Army of the Potomac, where he had served since the beginning of the war. Lincoln made clear that he expected Hooker to fight and win battles.

Letter to Joseph Hooker

January 26, 1863

Executive Mansion,
Washington

Major General Hooker:

General.

I have placed you at the head of the Army of the Potomac. Of course I have done this upon what appear to me to be sufficient reasons. And yet I think it best for you to know that there are some things in regard to which, I am not quite satisfied with you. I believe you to be a brave and a skilful soldier, which, of course, I like. I also believe you do not mix politics with your profession, in which you are right. You have confidence in yourself, which is a valuable, if not an indispensable quality. You are ambitious, which, within reasonable bounds, does good rather than harm. But I think that during Gen. Burnside's command of the Army, you have taken counsel of your ambition, and thwarted him as much as you could, in which you did a great wrong to the country, and to a most meritorious and honorable brother officer. I have heard, in such way as to believe it, of your recently saying that both the Army and the Government needed a Dictator. Of course it was not *for* this, but in spite of it, that I have given you the command. Only those generals who gain successes, can set up dictators. What I now ask of you is military success, and I will risk the dictatorship. The government will support you to the utmost of it's ability, which is neither more nor less than it has done and will do for all commanders. I much fear that the spirit which you have aided to infuse into the Army, of criticising their Commander, and withholding confidence from him, will now turn upon you. I shall assist you as far as I can, to put it down. Neither you, nor Napoleon, if he were alive again, could get any good out of an army, while such a spirit prevails in it.

And now, beware of rashness. Beware of rashness, but with energy, and sleepless vigilance, go forward, and give us victories.

Yours very truly
A. Lincoln

While Union forces across the country prepared for the spring campaign, Lincoln left Washington in early April to consult with General Hooker and to review the Army of the Potomac. Talking with Hooker and his officers, Lincoln began to worry that the generals were focusing on how to capture Richmond rather than on how to defeat General Robert E. Lee's Army of

Northern Virginia. Lincoln summarized his own view in a brief note written while he was still with Hooker's army in Virginia.

Memorandum on Joseph Hooker's Plan of Campaign against Richmond
Circa April 6–10, 1863

My opinion is, that just now, with the enemy directly ahead of us, there is *no* eligible route for us into Richmond; and consequently a question of preference between the Rappahannock route, and the James River route is a contest about nothing.[25] Hence our prime object is the enemies' army in front of us, and is not with, or about, Richmond—at all, unless it be incidental to the main object.

What then? The two armies are face to face with a narrow river between them. Our communications are shorter and safer than are those of the enemy. For this reason, we can, with equal powers fret him more than he can us. I do not think that by raids towards Washington he can derange the Army of the Potomac at all. He has no distant opperations which can call any of the Army of the Potomac away; we have such operations which may call him away, at least in part.[26] While he remains in tact, I do not think we should take the disadvantage of attacking him in his entrenchments; but we should continually harrass and menace him, so that he shall have no leisure, nor safety in sending away detachments. If he weakens himself, then pitch into him.

[25]Lincoln is referring to a debate among Hooker's staff about the best route to outflank Lee's army.
[26]Lincoln is referring to Union attacks at Charleston, South Carolina, Vicksburg, Mississippi, and elsewhere that might require Lee to divert soldiers from the Virginia front.

By the end of April 1863, Union armies seemed stalled on every front. In the West, General Grant's months-long campaign to assault Vicksburg remained stymied by the city's defenses and the marshy terrain along the Mississippi River. In the East, General Hooker still faced General Lee's army stretched along the Rappahannock River near Fredericksburg. Within the next three months, a series of ferocious battles in both the East and the West decisively improved the prospects of the Union and lifted Lincoln's spirits. In early May, however, Lincoln had few omens of the good fortune that lay ahead.

During the first week of May, General Hooker finally launched an attack on Lee's defenses near Chancellorsville. Although Hooker's men outnumbered the Confederates nearly two to one, Lee's soldiers outmaneuvered, outsmarted, and outfought the Yankees, inflicting another humiliating and costly defeat on the Army of the Potomac and forcing Hooker to retreat back to the northern side of the Rappahannock. Dismayed, Lincoln urged Hooker to come up with a new plan.

Letter to Joseph Hooker
May 7, 1863

Head-Quarters, Army of the Potomac

Major General Hooker
My dear Sir

The recent movement of your army is ended without effecting it's object, except perhaps some important breakings of the enemies communications.[27] What next? If possible I would be very glad of another movement early enough to give us some benefit from the fact of the enemies communications being broken, but neither for this reason or any other, do I wish anything done in desperation or rashness. An early movement would also help to supersede the bad moral effect of the recent one,[28] which is sure to be considerably injurious. Have you already in your mind a plan wholly, or partially formed? If you have, prossecute it without interference from me. If you have not, please inform me, so that I, incompetent as I may be, can try [to] assist in the formation of some plan for the Army.

Yours as ever
A. LINCOLN

[27]Hooker had sent a large force on a flanking movement toward the rear of Lee's army in order to interrupt its communications and supplies.
[28]That is, the defeat at Chancellorsville.

In mid-May, General Lee formulated a bold plan to capitalize on his victory at Chancellorsville and the fighting prowess of his men by racing up the Shenandoah Valley and invading Pennsylvania. Marching into the northern heartland would allow his army to forage supplies from Yankee civilians, to embarrass Lincoln, the Republican party, and the Union army, to encourage Democratic opponents of the war in the North, and maybe even to force Lincoln to concede defeat and recognize the independence of the Confederacy. A high-stakes gamble, Lee's invasion of the North represented the kind of inspired military leadership that Lincoln could not get from the commander of the Army of the Potomac. When Lee moved out of his defensive position along the Rappahannock in early June, General Hooker—not knowing where Lee was headed—was tempted to attack the weakened rebel defenses and speed toward the Confederate capital at Richmond, a course of action that Lincoln repeatedly advised against.

Letter to Joseph Hooker
June 5, 1863

Washington, D.C.

Major General Hooker

. . . I have but one idea which I think worth suggesting to you, and that is in case you find Lee coming to the North of the Rappahannock, I would by no means cross to the South of it. If he should leave a rear force at Fredericksburg, tempting you to fall upon it, it would fight in intrenchments, and have you at disadvantage, and so, man for man, worst you at that point, while his main force would in some way be getting an advantage of you Northward. In one word, I would not take any risk of being entangled upon the river, like an ox jumped half over a fence, and liable to be torn by dogs, front and rear, without a fair chance to gore one way or kick the other. If Lee would come to my side of the river, I would keep on the same side & fight him, or act on the defence, according as might be my estimate of his strength relatively to my own. But these are mere suggestions which I desire to be controlled by the judgment of yourself and Gen. Halleck.

A. LINCOLN

As Lee's movement toward the North became clear, Lincoln sensed a great opportunity. If Union commanders would attack Lee while his army was separated from secure supplies and easy reinforcements, the Army of Northern Virginia might finally be defeated. Lacking confidence that General Hooker would get in the mood for action, Lincoln replaced him with General George G. Meade in late June. In just a few days, Meade's army collided repeatedly with Lee's invaders at Gettysburg, Pennsylvania. In pivotal, deadly battles on July 1–3 that featured heroics on both sides, Union troops finally forced Lee's army to retreat from the battlefield and to abandon the northern invasion. For Lincoln, the Union triumph at Gettysburg was tempered by frustration that Lee's army escaped destruction.

Announcement of News from Gettysburg
July 4, 1863

Washington City, 10 A.M.

The President announces to the country that news from the Army of the Potomac, up to 10 P.M. of the 3rd. is such as to cover that Army with the highest honor, to promise a great success to the cause of the Union, and to claim the condolence of all for the many gallant fallen. And that for this, he especially desires that on this day, He whose will, not ours, should ever be done, be everywhere remembered and reverenced with profoundest gratitude.

ABRAHAM LINCOLN

Letter to Henry W. Halleck
July 6, 1863

Soldiers' Home,
[Washington]—7 P.M.

Major-General Halleck: I left the telegraph office a good deal dissatisfied. You know I did not like the phrase, in Orders, No. 68, I believe, "Drive the invaders from our soil."[29] Since that, I see a dispatch from General French,[30] saying the enemy is crossing his wounded over the [Potomac] river in flats, without saying why he [General French] does not stop it, or even intimating a thought that it ought to be stopped. Still later, another dispatch from General Pleasonton,[31] by direction of General Meade, to General French, stating that the main [Union] army is halted because it is believed the rebels are concentrating "on the road toward Hagerstown [Maryland], beyond Fairfield [Pennsylvania]," and is not to move until it is ascertained that the rebels intend to evacuate Cumberland Valley.[32]

---

[29]In his General Orders No. 68, issued on July 4, General Meade congratulated his army on their great victory at Gettysburg and declared, "Our task is not yet accomplished, and the commanding general looks to the army for greater efforts to drive from our soil every vestige of the presence of the invader." General Meade, like so many other Union generals, failed to grasp Lincoln's demand that the key military objective was not to occupy soil but to destroy the rebel army. *CW,* VI, 318.

[30]General William Henry French, a West Point graduate, had served in the Union army since the beginning of the war.

[31]General Alfred Pleasonton was another West Pointer who had commanded Union forces since 1861.

[32]In other words, rather than attacking the retreating Confederates, the Union army was waiting for the rebels to move out of Pennsylvania and Maryland via the Cumberland Valley, and back to Virginia.

These things all appear to me to be connected with a purpose [by Union commanders] to cover[33] Baltimore and Washington, and to get[34] the enemy across the [Potomac] river again without a further collision, and they do not appear connected with a purpose to prevent his crossing and to destroy him. I do fear the former purpose is acted upon and the latter is rejected.

If you are satisfied the latter purpose is entertained and is judiciously pursued, I am content. If you are not so satisfied, please look to it.

Yours, truly,

A. LINCOLN.

[33]That is, to defend.
[34]That is, to allow.

Response to a Serenade

July 7, 1863

Fellow-citizens:[35] I am very glad indeed to see you to-night, and yet I will not say I thank you for this call, but I do most sincerely thank Almighty God for the occasion on which you have called. [Cheers.] How long ago is it?—eighty odd years—since on the Fourth of July for the first time in the history of the world a nation by its representatives, assembled and declared as a self-evident truth that "all men are created equal." [Cheers.] That was the birth-day of the United States of America. Since then the Fourth of July has had several peculiar recognitions. The two most distinguished men in the framing and support of the Declaration were Thomas Jefferson and John Adams—the one having penned it and the other sustained it the most forcibly in debate—the only two of the fifty-five who sustained [signed?] it being elected President of the United States. Precisely fifty years after they put their hands to the paper it pleased Almighty God to take both from the stage of action.[36] This was indeed an extraordinary and remarkable event in our history. Another President, five years after, was called from this stage of existence on the same day and month of the year;[37] and now, on this last Fourth of July just passed, when we have a gigantic Rebellion, at the bottom of which is an effort to overthrow the principle that all men were created equal, we have the surrender of a most powerful position and army on that very day, [cheers] and not only so, but in a succession of battles in Pennsylvania, near to us, through three days, so rapidly fought that they might be called one great battle on the 1st, 2d and 3d of the month of July; and on the

[35]On July 8, 1863, the *New York Tribune* and other papers published this account of Lincoln's impromptu speech.
[36]Both Thomas Jefferson and John Adams died on July 4, 1826.
[37]James Monroe died July 4, 1831.

4th the cohorts of those who opposed the declaration that all men are created equal, "turned tail" and run. [Long and continued cheers.] Gentlemen, this is a glorious theme, and the occasion for a speech, but I am not prepared to make one worthy of the occasion. I would like to speak in terms of praise due to the many brave officers and soldiers who have fought in the cause of the Union and liberties of the country from the beginning of the war. These are trying occasions, not only in success, but for the want of success. I dislike to mention the name of one single officer lest I might do wrong to those I might forget. Recent events bring up glorious names, and particularly prominent ones, but these I will not mention. Having said this much, I will now take the music.

Celebrations of the great victory at Gettysburg were still under way when word reached Lincoln that General Grant, in a campaign Lincoln termed "one of the most brilliant in the world," had captured Vicksburg, Mississippi.[38] The heavily defended city perched atop high bluffs on the east bank of the Mississippi. After a fruitless effort to circumvent the city during the winter of 1862–63 by cutting a way through the tangled swamps west of the river, Grant marched his soldiers in April along the western bank of the river across a neck of land that jutted toward Vicksburg. Under cover of darkness in mid-April, Grant ran a fleet of troop transports and gunboats down the river, directly past Vicksburg's artillery batteries, which fired on but failed to destroy the Union flotilla. By the end of April, Grant's soldiers rendezvoused with the boats about thirty miles south of Vicksburg. Instead of continuing down the river to link up with the Union army under General Nathaniel Banks, which was attempting to capture the southernmost Confederate stronghold on the river at Port Hudson, Louisiana, Grant adopted a far bolder strategy, against the advice of his subordinate commanders. To divert Confederate defenders, he sent General William T. Sherman's men up the Yazoo River north of Vicksburg. Then Grant ferried his soldiers across the Mississippi unopposed, captured Port Gibson and Grand Gulf on May 1 and 2. Rather than then crossing the Big Black River and marching north directly to Vicksburg, Grant abandoned his source of supplies on the Mississippi and headed east toward Jackson, Mississippi, where a large Confederate army menaced the rear of any Union attack on Vicksburg. In a series of major engagements in mid-May, Grant's army defeated Confederate forces at Jackson and destroyed much

[38]Lincoln to Isaac N. Arnold, May 26, 1863, *CW,* VI, 230.

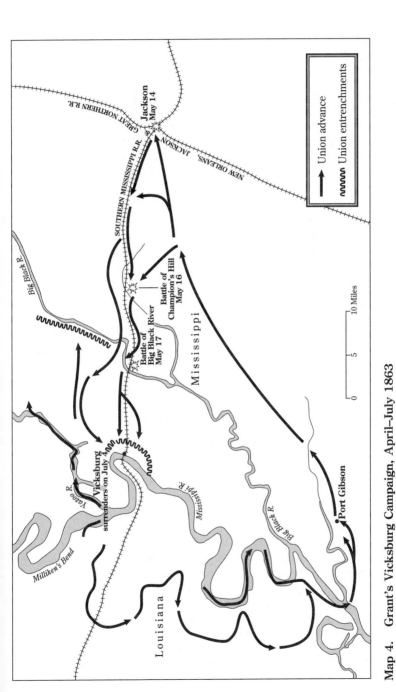

Map 4. Grant's Vicksburg Campaign, April–July 1863

Grant's bold campaign converted what seemed to be Vicksburg's impregnable position on the Mississippi River into an inescapable trap for Confederate defenders.

of the city, pushed west toward Vicksburg, defeating rebel defenders at Champion's Hill on May 16 and Big Black River on May 17, to bring Vicksburg under a siege, finally broken by Confederates' surrender of the city on July 4. Grant's Vicksburg campaign was the most brilliantly executed military strategy of the entire war; and, unlike Lee's invasion of the North, Grant's campaign achieved its objective, justifying Lincoln's praise of Grant's "almost inestimable service." For a brief time, Lincoln believed the end of the war was within sight.

Letter to Henry W. Halleck

July 7, 1863

Major-General Halleck:
We have certain information that Vicksburg surrendered to General Grant on the 4th of July. Now, if General Meade can complete his work, so gloriously prosecuted thus far, by the literal or substantial destruction of Lee's army, the rebellion will be over.

Yours, truly,
A. LINCOLN.

Letter to Ulysses S. Grant

July 13, 1863

Executive Mansion,
Washington

Major General Grant
My dear General
I do not remember that you and I ever met personally. I write this now as a grateful acknowledgment for the almost inestimable service you have done the country. I wish to say a word further. When you first reached the vicinity of Vicksburg, I thought you should do, what you finally did—march the troops across the neck, run the batteries with the transports, and thus go below; and I never had any faith, except a general hope that you knew better than I, that the Yazoo Pass expedition, and the like, could succeed. When you got below, and took Port-Gibson, Grand Gulf, and vicinity, I thought you should go down the river and join Gen. Banks; and when you turned North-

ward East of the Big Black, I feared it was a mistake. I now wish to make the personal acknowledgment that you were right, and I was wrong.

Yours very truly
A. LINCOLN

Lincoln remained frustrated that the commander of the Army of the Potomac failed to show the relentless will to engage and attempt to destroy the enemy that was exhibited by General Grant. He expressed his frustration in the following letter, which he decided not to send in order to avoid affronting General Meade.

Letter to George G. Meade
July 14, 1863

Executive Mansion,
Washington

Major General Meade

I have just seen your despatch to Gen. Halleck, asking to be relieved of your command, because of a supposed censure of mine.[39] I am very—*very*—grateful to you for the magnificent success you gave the cause of the country at Gettysburg; and I am sorry now to be the author of the slightest pain to you. But I was in such deep distress myself that I could not restrain some expression of it. I had been oppressed nearly ever since the battles at Gettysburg, by what appeared to be evidences that yourself, and Gen. Couch,[40] and Gen. Smith,[41] were not seeking a collision with the enemy, but were trying to get him across the [Potomac] river without another battle. What these evidences were, if you please, I hope to tell you at some time, when we shall both feel better. The case, summarily stated is this. You fought and beat the enemy at Gettysburg; and, of course, to say the least, his loss was as great as yours. He retreated; and you did not, as it seemed to me, pressingly pursue

[39] General Meade had offered his resignation in response to General Halleck's message urging him to pursue and attack Lee. Halleck explained that "the escape of Lee's army without another battle has created great dissatisfaction in the mind of the President, and it will require an active and energetic pursuit on your part to remove the impression that it has not been sufficiently active heretofore." *CW,* VI, 328.

[40] General Darius Nash Couch, a West Point graduate, commanded the Department of the Susquehanna at the time of the battle of Gettysburg.

[41] General William Farrar Smith, another West Pointer, also served in the Department of the Susquehanna during and after the battle of Gettysburg.

him; but a flood in the river detained him, till, by slow degrees, you were again upon him. You had at least twenty thousand veteran troops directly with you, and as many more raw ones within supporting distance, all in addition to those who fought with you at Gettysburg; while it was not possible that he had received a single recruit; and yet you stood and let the flood run down, bridges be built, and the enemy move away at his leisure, without attacking him. And Couch and Smith! The latter left Carlisle [Pennsylvania] in time, upon all ordinary calculation, to have aided you in the last battle at Gettysburg; but he did not arrive. At the end of more than ten days, I believe twelve, under constant urging, he reached Hagerstown [Maryland] from Carlisle, which is not an inch over fiftyfive miles, if so much. And Couch's movement was very little different.

Again, my dear general, I do not believe you appreciate the magnitude of the misfortune involved in Lee's escape. He was within your easy grasp, and to have closed upon him would, in connection with our other late successes, have ended the war. As it is, the war will be prolonged indefinitely. If you could not safely attack Lee last monday, how can you possibly do so South of the [Potomac] river, when you can take with you very few more than two thirds of the force you then had in hand? It would be unreasonable to expect, and I do not expect you can now effect much. Your golden opportunity is gone, and I am distressed immeasureably because of it.

I beg you will not consider this a prossecution, or persecution of yourself. As you had learned that I was dissatisfied, I have thought it best to kindly tell you why.

Letter to Oliver O. Howard

July 21, 1863

Executive Mansion,
Washington

My dear General Howard[42]

Your letter of the 18th. is received.[43] I was deeply mortified by the escape of Lee across the Potomac, because the substantial destruction of his army would have ended the war, and because I believed, such destruction was perfectly easy—believed that Gen. Meade and his noble army had expended all the skill, and toil, and blood, up to the ripe harvest, and then let the crop go

[42]General Howard, a West Point graduate, commanded soldiers throughout the Virginia theater, including at Gettysburg.

[43]General Howard's letter to Lincoln defended General Meade's leadership at Gettysburg in response to what he termed "the censure and misrepresentations which have grown out of the escape of Lee's army." *CW,* VI, 341.

to waste. Perhaps my mortification was heightened because I had always believed—making my belief a hobby possibly—that the main rebel army going North of the Potomac, could never return, if well attended to; and because I was so greatly flattered in this belief, by the operations at Gettysburg. A few days having passed, I am now profoundly grateful for what was done, without criticism for what was not done. Gen. Meade has my confidence as a brave and skillful officer, and a true man.

Yours very truly
A. LINCOLN

Although General Lee's army had been defeated at Gettysburg, it remained a formidable force, and Lincoln continued to insist that his commanders develop a plan to attack and destroy it.

Letter to Henry W. Halleck
September 19, 1863

Executive Mansion,
Washington

Major General Halleck:

By Gen. Meade's despatch to you of yesterday it appears that he desires your views and those of the government, as to whether he shall advance upon the enemy.[44] I am not prepared to order, or even advise an advance in this case, wherein I know so little of particulars, and wherein he, in the field, thinks the risk is so great, and the promise of advantage so small. And yet the case presents matter for very serious consideration in another aspect. These two armies confront each other across a small river [the Rapidan River], substantially midway between the two Capitals, each defending it's own Capital, and menacing the other. Gen Meade estimates the enemies infantry in front of him at not less than forty thousand. Suppose we add fifty per cent to this, for cavalry, artillery, and extra duty men stretching as far as Richmond, making the whole force of the enemy sixty thousand. Gen Meade ... has with him, and between him and Washington, of the same classes of well men, over ninety thousand. Neither [Meade nor Lee] can bring the whole of his men into a battle; but each can bring as large a per centage in as the other. For a

[44] General Meade's letter to Halleck expressed his view that "I can get a battle out of Lee under very disadvantageous circumstances which may render his inferior force my superior and which is not likely to result in any very decided advantage, even in case I should be victorious." *CW,* VI, 468.

battle, then, Gen. Meade has three men to Gen. Lee's two. Yet, it having been determined that choosing ground, and standing on the defensive, gives so great advantage that the three can not safely attack the two, the three are left simply standing on the defensive also. If the enemies sixty thousand are sufficient to keep our ninety thousand away from Richmond, why, by the same rule, may not forty thousand of ours keep their sixty thousand away from Washington, leaving us fifty thousand to put to some other use? Having practically come to the mere defensive, it seems to be no economy at all to employ twice as many men for that object as are needed. With no object, certainly, to misle[a]d myself, I can perceive no fault in this statement, unless we admit we are not the equal of the enemy man for man. I hope you will consider it.

To avoid misunderstanding, let me say that to attempt to fight the enemy slowly back into his intrenchments at Richmond, and there to capture him, is an idea I have been trying to repudiate for quite a year. My judgment is so clear against it, that I would scarcely allow the attempt to be made, if the general in command should desire to make it. My last attempt upon Richmond was to get McClellan, when he was nearer there than the enemy was, to run in ahead of him. Since then I have constantly desired the Army of the Potomac, to make Lee's army, and not Richmond, it's objective point. If our army can not fall upon the enemy and hurt him where he is, it is plain to me it can gain nothing by attempting to follow him over a succession of intrenched lines into a fortified city.

> Yours truly
> A. LINCOLN

POLITICS OF WAR AND FREEDOM

The Emancipation Proclamation, the draft law passed by Congress in March 1863, the halting progress of northern armies until the summer of 1863, the seemingly endless lists of dead and wounded published in newspapers throughout the Union, and Lincoln's continued willingness to suspend the writ of habeas corpus combined to strengthen a desire to end the war, especially among northern Democrats. Growing peace sentiment in the North threatened to undermine the recruitment of soldiers and to subvert Lincoln's dual war goals of union and freedom. Even the many Democratic politicians who supported the war often intensely opposed emancipation both because they considered black people inferior to whites and because the abolition of slavery fundamentally changed the character of the Union. Newly elected Democratic legislators in Illinois and Indiana, for example, passed resolutions calling for a cease-fire and a peace conference to restore the Union as it was, that is, with slavery. The seriousness of Democratic opposition to the war caused Lincoln, as he explained to a Republican senator in January 1863, to fear "'the fire in the rear'—meaning the Democracy . . . —more than our military chances."[45]

Lincoln responded to Democratic criticisms in two ways. First, he defended his legal and constitutional authority to enforce the draft, to suspend the writ of habeas corpus, and to issue the Emancipation Proclamation. Second, he explained his views of the historical significance of the war not just for the United States, but for the cause of democracy and freedom throughout the world.

[45]Charles Sumner to Francis Lieber, January 17, 1863, in Edward L. Pierce, ed., *Memoir and Letters of Charles Sumner* (4 vols.; Boston, 1877–93), IV, 114.

Letter to the Workingmen of Manchester, England
January 19, 1863

Executive Mansion,
Washington

To the workingmen of Manchester:

I have the honor to acknowledge the receipt of the address and resolutions which you sent to me on the eve of the new year.[46]

When I came, on the fourth day of March, 1861, through a free and constitutional election, to preside in the government of the United States, the country was found at the verge of civil war. Whatever might have been the cause, or whosoever the fault, one duty paramount to all others was before me, namely, to maintain and preserve at once the Constitution and the integrity of the federal republic. A conscientious purpose to perform this duty is a key to all the measures of administration which have been, and to all which will hereafter be pursued. Under our form of government, and my official oath, I could not depart from this purpose if I would. It is not always in the power of governments to enlarge or restrict the scope of moral results which follow the policies that they may deem it necessary for the public safety, from time to time, to adopt.

I have understood well that the duty of self-preservation rests solely with the American people. But I have at the same time been aware that favor or

[46]The resolutions praised Lincoln for the Emancipation Proclamation, even though "the war has so sorely distressed us." The war caused distress in Manchester and other British textile centers because it choked off the supply of cotton from the South and created unemployment for many textile workers. *CW,* VI, 65.

disfavor of foreign nations might have a material influence in enlarging and prolonging the struggle with disloyal men in which the country is engaged. A fair examination of history has seemed to authorize a belief that the past action and influences of the United States were generally regarded as having been beneficent towards mankind. I have therefore reckoned upon the forbearance of nations. Circumstances . . . induced me especially to expect that if justice and good faith should be practiced by the United States, they would encounter no hostile influence on the part of Great Britain.[47] It is now a pleasant duty to acknowledge the demonstration you have given of your desire that a spirit of peace and amity towards this country may prevail in the councils of your Queen, who is respected and esteemed in your own country only more than she is by the kindred nation which has its home on this side of the Atlantic.

I know and deeply deplore the sufferings which the workingmen at Manchester and in all Europe are called to endure in this crisis. It has been often and studiously represented that the attempt to overthrow this government, which was built upon the foundation of human rights, and to substitute for it one which should rest exclusively on the basis of human slavery, was likely to obtain the favor of Europe. Through the actions of our disloyal citizens the workingmen of Europe have been subjected to a severe trial, for the purpose of forcing their sanction to that attempt. Under these circumstances, I cannot but regard your decisive utterance upon the question as an instance of sublime Christian heroism which has not been surpassed in any age or in any country. It is, indeed, an energetic and reinspiring assurance of the inherent power of truth and of the ultimate and universal triumph of justice, humanity, and freedom. I do not doubt that the sentiments you have expressed will be sustained by your great nation, and, on the other hand, I have no hesitation in assuring you that they will excite admiration, esteem, and the most reciprocal feelings of friendship among the American people. I hail this interchange of sentiment, therefore, as an augury that, whatever else may happen, whatever misfortune may befall your country or my own, the peace and friendship which now exist between the two nations will be, as it shall be my desire to make them, perpetual.

ABRAHAM LINCOLN.

[47]Lincoln worried from the outset of the war that Britain might officially recognize the Confederacy and provide both aid and international respectability for the secessionists.

To replenish the army's manpower, Congress passed the nation's first draft law on March 3, 1863, bringing the war to the doorstep of nearly every household in the North. Each congressional district was required to supply a certain number of recruits, based on its population of men between twenty and forty-five years old. Since volunteers counted toward a district's quota, many places offered bounties to men who would enlist and thereby reduce the number of men subject to draft. To supplement the draft, Lincoln declared an amnesty for soldiers who were absent without leave and called on northern citizens to help enforce enlistments. When Erastus Corning, a prominent New York Democrat and president of the New York Central Railroad, led a group of New York Democrats in protest against what they termed Lincoln's "pretensions to more than regal authority,"[48] Lincoln responded with the following defense of his actions.

[48] *CW,* VI, 260.

Letter to Erastus Corning and Others
June 12, 1863

Executive Mansion,
Washington

Hon. Erastus Corning & others

Gentlemen   Your letter of May 19th. inclosing the resolutions of a public meeting held at Albany, N.Y. on the 16th. of the same month, was received several days ago.

The resolutions, as I understand them, are resolvable into two propositions—first, the expression of a purpose to sustain the cause of the Union, to secure peace through victory, and to support the administration in every constitutional, and lawful measure to suppress the rebellion; and secondly, a declaration of censure upon the administration for supposed unconstitutional action such as the making of military arrests.

And, from the two propositions a third is deduced, which is, that the gentlemen composing the meeting are resolved on doing their part to maintain our common government and country, despite the folly or wickedness, as they may conceive, of any administration. This position is eminently patriotic, and as such, I thank the meeting, and congratulate the nation for it. My own purpose is the same; so that the meeting and myself have a common object, and can have no difference, except in the choice of means or measures, for effecting that object.

And here I ought to close this paper, and would close it, if there were no apprehension that more injurious consequences, than any merely personal to myself, might follow the censures systematically cast upon me for doing what, in my view of duty, I could not forbear. The resolutions promise to support me in every constitutional and lawful measure to suppress the rebellion; and I have not knowingly employed, nor shall knowingly employ, any other. But the meeting, by their resolutions, assert and argue, that certain military arrests and proceedings following them for which I am ultimately responsible, are unconstitutional. I think they are not. The resolutions quote from the constitution, the definition of treason; and also the limiting safe-guards and guarrantees therein provided for the citizen, on trials for treason, and on his being held to answer for capital or otherwise infamous crimes, and, in criminal prossecutions, his right to a speedy and public trial by an impartial jury. They proceed to resolve "That these safe-guards of the rights of the citizen against the pretensions of arbitrary power, were intended more *especially* for his protection in times of civil commotion." And, apparantly, to demonstrate the proposition, the resolutions proceed "They were secured substantially to the English people, *after* years of protracted civil war, and were adopted into our constitution at the *close* of the revolution." Would not the demonstration have been better, if it could have been truly said that these safe-guards had been adopted, and applied *during* the civil wars and *during* our revolution, instead of *after* the one, and at the *close* of the other. I too am devotedly for them *after* civil war, and *before* civil war, and at all times "except when, in cases of Rebellion or Invasion, the public Safety may require" their suspension. The resolutions proceed to tell us that these safe-guards "have stood the test of seventysix years of trial, under our republican system, under circumstances which show that while they constitute the foundation of all free government, they are the elements of the enduring stability of the Republic." No one denies that they have so stood the test up to the beginning of the present rebellion . . . ; nor does any one question that they will stand the same test much longer after the rebellion closes. But these provisions of the constitution have no application to the case we have in hand, because the arrests complained of were not made for treason—that is, not for *the* treason defined in the constitution, and upon the conviction of which, the punishment is death—; nor yet were they made to hold persons to answer for any capital, or otherwise infamous crimes; nor were the proceedings following, in any constitutional or legal sense, "criminal prossecutions." The arrests were made on totally different grounds, and the proceedings following, accorded with the grounds of the arrests. Let us consider the real case with which we are dealing, and apply to it the parts of the constitution plainly made for such cases.

Prior to my instalation here it had been inculcated that any State had a lawful right to secede from the national Union; and that it would be expedient to exercise the right, whenever the devotees of the doctrine should fail to elect a President to their own liking. I was elected contrary to their liking; and accordingly, so far as it was legally possible, they had taken seven states out of the Union, had seized many of the United States Forts, and had fired upon the United States' Flag, all before I was inaugurated; and, of course, before I had done any official act whatever. The rebellion, thus began soon ran into the present civil war; and, in certain respects, it began on very unequal terms between the parties. The insurgents had been preparing for it more than thirty years, while the government had taken no steps to resist them. The former had carefully considered all the means which could be turned to their account. It undoubtedly was a well pondered reliance with them that in their own unrestricted effort to destroy Union, constitution, and law, all together, the government would, in great degree, be restrained by the same constitution and law, from arresting their progress. Their sympathizers pervaded all departments of the government, and nearly all communities of the people. From this material, under cover of "Liberty of speech" "Liberty of the press" and *"Habeas corpus"* they hoped to keep on foot amongst us a most efficient corps of spies, informers, supplyers, and aiders and abettors of their cause in a thousand ways. They knew that in times such as they were inaugerating, by the constitution itself, the "Habeas corpus" might be suspended; but they also knew they had friends who would make a question as to *who* was to suspend it; meanwhile their spies and others might remain at large to help on their cause. Or if, as has happened, the executive should suspend the writ, without ruinous waste of time, instances of arresting innocent persons might occur, as are always likely to occur in such cases; and then a clamor could be raised in regard to this, which might be, at least, of some service to the insurgent cause. It needed no very keen perception to discover this part of the enemies' programme, so soon as by open hostilities their machinery was fairly put in motion. Yet, thoroughly imbued with a reverence for the guarranteed rights of individuals, I was slow to adopt the strong measures, which by degrees I have been forced to regard as being within the exceptions of the constitution, and as indispensable to the public Safety. Nothing is better known to history than that courts of justice are utterly incompetent to such cases. Civil courts are organized chiefly for trials of individuals, or, at most, a few individuals acting in concert; and this in quiet times, and on charges of crimes well defined in the law. Even in times of peace, bands of horse-thieves and robbers frequently grow too numerous and powerful for the ordinary courts of justice. But what comparison, in numbers, have such bands ever borne to the insurgent sympathizers even in many of the loyal states? Again, a jury too frequently have at least one member, more ready to hang the panel than to hang the traitor. And yet again, he who dissuades one man from volunteering, or induces one soldier to desert, weakens the Union cause as much as he who kills a union soldier in battle. Yet this dissuasion, or inducement, may be so conducted as to be no defined crime of which any civil court would take cognizance.

Ours is a case of Rebellion—so called by the resolutions before me—in fact, a clear, flagrant, and gigantic case of Rebellion; and the provision of the constitution that "The previlege of the writ of Habeas Corpus shall not be suspended, unless when in cases of Rebellion or Invasion, the public Safety may require it" is *the* provision which specially applies to our present case. This provision plainly attests the understanding of those who made the constitution that ordinary courts of justice are inadequate to "cases of Rebellion"—attests their purpose that in such cases, men may be held in custody whom the courts acting on ordinary rules, would discharge. Habeas Corpus, does not discharge men who are proved to be guilty of defined crime; and its suspension is allowed by the constitution on purpose that, men may be arrested and held, who can not be proved to be guilty of defined crime, "when, in cases of Rebellion or Invasion the public Safety may require it." This is precisely our present case—a case of Rebellion, wherein the public Safety does require the suspension. Indeed, arrests by process of courts, and arrests in cases of rebellion, do not proceed altogether upon the same basis. The former is directed at the small per centage of ordinary and continuous perpetration of crime; while the latter is directed at sudden and extensive uprisings against the government, which, at most, will succeed or fail, in no great length of time. In the latter case, arrests are made, not so much for what has been done, as for what probably would be done. The latter is more for the preventive, and less for the vindictive, than the former. In such cases the purposes of men are much more easily understood, than in cases of ordinary crime. The man who stands by and says nothing, when the peril of his government is discussed, can not be misunderstood. If not hindered, he is sure to help the enemy. Much more, if he talks ambiguously—talks for his country with "buts" and "ifs" and "ands." Of how little value the constitutional provision I have quoted will be rendered, if arrests shall never be made until defined crimes shall have been committed, may be illustrated by a few notable examples. Gen. John C. Breckienridge, Gen. Robert E. Lee, Gen. Joseph E. Johnston, Gen. John B. Magruder, Gen. William B. Preston, Gen. Simon B. Buckner, and Comodore [Franklin] Buchanan, now occupying the very highest places in the rebel war service, were all within the power of the government since the rebellion began, and were nearly as well known to be traitors then as now. Unquestionably if we had seized and held them, the insurgent cause would be much weaker. But no one of them had then committed any crime defined in the law. Every one of them if arrested would have been discharged on Habeas Corpus, were the writ allowed to operate. In view of these and similar cases, I think the time not unlikely to come when I shall be blamed for having made too few arrests rather than too many.

By the third resolution the meeting indicate their opinion that military arrests may be constitutional in localities where rebellion actually exists; but that such arrests are unconstitutional in localities where rebellion, or insurrection, does not actually exist. They insist that such arrests shall not be made "outside of the lines of necessary military occupation, and the scenes of insurrection." In asmuch, however, as the constitution itself makes no such distinction, I am unable to believe that there is any such constitutional distinction. I concede that the class of arrests complained of, can be constitutional only when, in cases of Rebellion or Invasion, the public Safety may require them; and I insist that in such cases, they are constitutional *wherever* the public safety does require them—as well in places to which they may prevent the rebellion extending, as in those where it may be already prevailing—as well where they may restrain mischievous interference with the raising and supplying of armies, to suppress the rebellion, as where the rebellion may actually be—as well where they may restrain the enticing men out of the army, as where they would prevent mutiny in the army—equally constitutional at all places where they will conduce to the public Safety, as against the dangers of Rebellion or Invasion.

Take the particular case mentioned by the meeting. They assert in substance that Mr. [Clement] Vallandigham[49] was by a military commander, seized and tried "for no other reason than words addressed to a public meeting, in criticism of the course of the administration, and in condemnation of the military orders of that general." Now, if there be no mistake about this—if this assertion is the truth and the whole truth—if there was no other reason for the arrest, then I concede that the arrest was wrong. But the arrest, as I understand, was made for a very different reason. Mr. Vallandigham avows his hostility to the war on the part of the Union; and his arrest was made because he was laboring, with some effect, to prevent the raising of troops, to encourage desertions from the army, and to leave the rebellion without an adequate military force to suppress it. He was not arrested because he was damaging the political prospects of the administration, or the personal interests of the commanding general; but because he was damaging the army, upon the existence, and vigor of which, the life of the nation depends. He was warring upon the military; and this gave the military constitutional jurisdiction to lay hands upon him. If Mr. Vallandigham was not damaging the military power of the country, then his arrest was made on mistake of fact, which I would be glad to correct, on reasonably satisfactory evidence.

I understand the meeting, whose resolutions I am considering, to be in favor of suppressing the rebellion by military force—by armies. Long experience has shown that armies can not be maintained unless desertion shall be punished by the severe penalty of death. The case requires, and the law and the constitution, sanction this punishment. Must I shoot a simple-minded soldier boy who deserts, while I must not touch a hair of a wiley agitator who induces him to desert? This is none the less injurious when effected by getting a father, or brother, or friend, into a public meeting, and there working upon his feelings, till he is persuaded to write the soldier boy, that he is fighting in a bad cause, for a wicked administration of a contemptable government, too weak to arrest and punish him if he shall desert. I think that in such a case, to silence the agitator, and save the boy, is not only constitutional, but, withal, a great mercy.

If I be wrong on this question of constitutional power, my error lies in believing that certain proceedings are constitutional when, in cases of rebellion or Invasion, the public Safety requires them, which would not be constitutional when, in absence of rebellion or invasion, the public Safety does not require them—in other words, that the constitution is not in it's application

[49]Vallandigham, who sought to become the Democratic nominee for governor of Ohio, was a vehement opponent of the war and of emancipation. He was arrested on May 1, 1863, while advocating these ideas in a speech at Mount Vernon, Ohio.

in all respects the same, in cases of Rebellion or invasion, involving the public Safety, as it is in times of profound peace and public security. The constitution itself makes the distinction; and I can no more be persuaded that the government can constitutionally take no strong measure in time of rebellion, because it can be shown that the same could not be lawfully taken in time of peace, than I can be persuaded that a particular drug is not good medicine for a sick man, because it can be shown to not be good food for a well one. Nor am I able to appreciate the danger, apprehended by the meeting, that the American people will, by means of military arrests during the rebellion, lose the right of public discussion, the liberty of speech and the press, the law of evidence, trial by jury, and Habeas corpus, throughout the indefinite peaceful future which I trust lies before them, any more than I am able to believe that a man could contract so strong an appetite for emetics during temporary illness, as to persist in feeding upon them through the remainder of his healthful life.

In giving the resolutions that earnest consideration which you request of me, I can not overlook the fact that the meeting speak as "Democrats." Nor can I, with full respect for their known intelligence, and the fairly presumed deliberation with which they prepared their resolutions, be permitted to suppose that this occurred by accident, or in any way other than that they preferred to designate themselves "democrats" rather than "American citizens." In this time of national peril I would have preferred to meet you upon a level one step higher than any party platform; because I am sure that from such more elevated position, we could do better battle for the country we all love, than we possibly can from those lower ones, where from the force of habit, the prejudices of the past, and selfish hopes of the future, we are sure to expend much of our ingenuity and strength, in finding fault with, and aiming blows at each other. But since you have denied me this, I will yet be thankful, for the country's sake, that not all democrats have done so. He on whose discretionary judgment Mr. Vallandigham was arrested and tried, is a democrat,[50] having no old party affinity with me; and the judge[51] who rejected the constitutional view expressed in these resolutions, by refusing to discharge Mr. V. on Habeas Corpus, is a democrat of better days than these, having received his judicial mantle at the hands of President Jackson. And still more, of all those democrats who are nobly exposing their lives and shedding their blood on the battle-field, I have learned that many approve the course taken with Mr. V. while I have not heard of a single one condemning it. I can not assert that there are none such. . . .

And yet, let me say that in my own discretion, I do not know whether I would have ordered the arrest of Mr. V. While I can not shift the responsibility from myself, I hold that, as a general rule, the commander in the field is

[50]General Ambrose E. Burnside, a Democrat from Rhode Island, authorized Vallandigham's arrest.
[51]Judge Humphrey H. Leavitt of Ohio, a Democrat, ruled on Vallandigham's appeal.

the better judge of the necessity in any particular case. Of course I must practice a general directory and revisory power in the matter.

One of the resolutions expresses the opinion of the meeting that arbitrary arrests will have the effect to divide and distract those who should be united in suppressing the rebellion; and I am specifically called on to discharge Mr. Vallandigham. I regard this as, at least, a fair appeal to me, on the expediency of exercising a constitutional power which I think exists. In response to such appeal I have to say it gave me pain when I learned that Mr. V. had been arrested,—that is, I was pained that there should have seemed to be a necessity for arresting him—and that it will afford me great pleasure to discharge him so soon as I can, by any means, believe the public safety will not suffer by it.[52] I further say, that as the war progresses, it appears to me, opinion, and action, which were in great confusion at first, take shape, and fall into more regular channels; so that the necessity for arbitrary dealing with them gradually decreases. I have every reason to desire that it would cease altogether; and far from the least is my regard for the opinions and wishes of those who, like the meeting at Albany, declare their purpose to sustain the government in every constitutional and lawful measure to suppress the rebellion. Still, I must continue to do so much as may seem to be required by the public safety.

A. LINCOLN.

[52]In fact, Vallandigham's arrest embarrassed Lincoln. He quickly commuted Vallandigham's sentence of imprisonment and banished him to the Confederacy.

Like all presidents, Lincoln received countless requests for patronage appointments. In recognition of the great sacrifices being made by soldiers and their families, Lincoln urged Montgomery Blair, his postmaster general, to favor the requests of veterans. Such favors helped cement the loyalty of soldiers and their families to the Union cause.

Letter to Montgomery Blair

July 24, 1863

Executive Mansion,
Washington

Hon. Post-Master-General
Sir:
Yesterday little indorsements of mine went to you in two cases of Post-Masterships sought for widows whose husbands have fallen in the battles of this war. These cases occurring on the same day, brought me to reflect more

attentively than I had before done, as to what is fairly due from us here, in the dispensing of patronage, towards the men who, by fighting our battles, bear the chief burthen of saving our country. My conclusion is that, other claims and qualifications being equal, they have the better right; and this is especially applicable to the disabled soldier, and the deceased soldier's family.

Your Obt. Servt.

A. LINCOLN

Resistance to the draft broke out in communities across the North, especially where Democratic politicians denounced the war and emancipation. In New York City, resistance exploded into a full-scale riot on July 13, just as men were to be called for the draft. The rioters, many of them Irish laborers, pummeled any black person they could find, burned homes in black neighborhoods, and lynched several African Americans from lampposts. The riot continued for four days until order was restored by several regiments of Union soldiers who dashed from Pennsylvania, where they had fought at Gettysburg, to turn their weapons on fellow northerners. In all, more than one hundred people, mostly black Americans, died in the riots, and several hundred others suffered wounds. Above all, the New York riot illustrated that the draft could ignite a powder keg of political unrest, especially because drafted men would be fighting not just to restore the union of white people, but also to free black slaves. Fearing further disorder, New York governor Horatio Seymour, a rabidly anti-emancipation Democrat, petitioned Lincoln to suspend the draft in New York unless it became clear that volunteers alone would be insufficient to fill the state's quota.

Letter to Horatio Seymour

August 7, 1863

Executive Mansion,
Washington

His Excellency Horatio Seymour
Governor of New-York

... I can not consent to suspend the draft in New-York, as you request, because, among other reasons, *time* is too important....

I do not object to abide a decision of the United States Supreme Court, or of the judges thereof, on the constitutionality of the draft law. In fact, I should be willing to facilitate the obtaining of it; but I can not consent to lose the *time* while it is being obtained. We are contending with an enemy who, as I understand, drives every able bodied man he can reach, into his ranks, very much as a butcher drives bullocks into a slaughter-pen. No time is wasted, no argument is used. This produces an army which will soon turn upon our now victorious soldiers already in the field, if they shall not be sustained by recruits, as they should be. It produces an army with a rapidity not to be matched on our side, if we first waste time to re-experiment with the volunteer system, already deemed by congress, and palpably, in fact, so far exhausted, as to be inadequate; and then more time, to obtain a court decision, as to whether a law is constitutional, which requires a part of those not now in the service, to go to the aid of those who are already in it; and still more time, to determine with absolute certainty, that we get those, who are to go, in the precisely legal proportion, to those who are not to go.

My purpose is to be, in my action, just and constitutional; and yet practical, in performing the important duty, with which I am charged, of maintaining the unity, and the free principles of our common country.

Your Obt. Servt.
A. LINCOLN.

Lincoln took advantage of an invitation to address a Republican rally in Springfield, Illinois, to send a public letter that mounted a spirited defense of his policies.

Letter to James C. Conkling
August 26, 1863

Executive Mansion,
Washington

Hon. James C. Conkling[53]
My Dear Sir.
Your letter inviting me to attend a mass-meeting of unconditional Union-men, to be held at the Capital of Illinois, on the 3d day of September, has been received.

It would be very agreeable to me, to thus meet my old friends, at my own home; but I can not, just now, be absent from here, so long as a visit there, would require.

---

[53]James C. Conkling, a lawyer and ardent Republican in Springfield, Illinois, had been Lincoln's friend for many years.

The meeting is to be of all those who maintain unconditional devotion to the Union; and I am sure my old political friends will thank me for tendering, as I do, the nation's gratitude to those other noble men, whom no partizan malice, or partizan hope, can make false to the nation's life.

There are those who are dissatisfied with me. To such I would say: You desire peace; and you blame me that we do not have it. But how can we attain it? There are but three conceivable ways. First, to suppress the rebellion by force of arms. This, I am trying to do. Are you for it? If you are, so far we are agreed. If you are not for it, a second way is, to give up the Union. I am against this. Are you for it? If you are, you should say so plainly. If you are not for *force,* nor yet for *dissolution,* there only remains some imaginable *compromise.* I do not believe any compromise, embracing the maintenance of the Union, is now possible. All I learn, leads to a directly opposite belief. The strength of the rebellion, is its military—its army. That army dominates all the country, and all the people, within its range. Any offer of terms made by any man or men within that range, in opposition to that army, is simply nothing for the present; because such man or men, have no power whatever to enforce their side of a compromise, if one were made with them. To illustrate—Suppose refugees from the South, and peace men of the North, get together in convention, and frame and proclaim a compromise embracing a restoration of the Union; in what way can that compromise be used to keep Lee's army out of Pennsylvania? Meade's army can keep Lee's army out of Pennsylvania; and, I think, can ultimately drive it out of existence. But no paper compromise, to which the controllers of Lee's army are not agreed, can, at all, affect that army. In an effort at such compromise we should waste time, which the enemy would improve to our disadvantage; and that would be all. A compromise, to be effective, must be made either with those who control the rebel army, or with the people first liberated from the domination of that army, by the success of our own army. Now allow me to assure you, that no word or intimation, from that rebel army, or from any of the men controlling it, in relation to any peace compromise, has ever come to my knowledge or belief. All charges and insinuations to the contrary, are deceptive and groundless. And I promise you, that if any such proposition shall hereafter come, it shall not be rejected, and kept a secret from you. I freely acknowledge myself the servant of the people, according to the bond of service—the United States constitution; and that, as such, I am responsible to them.

But, to be plain, you[54] are dissatisfied with me about the negro. Quite likely there is a difference of opinion between you and myself upon that subject. I certainly wish that all men could be free, while I suppose you do not. Yet I have neither adopted, nor proposed any measure, which is not consistent with even your view, provided you are for the Union. I suggested com-

---

[54]Here and subsequently, Lincoln is referring to those who oppose his policies.

pensated emancipation, to which you replied you wished not to be taxed to buy negroes. But I had not asked you to be taxed to buy negroes, except in such way, as to save you from greater taxation to save the Union exclusively by other means.

You dislike the emancipation proclamation; and, perhaps, would have it retracted. You say it is unconstitutional—I think differently. I think the constitution invests its commander-in-chief, with the law of war, in time of war. The most that can be said, if so much, is, that slaves are property. Is there—has there ever been—any question that by the law of war, property, both of enemies and friends, may be taken when needed? And is it not needed when ever taking it, helps us, or hurts the enemy? Armies, the world over, destroy enemies' property when they can not use it; and even destroy their own to keep it from the enemy. Civilized belligerents do all in their power to help themselves, or hurt the enemy, except a few things regarded as barbarous or cruel. Among the exceptions are the massacre of vanquished foes, and non-combatants, male and female.

But the proclamation, as law, either is valid, or is not valid. If it is not valid, it needs no retraction. If it is valid, it can not be retracted, any more than the dead can be brought to life. Some of you profess to think its retraction would operate favorably for the Union. Why better *after* the retraction, than *before* the issue? There was more than a year and a half of trial to suppress the rebellion before the proclamation issued, the last one hundred days of which passed under an explicit notice[55] that it was coming, unless averted by those in revolt, returning to their allegiance. The war has certainly progressed as favorably for us, since the issue of the proclamation as before. I know as fully as one can know the opinions of others, that some of the commanders of our armies in the field who have given us our most important successes, believe the emancipation policy, and the use of colored troops, constitute the heaviest blow yet dealt to the rebellion; and that, at least one of those important successes, could not have been achieved when it was, but for the aid of black soldiers. Among the commanders holding these views are some who have never had any affinity with what is called abolitionism, or with republican party politics; but who hold them purely as military opinions. I submit these opinions as being entitled to some weight against the objections, often urged, that emancipation, and arming the blacks, are unwise as military measures, and were not adopted, as such, in good faith.

You say you will not fight to free negroes. Some of them seem willing to fight for you; but, no matter. Fight you, then, exclusively to save the Union. I issued the proclamation on purpose to aid you in saving the Union. Whenever you shall have conquered all resistance to the Union, if I shall urge you to continue fighting, it will be an apt time, then, for you to declare you will not fight to free negroes.

[55] That is, the preliminary Emancipation Proclamation issued September 22, 1862.

I thought that in your struggle for the Union, to whatever extent the negroes should cease helping the enemy, to that extent it weakened the enemy in his resistance to you. Do you think differently? I thought that whatever negroes can be got to do as soldiers, leaves just so much less for white soldiers to do, in saving the Union. Does it appear otherwise to you? But negroes, like other people, act upon motives. Why should they do any thing for us, if we will do nothing for them? If they stake their lives for us, they must be prompted by the strongest motive—even the promise of freedom. And the promise being made, must be kept.

The signs look better. The Father of Waters[56] again goes unvexed to the sea. Thanks to the great North-West for it. Nor yet wholly to them. Three hundred miles up, they met New-England, Empire, Key-Stone, and Jersey, hewing their way right and left.[57] The Sunny South too, in more colors than one, also lent a hand. On the spot, their part of the history was jotted down in black and white. The job was a great national one; and let none be banned who bore an honorable part in it. And while those who have cleared the great river may well be proud, even that is not all. It is hard to say that anything has been more bravely, and well done, than at Antietam, Murfreesboro, Gettysburg, and on many fields of lesser note. Nor must Uncle Sam's Web-feet[58] be forgotten. At all the watery margins they have been present. Not only on the deep sea, the broad bay, and the rapid river, but also up the narrow muddy bayou, and wherever the ground was a little damp, they have been, and made their tracks. Thanks to all. For the great republic—for the principle it lives by, and keeps alive—for man's vast future,—thanks to all.

Peace does not appear so distant as it did. I hope it will come soon, and come to stay; and so come as to be worth the keeping in all future time. It will then have been proved that, among free men, there can be no successful appeal from the ballot to the bullet; and that they who take such appeal are sure to lose their case, and pay the cost. And then, there will be some black men who can remember that, with silent tongue, and clenched teeth, and steady eye, and well-poised bayonet, they have helped mankind on to this great consummation; while, I fear, there will be some white ones, unable to forget that, with malignant heart, and deceitful speech, they have strove to hinder it.

Still let us not be over-sanguine of a speedy final triumph. Let us be quite sober. Let us diligently apply the means, never doubting that a just God, in his own good time, will give us the rightful result.

Yours very truly
A. LINCOLN.

[56] That is, the Mississippi River.

[57] Lincoln is referring to Union regiments from the different regions and states of the North responsible for the great victories during the summer.

[58] That is, the Union navy.

Lincoln believed that although the draft was undesirable, it was absolutely necessary to maintain the strength of the Union army and ultimately to win the war. He prepared the following defense of the draft—evidently for a public speech or letter; it was discussed by his cabinet but never made public. On September 15, Lincoln suspended the writ of habeas corpus throughout the country for any person drafted or currently serving in uniform, in order to prevent state officials hostile to the war from using writs to release men from military service.

Opinion on the Draft
September 14?, 1863

It is at all times proper that misunderstanding between the public and the public servant should be avoided; and this is far more important now, than in times of peace and tranquility. I therefore address you without searching for a precedent upon which to do so. Some of you are sincerely devoted to the republican institutions, and territorial integrity of our country, and yet are opposed to what is called the draft, or conscription.

At the beginning of the war, and ever since, a variety of motives pressing, some in one direction and some in the other, would be presented to the mind of each man physically fit for a soldier, upon the combined effect of which motives, he would, or would not, voluntarily enter the service. Among these motives would be patriotism, political bias, ambition, personal courage, love of adventure, want of employment, and convenience, or the opposites of some of these. We already have, and have had in the service, as appears, substantially all that can be obtained upon this voluntary weighing of motives. And yet we must somehow obtain more, or relinquish the original object of the contest, together with all the blood and treasure already expended in the effort to secure it. To meet this necessity the law for the draft has been enacted. You who do not wish to be soldiers, do not like this law. This is natural; nor does it imply want of patriotism. Nothing can be so just, and necessary, as to make us like it, if it is disagreeable to us. We are prone, too, to find false arguments with which to excuse ourselves for opposing such disagreeable things. In this case those who desire the rebellion to succeed, and others who seek reward in a different way, are very active in accomodating us with this class of arguments. They tell us the law is unconstitutional. It is the first instance, I believe, in which the power of congress to do a thing has ever been questioned, in a case when the power is given by the constitution in express terms. Whether a power can be implied, when it is not expressed, has often been the subject of controversy; but this is the first case in which the degree of effrontery has been ventured upon, of denying a power which is plainly and distinctly written down in the constitution. The constitution declares that "The congress shall have power ... To raise and support armies; but no appropriation of money to that use shall be for a longer term than two years." The whole scope of the conscription act is "to raise and support armies." There is nothing else in it.... The power is given fully, completely, unconditionally. It is not a power to raise armies *if* State authorities consent; nor *if* the men to compose the armies are entirely willing; but it is a power to raise and support armies given to congress by the constitution, without an if.

It is clear that a constitutional law may not be expedient or proper. Such would be a law to raise armies when no armies were needed. But this is not such. The republican institutions, and territorial integrity of our country can not be maintained without the further raising and supporting of armies. There can be no army without men. Men can be had only voluntarily, or involuntarily. We have ceased to obtain them voluntarily; and to obtain them involuntarily, is the draft—the conscription. If you dispute the fact, and declare that men can still be had voluntarily in sufficient numbers prove the assertion by yourselves volunteering in such numbers, and I shall gladly give up the draft. Or if not a sufficient number, but any one of you will volunteer, he for his single self, will escape all the horrors of the draft; and will thereby do only what each one of at least a million of his manly brethren have already done. Their toil and blood have been given as much for you as for themselves. Shall it all be lost rather than you too, will bear your part?

I do not say that all who would avoid serving in the war, are unpatriotic; but I do think every patriot should willingly take his chance under a law made with great care in order to secure entire fairness. This law was considered, discussed, modified, and amended, by congress, at great length, and with much labor; and was finally passed, by both branches, with a near approach to unanimity....

Much complaint is made of that provision of the conscription law which allows a drafted man to substitute three hundred dollars for himself;[59] while, as I believe, none[60] is made of that provision which allows him to substitute another man for himself. Nor is the three hundred dollar provision objected to for unconstitutionality; but for inequality—for favoring the rich against

[59] The draft law allowed a drafted man two ways to avoid serving in the military: pay a $300 commutation fee or find a substitute, another man willing to serve in the drafted man's place. The vast majority of drafted men paid the commutation fee; beginning in October 1863 the government used these fees to finance a bounty of $300 for volunteers and soldiers who re-enlisted. About seventy-five thousand other drafted men obtained substitutes. In all, fewer than fifty thousand draftees actually served in uniform—or about 7 percent of those who were drafted—a measure of the strong popular opposition to the draft.

[60] That is, no complaint.

the poor. The substitution of men is the provision if any, which favors the rich to the exclusion of the poor. But this being a provision in accordance with an old and well known practice, in the raising of armies, is not objected to. . . . It is true that by this law a some what larger number will escape than could under a law allowing personal substitutes only; but each additional man thus escaping will be [a] poorer man than could have escaped by the law in the other form. The money provision enlarges the class of exempts from actual service simply by admitting poorer men into it. How, then can this money provision be a wrong to the poor man? . . .

The principle of the draft, which simply is involuntary, or enforced service, is not new. It has been practiced in all ages of the world. It was well known to the framers of our constitution as one of the modes of raising armies, at the time they placed in that instrument the provision that "the congress shall have power to raise and support armies." It has been used, just before, in establishing our independence; and it was also used under the constitution in 1812. Wherein is the peculiar hardship now? Shall we shrink from the necessary means to maintain our free government, which our grandfathers employed to establish it, and our own fathers have already employed once to maintain it? Are we degenerate? Has the manhood of our race run out? . . .

With these views, and on these principles, I feel bound to tell you it is my purpose to see the draft law faithfully executed.

Lincoln crystallized his thoughts about the historical significance of the war in his brief speech at the dedication of the massive military cemetery at Gettysburg. Eventually recognized as the most eloquent speech ever given by an American president, the Gettysburg Address explained Lincoln's view of why the war must go on, despite the horrendous sacrifices of life and limb. Without mentioning slavery, the address answered those who were tired of the war and were opposed to emancipation by proclaiming that the soldiers at Gettysburg died to defend democracy and to give the nation "a new birth of freedom." Lincoln ennobled the Union cause by attaching the profession of human equality in the Declaration of Independence to both the Union and the war. The address fused his war goals of Union and freedom with equality.

Four score and seven years ago our fathers brought forth upon this continent, a new nation, conceived in Liberty, and dedicated to the proposition that all men are created equal.

Now we are engaged in a great civil war, testing whether that nation, or any nation so conceived, and so dedicated, can long endure. We are met on a great battle-field of that war. We have come to dedicate a portion of that field, as a final resting place for those who here gave their lives, that that nation might live. It is altogether fitting and proper that we should do this.

But, in a larger sense, we can not dedicate— we can not consecrate— we can not hallow— this ground. The brave men, living and dead, who struggled here, have consecrated it, far above our poor power to add or detract. The world will little note, nor long remember, what we say here, but it can never forget what they did here. It is for us the living, rather, to be dedicated here to the unfinished work which they who fought here, have, thus far, so nobly advanced. It is rather for us to be here dedicated to the great task remaining before

us— that from these honored dead we take increased devotion to that cause for which they here gave the last full measure of devotion— that we here highly resolve that these dead shall not have died in vain— that this nation, under God, shall have a new birth of freedom— and that, government of the people, by the people, for the people, shall not perish from the earth.

The Gettysburg Address

November 19, 1863

Four score and seven years ago our fathers brought forth on this continent, a new nation, conceived in Liberty, and dedicated to the proposition that all men are created equal.

Now we are engaged in a great civil war, testing whether that nation, or any nation so conceived and so dedicated, can long endure. We are met on a great battle-field of that war. We have come to dedicate a portion of that field, as a final resting place for those who here gave their lives that that nation might live. It is altogether fitting and proper that we should do this.

But, in a larger sense, we can not dedicate—we can not consecrate—we can not hallow—this ground. The brave men, living and dead, who struggled here, have consecrated it, far above our poor power to add or detract. The world will little note, nor long remember what we say here, but it can never forget what they did here. It is for us the living, rather, to be dedicated here to the unfinished work which they who fought here have thus far so nobly advanced. It is rather for us to be here dedicated to the great task remaining before us—that from these honored dead we take increased devotion to that cause for which they gave the last full measure of devotion—that we here highly resolve that these dead shall not have died in vain—that this nation, under God, shall have a new birth of freedom—and that government of the people, by the people, for the people, shall not perish from the earth.

ABRAHAM LINCOLN.

Figure 7. The Gettysburg Address

Lincoln wrote out this neat copy of his most famous speech for publication and sale by the U.S. Sanitary Commission in 1864 to raise funds to aid Union soldiers. It differs slightly from the so-called final text above. Five copies of the Gettysburg Address in Lincoln's handwriting still exist, but none has been conclusively identified as the one he held in his hand when he delivered the address.

9

Defending a New Birth of Freedom

For Lincoln, defending the nation's new birth of freedom required action on three closely related fronts. First, the Union army had to make progress on the battlefield. But the army could not be reinforced with the necessary men and supplies unless the increasingly war-weary people of the North supported Lincoln's determination to fight to restore the Union without slavery. In regions of the Confederacy occupied by the Union army, a second front demanded attention. Some pathway needed to be marked out for bringing seceded states back into the Union without empowering rebels—thereby undermining rather than reuniting the nation—or violating the pledge of freedom to millions of slaves. Any plan for reconstruction of the Union consistent with a new birth of freedom depended, of course, on the success of federal armies and the willingness of northern citizens to insist that reunion could only be achieved without slavery. The third front lay along the partisan divide within the northern electorate. Lincoln had to defend his Republican vision of the Union reunited by defeating Confederate armies against some Democrats' promise to stop the war and restore the Union as it was, with slavery. Unless the Union army achieved military victory by Election Day in November 1864, a new birth of freedom for the nation depended upon Lincoln's re-election to a second term. Lincoln had to match his generals' military strategy with his own adroit maneuvers through dangerous political terrain.

WAR WITHOUT END

Even after the failure of General Robert E. Lee's invasion of the North in the summer of 1863, the military strategy of the Confederacy focused ultimately on peace sentiment in the North. If Confederate armies could continue to inflict heavy casualties on Union forces and prolong the war, then northern citizens might decide that it was preferable to stop fighting and to recognize Confederate independence. Confederate armies did not necessarily need to win battles to contribute to this strategy. They had to stay intact, adopt a largely defensive posture, and maintain their ability to send potent political messages northward in the reports of Union men killed and wounded. At bottom, the Confederacy gambled that the awful arithmetic that heartened Lincoln (see the introduction to Chapter 8) would instead demoralize the northern people.

Lincoln understood that time favored the Confederate strategy, especially if the Union army could not make readily visible progress in capturing rebel strongholds and destroying southern armies. The North's superior resources of manpower and supplies would not matter if northerners decided that the war was not worth fighting, that they had had enough of sacrificing their men to a war with no end in sight. Lincoln needed victories now to reassure northern families that the war would end soon, before they were willing to accept peace at the price of Confederate independence.

After his spectacular success at Vicksburg, General Grant took command of federal forces in eastern Tennessee and, in a series of complex and hard-fought engagements, succeeded in driving Confederate defenders from Chattanooga and Knoxville. Grant's multiple victories earned him fame throughout the North and made him an obvious choice to become commander of all Union armies. In February, Congress revived the rank of lieutenant general, last held by George Washington, and early in March Lincoln promoted Grant to that rank and made him general in chief, second in command only to the president. Grant quickly moved his headquarters from the West to the Virginia theater and prepared for a campaign to replicate his western successes in the east. When Grant came to Washington to receive his promotion, Lincoln held a small ceremony in his office and made the following remarks in the presence of his cabinet and a few others.

Speech to Ulysses S. Grant
March 9, 1864

General Grant

The nation's appreciation of what you have done, and it's reliance upon you for what remains to do, in the existing great struggle, are now presented with this commission, constituting you Lieutenant General in the Army of the United States. With this high honor devolves upon you also, a corresponding responsibility. As the country herein trusts you, so, under God, it will sustain you. I scarcely need to add that with what I here speak for the nation goes my own hearty personal concurrence.

Lincoln's confidence in Grant—in contrast, for example, to his previous doubts about Generals McClellan and Hooker—could hardly have been expressed more forthrightly than in the following letter, written shortly before the start of Grant's campaign.

Letter to Ulysses S. Grant

April 30, 1864

Executive Mansion,
Washington

Lieutenant General Grant.

Not expecting to see you again before the Spring campaign opens, I wish to express, in this way, my entire satisfaction with what you have done up to this time, so far as I understand it. The particulars of your plans I neither know, or seek to know. You are vigilant and self-reliant; and, pleased with this, I wish not to obtrude any constraints or restraints upon you. While I am very anxious that any great disaster, or the capture of our men in great numbers, shall be avoided, I know these points are less likely to escape your attention than they would be mine. If there is anything wanting which is within my power to give, do not fail to let me know it.

And now with a brave Army, and a just cause, may God sustain you.

Yours very truly
A. LINCOLN

Grant's plan called for an attack by all Union armies to begin on May 5. A simultaneous assault across the entire line from Virginia to Mississippi was intended to immobilize Confederate defenders and to prevent reinforcements from being shifted to repulse major Union offensives. When Grant explained his plan, Lincoln—who had advocated the concept for a long time—declared, "As we say out West, if a man can't skin he must hold a leg while somebody else does."[1] Confederate armies, however, did not hold still to be skinned; they fought back fiercely.

[1] Ulysses S. Grant, *Personal Memoirs of U. S. Grant* (2 vols.; New York, 1885–86), II, 143.

Figure 8.   General Grant at City Point, Virginia

This photograph, taken during the siege of Petersburg, Virginia, between mid-June 1864 and early April 1865, portrays Grant wearing the insignia of his rank but obviously not concerned with a spit-and-polish image. It conveys Grant's relentless focus and composure, so admired by Lincoln.

Grant, like other commanders before him in the Virginia theater, became bogged down. Between May 15 and 19, the ferocity and skill of Confederate defenders turned back Yankee attacks in the Wilderness—a heavily wooded region about fifteen miles west of Fredericksburg—and at Spottsylvania—about ten miles southeast of the Wilderness. During these two weeks, Grant suffered more than thirty thousand casualties. But unlike other commanders in the East, Grant did not retreat. He continued to engage Lee's army, relentlessly moving southeast toward Richmond. In early June at Cold Harbor about ten miles outside the city, Lee inflicted another bloody defeat on Grant's men. Grant then moved most of his army south of Richmond to attack Petersburg. After the failure of his initial assaults on Petersburg's defenses, Grant settled into a siege by June 18. For the next ten months, Grant besieged the city, largely immobilizing both Lee's army and his own. By mid-August, with the November presidential election on the horizon, the discouraging reports from the battlefield and the continuing draft created great unease in the North.

PLANNING RECONSTRUCTION

Union military successes in the Mississippi Valley during the summer of 1863 presented Lincoln with an opportunity to design a plan for bringing rebel states back into the Union, a plan he continued to promote for the remainder of his presidency. In theory, any such plan contradicted Lincoln's refusal to recognize secession as a reality. In practice, however, Lincoln knew that he could not permit rebel states that had been conquered by the federal army to come back into the Union as if nothing had happened and to continue to fight politically for what they had lost on the battlefield. Lincoln proposed that, as a prerequisite for the restoration of a rebel state to the Union, a small core of loyal unionists would adopt a new state constitution that recognized emancipation. Lincoln was willing to allow the reconstructed states a great deal of latitude in defining the new status of former slaves. By setting a relatively low and minimally punitive threshold for readmission, Lincoln hoped to show Confederates that, if they stopped fighting, it would be fairly easy and painless for them to regain their former status in the Union. Lincoln was also fully aware that, if new state governments were formed by unionists, the elected officials from those states would likely be Republicans who—not coincidentally—would support his policies and his re-election to a second term. Lincoln's plan for reconstruction would both restore the Union

and strengthen Republican control of the federal government by supplement-
ing northern Republicans with newly hatched southern Republicans. Design-
ing such a plan, however, proved easier than implementing it.

Letter to Nathaniel P. Banks
August 5, 1863

Executive Mansion,
Washington

My dear General Banks[2]
Being a poor correspondent is the only apology I offer for not having sooner
tendered my thanks for your very successful, and very valuable military
operations this year. The final stroke in opening the Mississippi never
should, and I think never will, be forgotten. . . .

Governor Boutwell[3] read me to-day that part of your letter to him, which
relates to Louisiana affairs. While I very well know what I would be glad for
Louisiana to do, it is quite a different thing for me to assume direction of the
matter. I would be glad for her to make a new Constitution recognizing the
emancipation proclamation, and adopting emancipation in those parts of the
state to which the proclamation does not apply.[4] And while she is at it, I
think it would not be objectionable for her to adopt some practical system by
which the two races could gradually live themselves out of their old relation
to each other, and both come out better prepared for the new. Education for
young blacks should be included in the plan. After all, the power, or element,
of "contract" may be sufficient for this probationary period; and, by it's sim-
plicity, and flexibility, may be the better.[5]

As an anti-slavery man I have a motive to desire emancipation, which
pro-slavery men do not have; but even they have strong enough reason to
thus place themselves again under the shield of the Union; and to thus per-
petually hedge against the recurrence of the scenes through which we are
now passing.

[2]General Banks, a former governor of Massachusetts and a prominent Republican, had
commanded the Union force that captured Port Hudson, Louisiana, on July 9, 1863, finally
eliminating the last Confederate choke point on the Mississippi River. He currently commanded the Department of the Gulf, which included Louisiana.
[3]George S. Boutwell, a former governor of Massachusetts and a fervently antislavery
Republican, was elected to the Congress in 1863.
[4]The Emancipation Proclamation did not apply to those parts of Louisiana under the control of the Union army on January 1, 1863, which included New Orleans and surrounding
parishes.
[5]In other words, Lincoln is suggesting that former slaves may enter into contracts to work
for white people. In theory, the legal limits of written contracts, mutually agreed upon, would
replace the almost limitless coercions of slavery.

Gov. Shepley[6] has informed me that Mr. Durant[7] is now taking a registry, with a view to the election of a Constitutional convention in Louisiana. This, to me, appears proper. If such convention were to ask my views, I could present little else than what I now say to you. I think the thing should be pushed forward, so that if possible, it's mature work may reach here by the meeting of Congress.

For my own part I think I shall not, in any event, retract the emancipation proclamation; nor, as executive, ever return to slavery any person who is free by the terms of that proclamation, or by any of the acts of Congress.

If Louisiana shall send members to Congress, their admission to seats will depend, as you know, upon the respective Houses, and not upon the President.

If these views can be of any advantage in giving shape, and impetus, to action there, I shall be glad for you to use them prudently for that object. Of course you will confer with intelligent and trusty citizens of the State.... Still it is perhaps better to not make the letter generally public.

Yours very truly
A. LINCOLN

[6]George F. Shepley, a Union general who had been a well-known lawyer in Maine, was appointed military governor of Louisiana by Lincoln in June 1862.

[7]Thomas J. Durant was attorney general of Louisiana. Lincoln was informed that Durant was registering voters who would participate in electing delegates to a state constitutional convention.

Letter to Andrew Johnson

September 11, 1863

Private

Executive Mansion,
Washington

Hon. Andrew Johnson:[8]
My dear Sir:
All Tennessee is now clear of armed insurrectionists. You need not to be reminded that it is the nick of time for re-inaugerating a loyal State government. Not a moment should be lost. You, and the co-operating friends there, can better judge of the ways and means, than can be judged by any here. I only offer a few suggestions. The re-inauguration must not be such as to give control of the State, and it's representation in Congress, to the enemies of the Union, driving it's friends there into political exile. The whole struggle for Tennessee will have been profitless to both State and Nation, if it so ends

[8]Andrew Johnson was serving as military governor of Tennessee.

that Gov. Johnson[9] is put down, and Gov. Harris[10] is put up. It must not be so. You must have it otherwise. Let the reconstruction be the work of such men only as can be trusted for the Union. Exclude all others, and trust that your government, so organized, will be recognized here, as being the one of republican form,[11] to be guarranteed to the state, and to be protected against invasion and domestic violence.

It is something on the question of *time,* to remember that it can not be known who is next to occupy the position I now hold, nor what he will do.

I see that you have declared in favor of emancipation in Tennessee, for which, may God bless you. Get emancipation into your new State government—Constitution—and there will be no such word as fail for your case.

The raising of colored troops I think will greatly help every way.

Yours very truly
A. LINCOLN

[9]That is, Andrew Johnson.
[10]Isham G. Harris, the Democratic governor of Tennessee at the time of the secession crisis, supported the Confederacy.
[11]Lincoln is referring not to the Republican party but to the federal Constitution's guarantee of a republican form of government.

Letter to Nathaniel P. Banks
November 5, 1863

Executive Mansion,
Washington

Major General Banks

Three months ago to-day I wrote you about Louisiana affairs, stating, on the word of Gov. Shepley, as I understood him, that Mr. Durant was taking a registry of Citizens, preparatory to the election of a constitutional convention for that State. I sent a copy of the letter to Mr. Durant; and I now have his letter, written two months after, acknowledging receipt, and saying he is not taking such registry; and he does not let me know that he personally is expecting to do so. Mr. Flanders,[12] to whom I also sent a copy, is now here, and he says nothing has yet been done. This disappoints me bitterly; yet I do not throw blame on you or on them. I do however, urge both you and them, to lose no more time. Gov. Shepley has special instructions from the War Department. I wish him—these gentlemen and others co-operating—without waiting for more territory, to go to work and give me a tangible nucleus which the remainder of the State may rally around as fast as it can, and

[12]Benjamin F. Flanders was a unionist resident of New Orleans who took a leading role in trying to organize a new state government.

which I can at once recognize and sustain as the true State government. And in that work I wish you, and all under your command, to give them a hearty sympathy and support. The instruction to Gov. Shepley bases the movement (and rightfully too) upon the loyal element. Time is important. There is danger, even now, that the adverse element seeks insidiously to pre-occupy the ground. If a few professedly loyal men shall draw the disloyal about them, and colorably set up a State government, repudiating the emancipation proclamation, and re-establishing slavery, I can not recognize or sustain their work. I should fall powerless in the attempt. This government, in such an attitude, would be a house divided against itself. I have said, and say again, that if a new State government, acting in harmony with this government, and consistently with general freedom, shall think best to adopt a reasonable temporary arrangement, in relation to the landless and homeless freed people, I do not object; but my word is out to be *for* and not *against* them on the question of their permanent freedom. I do not insist upon such temporary arrangement, but only say such would not be objectionable to me.

Yours very truly
A. LINCOLN.

In his annual address to Congress in December 1863, Lincoln reviewed military and political developments during the last year and publicly outlined his plans for reconstruction. He explained that he believed rebels should be required to take an oath to uphold both the federal constitution and emancipation and that such a requirement was within his constitutional authority.

Annual Message to Congress
December 8, 1863

... When Congress assembled a year ago the war had already lasted nearly twenty months, and there had been many conflicts on both land and sea, with varying results.

The rebellion had been pressed back into reduced limits; yet the tone of public feeling and opinion, at home and abroad, was not satisfactory. With other signs, the popular elections, then just past, indicated uneasiness among ourselves, while amid much that was cold and menacing the kindest words coming from Europe were uttered in accents of pity, that we were too blind to surrender a hopeless cause. Our commerce was suffering greatly by a few armed vessels built upon and furnished from foreign shores, and we were threatened with such additions from the same quarter as would sweep our trade from the sea and raise our blockade. We had failed to elicit from European governments anything hopeful upon this subject. The preliminary emancipation proclamation, issued in September, was running its assigned period to the beginning of the new year. A month later the final proclamation came, including the announcement that colored men of suitable condition would be received into the war service. The policy of emancipation, and of employing black soldiers, gave to the future a new aspect, about which hope, and fear, and doubt contended in uncertain conflict. According to our political system, as a matter of civil administration, the general government had no lawful power to effect emancipation in any State, and for a long time it had been hoped that the rebellion could be suppressed without resorting to it as a military measure. It was all the while deemed possible that the necessity for it might come, and that if it should, the crisis of the contest would then be presented. It came, and as was anticipated, it was followed by dark and doubtful days. Eleven months having now passed, we are permitted to take another review. The rebel borders are pressed still further back, and by the complete opening of the Mississippi the country dominated by the rebellion is divided into distinct parts, with no practical communication between them. Tennessee and Arkansas have been substantially cleared of insurgent control, and influential citizens in each, owners of slaves and advocates of slavery at the beginning of the rebellion, now declare openly for emancipation in their respective States. Of those States not included in the emancipation proclamation, Maryland, and Missouri, neither of which three years ago would tolerate any restraint upon the extension of slavery into new territories, only dispute now as to the best mode of removing it within their own limits.

Of those who were slaves at the beginning of the rebellion, full one hundred thousand are now in the United States military service, about one-half of which number actually bear arms in the ranks; thus giving the double advantage of taking so much labor from the insurgent cause, and supplying the places which otherwise must be filled with so many white men. So far as tested, it is difficult to say they are not as good soldiers as any. No servile insurrection, or tendency to violence or cruelty, has marked the measures of emancipation and arming the blacks. These measures have been much discussed in foreign countries, and contemporary with such discussion the tone of public sentiment there is much improved. At home the same measures have been fully discussed, supported, criticised, and denounced, and the annual elections following are highly encouraging to those whose official duty it is to bear the country through this great trial. Thus we have the new reckoning. The crisis which threatened to divide the friends of the Union is past.

Looking now to the present and future, and with reference to a resumption of the national authority within the States wherein that authority has been suspended, I have thought fit to issue a proclamation, a copy of which is herewith transmitted. On examination of this proclamation it will appear, as is believed, that nothing is attempted beyond what is amply justified by the Constitution. True, the form of an oath is given, but no man is coerced to take it. The man is only promised a pardon in case he voluntarily takes the oath. The Constitution authorizes the Executive to grant or withhold the pardon at his own absolute discretion; and this includes the power to grant on terms, as is fully established by judicial and other authorities.

It is also proffered that if, in any of the States named, a State government shall be, in the mode prescribed, set up, such government shall be recognized and guarantied by the United States, and that under it the State shall, on the constitutional conditions, be protected against invasion and domestic violence. The constitutional obligation of the United States to guaranty to every State in the Union a republican form of government, and to protect the State, in the cases stated, is explicit and full. But why tender the benefits of this provision only to a State government set up in this particular way? This section of the Constitution contemplates a case wherein the element within a State, favorable to republican government, in the Union, may be too feeble for an opposite and hostile element external to, or even within the State; and such are precisely the cases with which we are now dealing.

An attempt to guaranty and protect a revived State government, constructed in whole, or in preponderating part, from the very element against whose hostility and violence it is to be protected, is simply absurd. There must be a test by which to separate the opposing elements, so as to build only from the sound; and that test is a sufficiently liberal one, which accepts as sound whoever will make a sworn recantation of his former unsoundness.

But if it be proper to require, as a test of admission to the political body, an oath of allegiance to the Constitution of the United States, and to the Union under it, why also to the laws and proclamations in regard to slavery? Those laws and proclamations were enacted and put forth for the purpose of aiding in the suppression of the rebellion. To give them their fullest effect, there had to be a pledge for their maintenance. In my judgment they have aided, and will further aid, the cause for which they were intended. To now abandon them would be not only to relinquish a lever of power, but would also be a cruel and an astounding breach of faith. I may add at this point, that while I remain in my present position I shall not attempt to retract or modify the emancipation proclamation; nor shall I return to slavery any person who is free by the terms of that proclamation, or by any of the acts of Congress. For these and other reasons it is thought best that support of these measures shall be included in the oath; and it is believed the Executive may lawfully claim it in return for pardon and restoration of forfeited rights, which he has clear constitutional power to withhold altogether, or grant upon the terms which he shall deem wisest for the public interest. It should be observed, also, that this part of the oath is subject to the modifying and abrogating power of legislation and supreme judicial decision.

The proposed acquiescence of the national Executive in any reasonable temporary State arrangement for the freed people is made with the view of possibly modifying the confusion and destitution which must, at best, attend all classes by a total revolution of labor throughout whole States. It is hoped that the already deeply afflicted people in those States may be somewhat more ready to give up the cause of their affliction, if, to this extent, this vital matter be left to themselves; while no power of the national Executive to prevent an abuse is abridged by the proposition.

The suggestion in the proclamation as to maintaining the political framework of the States on what is called reconstruction, is made in the hope that it may do good without danger of harm. It will save labor and avoid great confusion.

But why any proclamation now upon this subject? This question is beset with the conflicting views that the step might be delayed too long or be taken too soon. In some States the elements for resumption seem ready for action, but remain inactive, apparently for want of a rallying point—a plan of action. Why shall A adopt the plan of B, rather than B that of A? And if A and B should agree, how can they know but that the general government here will reject their plan? By the proclamation a plan is presented which may be accepted by them as a rallying point, and which they are assured in advance will not be rejected here. This may bring them to act sooner than they otherwise would.

The objections to a premature presentation of a plan by the national Executive consists in the danger of committals on points which could be more safely left to further developments. Care has been taken to so shape the document as to avoid embarrassments from this source. Saying that, on certain terms, certain classes will be pardoned, with rights restored, it is not said that other classes, or other terms, will never be included. Saying that reconstruction will be accepted if presented in a specified way, it is not said it will never be accepted in any other way.

The movements, by State action, for emancipation in several of the States, not included in the emancipation proclamation, are matters of profound gratulation. And while I do not repeat in detail what I have hertofore so earnestly urged upon this subject, my general views and feelings remain unchanged; and I trust that Congress will omit no fair opportunity of aiding these important steps to a great consummation.

In the midst of other cares, however important, we must not lose sight of the fact that the war power is still our main reliance. To that power alone can we look, yet for a time, to give confidence to the people in the contested regions, that the insurgent power will not again overrun them. Until that confidence shall be established, little can be done anywhere for what is called reconstruction. Hence our chiefest care must still be directed to the army and navy, who have thus far borne their harder part so nobly and well. And it may be esteemed fortunate that in giving the greatest efficiency to these indispensable arms, we do also honorably recognize the gallant men, from commander to sentinel, who compose them, and to whom, more than to others, the world must stand indebted for the home of freedom disenthralled, regenerated, enlarged, and perpetuated.

ABRAHAM LINCOLN

Proclamation of Amnesty and Reconstruction

December 8, 1863

BY THE PRESIDENT OF THE UNITED STATES OF AMERICA: A PROCLAMATION.

Whereas, in and by the Constitution of the United States, it is provided that the President "shall have power to grant reprieves and pardons for offences against the United States, except in cases of impeachment;" and

Whereas a rebellion now exists whereby the loyal State governments of several States have for a long time been subverted, and many persons have committed and are now guilty of treason against the United States; and

Whereas, with reference to said rebellion and treason, laws have been enacted by Congress declaring forfeitures and confiscation of property and liberation of slaves, all upon terms and conditions therein stated, and also declaring that the President was thereby authorized at any time thereafter, by proclamation, to extend to persons who may have participated in the existing rebellion, . . . pardon and amnesty,[13] with such exceptions and at such times and on such conditions as he may deem expedient for the public welfare; and . . .

Whereas, with reference to said rebellion, the President of the United States has issued several proclamations, with provisions in regard to the liberation of slaves; and

Whereas it is now desired by some persons heretofore engaged in said rebellion to resume their allegiance to the United States, and to reinaugurate loyal State governments within and for their respective States; therefore,

I, Abraham Lincoln, President of the United States, do proclaim, declare, and make known to all persons who have, directly or by implication, participated in the existing rebellion, except as hereinafter excepted, that a full pardon is hereby granted to them and each of them, with restoration of all rights of property, except as to slaves, . . . and upon the condition that every such person shall take and subscribe an oath, and thenceforward keep and maintain said oath inviolate; and which oath shall be registered for permanent preservation, and shall be of the tenor and effect following, to wit:

"I, ———, do solemnly swear, in presence of Almighty God, that I will henceforth faithfully support, protect and defend the Constitution of the United States, and the union of the States thereunder; and that I will, in like

---

[13] An amnesty is an exemption from prosecution for a criminal act, in this case treason. A pardon is an exemption from punishment for a crime (again, treason) for which a person has already been convicted.

manner, abide by and faithfully support all acts of Congress passed during the existing rebellion with reference to slaves, so long and so far as not repealed, modified or held void by Congress, or by decision of the Supreme Court; and that I will, in like manner, abide by and faithfully support all proclamations of the President made during the existing rebellion having reference to slaves, so long and so far as not modified or declared void by decision of the Supreme Court. So help me God."

The persons excepted from the benefits of the foregoing provisions are all who are, or shall have been, civil or diplomatic officers or agents of the so-called confederate government; all who have left judicial stations under the United States to aid the rebellion; all who are, or shall have been, military or naval officers of said so-called confederate government above the rank of colonel in the army, or of lieutenant in the navy; all who left seats in the United States Congress to aid the rebellion; all who resigned commissions in the army or navy of the United States, and afterwards aided the rebellion; and all who have engaged in any way in treating colored persons or white persons, in charge of such, otherwise than lawfully as prisoners of war, and which persons may have been found in the United States service, as soldiers, seamen, or in any other capacity.

And I do further proclaim, declare, and make known, that whenever, in any of the States of Arkansas, Texas, Louisiana, Mississippi, Tennessee, Alabama, Georgia, Florida, South Carolina, and North Carolina, a number of persons, not less than one-tenth in number of the votes cast in such State at the Presidential election of the year of our Lord one thousand eight hundred and sixty, each having taken the oath aforesaid and not having since violated it, and being a qualified voter by the election law of the State existing immediately before the so-called act of secession, and excluding all others, shall re-establish a State government which shall be republican, and in no wise contravening said oath, such shall be recognized as the true government of the State, and the State shall receive thereunder the benefits of the constitutional provision which declares that "The United States shall guaranty to every State in this union a republican form of government, and shall protect each of them against invasion; and, on application of the legislature, or the executive, (when the legislature cannot be convened,) against domestic violence."

And I do further proclaim, declare, and make known that any provision which may be adopted by such State government in relation to the freed people of such State, which shall recognize and declare their permanent freedom, provide for their education, and may yet be consistent, as a temporary arrangement, with their present condition as a laboring, landless, and homeless class, will not be objected to by the national Executive. And it is suggested as not improper, that, in constructing a loyal State government in any State, the name of the State, the boundary, the subdivisions, the constitution, and the general code of laws, as before the rebellion, be maintained, subject only to the modifications made necessary by the conditions hereinbefore stated. . . .

To avoid misunderstanding, it may be proper to say that this proclamation, so far as it relates to State governments, has no reference to States wherein loyal State governments have all the while been maintained. And for the same reason, it may be proper to further say that whether members sent to Congress from any State shall be admitted to seats, constitutionally rests exclusively with the respective Houses, and not to any extent with the Executive. And still further, that this proclamation is intended to present the people of the States wherein the national authority has been suspended, and loyal State governments have been subverted, a mode in and by which the national authority and loyal State governments may be re-established within said States, or in any of them; and, while the mode presented is the best the Executive can suggest, with his present impressions, it must not be understood that no other possible mode would be acceptable. . . .

ABRAHAM LINCOLN

Letter to Alpheus Lewis
January 23, 1864

Executive Mansion,
Washington

Alpheus Lewis, Esq.[14]
My dear Sir

You have enquired how the government would regard and treat cases wherein the owners of plantations, in Arkansas, for instance, might fully recognize the freedom of those formerly slaves, and by fair contracts of hire with them, recommence the cultivation of their plantations. I answer I should regard such cases with great favor, and should, as the principle, treat them precisely as I would treat the same number of free white people in the same relation and condition. Whether white or black, reasonable effort should be made to give government protection. In neither case should the giving of aid and comfort to the rebellion, or other practices injurious to the government, be allowed on such plantations; and in either, the government would claim the right to take if necessary those of proper ages and conditions into the military service. Such plan must not be used to break up existing leases or arrangements of abandoned plantations which the government may have made to give employment and sustenance to the idle and destitute people. With the foregoing qual-

[14]Several members of Congress from Kentucky recommended Alpheus Lewis, a relative of prominent cotton planters in Mississippi and Arkansas, to Lincoln as a person who could help introduce free labor among former slaves.

ifications and explanations, and in view of it's tendency to advance freedom, and restore peace and prosperity, such hireing and employment of the freed people, would be regarded by me with rather especial favor.

> Yours truly
> A. LINCOLN

P.S. To be more specific I add that all the Military, and others acting by authority of the United States, are to favor and facilitate the introduction and carrying forward, in good faith, the free-labor system as above indicated, by allowing the necessary supplies therefor to be procured and taken to the proper points, and by doing and forbearing whatever will advance it. . . .[15]

> A. L.

[15]Several weeks later, General Lorenzo Thomas, who was in charge of freedmen in the Mississippi Valley, reported to Lincoln that Lewis was charging planters 5 percent of their crops for protection and that "Lewis's plan is a selfish one, having his own interest at stake." In response, Lincoln explained that he had not authorized Lewis to receive payments. Lincoln to Lorenzo Thomas, March 1, 1864, *CW,* VII, 217–18.

Letter to Michael Hahn

March 13, 1864

Private

> Executive Mansion,
> Washington

Hon. Michael Hahn[16]
My dear Sir:
I congratulate you on having fixed your name in history as the first-free-state Governor of Louisiana.[17] Now you are about to have a Convention which, among other things, will probably define the elective franchise. I barely suggest for your private consideration, whether some of the colored people may not be let in — as, for instance, the very intelligent, and especially those who have fought gallantly in our ranks. They would probably help, in some trying time to come, to keep the jewel of liberty within the family of freedom. But this is only a suggestion, not to the public, but to you alone.[18]

> Yours truly
> A. LINCOLN

[16]Michael Hahn was a New Orleans unionist.
[17]Hahn, supported by General Banks, was elected governor on February 22, 1864, winning the majority of the 11,000 Louisiana voters who met the requirements of Lincoln's Proclamation of Amnesty and Reconstruction.
[18]In fact, the new state constitution adopted in September 1864 did not allow African Americans to vote.

Many Republicans in Congress believed that Lincoln's reconstruction plan was far too generous toward Confederates who were, after all, killing and maiming thousands of Union soldiers. On July 2, 1864, only a few days before adjournment, Congress passed a more demanding formula for reconstruction. The Wade-Davis Bill—named for Benjamin F. Wade, the Ohio abolitionist who chaired the Senate committee that sponsored the bill, and for Henry Winter Davis, the Maryland Republican who headed the House committee—required the abolition of slavery by an electorate composed of 50 percent of the 1860 presidential voters (as opposed to 10 percent in Lincoln's plan) who swore an oath that they had never aided the rebellion or voluntarily borne arms against the Union (an "ironclad oath" compared to the oath of future loyalty under Lincoln's plan). In addition to the more stringent criteria for readmission, the Wade-Davis Bill asserted congressional rather than presidential power over reconstruction. Rather than veto the bill, Lincoln simply refused to sign it. He explained his pocket veto in a public proclamation that reasserted both his authority and the general outline of his plan for reconstruction.

Proclamation Concerning Reconstruction

July 8, 1864

BY THE PRESIDENT OF THE UNITED STATES.
A PROCLAMATION.

Whereas, at the late Session, Congress passed a Bill, "To guarantee to certain States, whose governments have been usurped or overthrown, a republican form of Government," . . .

And whereas, the said Bill was presented to the President of the United States, for his approval, less than one hour before the . . . adjournment of said Session, and was not signed by him:

And whereas, the said Bill contains, among other things, a plan for restoring the States in rebellion to their proper practical relation in the Union, which plan expresses the sense of Congress upon that subject, and which plan it is now thought fit to lay before the people for their consideration:

Now, therefore, I, Abraham Lincoln, President of the United States, do proclaim, declare, and make known, that, while I am, (as I was in December last, when by proclamation I propounded a plan for restoration) unprepared, by a formal approval of this Bill, to be inflexibly committed to any single plan of restoration; and, while I am also unprepared to declare, that the free-state constitutions and governments, already adopted and installed in

Arkansas and Louisiana, shall be set aside and held for nought, thereby re-pelling and discouraging the loyal citizens who have set up the same, as to further effort; or to declare a constitutional competency in Congress to abolish slavery in States, but am at the same time sincerely hoping and expecting that a constitutional amendment, abolishing slavery throughout the nation, may be adopted, nevertheless, I am fully satisfied with the system for restoration contained in the Bill, as one very proper plan for the loyal people of any State choosing to adopt it; and that I am, and at all times shall be, prepared to give the Executive aid and assistance to any such people, so soon as the military resistance to the United States shall have been suppressed in any such State, and the people thereof shall have sufficiently returned to their obedience to the Constitution and the laws of the United States,—in which cases, military Governors will be appointed according to the Bill. . . .

ABRAHAM LINCOLN.

THE POLITICAL CAMPAIGN FOR UNION, FREEDOM, AND WAR

Beset by Republican critics for his caution and by Democratic foes for his refusal to stop the war and to abandon emancipation, Lincoln used the bully pulpit of the presidency to declare again and again his conviction that war was absolutely necessary to achieve the inseparable goals of Union and freedom. Without explicitly saying so, Lincoln was at the same time campaigning for re-election. Discouraging news from the battlefield made many northerners receptive to the idea of peace. Lincoln firmly believed that without military victory the Union's new birth of freedom would be sacrificed to war weariness and revitalization of slavery. Accordingly, when rumors came to his attention of peace overtures from the Confederacy, he responded warily.

Although women could not vote, Lincoln had no doubts about their political influence. He seized opportunities to praise their contributions to the war effort and to solicit their continued support. Throughout the North, women organized local voluntary associations to send soldiers clothing, bandages, medicines, food, and other items. In June 1861, local groups coalesced into the United States Sanitary Commission, which, with Lincoln's approval, funneled goods purchased with private funds into the hands of soldiers at the front for the duration of the war. The Sanitary Commission held fairs in many northern cities, selling homemade goods to raise money to aid soldiers. Lincoln's brief speech at a Sanitary Fair in March 1864 was printed in the *Washington Evening Star*.

Remarks at Closing of Sanitary Fair, Washington, D.C.

March 18, 1864

Ladies and Gentlemen: I appear to say but a word. This extraordinary war in which we are engaged falls heavily upon all classes of people, but the most heavily upon the soldier. For it has been said, all that a man hath will he give for his life; and while all contribute of their substance the soldier puts his life at stake, and often yields it up in his country's cause. The highest merit, then, is due to the soldier. [Cheers.]

In this extraordinary war extraordinary developments have manifested themselves, such as have not been seen in former wars; and amongst these manifestations nothing has been more remarkable than these fairs for the relief of suffering soldiers and their families. And the chief agents in these fairs are the women of America. [Cheers.]

I am not accustomed to the use of language of eulogy; I have never studied the art of paying compliments to women; but I must say that if all that has been said by orators and poets since the creation of the world in praise of woman were applied to the women of America, it would not do them justice for their conduct during this war. I will close by saying God bless the women of America! [Great applause.]

When a delegation of a New York workingmen's association visited Lincoln to inform him that they had elected him an honorary member and that their association "binds them together in support of the Union, and induces them at all sacrifices to sustain it," Lincoln emphasized that the war for the Union served the cause of working people.[19]

[19]*New York Tribune,* March 22, 1864, quoted in *CW,* VII, 260.

Reply to New York Workingmen's Democratic Republican Association

March 21, 1864

Gentlemen of the Committee.

The honorary membership in your Association, as generously tendered, is gratefully accepted.

You comprehend, as your address shows, that the existing rebellion, means more, and tends to more, than the perpetuation of African Slavery — that it is, in fact, a war upon the rights of all working people.... None are so deeply interested to resist the present rebellion as the working people. Let them beware of prejudice, working division and hostility among themselves. The most notable feature of a disturbance in your city last summer, was the hanging of some working people by other working people.[20] It should never be so. The strongest bond of human sympathy, outside of the family relation, should be one uniting all working people, of all nations, and tongues, and kindreds. Nor should this lead to a war upon property, or the owners of property. Property is the fruit of labor—property is desirable—is a positive good in the world. That some should be rich, shows that others may become rich, and hence is just encouragement to industry and enterprize. Let not him who is houseless pull down the house of another; but let him labor diligently and build one for himself, thus by example assuring that his own shall be safe from violence when built.

[20]Lincoln is referring to the July 1863 draft riots in New York City. He did not mention that the hanged workers were African Americans.

Wartime demand for production, combined with military service of many able-bodied men, created new employment opportunities for women in factories and government offices. Women employed at the Philadelphia arsenal petitioned Secretary of War Edwin Stanton to raise wages to compensate for wartime inflation. Their petition read, in part,

Sir: Twenty thousand Working Women of Philadelphia, Pennsylvania, respectfully ask your indulgence, while they narrate the causes which compel them to petition for relief at your hands.

At the breaking out of the rebellion that is now deluging our land with blood, and which for a time threatened the destruction of the Nation, the prices paid at the United States Arsenal in this city were barely sufficient to enable the women engaged upon Government work to earn a scanty respectable subsistence. Since the period referred to, board, provisions, and all other articles of female consumption, have advanced to such an extent as to make an average of at least seventy-five per cent.,—while woman's labor has been *reduced thirty per cent*. What need of argument? To an intelligent mind, the result must be apparent; and it is perhaps superfluous to say, that it has produced great suffering, privation, and, in many instances, actual hunger. Such, however, is the *truth*.

To alleviate this misery, feed the hungry, clothe the naked, and house the houseless, we appeal to those in authority for a just and reasonable compensation for our labor.

What we need most IS IMMEDIATE AID. You can give it; the power is lodged with you; issue an Order to the Quartermaster-General, authorizing or ordering him to increase the price of female labor until it shall approximate to the price of living.

Let it be done without delay. Send the order at once, and you will have the proud satisfaction of knowing that you have done all in your power to ameliorate the condition of those who have given *their all* to their country; and who now come to that country, not as beggars, asking alms, but as American matrons and daughters, asking an equitable price for their labor.[21]

[21] *CW,* VII, 467.

Letter to Edwin M. Stanton
July 27, 1864

I know not how much is within the legal power of the government in this case; but it is certainly true in equity, that the laboring women in our employment, should be paid at the least as much as they were at the beginning of the war. Will the Secretary of War please have the case fully examined, and so much relief given as can be consistently with the law and the public service.

A. LINCOLN

When a delegation from Kentucky met with Lincoln to express the dissatisfaction in their state about the enlistment of slaves in the Union army, Lincoln explained why he had concluded that the Union could not be saved without the black soldiers made available by emancipation. In a widely reprinted letter, Lincoln summarized his argument for the absolute necessity of emancipation, thereby undercutting claims made by many northern Democrats that the Union could be restored without further bloodshed by negotiating a peace settlement that did not demand emancipation.

Letter to Albert G. Hodges

April 4, 1864

Executive Mansion,
Washington

A. G. Hodges, Esq.[22]
Frankfort, Ky.
My dear Sir:

You ask me to put in writing the substance of what I verbally said the other day, in your presence, to Governor Bramlette[23] and Senator Dixon.[24] It was about as follows:

"I am naturally anti-slavery. If slavery is not wrong, nothing is wrong. I can not remember when I did not so think, and feel. And yet I have never understood that the Presidency conferred upon me an unrestricted right to act officially upon this judgment and feeling. It was in the oath I took that I would, to the best of my ability, preserve, protect, and defend the Constitution of the United States. I could not take the office without taking the oath. Nor was it my view that I might take an oath to get power, and break the oath in using the power. I understood, too, that in ordinary civil administration this oath even forbade me to practically indulge my primary abstract judgment on the moral question of slavery. I had publicly declared this many times, and in many ways. And I aver that, to this day, I have done no official act in mere deference to my abstract judgment and feeling on slavery. I did understand however, that my oath to preserve the constitution to the best of my ability, imposed upon me the duty of preserving, by every indispensable means, that government—that nation—of which that constitution was the organic law. Was it possible to lose the nation, and yet preserve the constitution? By general law life *and* limb must be protected; yet often a limb must be amputated to save a life; but a life is never wisely given to save a limb. I felt that measures, otherwise unconstitutional, might become lawful, by becoming indispensable to the preservation of the constitution, through the preservation of the nation. Right or wrong, I assumed this ground, and now avow it. I could not feel that, to the best of my ability, I had even tried to preserve the constitution, if, to save slavery, or any minor matter, I should permit the wreck of government, country, and Constitution all together. When, early in the war, Gen. Fremont attempted military emancipation,[25] I forbade it, because I did not then think it an indispensable necessity. When a little later, Gen. Cameron,[26] then Secretary of War, suggested the arming of

---

[22] Albert G. Hodges was the editor of the *Frankfort (Kentucky) Commonwealth.*
[23] Thomas E. Bramlette was governor of Kentucky.
[24] Archibald Dixon was a former U.S. senator from Kentucky.
[25] See Lincoln to Frémont, September 2 and 11, 1861, in chapter 7.

---

blacks, I objected, because I did not yet think it an indispensable necessity. When, still later, Gen. Hunter attempted military emancipation,[27] I again forbade it, because I did not yet think the indispensable necessity had come. When, in March, and May, and July 1862 I made earnest, and successive appeals to the border states to favor compensated emancipation,[28] I believed the indispensable necessity for military emancipation, and arming the blacks would come, unless averted by that measure. They declined the proposition; and I was, in my best judgment, driven to the alternative of either surrendering the Union, and with it, the Constitution, or of laying strong hand upon the colored element. I chose the latter. In choosing it, I hoped for greater gain than loss; but of this, I was not entirely confident. More than a year of trial now shows no loss by it in our foreign relations, none in our home popular sentiment, none in our white military force,—no loss by it any how or any where. On the contrary, it shows a gain of quite a hundred and thirty thousand soldiers, seamen, and laborers. These are palpable facts, about which, as facts, there can be no cavilling. We have the men; and we could not have had them, without the measure.

"And now let any Union man who complains of the measure, test himself by writing down in one line that he is for subduing the rebellion by force of arms; and in the next, that he is for taking these hundred and thirty thousand men from the Union side, and placing them where they would be but for the measure he condemns. If he can not face his case so stated, it is only because he can not face the truth."

I add a word which was not in the verbal conversation. In telling this tale I attempt no compliment to my own sagacity. I claim not to have controlled events, but confess plainly that events have controlled me. Now, at the end of three years struggle the nation's condition is not what either party, or any man devised, or expected. God alone can claim it. Whither it is tending seems plain. If God now wills the removal of a great wrong, and wills also that we of the North as well as you of the South, shall pay fairly for our complicity in that wrong, impartial history will find therein new cause to attest and revere the justice and goodness of God.

Yours truly
A. LINCOLN

[26]Secretary of War Simon Cameron's annual report in November 1861 declared, "It is as clearly a right of the Government to arm slaves, when it may become necessary, as it is to use gun-powder taken from the enemy." Cameron leaked this statement to newspapers before Lincoln had seen it. Lincoln forced Cameron to excise the passage from his report. Because of this and other embarrassments, Lincoln made Cameron minister to Russia in January 1862 and appointed Edwin Stanton to take Cameron's place as secretary of war. John G. Nicolay and John Hay, *Abraham Lincoln: A History* (10 vols., New York, 1890), V, 125–26.

[27]See Lincoln's proclamation, May 19, 1862, in chapter 7.

[28]See, for example, Lincoln's appeal to border-state representatives, July 12, 1862, in chapter 7.

Although Lincoln favored the end of slavery throughout the nation, he continued to insist that he lacked constitutional authority to emancipate slaves in the loyal states or in the regions excepted from the Emancipation Proclamation, as he noted in response to a petition from 195 children.

Letter to Mrs. Horace Mann
April 5, 1864

Executive Mansion,
Washington

Mrs. Horace Mann,[29]
Madam,
The petition of persons under eighteen, praying that I would free all slave children, and the heading of which petition it appears you wrote, was handed me a few days since by Senator [Charles] Sumner.[30] Please tell these little people I am very glad their young hearts are so full of just and generous sympathy, and that, while I have not the power to grant all they ask, I trust they will remember that God has, and that, as it seems, He wills to do it.

Yours truly
A. LINCOLN

[29]Mrs. Horace Mann was the widow of the famed Massachusetts educator who had died in 1859. In response to Lincoln's letter, Mrs. Mann promised to "scatter fac-similes of your sweet words to the children like apple blossoms all over the country—and we look with more hope than ever for the day when perfect justice shall be decreed, which shall make every able bodied colored man spring to the defence of the nation which it is plain the white man alone cannot save." *CW,* VII, 287.
[30]Charles Sumner, a devout abolitionist, was a Republican senator from Massachusetts.

Most Republican officials throughout the North supported Lincoln's nomination for a second term. In an effort to garner votes from Democrats who favored continued war in order to preserve the Union, the Republican party adopted a new name for the 1864 presidential election: the National Union party. Meeting in Baltimore early in June, the party easily nominated Lincoln and, after considerable maneuvering, selected Andrew Johnson—a war Democrat and military governor of Tennessee—as Lincoln's running mate. The party platform called for a constitutional amendment abolishing slavery, demanded unconditional surrender of Confederate forces, applauded the wisdom of Lincoln's Emancipation Proclamation and "employment as

Union soldiers of men heretofore held in slavery," and promoted such Republican projects as "the speedy construction of the Railroad to the Pacific coast," the encouragement of foreign immigration, and "economy and rigid responsibility in the public expenditures."[31] In sum, the platform endorsed the policies of Lincoln's presidency and promised to continue them.

In mid-June, Lincoln left Washington for a day to attend the Sanitary Fair in Philadelphia, where he responded to a toast with a de facto campaign speech, published in Philadelphia newspapers.

[31]*CW,* VII, 381–82.

Speech at Great Central Sanitary Fair, Philadelphia, Pennsylvania

June 16, 1864

... War, at the best, is terrible, and this war of ours, in its magnitude and in its duration, is one of the most terrible. It has deranged business, totally in many localities, and partially in all localities. It has destroyed property, and ruined homes; it has produced a national debt and taxation unprecedented, at least in this country. It has carried mourning to almost every home, until it can almost be said that the "heavens are hung in black." Yet it continues, and several relieving coincidents have accompanied it from the very beginning, which have not been known, as I understood, or have any knowledge of, in any former wars in the history of the world. The Sanitary Commission, with all its benevolent labors, the Christian Commission,[32] with all its Christian and benevolent labors, and the various places, arrangements, so to speak, and institutions, have contributed to the comfort and relief of the soldiers. ... And ... these fairs, which, I believe, began only in last August, if I mistake not, in Chicago; then at Boston, at Cincinnati, Brooklyn, New York, at Baltimore, and those at present held at St. Louis, Pittsburg, and Philadelphia. The motive and object that lie at the bottom of all these are most worthy; for, say what you will, after all the most is due to the soldier, who takes his life in his hands and goes to fight the battles of his country. [Cheers.] In what is contributed to his comfort when he passes to and fro, and in what is contributed to him when he is sick and wounded, in whatever shape it comes, whether from the fair and tender hand of woman, or from any other source, is much, very much; but, I think there is still that which has as much value to him [*in the continual reminders he sees in the newspapers, that while he is absent he*

[32]Founded in 1861 by leaders of the Young Men's Christian Association, the Christian Commission provided religious tracts to Union soldiers, as well as clothing and other supplies.

is yet remembered by the loved ones at home.]—he is not forgotten. [Cheers.]
Another view of these various institutions is worthy of consideration, I
think; they are voluntary contributions, given freely, zealously, and earnestly,
on top of all the disturbances of business, the taxation and burdens that the
war has imposed upon us, giving proof that the national resources are not at
all exhausted, [cheers;] that the national spirit of patriotism is even stronger
than at the commencement of the rebellion.

It is a pertinent question often asked in the mind privately, and from one
to the other, when is the war to end? Surely I feel as deep an interest in this
question as any other can, but I do not wish to name a day, or month, or a
year when it is to end. I do not wish to run any risk of seeing the time come,
without our being ready for the end, and for fear of disappointment, because
the time had come and not the end. [*We accepted this war; we did not begin
it.*] We accepted this war for an object, a worthy object, and the war will end
when that object is attained. Under God, I hope it never will until that time.
[Great cheering.] Speaking of the present campaign, General Grant is
reported to have said, I am going through on this line if it takes all summer.
[Cheers.] This war has taken three years; it was begun or accepted upon the
line of restoring the national authority over the whole national domain, and
for the American people, as far as my knowledge enables me to speak, I say
we are going through on this line if it takes three years more. [Cheers.] My
friends, I did not know but that I might be called upon to say a few words
before I got away from here, but I did not know it was coming just here.
[Laughter.] I have never been in the habit of making predictions in regard to
the war, but I am almost tempted to make one. *[(Do it—do it!)]*—If I were
to hazard it, it is this: That Grant is this evening, with General Meade and
General Hancock,[33] of Pennsylvania, and the brave officers and soldiers with
him, in position from whence he will never be dislodged until Richmond is
taken [loud cheering], and I have but one single proposition to put now, and,
perhaps, I can best put it in form of an interrogative. If I shall discover that
General Grant and the noble officers and men under him can be greatly facil-
itated in their work by a sudden pouring forward of men and assistance, will
you give them to me? [Cries of "yes."] Then, I say, stand ready, for I am
watching for the chance. [Laughter and cheers.] I thank you, gentlemen.

[33]General Winfield Scott Hancock, a West Point graduate from Pennsylvania, was one of
Grant's subordinates in the siege of Petersburg.

Despite Lincoln's public optimism about the military prospects, Grant's
spring campaign had caused a bloodbath of more than one hundred thousand Union casualties before digging in to besiege Petersburg in mid-June.
As Confederate General Jubal Early's army rampaged near Washington in
early July, Horace Greeley, editor of the *New York Tribune* wrote Lincoln

urging him to meet with two Confederate ambassadors who were in Canada with "full & complete power for a peace."[34] Greeley went on to "remind" Lincoln—who needed no reminding—"that our bleeding, bankrupt, almost dying country also longs for peace—shudders at the prospect of fresh conscriptions, of further wholesale devastations, and of new rivers of human blood.... Mr. President, I fear you do not realize how intently the people desire any peace consistent with the national integrity and honor.... With United States stocks worth but forty cents in gold per dollar, and drafting about to commence on the third million of Union soldiers, can this be wondered at?"[35] Shrewdly, Lincoln delegated Greeley to contact the Confederate representatives and sound them out. He gave Greeley a brief statement of terms for initiating serious peace negotiations, fully expecting them to be rejected as unacceptable, and they were.

[34]William Cornell Jewett to Horace Greeley, enclosed in Greeley to Lincoln, July 7, 1864, *CW,* VII, 436.
[35]Greeley to Lincoln, July 7, 1864, *CW,* VII, 435.

Letter to Horace Greeley
July 9, 1864

Washington, D.C.
Hon. Horace Greely
Dear Sir
Your letter of the 7th., with inclosures, received. If you can find, any person anywhere professing to have any proposition of Jefferson Davis in writing, for peace, embracing the restoration of the Union and abandonment of slavery, what ever else it embraces, say to him he may come to me with you, and that if he really brings such proposition, he shall, at the least, have safe conduct, with the paper (and without publicity, if he choose) to the point where you shall have met him. The same, if there be two or more persons.

Yours truly
A. LINCOLN

After receiving the following statement of Lincoln's terms for peace, Greeley telegraphed Lincoln, "I have communicated with the Gentlemen in question & do not find them so empowered as I was previously assured."[36]

[36]Greeley to Lincoln, July 18, 1864, *CW,* VII, 451.

To Whom It May Concern
July 18, 1864

Executive Mansion,
Washington

To Whom it may concern:
Any proposition which embraces the restoration of peace, the integrity of the whole Union, and the abandonment of slavery, and which comes by and with an authority that can control the armies now at war against the United States will be received and considered by the Executive government of the United States, and will be met by liberal terms on other substantial and collateral points; and the bearer, or bearers thereof shall have safe-conduct both ways.

ABRAHAM LINCOLN

The Confederate emissaries arranged to have Lincoln's peace terms published in northern newspapers, creating unease among many war Democrats in the North. Charles D. Robinson, editor of the *Green Bay (Wisconsin) Advocate,* wrote Lincoln, explaining that as a war Democrat he had supported Lincoln's war policies, including emancipation, but that Lincoln's recent statement of the prerequisites for peace negotiations seemed to say "that no steps can be taken towards peace . . . unless accompanied with an abandonment of slavery. This puts the whole war question on a new basis, and takes us War Democrats clear off our feet, leaving us no ground to stand upon." Robinson asked Lincoln to "suggest some interpretation . . . [that will] make it tenable ground on which we War democrats may stand."[37] Robinson's letter prompted Lincoln to draft the following reply. After consulting with several advisers, including the famous African American leader Frederick Douglass, Lincoln decided not to send the letter, fearing that it would be likely to alienate many loyal Republicans by offering to discuss peace and reunion without regard to slavery. The letter nonetheless reflected Lincoln's insistence on the military necessity of emancipation and his awareness that northerners' intense desire for an end to the war might well undermine his dual goals of union and freedom.

[37]Robinson to Lincoln, August 7, 1864, *CW,* VII, 501.

Letter to Charles D. Robinson
August 17, 1864

Executive Mansion,
Washington

Hon. Charles D. Robinson
My dear Sir:
Your letter of the 7th. was placed in my hand yesterday by Gov. Randall.[38]

To me it seems plain that saying re-union and abandonment of slavery would be considered, if offered, is not saying that nothing *else* or *less* would be considered, if offered. But I will not stand upon the mere construction of language. It is true, as you remind me, that in the Greeley letter of 1862,[39] I said. "If I could save the Union without freeing any slave I would do it; and if I could save it by freeing all the slaves I would do it; and if I could save it by freeing some, and leaving others alone I would also do that." I continued in the same letter as follows: "What I do about slavery and the colored race, I do because I believe it helps to save the Union; and what I forbear I forbear because I do not believe it would help to save the Union. I shall do less whenever I shall believe what I am doing hurts the cause; and I shall do more whenever I shall believe doing more will help the cause." All this I said in the utmost sincerety; and I am as true to the whole of it now, as when I first said it. When I afterwards proclaimed emancipation, and employed colored soldiers, I only followed the declaration just quoted from the Greeley letter that "I shall do *more* whenever I shall believe *doing* more will help the cause." The way these measures were to help the cause, was not to be by magic, or miracles, but by inducing the colored people to come bodily over from the rebel side to ours. On this point, nearly a year ago, in a letter to Mr. Conkling,[40] made public at once, I wrote as follows: "But negroes, like other people, act upon motives. Why should they do anything for us if we will do nothing for them? If they stake their lives for us they must be prompted by the strongest motive—even the promise of freedom. And the promise, being made, must be kept." I am sure you will not, on due reflection, say that the promise being made, must be *broken* at the first opportunity. I am sure you would not desire me to say, or to leave an inference, that I am ready, whenever convenient, to join in re-enslaving those who shall have served us in consideration of our promise. As matter of morals, could such treachery by any possibility, escape the curses of Heaven, or of any good man? As matter of policy, to *announce* such a purpose, would ruin the Union cause itself. All

---

[38] Alexander W. Randall was a former governor of Wisconsin.
[39] See Lincoln to Greeley, August 22, 1862, in chapter 7.
[40] See Lincoln to Conkling, August 26, 1863, in chapter 8.

recruiting of colored men would instantly cease, and all colored men now in our service, would instantly desert us. And rightfully too. Why should they give their lives for us, with full notice of our purpose to betray them? Drive back to the support of the rebellion the physical force which the colored people now give, and promise us, and neither the present, nor any coming administration, *can* save the Union. Take from us, and give to the enemy, the hundred and thirty, forty, or fifty thousand colored persons now serving us as soldiers, seamen, and laborers, and we can not longer maintain the contest. The party who could elect a President on a War & Slavery Restoration platform, would, of necessity, lose the colored force; and that force being lost, would be as powerless to save the Union as to do any other impossible thing. It is not a question of sentiment or taste, but one of physical force, which may be measured, and estimated as horsepower, and steam power, are measured and estimated. And by measurement, it is more than we can lose, and live. Nor can we, by discarding it, get a white force in place of it. There is a witness in every white mans bosom that he would rather go to the war having the negro to help him, than to help the enemy against him. It is not the giving of one class for another. It is simply giving a large force to the enemy, for *nothing* in return.

In addition to what I have said, allow me to remind you that no one, having control of the rebel armies, or, in fact, having any influence whatever in the rebellion, has offered, or intimated a willingness to, a restoration of the Union, in any event, or on any condition whatever. Let it be constantly borne in mind that no such offer has been made or intimated. Shall we be weak enough to allow the enemy to distract us with an abstract question which he himself refuses to present as a practical one? In the Conkling letter before mentioned, I said: "Whenever you shall have conquered all resistance to the Union, if I shall urge you to continue fighting, it will be an apt time *then* to declare that you will not fight to free negroes." I repeat this now. If Jefferson Davis wishes, for himself, or for the benefit of his friends at the North, to know what I would do if he were to offer peace and re-union, saying nothing about slavery, let him try me.

Lincoln's consultation about the Robinson letter with former Wisconsin governor Alexander Randall and Joseph T. Mills, a Wisconsin judge, was summarized by Mills in the following excerpt from his diary, and a version was subsequently published in the *New York Tribune* on September 10, 1864.

Interview with Alexander W. Randall
and Joseph T. Mills
August 19, 1864

The President was free & animated in conversation. I [Mills] was astonished at his elasticity of spirits. Says Gov Randall, why cant you Mr P. seek some place of retirement for a few weeks. You would be reinvigorated. Aye said the President, 3 weeks would do me no good—my thoughts my solicitude for this great country follow me where ever I go. I don't think it is personal vanity, or ambition—but I cannot but feel that the weal or woe of this great nation will be decided in the approaching canvas.[41] My own experience has proven to me, that there is no program intended by the democratic party but that will result in the dismemberment of the Union. But Genl McClellan is in favor of crushing out the rebellion, & he will probably be the Chicago candidate.[42] The slightest acquaintance with arithmetic will prove to any man that the rebel armies cannot be destroyed with democratic [party] strategy. It would sacrifice all the white men of the north to do it. There are now between 1 & 200 thousand black men now in the service of the Union. These men will be disbanded, returned to slavery & we will have to fight two nations instead of one. I have tried it. You cannot concilliate the South, when the mastery & control of millions of blacks makes them sure of ultimate success. You cannot conciliate the South, when you place yourself in such a position, that they see they can achieve their independence. The war democrat depends upon conciliation. He must confine himself to that policy entirely. If he fights at all in such a war as this he must economise life & use all the means which God & nature puts in his power. Abandon all the posts now possessed by black men surrender all these advantages to the enemy, & we would be compelled to abandon the war in 3 weeks. We have to hold territory. Where are the war democrats to do it. The field was open to them to have enlisted & put down this rebellion by force of arms, by concilliation, long before the present policy was inaugurated. There have been men who have proposed to me to return to slavery the black warriors of Port Hudson & Olustee[43] to their masters to conciliate the South. I should be damned in time & in eternity for so doing. The world shall know that I will keep my

[41] That is, the presidential election in November.
[42] In fact, General McClellan did become the Democratic nominee, on a platform that called for an immediate end to the war, postponing for future negotiations the questions of the abolition of slavery and whether the Union would be restored or Confederate independence would be allowed. McClellan himself, as Lincoln noted, was a war Democrat who insisted that the Union must be preserved. The contrast between the Democrats' peace platform and the war candidate reflected the deep divisions among party members.
[43] Black soldiers fought in the battles for Port Hudson, Louisiana, and Olustee, Florida.

faith to friends & enemies, come what will. My enemies say I am now carrying on this war for the sole purpose of abolition. It is & will be carried on so long as I am President for the sole purpose of restoring the Union. But no human power can subdue this rebellion without using the Emancipation lever as I have done. Freedom has given us the control of 200 000 able bodied men, born & raised on southern soil. It will give us more yet. Just so much it has sub[t]racted from the strength of our enemies, & instead of alienating the south from us, there are evidences of a fraternal feeling growing up between our own & rebel soldiers. My enemies condemn my emancipation policy. Let them prove by the history of this war, that we can restore the Union without it. . . .

Lincoln hoped soldiers would vote for him. In a speech to an Ohio regiment passing through Washington, Lincoln emphasized the significance of the issues at stake in the war, and—implicitly—in the impending presidential election. The speech was published in many newspapers.

Speech to 166th Ohio Regiment
August 22, 1864

I suppose you are going home to see your families and friends. For the service you have done in this great struggle in which we are engaged I present you sincere thanks for myself and the country. I almost always feel inclined, when I happen to say anything to soldiers, to impress upon them in a few brief remarks the importance of success in this contest. It is not merely for to-day, but for all time to come that we should perpetuate for our children's children this great and free government, which we have enjoyed all our lives. I beg you to remember this, not merely for my sake, but for yours. I happen temporarily to occupy this big White House. I am a living witness that any one of your children may look to come here as my father's child has. It is in order that each of you may have through this free government which we have enjoyed, an open field and a fair chance for your industry, enterprise and intelligence; that you may all have equal privileges in the race of life, with all its desirable human aspirations. It is for this the struggle should be maintained, that we may not lose our birthright—not only for one, but for two or three years. The nation is worth fighting for, to secure such an inestimable jewel.

Notwithstanding Lincoln's public statements, privately he was deeply pes-
simistic about the prospects of his re-election. On August 23, he received a
gloomy letter from the chairman of the National Union Executive Committee, Henry J. Raymond, reporting that the president's "staunchest friends in
every state" unanimously agreed, "The tide is setting strongly against us."
Raymond wrote that "this great reaction in public sentiment" was caused
by "the want of military successes, and the impression in some minds, the
fear and suspicion in others, that we are not to have peace in any event
under this administration until Slavery is abandoned." Raymond urged Lincoln to counteract this sentiment and "save the country from falling into
hostile hands" by making "distinct proffers of peace to [Jefferson] Davis, as
the head of the rebel armies, on the sole condition of acknowledging the
supremacy of the constitution,—all other questions to be settled in a convention of the people of all the States."[44]

[44]Raymond to Lincoln, August 22, 1864, *CW,* VII, 517–18.

Memorandum Concerning Lincoln's
Probable Failure of Re-election
August 23, 1864

Executive Mansion,
Washington
This morning, as for some days past, it seems exceedingly probable that this
Administration will not be re-elected. Then it will be my duty to so co-
operate with the President elect,[45] as to save the Union between the election
and the inauguration; as he will have secured his election on such ground
that he can not possibly save it afterwards.

A. LINCOLN

[45]That is, George McClellan, the Democratic candidate.

Lincoln initially accepted Raymond's advice about making an overture to
Jefferson Davis, and he drafted instructions for Raymond to serve as an
emissary—powerful testimony of Lincoln's political desperation. But after discussing the document the next day with Raymond and several members of his cabinet, Lincoln concluded that to send such "a commission to

Richmond would be worse than losing the Presidential contest—it would be ignominiously surrendering it in advance."[46] Accordingly, the plan was scrapped.

GLORIOUS VICTORIES

Dramatic news from the battlefield transformed Lincoln's political prospects. General William Tecumseh Sherman's campaign to push south from Chattanooga toward Atlanta had been under way since mid-May. Despite Sherman's skillful military maneuvers, progress was slowed by the terrain and by Confederate General Joseph E. Johnston's shrewd defensive tactics. Eager to stop Sherman with a bold offensive, Jefferson Davis replaced General Johnston with General John Bell Hood in mid-July. While Sherman approached Atlanta, Admiral David G. Farragut took his Union fleet into Mobile Harbor on the Gulf Coast of Alabama and in three weeks of battles captured the three forts that guarded the harbor, effectively closing Mobile to Confederate shipping. Hood delayed Sherman with costly attacks, but Sherman's relentless flanking movements forced Confederate forces to evacuate Atlanta, and Union soldiers marched into the city on September 2, 1864. Lincoln's response to these great victories was immediate and heartfelt.

[46]Nicolay and Hay, *Abraham Lincoln,* IX, 221.

Order of Thanks to David G. Farragut and Others
September 3, 1864

Executive Mansion
The national thanks are tendered by the President to Admiral Farragut and Major General Canby[47] for the skill and harmony with which the recent operations in Mobile Harbor, and against Fort Powell, Fort Gaines, and Fort Morgan,[48] were planned and carried into execution. Also, to Admiral Farragut and Major General Granger,[49] under whose immediate command they were conducted, and to the gallant commanders on sea and land, and to the sailors

[47]General Edward R. S. Canby, a West Pointer from Kentucky, commanded the Military Division of Western Mississippi, which included Mobile.
[48]These forts guarded Mobile Harbor.
[49]General Gordon Granger, a West Point graduate from New York, commanded Union troops in the successful assault on the harbor forts.

and soldiers engaged in the operations, for their energy and courage, which, under the blessing of Providence, have been crowned with brilliant success, and have won for them the applause and thanks of the nation.

ABRAHAM LINCOLN

Order of Thanks to William T. Sherman and Others
September 3, 1864

Executive Mansion

The national thanks are herewith tendered by the President to Major General William T. Sherman, and the gallant officers and soldiers of his command before Atlanta, for the distinguished ability, courage, and perseverance displayed in the campaign in Georgia, which, under Divine favor, has resulted in the capture of the City of Atlanta. The marches, battles, sieges, and other military operations that have signalized this campaign must render it famous in the annals of war, and have entitled those who have participated therein to the applause and thanks of the nation.

ABRAHAM LINCOLN

Proclamation of Thanksgiving and Prayer
September 3, 1864

Executive Mansion,
Washington City

The signal success that Divine Providence has recently vouchsafed to the operations of the United States fleet and army in the harbor of Mobile and the reduction of Fort-Powell, Fort-Gaines, and Fort-Morgan, and the glorious achievements of the Army under Major General Sherman in the State of Georgia, resulting in the capture of the City of Atlanta, call for devout acknowledgment to the Supreme Being in whose hands are the destinies of nations. It is therefore requested that on next Sunday, in all places of public worship in the United-States, thanksgiving be offered to Him for His mercy in preserving our national existence against the insurgent rebels who so long have been waging a cruel war against the Government of the United-States, for its overthrow; and also that prayer be made for the Divine protection to our brave soldiers and their leaders in the field, who have so often and so gallantly perilled their lives in battling with the enemy; and for blessing and comfort from the Father of Mercies to the sick, wounded, and prisoners, and to the orphans and widows of those who have fallen in the service of their country, and that he will continue to uphold the Government of the United-States against all the efforts of public enemies and secret foes.

ABRAHAM LINCOLN

The welcome military victories heightened Lincoln's growing conviction that, somehow, a divine purpose was being served by the seemingly endless slaughter, a sentiment he expressed in a long-delayed response to a letter he had received more than a year earlier from Eliza P. Gurney, a member of the Society of Friends, or Quakers. Early in August 1863, Gurney had written Lincoln that "the prayer of many thousands whose hearts thou hast gladdened by thy praiseworthy and successful effort 'to burst the bands of wickedness, and let the oppressed go free' [is] that the Almighty . . . may strengthen thee."[50]

[50]Gurney to Lincoln, August 8, 1863, *CW,* VII, 535–36.

Letter to Eliza P. Gurney
September 4, 1864

Executive Mansion,
Washington

Eliza P. Gurney.

My esteemed friend.

I have not forgotten—probably never shall forget—the very impressive occasion when yourself and friends visited me on a Sabbath forenoon two years ago.[51] Nor has your kind letter, written nearly a year later, ever been forgotten. In all, it has been your purpose to strengthen my reliance on God. I am much indebted to the good christian people of the country for their constant prayers and consolations; and to no one of them, more than to yourself. The purposes of the Almighty are perfect, and must prevail, though we erring mortals may fail to accurately perceive them in advance. We hoped for a happy termination of this terrible war long before this; but God knows best, and has ruled otherwise. We shall yet acknowledge His wisdom and our own error therein. Meanwhile we must work earnestly in the best light He gives us, trusting that so working still conduces to the great ends He ordains. Surely He intends some great good to follow this mighty convulsion, which no mortal could make, and no mortal could stay.

[51]Gurney and other Friends visited Lincoln in October 1862 and, in his presence, prayed for him to be guided by divine wisdom.

Your people—the Friends—have had, and are having, a very great trial. On principle, and faith, opposed to both war and oppression, they can only practically oppose oppression by war. In this hard dilemma, some have chosen one horn and some the other. For those appealing to me on conscientious grounds,[52] I have done, and shall do, the best I could and can, in my own conscience, under my oath to the law. That you believe this I doubt not; and believing it, I shall still receive, for our country and myself, your earnest prayers to our Father in Heaven.

> Your sincere friend
> A. LINCOLN.

[52]That is, Friends who refused to serve in the military because of their religious opposition to war.

General Philip Sheridan gave Lincoln more good military news on the eve of the presidential election. In pursuit of Confederate General Jubal Early's army since early August, Sheridan led his men to a decisive victory at Cedar Creek, Virginia, on October 19. During this unrelenting campaign through the Shenandoah Valley, Sheridan, with Grant's encouragement, destroyed everything in his path—crops, barns, farm animals, and implements—anything that might be used to supply hungry Confederates.

Letter to Philip H. Sheridan
October 22, 1864

> Executive Mansion,
> Washington

Major General Sheridan

With great pleasure I tender to you and your brave army, the thanks of the Nation, and my own personal admiration and gratitude for the month's operations in the Shenandoah Valley; and especially for the splendid work of October 19, 1864.

> Your Obt. Servt.
> ABRAHAM LINCOLN.

Lincoln also expressed thanks for soldiers' political support in a brief speech to a New York regiment, published in northern newspapers just days before the presidential election.

Speech to 189th New York Volunteers
October 24, 1864

SOLDIERS: I am exceedingly obliged to you for this mark of respect. It is said that we have the best Government the world ever knew, and I am glad to meet you, the supporters of that Government. To you who render the hardest work in its support should be given the greatest credit. Others who are connected with it, and who occupy higher positions, their duties can be dispensed with, but we cannot get along without your aid. While others differ with the Administration,[53] and, perhaps, honestly, the soldiers generally have sustained it; they have not only fought right, but, so far as could be judged from their actions, they have voted right, and I for one thank you for it. I know you are en route for the front, and therefore do not expect me to detain you long, and will therefore bid you good morning.

[53]That is, his political foes, the peace Democrats and their presidential candidate, General McClellan.

A VOTE FOR UNION, FREEDOM, AND WAR?

The 1864 presidential election amounted to a referendum on Lincoln's presidency: Should a war for freedom and Union continue with Lincoln at the helm, or should the Democratic candidate, General George McClellan, be entrusted to somehow find a way to preserve the Union and postpone emancipation pending the outcome of postwar negotiations? Lincoln spelled out his opposition to peace at any price in a draft of a letter to Isaac M. Schermerhorn, organizer of a mass meeting of Union men in Buffalo. Lincoln did not finish the letter, and he explained to Schermerhorn that, in any case, he could not spare time to address the Buffalo gathering.

Letter to Isaac M. Schermerhorn

September 12, 1864

Executive Mansion,
Washington

Isaac M. Schermerhorn

My dear Sir.

Yours inviting me to attend a Union Mass Meeting at Buffalo is received. Much is being said about peace; and no man desires peace more ardently than I. Still I am yet unprepared to give up the Union for a peace which, so achieved, could not be of much duration. The preservation of our Union was *not* the sole avowed object for which the war was commenced. It was commenced for precisely the reverse object—*to destroy our Union*. The insurgents commenced it by firing upon the Star of the West,[54] and on Fort Sumpter, and by other similar acts. It is true, however, that the administration accepted the war thus commenced, for the sole avowed object of preserving our Union; and it is not true that it has since been, or will be, prossecuted by this administration, for any other object. In declaring this, I only declare what I can know, and do know to be true, and what no other man can know to be false.

In taking the various steps which have led to my present position in relation to the war, the public interest and my private interest, have been perfectly paralel, because in no other way could I serve myself so well, as by truly serving the Union. The whole field has been open to me, where to choose. No place-hunting necessity has been upon me urging me to seek a position of antagonism to some other man, irrespective of whether such position might be favorable or unfavorable to the Union.

Of course I may err in judgment, but my present position in reference to the rebellion is the result of my best judgment, and according to that best judgment, it is the only position upon which any Executive can or could save the Union. Any substantial departure from it insures the success of the rebellion. An armistice—a cessation of hostilities—is the end of the struggle, and the insurgents would be in peaceable possession of all that has been struggled for. Any different policy in regard to the colored man, deprives us of his help, and this is more than we can bear. We can not spare the hundred and forty or fifty thousand now serving us as soldiers, seamen, and laborers. This is not a question of sentiment or taste, but one of physical force which may be measured and estimated as horse-power and Steam-power are measured and estimated. Keep it and you can save the Union. Throw it away, and

---

[54]The *Star of the West* was a merchant ship sent to supply the federal garrison at Fort Sumter in Charleston Harbor. Confederate batteries fired on the ship on January 9, 1861, forcing it to turn back.

Figure 9.   Soldiers Vote for President in 1864

This sketch by eyewitness William Waud shows Union soldiers near Petersburg, Virginia, casting ballots for president in 1864. Soldiers voted overwhelmingly for Lincoln, indicating their willingness to continue to fight for both Union and freedom.

the Union goes with it. Nor is it possible for any Administration to retain the service of these people with the express or implied understanding that upon the first convenient occasion, they are to be re-inslaved. It *can* not be; and it *ought* not to be.

Keenly aware of the delicate political balance in the North, Lincoln urged General Sherman to do what he safely could to allow Indiana soldiers to go home to vote.

Letter to William T. Sherman

September 19, 1864

Executive Mansion,
Washington, D.C.

Major General Sherman,
The State election of Indiana occurs on the 11th. of October, and the loss of it to the friends of the Government would go far towards losing the whole Union cause. The bad effect upon the November election,[55] and especially the giving the State Government to those who will oppose the war in every possible way,[56] are too much to risk, if it can possibly be avoided. The draft proceeds, notwithstanding its strong tendency to lose us the State. Indiana is the only important State, voting in October, whose soldiers cannot vote in the field. Any thing you can safely do to let her soldiers, or any part of them, go home and vote at the State election, will be greatly in point. They need not remain for the Presidential election, but may return to you at once. This is, in no sense, an order, but is merely intended to impress you with the importance, to the army itself, of your doing all you safely can, yourself being the judge of what you can safely do.

Yours truly
A. LINCOLN

[55] That is, the November presidential election.
[56] In other words, the Democrats.

At 7 P.M. on Election Day, Lincoln went to the War Department with a few other officials to await telegraphed reports of election returns. Late in the night, it became almost certain that he had been re-elected. He learned later that he had carried every state except Delaware, Kentucky, and New Jersey, for an electoral vote tally of 212 to 21, a popular vote majority of 55 percent, and the support of more than three out of four soldiers whose votes were tabulated separately. It was a smashing victory, made possible by Lincoln's success in maintaining the support of the coalition of voters who had elected him in 1860. Lincoln reflected on the larger meaning of his victory in remarks, subsequently published in the *Washington Chronicle,* to serenaders from the Lincoln and Johnson clubs of Washington and Georgetown.

Response to a Serenade
November 10, 1864

It has long been a grave question whether any government, not *too* strong for the liberties of its people, can be strong *enough* to maintain its own existence, in great emergencies.

On this point the present rebellion brought our republic to a severe test; and a presidential election occurring in regular course during the rebellion added not a little to the strain. If the loyal people, *united,* were put to the utmost of their strength by the rebellion, must they not fail when *divided,* and partially paralized, by a political war among themselves?

But the election was a necessity.

We can not have free government without elections; and if the rebellion could force us to forego, or postpone a national election, it might fairly claim to have already conquered and ruined us. The strife of the election is but human-nature practically applied to the facts of the case. What has occurred in this case, must ever recur in similar cases. Human-nature will not change. In any future great national trial, compared with the men of this, we shall have as weak, and as strong; as silly and as wise; as bad and good. Let us, therefore, study the incidents of this, as philosophy to learn wisdom from, and none of them as wrongs to be revenged.

But the election, along with its incidental, and undesirable strife, has done good too. It has demonstrated that a people's government can sustain a national election, in the midst of a great civil war. Until now it has not been known to the world that this was a possibility. It shows also how *sound,* and how *strong* we still are. It shows that, even among candidates of the same party, he who is most devoted to the Union, and most opposed to treason, can receive most of the people's votes. It shows also, to the extent yet known, that we have more men now, than we had when the war began. Gold is good in its place; but living, brave, patriotic men, are better than gold.

But the rebellion continues; and now that the election is over, may not all, having a common interest, re-unite in a common effort, to save our common country? For my own part I have striven, and shall strive to avoid placing any obstacle in the way. So long as I have been here I have not willingly planted a thorn in any man's bosom.

While I am deeply sensible to the high compliment of a re-election; and duly grateful, as I trust, to Almighty God for having directed my countrymen to a right conclusion, as I think, for their own good, it adds nothing to my satisfaction that any other man may be disappointed or pained by the result.

May I ask those who have not differed with me, to join with me, in this same spirit towards those who have?

And now, let me close by asking three hearty cheers for our brave soldiers and seamen and their gallant and skilful commanders.

Lincoln acknowledged the ultimate sacrifice made by so many thousands of families throughout the Union in an eloquent letter to Mrs. Lydia Bixby, a widowed mother who lived in Boston. The *Boston Transcript* soon published the letter. Significantly, Lincoln remarked Mrs. Bixby's costly sacrifice "upon the altar of Freedom," not the altar of Union. Now that he had been re-elected, Lincoln knew that still more sacrifices would be required to ensure the nation's new birth of freedom.

Letter to Lydia Bixby
November 21, 1864

Executive Mansion,
Washington

Dear Madam,—I have been shown in the files of the War Department a statement of the Adjutant General of Massachusetts, that you are the mother of five sons who have died gloriously on the field of battle.[57]

I feel how weak and fruitless must be any words of mine which should attempt to beguile you from the grief of a loss so overwhelming. But I cannot refrain from tendering to you the consolation that may be found in the thanks of the Republic they died to save.

I pray that our Heavenly Father may assuage the anguish of your bereavement, and leave you only the cherished memory of the loved and lost, and the solemn pride that must be yours, to have laid so costly a sacrifice upon the altar of Freedom.

Yours, very sincerely and respectfully,[58]
A. LINCOLN.

[57]In fact, Mrs. Bixby had five sons in the Union army, but the adjutant general misinformed Lincoln about their deaths; two of the five were killed.

[58]Lincoln signed this famous letter and there is no doubt that it conveyed his sentiments, but the original manuscript letter was evidently destroyed by Mrs. Bixby. Years later, Lincoln's secretary, John Hay, claimed that he wrote the letter; the evidence that he did is intriguing but not conclusive. The strongest case for Hay's authorship is made by Michael Burlingame, "New Light on the Bixby Letter," *Journal of the Abraham Lincoln Association,* 16 (1995), 59–71.

10

"To Finish the Work We Are In"

Re-election boosted Lincoln's confidence that he could—as he put it in his second inaugural address—"finish the work we are in." Lincoln's re-election defeated at the ballot box the Confederates' hope that northerners would vote for peace under Democrats rather than for continuing the war under Lincoln. Having won the battle on the political front at home, Lincoln gained a decisive advantage he had lacked before re-election: time. Lincoln's re-election made time an enemy of the Confederacy. With four more years as president ahead of him, Lincoln had every reason to believe that the Confederate army could not hold out against the unrelenting attacks of Union commanders.

THE WAR CONTINUES

Lincoln expressed his renewed confidence in his annual message to Congress early in December 1864. He reviewed evidence of northern strength to show that the war could be continued "indefinitely," a statement no sensible Confederate leader could match. Reports of Union successes on the battlefield soon confirmed Lincoln's optimism.

Annual Message to Congress
December 6, 1864

Fellow-citizens of the Senate and House of Representatives:
. . . The war continues. Since the last annual message all the important lines and positions then occupied by our forces have been maintained, and our arms have steadily advanced; thus liberating the regions left in rear, so that Missouri, Kentucky, Tennessee and parts of other States have again produced reasonably fair crops.

The most remarkable feature in the military operations of the year is General Sherman's attempted march of three hundred miles directly through the insurgent region.[1] It tends to show a great increase of our relative strength that our General-in-Chief[2] should feel able to confront and hold in check every active force of the enemy, and yet to detach a well-appointed large army[3] to move on such an expedition. The result not yet being known, conjecture in regard to it is not here indulged.

Important movements have also occurred during the year to the effect of moulding society for durability in the Union. Although short of complete success, it is much in the right direction, that twelve thousand citizens in each of the States of Arkansas and Louisiana have organized loyal State governments with free constitutions, and are earnestly struggling to maintain and administer them. The movements in the same direction, more extensive, though less definite in Missouri, Kentucky and Tennessee, should not be overlooked. But Maryland presents the example of complete success. Maryland is secure to Liberty and Union for all the future.[4] The genius of rebellion will no more claim Maryland. Like another foul spirit, being driven out, it may seek to tear her, but it will woo her no more.

At the last session of Congress a proposed amendment of the Constitution abolishing slavery throughout the United States, passed the Senate, but failed for lack of the requisite two-thirds vote in the House of Representatives. Although the present is the same Congress, and nearly the same members, and without questioning the wisdom or patriotism of those who stood in opposition, I venture to recommend the reconsideration and passage of the measure at the present session. Of course the abstract question is not changed; but an intervening election shows, almost certainly, that the next Congress will pass the measure if this does not. Hence there is only a question of *time* as to when the proposed amendment will go to the States for their action. And as it is to so go, at all events, may we not agree that the sooner the better? It is not claimed that the election has imposed a duty on members to change their views or their votes, any further than, as an additional element to be considered, their judgment may be affected by it. It is the voice of the people now, for the first time, heard upon the question. In a great national crisis, like ours, unanimity of action among those seeking a common end is very desirable—almost indispensable. And yet no approach to such unanimity is attainable, unless some deference shall be paid to the will of the majority, simply because it is the will of the majority. In this case the common end is the maintenance of the Union; and, among the means to secure that end, such will, through the election, is most clearly declared in favor of such constitutional amendment.

[1]On September 15, General Sherman left Atlanta, cutting his lines of communication and supply, and began his famous march through enemy territory toward Savannah.
[2]That is, General Grant.
[3]That is, Sherman's army of more than sixty thousand battle-hardened veterans.
[4]Lincoln is referring to Maryland's new constitution abolishing slavery.

The most reliable indication of public purpose in this country is derived through our popular elections. Judging by the recent canvass and its result, the purpose of the people, within the loyal States, to maintain the integrity of the Union, was never more firm, nor more nearly unanimous, than now. The extraordinary calmness and good order with which the millions of voters met and mingled at the polls, give strong assurance of this. Not only all those who supported the Union ticket, so called, but a great majority of the opposing party also, may be fairly claimed to entertain, and to be actuated by, the same purpose. It is an unanswerable argument to this effect, that no candidate for any office whatever, high or low, has ventured to seek votes on the avowal that he was for giving up the Union. There have been much impugning of motives, and much heated controversy as to the proper means and best mode of advancing the Union cause; but on the distinct issue of Union or no Union, the politicians have shown their instinctive knowledge that there is no diversity among the people. In affording the people the fair opportunity of showing, one to another and to the world, this firmness and unanimity of purpose, the election has been of vast value to the national cause.

The election has exhibited another fact not less valuable to be known—the fact that we do not approach exhaustion in the most important branch of national resources—that of living men. While it is melancholy to reflect that the war has filled so many graves, and carried mourning to so many hearts, it is some relief to know that, compared with the surviving, the fallen have been so few. While corps, and divisions, and brigades, and regiments have formed, and fought, and dwindled, and gone out of existence, a great majority of the men who composed them are still living. The same is true of the naval service.... The important fact remains demonstrated, that we have *more* men *now* than we had when the war *began;* that we are not exhausted, nor in process of exhaustion; that we are *gaining* strength, and may, if need be, maintain the contest indefinitely. This as to men. Material resources are now more complete and abundant than ever.

The national resources, then, are unexhausted, and, as we believe, inexhaustible. The public purpose to re-establish and maintain the national authority is unchanged, and, as we believe, unchangeable. The manner of continuing the effort remains to choose. On careful consideration of all the evidence accessible it seems to me that no attempt at negotiation with the insurgent leader[5] could result in any good. He would accept nothing short of severance of the Union—precisely what we will not and cannot give. His declarations to this effect are explicit and oft-repeated. He does not attempt to deceive us. He affords us no excuse to deceive ourselves. He cannot voluntarily reaccept the Union; we cannot voluntarily yield it. Between him and us the issue is distinct, simple, and inflexible. It is an issue which can only be tried by war, and decided by victory. If we yield, we are beaten; if the Southern

[5]That is, Jefferson Davis.

people fail him, he is beaten. Either way, it would be the victory and defeat following war. What is true, however, of him who heads the insurgent cause, is not necessarily true of those who follow. Although he cannot reaccept the Union, they can. Some of them, we know, already desire peace and reunion. The number of such may increase. They can, at any moment, have peace simply by laying down their arms and submitting to the national authority under the Constitution. After so much, the government could not, if it would, maintain war against them. The loyal people would not sustain or allow it. If questions should remain, we would adjust them by the peaceful means of legislation, conference, courts, and votes, operating only in constitutional and lawful channels. . . .

A year ago general pardon and amnesty, upon specified terms, were offered to all, except certain designated classes; and, it was, at the same time, made known that the excepted classes were still within contemplation of special clemency.[6] . . . Thus, practically, the door has been, for a full year, open to all, except such as were not in condition to make free choice—that is, such as were in custody or under constraint. It is still so open to all. But the time may come—probably will come—when public duty shall demand that it be closed; and that, in lieu, more rigorous measures than heretofore shall be adopted.

In presenting the abandonment of armed resistance to the national authority on the part of the insurgents, as the only indispensable condition to ending the war on the part of the government, I retract nothing heretofore said as to slavery. I repeat the declaration made a year ago, that "while I remain in my present position I shall not attempt to retract or modify the emancipation proclamation, nor shall I return to slavery any person who is free by the terms of that proclamation, or by any of the Acts of Congress." If the people should, by whatever mode or means, make it an Executive duty to re-enslave such persons, another, and not I, must be their instrument to perform it.

In stating a single condition of peace, I mean simply to say that the war will cease on the part of the government, whenever it shall have ceased on the part of those who began it.

ABRAHAM LINCOLN

[6]See Lincoln's Proclamation of Amnesty and Reconstruction, December 8, 1863, in chapter 9.

While General Sherman burned a wide swath across central Georgia, Confederate General John B. Hood initiated a bold and reckless advance into Tennessee that culminated in a devastating defeat at Nashville by Union forces under General George H. Thomas.

Letter to George H. Thomas

December 16, 1864

Office U.S. Military Telegraph,
War Department,
Washington, D.C.

Major General Thomas
Nashville, Tenn.
Please accept for yourself, officers, and men, the nation's thanks for your good work of yesterday. You made a magnificent beginning. A grand consummation is within your easy reach. Do not let it slip.[7]

A. LINCOLN

[7]Lincoln and Grant feared that Thomas, like other Union commanders in the past, might not press on to destroy Hood's army. In fact, Thomas did not let this opportunity slip, pursuing Hood's army all the way back to Mississippi, where Hood finally resigned his command in early January 1865.

Lincoln soon received news of an even greater military achievement. A day after marching into Savannah, Georgia, General Sherman telegraphed Lincoln on December 22, 1864, "I beg to present you as a Christmas gift the city of Savannah, with 150 heavy guns & plenty of ammunition & also about 25000 bales of cotton."[8] Sherman's army had proven that the Confederate military was incapable of protecting its homeland, profoundly demoralizing Confederate military and civilian leaders alike.

[8]Sherman to Lincoln, December 22, 1864, *CW,* VIII, 182.

Letter to William T. Sherman

December 26, 1864

Executive Mansion,
Washington

My dear General Sherman.
Many, many, thanks for your Christmas-gift—the capture of Savannah.

When you were about leaving Atlanta for the Atlantic coast, I was *anxious,* if not fearful; but feeling that you were the better judge, and remembering that "nothing risked, nothing gained" I did not interfere. Now, the undertaking being a success, the honor is all yours; for I believe none of us went farther than to acquiesce. And, taking the work of Gen. Thomas into the count, as it should be taken, it is indeed a great success. Not only does it afford the obvious and immediate military advantages; but, in showing to the world that your army could be divided, putting the stronger part to an important new service,[9] and yet leaving enough[10] to vanquish the old opposing force of the whole—Hood's army—it brings those who sat in darkness, to see a great light. But what next? I suppose it will be safer if I leave Gen. Grant and yourself to decide.

Please make my grateful acknowledgments to your whole army, officers and men.

Yours very truly
A. Lincoln.

[9]That is, Sherman's army, which marched from Atlanta to Savannah.
[10]That is, Thomas's army, which had been part of Sherman's command in the assault on Atlanta.

General Sherman, with General Grant's concurrence, proposed to follow his march across Georgia with an even more dangerous but eagerly anticipated march through the heartland of secession, South Carolina. Sherman wrote that his strategy would still be to "make a good ready and then move rapidly to my objective, avoiding a battle at points where I would be encumbered by wounded, but striking boldly and quickly when my objective is reached ... [in order to] conduct war as though it could only terminate with the destruction of the enemy."[11]

[11]Sherman to Henry W. Halleck, December 31, 1864, *CW*, VIII, 201.

Letter to Edwin M. Stanton

January 5, 1865

Executive Mansion,
Washington

Hon. Sec. of War
Dear Sir,
Since parting with you, it has occurred to me to say that while Gen. Sherman's *"get a good ready"* is appreciated, and is not to be overlooked, *time,*

[12]In other words, Lincoln did not want Sherman to take too much time getting ready for the attack on South Carolina.

now that the enemy is wavering, is more important than ever before.[12] Being on the down-hill, & some what confused, keeping him[13] going. Please say so much to Genl. S[herman].

> Yours truly
> A. LINCOLN

[13] That is, the enemy.

While millions of northern men served in uniform, Lincoln's eldest son, Robert Todd Lincoln, remained a student at Harvard until he graduated in 1864. Criticized as a shirker, Robert wanted to enlist, but his parents feared for his safety. Although the president himself obviously could not serve in the army, he nonetheless paid $750 to a substitute—a man from Strouds-burg, Pennsylvania, named John Summerfield Staples—to serve as his personal representative in the ranks. Lincoln also interceded with Grant and asked for a safe, token position for Robert.

Letter to Ulysses S. Grant

January 19, 1865

> Executive Mansion,
> Washington

Lieut. General Grant:
Please read and answer this letter as though I was not President, but only a friend. My son, now in his twenty second year, having graduated at Harvard, wishes to see something of the war before it ends. I do not wish to put him in the ranks, nor yet to give him a commission, to which those who have already served long, are better entitled, and better qualified to hold. Could he, without embarrassment to you, or detriment to the service, go into your Military family with some nominal rank, I, and not the public, furnishing his necessary means? If no, say so without the least hesitation, because I am as anxious, and as deeply interested, that you shall not be encumbered as you can be yourself.[14]

> Yours truly
> A. LINCOLN

[14] Grant arranged for Robert to receive a captain's commission on his staff with the primary duty of serving as an escort for visitors to the army.

TOWARD PEACE AND FREEDOM

Union military success made the terms of peace a pressing concern for Lincoln. In early January 1865, Lincoln agreed to permit Francis P. Blair, a longtime supporter and editor of the *Congressional Globe,* to go to Richmond and sound out Jefferson Davis about possible peace negotiations. Davis told Blair that he was willing to send representatives to a "conference with a view to secure peace to the two countries."[15] Lincoln, of course, found Davis's "two countries" formula unacceptable. He sent Blair back to Richmond with an expression of willingness to meet informally with Confederate representatives "with the view of securing peace to the people of our one common country."[16] After numerous memos back and forth, Lincoln agreed to informal discussion at Hampton Roads, Virginia,[17] with three Confederate representatives: Alexander H. Stephens, the Confederate vice president and a former Whig from Georgia whom Lincoln had known when both served in Congress almost twenty years earlier; John A. Campbell, a former Supreme Court justice who resigned to become the Confederate assistant secretary of war; and Robert M. T. Hunter, a former U.S. congressman and Speaker of the House who served as Confederate secretary of state before being elected to represent Virginia in the Confederate Senate. Lincoln specified his conditions for the Hampton Roads discussions in a letter to Secretary of State William Seward.

[15]Jefferson Davis to F. P. Blair, January 12, 1865, *CW,* VIII, 275.
[16]Lincoln to F. P. Blair, January 18, 1865, *CW,* VIII, 220.
[17]Hampton Roads is the entrance to the harbor of Norfolk, Virginia, at the mouth of the James River.

Letter to William H. Seward

January 31, 1865

Executive Mansion,
Washington

Hon. William H. Seward
Secretary of State
You will proceed to Fortress-Monroe, Virginia, there to meet, and informally confer with Messrs. Stephens, Hunter, and Campbell. . . .
    You will make known to them that three things are indispensable, towit:
    1. The restoration of the national authority throughout all the States.

2. No receding, by the Executive of the United States on the Slavery question, from the position assumed thereon, in the late Annual Message to Congress, and in preceding documents.

3. No cessation of hostilities short of an end of the war, and the disbanding of all forces hostile to the government.

You will inform them that all propositions of theirs not inconsistent with the above, will be considered and passed upon in a spirit of sincere liberality. You will hear all they may choose to say, and report it to me.

You will not assume to definitely consummate anything.

Yours &c.
ABRAHAM LINCOLN.

Lincoln made clear that, despite this peace overture, General Grant should press on with the more certain approach to peace, namely the destruction of Lee's army.

Letter to Ulysses S. Grant

February 1, 1865

"Cypher"

Office U.S. Military Telegraph,
War Department,
Washington, D.C.

Lieut. Genl. Grant
City-Point.
Let nothing which is transpiring, change, hinder, or delay your Military movements, or plans.

A LINCOLN

Lincoln met with Seward and the Confederate representatives aboard the presidential steamboat, *River Queen,* at Hampton Roads on February 3. After several hours, it became clear that the Confederates were unwilling to accept Lincoln's terms. Although the meeting had been held in secret, a few days later Lincoln sent to the House of Representatives a full documentary record of the discussions, which, as he wrote, "ended without result."[18]

---

[18]Lincoln to the House of Representatives, February 10, 1865, *CW,* VIII, 285.

Lincoln insisted that only he, not his military commanders, had the authority to negotiate terms for ending the war, as he relayed to General Grant via the following letter from Secretary of War Stanton.

Letter to Ulysses S. Grant
March 3, 1865

Lieutenant General Grant[19]
The President directs me to say to you that he wishes you to have no conference with General Lee unless it be for the capitulation of Gen. Lee's army, or on some minor, and purely, military matter. He instructs me to say that you are not to decide, discuss, or confer upon any political question. Such questions the President holds in his own hands; and will submit them to no military conferences or conventions. Meantime you are to press to the utmost, your military advantages.

Edwin M Stanton
Secretary of War

[19]Grant had asked Stanton for instructions about how to respond to a letter from General Lee asking to meet with Grant to discuss "the possibility of arriving at a satisfactory adjustment of the present unhappy difficulties, by means of a military convention." Grant to Stanton, March 2, 1865, *CW,* VIII, 331.

While the Union army pressed forward on the military front as Lincoln directed, Congress responded to Lincoln's request for a thirteenth amendment abolishing slavery throughout the nation. Although Lincoln's signature was not required before submitting the congressional resolution to the states for ratification, Lincoln signed it anyway and explained its significance to a group of serenaders.

Resolution Submitting the
Thirteenth Amendment to the States

February 1, 1865

A RESOLUTION

Submitting to the legislatures of the several States a proposition to amend the Constitution of the United States.

Resolved by the Senate and House of Representatives of the United States of America in Congress assembled, (two-thirds of both houses concurring), That the following article be proposed to the legislatures of the several States as an amendment to the constitution of the United States, which, when ratified by three-fourths of said Legislatures, shall be valid, to all intents and purposes, as a part of the said Constitution, namely: Article XIII. Section 1. Neither slavery nor involuntary servitude, except as a punishment for crime whereof the party shall have been duly convicted, shall exist within the United States, or any place subject to their jurisdiction. Section 2. Congress shall have power to enforce this article by appropriate legislation.

SCHUYLER COLFAX
Speaker of the House of Representatives.
H. HAMLIN
Vice President of the United States, and
President of the Senate.

Approved, February 1. 1865.   ABRAHAM LINCOLN

Response to a Serenade

February 1, 1865

The President said he supposed the passage through Congress of the Constitutional amendment for the abolishment of Slavery throughout the United States, was the occasion to which he was indebted for the honor of this call. [Applause.] The occasion was one of congratulation to the country and to the whole world. But there is a task yet before us—to go forward and consummate by the votes of the States that which Congress so nobly began yesterday.[20] [Applause and cries—"They will do it," &c.] He had the honor to inform those present that Illinois had already to-day done the work. [Applause.] Maryland was about half through; but he felt proud that Illinois

---

[20]The requisite states officially ratified the amendment by December 18, 1865.

was a little ahead. He thought this measure was a very fitting if not an indispensable adjunct to the winding up of the great difficulty. He wished the reunion of all the States perfected and so effected as to remove all causes of disturbance in the future; and to attain this end it was necessary that the original disturbing cause[21] should, if possible, be rooted out. He thought all would bear him witness that he had never shrunk from doing all that he could to eradicate Slavery by issuing an emancipation proclamation. [Applause.] But that proclamation falls far short of what the amendment will be when fully consummated. A question might be raised whether the proclamation was legally valid. It might be added that it only aided those who came into our lines and that it was inoperative as to those who did not give themselves up, or that it would have no effect upon the children of the slaves born hereafter. In fact it would be urged that it did not meet the evil. But this amendment is a King's cure for all the evils. [Applause.] It winds the whole thing up. He would repeat that it was the fitting if not indispensable adjunct to the consummation of the great game we are playing. He could not but congratulate all present, himself, the country and the whole world upon this great moral victory.

[21] That is, slavery.

Although Lincoln resolutely supported the end of slavery, he nonetheless favored federal compensation to masters for the loss of slave property. He had offered compensation to border-state masters back in 1862,[22] but only in Washington, D.C., was compensated emancipation actually put into practice. There the federal government paid masters for 2,989 slaves, hiring a Baltimore slave trader to determine a reasonable value for each one.[23] By February 1865, Lincoln was so eager to end the war that he proposed privately to his cabinet that the government compensate all slave states— including Confederate states—for their loss of slave property. Lincoln believed the proposal might drive a wedge between Confederate leaders, who refused to stop fighting, and the Confederate people, who might well respond to this incentive to abandon the war and support emancipation. Lincoln also maintained that the $400 million offer of compensation was small compared to the cost of continuing the war, which he estimated at $3 million a day. Lincoln's cabinet persuaded him that this compensation pro-

[22] See, for example, Lincoln's message to Congress, March 6, 1862, and his appeal to border-state representatives, July 12, 1862, in chapter 7.

[23] Ira Berlin et al., eds., *Freedom: A Documentary History of Emancipation,* Series I, Volume I, *The Destruction of Slavery* (Cambridge, 1985), 165.

posal would never be approved by Congress; he took their advice, and the proposal was quietly shelved. The proposal illustrates Lincoln's astonishing willingness to recognize masters'—even rebel masters'—property rights in slaves at the same time that he urged ratification of the Thirteenth Amendment to guarantee slaves' rights to freedom.

Message to the Senate and House of Representatives
February 5, 1865

Fellow citizens of the Senate, and House of Representatives.

I respectfully recommend that a Joint Resolution, substantially as follows, be adopted so soon as practicable, by your honorable bodies.

"Resolved by the Senate and House of Representatives, of the United States of America in congress assembled: That the President of the United States is hereby empowered, in his discretion, to pay four hundred millions of dollars to the States of Alabama, Arkansas, Delaware, Florida, Georgia, Kentucky, Louisiana, Maryland, Mississippi, Missouri, North Carolina, South Carolina, Tennessee, Texas, Virginia, and West-Virginia, in the manner, and on the conditions following, towit: The payment to be made in six per cent government bonds, and to be distributed among said States *pro rata* on their respective slave populations, as shown by the census of 1860; and no part of said sum to be paid unless all resistance to the national authority shall be abandoned and cease, on or before the first day of April next; and upon such abandonment and ceasing of resistance, one half of said sum to be paid in manner aforesaid, and the remaining half to be paid only upon the amendment of the national constitution recently proposed by congress, becoming valid law, on or before the first day of July next, by the action thereon of the requisite number of States."

The adoption of such resolution is sought with a view to embody it, with other propositions, in a proclamation looking to peace and re-union.

Whereas a Joint Resolution has been adopted by congress in the words following, towit

Now therefore I, Abraham Lincoln, President of the United States, do proclaim, declare, and make known, that on the conditions therein stated, the power conferred on the Executive in and by said Joint Resolution, will be fully exercised; that war will cease, and armies be reduced to a basis of peace; that all political offences will be pardoned; that all property, except slaves, liable to confiscation or forfeiture, will be released therefrom, except in cases of intervening interests of third parties; and that liberality will be recommended to congress upon all points not lying within executive control.

[Endorsement]

Feb. 5. 1865

To-day these papers, which explain themselves, were drawn up and submitted to the Cabinet & unanamously disapproved by them.

A LINCOLN

"THAT THIS MIGHTY SCOURGE OF WAR MAY SPEEDILY PASS AWAY"

By inauguration day, the end of the war, at long last, seemed near. In his eloquent Second Inaugural Address, Lincoln attributed "this terrible war" to God's will to end slavery, for which the entire nation must suffer. In contrast to a vengeful God, Lincoln promised a magnanimous peace, "with malice toward none; with charity for all," vanquished and victor alike. Lincoln's calm, elegiac address offered an interpretation of "this mighty scourge of war" that could help "to bind up the nation's wounds." It set a standard of presidential rhetoric that has seldom been equaled and never surpassed.

Lincoln's remarkable generosity toward rebellious southerners looked forward to a peaceful reunion of the nation. But it did not cause Lincoln to moderate his insistence on military victory; he wanted peace and reconstruction not as an alternative to war, but as its result.

Second Inaugural Address
March 4, 1865

[Fellow Countrymen:]

At this second appearing to take the oath of the presidential office, there is less occasion for an extended address than there was at the first. Then a statement, somewhat in detail, of a course to be pursued, seemed fitting and proper. Now, at the expiration of four years, during which public declarations have been constantly called forth on every point and phase of the great contest which still absorbs the attention, and engrosses the enerergies [sic] of the nation, little that is new could be presented. The progress of our arms, upon which all else chiefly depends, is as well known to the public as to myself; and it is, I trust, reasonably satisfactory and encouraging to all. With high hope for the future, no prediction in regard to it is ventured.

On the occasion corresponding to this four years ago, all thoughts were anxiously directed to an impending civil-war. All dreaded it—all sought to avert it. While the inaugeral address was being delivered from this place, devoted altogether to *saving* the Union without war, insurgent agents were in the city seeking to *destroy* it without war—seeking to dissol[v]e the Union, and divide effects, by negotiation. Both parties deprecated war; but one of them[24] would *make* war rather than let the nation survive; and the other would *accept* war rather than let it perish. And the war came.

One eighth of the whole population were colored slaves, not distributed generally over the Union, but localized in the Southern part of it. These slaves constituted a peculiar and powerful interest. All knew that this interest was, somehow, the cause of the war. To strengthen, perpetuate, and extend this interest was the object for which the insurgents would rend the Union, even by war; while the government claimed no right to do more than to restrict the territorial enlargement of it. Neither party expected for the war, the magnitude, or the duration, which it has already attained. Neither anticipated that the *cause*[25] of the conflict might cease with, or even before, the conflict itself should cease. Each looked for an easier triumph, and a result less fundamental and astounding. Both read the same Bible, and pray to the same God; and each invokes His aid against the other. It may seem strange that any men should dare to ask a just God's assistance in wringing their bread from the sweat of other men's faces; but let us judge not that we be not judged. The prayers of both could not be answered; that of neither has been answered fully. The Almighty has His own purposes. "Woe unto the world because of offences! for it must needs be that offences come; but woe to that man by whom the offence cometh!"[26] If we shall suppose that American Slavery is one of those offences which, in the providence of God must needs come, but which, having continued through His appointed time, He now wills to remove, and that He gives to both North and South, this terrible war, as the woe due to those by whom the offence came, shall we discern therein any departure from those divine attributes which the believers in a Living God always ascribe to Him? Fondly do we hope—fervently do we pray—that this mighty scourge of war may speedily pass away. Yet, if God wills that it continue, until all the wealth piled by the bond-man's two hundred and fifty years of unrequited toil shall be sunk, and until every drop of blood drawn with the lash, shall be paid by another drawn with the sword, as was said three thousand years ago, so still it must be said "the judgments of the Lord, are true and righteous altogether."[27]

With malice toward none; with charity for all; with firmness in the right, as God gives us to see the right, let us strive on to finish the work we are in; to bind up the nation's wounds; to care for him who shall have borne the battle, and for his widow, and his orphan—to do all which may achieve and cherish a just, and a lasting peace, among ourselves, and with all nations.

[24]That is, the Confederacy.
[25]That is, slavery.
[26]Matthew 18: 17.
[27]Psalms 19: 9.

The Second Inaugural Address did not immediately receive the acclaim it has subsequently earned. Lincoln explained his own assessment of the address in a letter to the prominent New York Republican Thurlow Weed.

Letter to Thurlow Weed
March 15, 1865

Executive Mansion,
Washington

Thurlow Weed, Esq.

My dear Sir.

Every one likes a compliment. Thank you for yours on my little notification speech,[28] and on the recent Inaugeral Address.[29] I expect the latter to wear as well as—perhaps better than—any thing I have produced; but I believe it is not immediately popular. Men are not flattered by being shown that there has been a difference of purpose between the Almighty and them. To deny it, however, in this case, is to deny that there is a God governing the world. It is a truth which I thought needed to be told; and as whatever of humiliation there is in it, falls most directly on myself, I thought others might afford for me to tell it.

Yours truly
A. LINCOLN

[28]On March 1, 1865, Lincoln made the following three-sentence speech to a committee of Congress officially notifying him of his re-election: "Having served four years in the depths of a great, and yet unended national peril, I can view this call to a second term, in nowise more flatteringly to myself, than as an expression of the public judgment, that I may better finish a difficult work, in which I have labored from the first, than could any one less severely schooled to the task.

In this view, and with assured reliance on that Almighty Ruler who has so graceously sustained us thus far; and with increased gratitude to the generous people for their continued confidence, I accept the renewed trust, with it's onerous and perplexing duties and responsibilities.

Please communicate this to the two Houses of Congress." Weed praised this speech as "not only the neatest but the most pregnant and effective use to which the English Language was ever put." Lincoln to Notification Committee, March 1, 1865; Weed to Lincoln, March 4, 1865; *CW,* VIII, 326, 356.

[29]No mention of the inaugural address has been found in correspondence from Weed. Lincoln evidently remembered Weed's extravagant praise of the notification speech as applying also—or instead—to the inaugural address.

Lincoln often received petitions to pardon men facing execution for desertion or other serious military crimes. In 1864, he told a Republican congressman, "Some of my generals complain that I impair discipline and sub-ordination in the army by my pardons and respites, but it makes me rested, after a day's hard work if I can find some good excuse for saving a man's life, and I go to bed happy as I think how joyous the signing of my name will make him and his family and friends."[30] General Grant telegraphed just such a complaint to Secretary of War Stanton in early March. Grant said it was "wrong" for Confederate prisoners in the North to take the oath of allegiance to the Union and then go free; they should instead be exchanged for Union prisoners in Confederate hands.[31] Lincoln explained that his pardons, in effect, put into practice his inaugural pledge "to bind up the nation's wounds."

[30]Schuyler Colfax, *Life and Principles of Abraham Lincoln* (Philadelphia, 1865), 18.
[31]Grant to Stanton, March 8, 1865, *CW,* VIII, 348.

Letter to Ulysses S. Grant
March 9, 1865

Office U.S. Military Telegraph,
War Department,
Washington, D.C.

Lieut. Genl. Grant
City-Point, Va.

I see your despatch to the Sec. of War, objecting to rebel prisoners being allowed to take the oath and go free. Supposing that I am responsible for what is done in this way, I think fit to say that there is no general rule, or action, allowing prisoners to be discharged merely on taking the oath. What has been done is that Members of Congress come to me from time to time with lists of names alleging that from personal knowledge, and evidence of reliable persons they are satisfied that it is safe to discharge the particular persons named on the lists, and I have ordered their discharge.[32] These Members are chiefly from the border states; and those they get discharged are their neighbors and neighbors sons. They tell me that they do not bring to me one tenth of the names which are brought to them, bringing only such as their knowledge or the proof satisfies them about. I have, on the same principle, discharged some on the representations of others than Members of Congress, as, for instance, Gov. [Andrew] Johnson of Tennessee. The number I have discharged has been rather larger than I liked—reaching I should

[32]That is, the men on the lists fought for the Confederacy, although they were from the loyal border states.

think an average of fifty a day, since the recent general exchange commenced.[33] On the same grounds, last year, I discharged quite a number at different times, aggregating perhaps a thousand, Missourians and Kentuckians; and their Members returning here since the prisoner's return to their homes, report to me only two cases of proving false.[34] Doubtless some more have proved false; but, on the whole I believe what I have done in this way has done good rather than harm.

A. LINCOLN

[33] A general exchange of prisoners had been agreed to in January 1865. No regular exchange had existed since May 1863 because the Union refused to exchange captured Confederates until the Confederacy changed its policy of considering black soldiers slaves or traitors, rather than prisoners of war who were eligible for exchange.

[34] That is, men who took the oath of allegiance to the Union in order to be pardoned but subsequently continued their loyalty to the Confederacy.

As Confederate military prospects became gloomier, rebel leaders began to discuss seriously the possibility of arming slaves. With the endorsement of General Lee, a bill to conscript a quota of black soldiers from each state was considered by the Confederate Congress, where the Senate passed it but the House defeated it by one vote. Lincoln commented on this act of Confederate desperation in a speech to an Indiana regiment that was subsequently published in the *New York Herald* and other newspapers.

Speech to 140th Indiana Regiment
March 17, 1865

FELLOW CITIZENS—It will be but a very few words that I shall undertake to say. I was born in Kentucky, raised in Indiana and lived in Illinois. (Laughter.) And now I am here, where it is my business to care equally for the good people of all the States. I am glad to see an Indiana regiment on this day able to present the captured flag to the Governor of Indiana. (Applause.) I am not disposed, in saying this, to make a distinction between the states, for all have done equally well. (Applause.) There are but few views or aspects of this great war upon which I have not said or written something whereby my own opinions might be known. But there is one—the recent attempt of our erring brethren, as they are sometimes called—(laughter)—to employ the negro to fight for them. I have neither written nor made a speech on that subject, because that was their business, not mine; and if I had a wish upon the subject I had not the power to introduce it, or make it effective. The great ques-

Figure 10.   Reburial of Union Dead
Soldiers killed in battle were often buried hastily in shallow graves that were soon
opened by rainstorms and rummaging animals. As shown in this April 1865 photograph of the Cold Harbor, Virginia, battlefield, black soldiers were frequently
assigned the heavy labor of reburial of soldiers' remains in proper graves.

tion with them was, whether the negro, being put into the army, would fight
for them. I do not know, and therefore cannot decide. (Laughter.) They ought
to know better than we. I have in my lifetime heard many arguments why the
negroes ought to be slaves; but if they fight for those who would keep them
in slavery it will be a better argument than any I have yet heard.[35] (Laughter
and applause.) He who will fight for that ought to be a slave. (Applause.)
They have concluded at last to take one out of four of the slaves, and put
them in the army; and that one of the four who will fight to keep the others
in slavery ought to be a slave himself unless he is killed in a fight.
(Applause.) While I have often said that all men ought to be free, yet I would

[35]The Virginia legislature passed a law on March 13, 1865, authorizing slaves to fight
against the Union, and two black companies were hurriedly assembled, but they were never in
combat.

allow those colored persons to be slaves who want to be; and next to them those white persons who argue in favor of making other people slaves. (Applause.) I am in favor of giving an opportunity to such white men to try it on for themselves. (Applause.) I will say one thing in regard to the negro being employed to fight for them. I do know he cannot fight and stay at home and make bread too—(laughter and applause)—and as one is about as important as the other to them, I don't care which they do. (Renewed applause.) I am rather in favor of having them try them as soldiers. (Applause.) They lack one vote of doing that, and I wish I could send my vote over the river so that I might cast it in favor of allowing the negro to fight. (Applause.) But they cannot fight and work both. We must now see the bottom of the enemy's resources. They will stand out as long as they can, and if the negro will fight for them, they must allow him to fight. They have drawn upon their last branch of resources. (Applause.) And we can now see the bottom. (Applause.) I am glad to see the end so near at hand. (Applause.) I have said now more than I intended, and will therefore bid you goodby.

As Lincoln predicted, the end was near. Grant's long siege of Petersburg finally succeeded on April 2, causing Lee to pull out of the city and retreat toward the west in an attempt to prevent Grant from capturing his entire army. Grant invited Lincoln to visit the army, and the president set out for Virginia on April 3, accompanied by his young son Tad. Lincoln went to Richmond on April 4 and walked the streets of the Confederate capital, even visiting the recently evacuated Confederate White House and sitting in Jefferson Davis's chair. While in Richmond, Lincoln also talked with John A. Campbell—who had participated in the Hampton Roads peace discussions—one of the few Confederate officials still in the city. The next day, Lincoln summarized the terms he had offered to Campbell.

Letter to John A. Campbell

April 5, 1865

As to peace, I have said before, and now repeat, that three things are indispensable.

1. The restoration of the national authority throughout all the States.

2. No receding by the Executive of the United States on the slavery question, from the position assumed thereon, in the late Annual Message to Congress, and in preceding documents.

3. No cessation of hostilities short of an end of the war, and the disbanding of all force hostile to the government.

That all propositions coming from those now in hostility to the government; and not inconsistent with the foregoing, will be respectfully considered, and passed upon in a spirit of sincere liberality.

I now add that it seems useless for me to be more specific with those who will not say they are ready for the indispensable terms, even on conditions to be named by themselves. If there be any who are ready for those indispensable terms, on any conditions whatever, let them say so, and state their conditions, so that such conditions can be distinctly known, and considered.

It is further added that, the remission of confiscations being within the executive power, if the war be now further persisted in, by those opposing the government, the making of confiscated property at the least to bear the additional cost, will be insisted on; but that confiscations (except in cases of third party intervening interests) will be remitted to the people of any State which shall now promptly, and in good faith, withdraw it's troops and other support, from further resistance to the government.[36]

What is now said as to remission of confiscations has no reference to supposed property in slaves.

---

[36]Lincoln was offering an incentive for the Virginia legislature to withdraw its soldiers from the army. But Lincoln told his adviser Charles A. Dana "that [General] Sheridan seemed to be getting Virginia soldiers out of the war faster than this legislature could think." Dana to Stanton, April 7, 1865, *CW,* VIII, 387.

Upon receiving news that General Sheridan had almost succeeded in cutting off Lee's retreat, Lincoln telegraphed his encouragement to Grant.

Letter to Ulysses S. Grant
April 7, 1865

Head Quarters Armies of the United States,
City-Point,
11 AM.

Lieut Gen. Grant.
Gen. Sheridan says "If the thing is pressed I think that Lee will surrender."
Let the *thing* be pressed.

A LINCOLN

Figure 11.   Lincoln in 1865
One of the last photographs of Lincoln, this portrait made in February 1865 documents the war's personal toll on the president. Two and a half months later, following Lee's surrender at Appomattox, Lincoln was assassinated.

Grant needed no reminder to press on. He accepted the surrender of Lee's
army in the home of Virginia farmer Wilmer McLean at Appomattox
Courthouse about 1 P.M. on April 9. Lincoln learned of the surrender that
night after he had returned to Washington from Virginia. The next day, he
spoke briefly to a jubilant crowd gathered at the White House. His remarks
were published by the *Washington Daily National Intelligencer* and other
newspapers.

Response to a Serenade

FELLOW CITIZENS: I am very greatly rejoiced to find that an occasion has occurred so pleasurable that the people cannot restrain themselves. [Cheers.] I suppose that arrangements are being made for some sort of a formal demonstration, this, or perhaps, to-morrow night. [Cries of 'We can't wait,' 'We want it now,' &c.] If there should be such a demonstration, I, of course, will be called upon to respond, and I shall have nothing to say if you dribble it all out of me before. [Laughter and applause.] I see you have a band of music with you. [Voices, 'We have two or three.'] I propose closing up this interview by the band performing a particular tune which I will name. Before this is done, however, I wish to mention one or two little circumstances connected with it. I have always thought 'Dixie' one of the best tunes I have ever heard. Our adversaries over the way attempted to appropriate it, but I insisted yesterday that we fairly captured it. [Applause.] I presented the question to the Attorney General, and he gave it as his legal opinion that it is our lawful prize. [Laughter and applause.] I now request the band to favor me with its performance.[37]

[37]While the President remained in view, the band played "Dixie," followed by "Yankee Doodle," then Lincoln called for "three good hearty cheers for General Grant and all under his command," then "three more cheers for our gallant Navy." *Washington Daily National Intelligencer,* April 11, 1865, *CW,* VIII, 393–94.

The next evening, in the midst of the joyous celebration of Lee's surrender and the impending collapse of the rebellion, Lincoln delivered what turned out to be his last public address, a serious and detailed defense of his plans for reconstruction.

Last Public Address

April 11, 1865

We meet this evening, not in sorrow, but in gladness of heart. The evacuation of Petersburg and Richmond, and the surrender of the principal insurgent army, give hope of a righteous and speedy peace whose joyous expression can not be restrained. In the midst of this, however, He, from Whom all blessings flow, must not be forgotten. A call for a national thanksgiving is being prepared, and will be duly promulgated. Nor must those whose harder part gives us the cause of rejoicing, be overlooked. Their honors must not be parcelled out with others. I myself, was near the front, and had the high pleasure of transmitting much of the good news to you; but no part of the honor, for plan or execution, is mine. To Gen. Grant, his skilful officers, and brave men, all belongs. The gallant Navy stood ready, but was not in reach to take active part.

By these recent successes the re-inauguration of the national authority—reconstruction—which has had a large share of thought from the first, is pressed much more closely upon our attention. It is fraught with great difficulty. Unlike the case of a war between independent nations, there is no authorized organ for us to treat with. No one man has authority to give up the rebellion for any other man. We simply must begin with, and mould from, disorganized and discordant elements. Nor is it a small additional embarrassment that we, the loyal people, differ among ourselves as to the mode, manner, and mean, of reconstruction.

As a general rule, I abstain from reading the reports of attacks upon myself, wishing not to be provoked by that to which I can not properly offer an answer. In spite of this precaution, however, it comes to my knowledge that I am much censured for some supposed agency in setting up, and seeking to sustain, the new State Government of Louisiana. In this I have done just so much as, and no more than, the public knows. In the Annual Message of Dec. 1863 and accompanying Proclamation,[38] I presented *a* plan of reconstruction (as the phrase goes) which, I promised, if adopted by any State, should be acceptable to, and sustained by, the Executive government of the nation. I distinctly stated that this was not the only plan which might possibly be acceptable; and I also distinctly protested that the Executive claimed no right to say when, or whether members should be admitted to seats in Congress from such States. This plan was, in advance, submitted to the then Cabinet, and distinctly approved by every member of it. One[39] of them suggested that I should then, and in that connection, apply the Emancipation Proclamation to the theretofore excepted parts of Virginia and Louisiana; that I should drop the suggestion about apprenticeship for freed-people, and that I should omit the protest against my own power, in regard to the admission of members to Congress; but even he approved every part and parcel of the plan which has since been employed or touched by the action of Louisiana. The new constitution of Louisiana, declaring emancipation for the whole State, practically applies the Proclamation to the part previously excepted. It does not adopt apprenticeship for freed-people; and it is silent, as it could not well be otherwise, about the admission of members to Congress.

[38]Both documents are in chapter 9.

[39]Salmon P. Chase, Secretary of the Treasury until July 1864, after which Lincoln appointed him Chief Justice of the Supreme Court. Chase had just written Lincoln urging him to insist on "suffrage to all citizens," that is, including freedmen. Chase to Lincoln, April 11, 1865, *CW,* VIII, 399.

So that, as it applies to Louisiana, every member of the Cabinet fully approved the plan. The Message went to Congress, and I received many commendations of the plan, written and verbal; and not a single objection to it, from any professed emancipationist, came to my knowledge, until after the news reached Washington that the people of Louisiana had begun to move in accordance with it. From about July 1862, I had corresponded with different persons, supposed to be interested, seeking a reconstruction of a State government for Louisiana.[40] When the Message of 1863, with the plan before mentioned, reached New-Orleans, Gen. Banks wrote me that he was confident the people, with his military co-operation, would reconstruct, substantially on that plan. I wrote him, and some of them to try it; they tried it, and the result is known. Such only has been my agency in getting up the Louisiana government. As to sustaining it, my promise is out, as before stated. But, as bad promises are better broken than kept, I shall treat this as a bad promise, and break it, whenever I shall be convinced that keeping it is adverse to the public interest. But I have not yet been so convinced.

I have been shown a letter on this subject, supposed to be an able one, in which the writer[41] expresses regret that my mind has not seemed to be definitely fixed on the question whether the seceded States, so called, are in the Union or out of it. It would perhaps, add astonishment to his regret, were he to learn that since I have found professed Union men endeavoring to make that question, I have *purposely* forborne any public expression upon it. As appears to me that question has not been, nor yet is, a practically material one, and that any discussion of it, while it thus remains practically immaterial, could have no effect other than the mischievous one of dividing our friends. As yet, whatever it may hereafter become, that question is bad, as the basis of a controversy, and good for nothing at all—a merely pernicious abstraction.

We all agree that the seceded States, so called, are out of their proper practical relation with the Union; and that the sole object of the government, civil and military, in regard to those States is to again get them into that proper practical relation. I believe it is not only possible, but in fact, easier, to do this, without deciding, or even considering, whether these states have even been out of the Union, than with it. Finding themselves safely at home, it would be utterly immaterial whether they had ever been abroad. Let us all join in doing the acts necessary to restoring the proper practical relations between these states and the Union; and each forever after, innocently indulge his own opinion whether, in doing the acts, he brought the States from without, into the Union, or only gave them proper assistance, they never having been out of it.

The amount of constituency, so to to [*sic*] speak, on which the new Louisiana government rests, would be more satisfactory to all, if it contained

---

[40] See, for example, Lincoln to Banks, August 5 and November 5, 1863, in chapter 9.
[41] Salmon P. Chase.

fifty, thirty, or even twenty thousand, instead of only about twelve thousand, as it does. It is also unsatisfactory to some that the elective franchise is not given to the colored man. I would myself prefer that it were now conferred on the very intelligent, and on those who serve our cause as soldiers. Still the question is not whether the Louisiana government, as it stands, is quite all that is desirable. The question is "Will it be wiser to take it as it is, and help to improve it; or to reject, and disperse it?" "Can Louisiana be brought into proper practical relation with the Union *sooner* by *sustaining,* or by *discarding* her new State Government?"

Some twelve thousand voters in the heretofore slave-state of Louisiana have sworn allegiance to the Union, assumed to be the rightful political power of the State, held elections, organized a State government, adopted a free-state constitution, giving the benefit of public schools equally to black and white, and empowering the Legislature to confer the elective franchise upon the colored man. Their Legislature has already voted to ratify the constitutional amendment recently passed by Congress, abolishing slavery throughout the nation. These twelve thousand persons are thus fully committed to the Union, and to perpetual freedom in the state—committed to the very things, and nearly all the things the nation wants—and they ask the nations recognition, and it's assistance to make good their committal. Now, if we reject, and spurn them, we do our utmost to disorganize and disperse them. We in effect say to the white men "You are worthless, or worse—we will neither help you, nor be helped by you." To the blacks we say, "This cup of liberty which these, your old masters, hold to your lips, we will dash from you, and leave you to the chances of gathering the spilled and scattered contents in some vague and undefined when, where, and how." If this course, discouraging and paralyzing both white and black, has any tendency to bring Louisiana into proper practical relations with the Union, I have, so far, been unable to perceive it. If, on the contrary, we recognize, and sustain the new government of Louisiana the converse of all this is made true. We encourage the hearts, and nerve the arms of the twelve thousand to adhere to their work, and argue for it, and proselyte for it, and fight for it, and feed it, and grow it, and ripen it to a complete success. The colored man too, in seeing all united for him, is inspired with vigilance, and energy, and daring, to the same end. Grant that he desires the elective franchise, will he not attain it sooner by saving the already advanced steps toward it, than by running backward over them? Concede that the new government of Louisiana is only to what it should be as the egg is to the fowl, we shall sooner have the fowl by hatching the egg than by smashing it? Again, if we reject Louisiana, we also reject one vote in favor of the proposed amendment[42] to the national constitution. To meet this proposition, it has been argued that no more than three fourths of those States which have not attempted secession are necessary to validly ratify the amendment. I do not commit myself against this,

[42]That is, the Thirteenth Amendment abolishing slavery.

further than to say that such a ratification would be questionable, and sure to be persistently questioned; while a ratification by three fourths of all the States would be unquestioned and unquestionable.

I repeat the question. "Can Louisiana be brought into proper practical relation with the Union *sooner* by *sustaining* or by *discarding* her new State Government?"

What has been said of Louisiana will apply generally to other States. And yet so great peculiarities pertain to each state; and such important and sudden changes occur in the same state; and, withal, so new and unprecedented is the whole case, that no exclusive, and inflexible plan can safely be prescribed as to details and colatterals. Such exclusive, and inflexible plan, would surely become a new entanglement. Important principles may, and must, be inflexible.

In the present *"situation"* as the phrase goes, it may be my duty to make some new announcement to the people of the South.[43] I am considering, and shall not fail to act, when satisfied that action will be proper.

---

[43]Lincoln left no record that documents the gist of the announcement he had in mind. Eminent Lincoln scholar David Herbert Donald points out that Lincoln probably had in mind a plan to allow state legislatures to assemble and formally vote to withdraw from the Confederacy as a practical and expedient way to speed reconstruction and restore civil order in the defeated South. David Herbert Donald, *Lincoln* (New York, 1995), 583–85.

Three days later, a relaxed and cheerful President and Mrs. Lincoln went to Ford's Theater to enjoy a performance of the comedy *Our American Cousin.* During the third act, a little after 10 P.M., the actor John Wilkes Booth, a fanatical Confederate sympathizer, made his way into the presidential box, sneaked up behind Lincoln, and shot him in the back of the head. In the pandemonium, Booth escaped.[44] The comatose Lincoln was carried to a private home across the street from the theater; he died there a little before 7:30 A.M. on April 15. At the deathbed, a tearful Secretary of War Stanton solemnly pronounced the benediction, "Now he belongs to the ages."[45]

[44]Booth was subsequently tracked down near Bowling Green, Virginia, and killed on April 26 as he tried to get away.

[45]Stanton quoted in John G. Nicolay and John Hay, *Abraham Lincoln: A History* (10 vols.; New York, 1890), X, 302.

An Abraham Lincoln Chronology
(1809–1865)

1809 *February 12:* Abraham Lincoln is born in Hardin County, Kentucky, the son of Thomas Lincoln (born 1778) and Nancy Hanks Lincoln (born about 1784).

1816 Thomas Lincoln moves his family to Little Pigeon Creek, Indiana.

1818 Nancy Hanks Lincoln dies of milk sickness.

1819 Thomas Lincoln marries Sarah Bush Johnston.

1828 Lincoln and a friend take a cargo of farm products on a flatboat down the Ohio and Mississippi Rivers to New Orleans.

1830 Lincoln moves with his father, stepmother, and family to Macon County, Illinois.

1831 Lincoln, his stepbrother, and a cousin take a second flatboat trip to New Orleans with farm produce. Lincoln's father, stepmother, and family move to Coles County, Illinois. When Lincoln returns to Illinois, he moves to the village of New Salem in Sangamon County, where he works as a clerk and does odd jobs.

1832 Lincoln volunteers for the Illinois militia to serve in the Black Hawk War and is elected company captain. He runs for the Illinois House of Representatives but is not elected. He becomes a partner in a New Salem general store.

1833 Lincoln is deeply in debt after the general store fails, works as a hired hand, and is appointed postmaster of New Salem and deputy surveyor of Sangamon County.

1834 Lincoln is elected to the Illinois House of Representatives as a Whig in one of four seats from Sangamon County. He begins to study law.

1835 Lincoln supports banks, canals, and other internal improvements in the Illinois legislature.

1836 Lincoln is re-elected to the legislature as one of seven Sangamon County representatives. He earns a license to practice law.

1837 Lincoln continues to support internal improvements in the legislature. With another Whig, Lincoln proposes an antislavery resolution. He moves to Springfield and begins law practice as a partner of John T. Stuart.

1838 Lincoln is re-elected to the Illinois legislature, where he serves as the Whig floor leader.

1840 Lincoln campaigns for Whig presidential candidate William Henry Harrison. Lincoln is re-elected to the legislature.

1841 Lincoln forms a new law partnership with Stephen T. Logan. He visits friend Joshua Speed near Lexington, Kentucky.

1842 Lincoln decides not to run again for state legislature. He marries Mary Todd, and the couple moves into a room in the Globe Tavern in Springfield.

1843 Son Robert Todd Lincoln is born.

1844 Lincoln moves his family into a house he buys in Springfield. He campaigns for Whig presidential candidate Henry Clay. Lincoln sets up a law practice and takes William H. Herndon as a partner.

1846 Son Edward Baker Lincoln is born. Lincoln is elected as a Whig to the U.S. House of Representatives.

1847 Lincoln goes to Washington, D.C., with his family and serves in the Thirtieth Congress.

1848 Lincoln opposes the Mexican war policy of President James Polk. He does not seek re-election to Congress. He campaigns for Whig presidential candidate Zachary Taylor and votes for the Wilmot Proviso.

1849 Lincoln returns to Springfield and resumes his law practice.

1850 Son Edward dies. Son William Wallace Lincoln born.

1851 Lincoln's father, Thomas Lincoln, dies.

1852 Lincoln campaigns for Whig presidential candidate Winfield Scott.

1853 Son Thomas (Tad) Lincoln born.

1854 Lincoln speaks out against the Kansas-Nebraska Act. He wins election to the Illinois legislature but declines to serve to be eligible for election by the legislature to the U.S. Senate.

1856 Lincoln fails to be elected to the U.S. Senate. He becomes a founding member of the Republican party in Illinois and campaigns for Republican presidential candidate John C. Frémont.

1857 Lincoln speaks out against the *Dred Scott* decision.

1858 Lincoln gives his "House Divided" speech as the Republican candidate for a U.S. Senate seat. He debates incumbent Democratic senator Stephen A. Douglas.

1859   Lincoln loses the senatorial election to Douglas, campaigns for Republicans in the Midwest, and begins to be mentioned as a possible presidential candidate.

1860   *February 27:* Lincoln speaks at Cooper Union in New York City.

May 18:   Lincoln wins the presidential nomination of the Republican national convention meeting in Chicago. He remains in Springfield during the presidential campaign.

November 6: Lincoln wins the presidential election.

December 20: South Carolina secedes.

1861   *January:* Mississippi, Florida, Alabama, Georgia, and Louisiana secede. Kansas becomes a state.

February: Texas secedes. The Confederate government meeting in Montgomery, Alabama, chooses Jefferson Davis as provisional president.

February 11: Lincoln leaves Springfield on a train to Washington and arrives there February 23.

March 4: Lincoln is inaugurated as president of the United States. Congress passes the Morrill Tariff Act, which sets high protective tariffs on imports.

April 12: Confederates bombard Fort Sumter.

April 13: Major Robert Anderson surrenders.

April 15: Lincoln calls for 75,000 militia.

April 17: Virginia convention adopts secession ordinance.

April 19: Massachusetts regiment is attacked by a mob in Baltimore. Lincoln proclaims a blockade of Confederate ports.

May: Lincoln calls for 42,304 three-year volunteers. Arkansas, Tennessee, North Carolina, and Virginia secede. Great Britain declares neutrality.

July 21: At the Battle of Bull Run (Manassas), Union forces under General Irvin McDowell suffer defeat.

July 27: General George B. McClellan replaces McDowell as commander of the Department of the Potomac. France declares neutrality.

August 6: Congress passes the First Confiscation Act. General John C. Frémont declares martial law in Missouri and proclaims that slaves of Missouri rebels are free.

September: Lincoln rescinds Frémont's emancipation order.

November: General McClellan is appointed general in chief. Union forces capture Port Royal, South Carolina. Confederate envoys James M. Mason and John Slidell are captured from the British ship *Trent.*

December: The *Trent* crisis is resolved by the release of the Confederate envoys.

1862 *February:* General Ulysses S. Grant defeats the Confederate forces at Fort Henry and Fort Donelson, Tennessee. Lincoln's son Willie dies.

March: Lincoln proposes gradual, compensated emancipation of slaves in loyal border states. General McClellan starts to deploy his Army of the Potomac for the Peninsula campaign.

April: General McClellan begins the Peninsula campaign. General Grant suffers a surprise attack at Shiloh, Tennessee, but forces Confederate retreat. Lincoln signs a law abolishing slavery in the District of Columbia. Union forces capture New Orleans.

May: General McClellan advances toward Richmond. Lincoln visits McClellan and the Army of the Potomac. Congress passes the Homestead Law opening federal land to settlement on easy terms.

June: Lincoln signs a law prohibiting slavery in federal territories. General McClellan begins an attack that becomes the Seven Days' Battle. McClellan retreats under counterattack by General Robert E. Lee.

July: Lincoln calls for 300,000 men to enlist for three years. He visits General McClellan and the Army of the Potomac dug in at Harrison Landing, Virginia. Lincoln appoints General Henry Halleck general in chief. He signs the Second Confiscation Act, which provides freedom for slaves of rebel masters.

July 22: Lincoln reads a draft of the Preliminary Emancipation Proclamation to his cabinet. During the month, Congress passes the Morrill Act, which grants federal land to states for agricultural colleges and approves the construction of a transcontinental railroad.

August: Lincoln calls for 300,000 militia to serve for nine months. General McClellan begins to withdraw the Army of the Potomac from the Peninsula. Union forces are defeated at the Second Battle of Bull Run.

September: General Lee begins an invasion of the North by crossing the Potomac River into Maryland.

September 17: In the battle of Antietam, General McClellan repulses Lee's northern advance.

September 22: Lincoln issues the Preliminary Emancipation Proclamation.

November: General Grant begins a campaign to capture Vicksburg, Mississippi. Democratic candidates make gains in congressional elections. General Ambrose E. Burnside replaces General McClellan as commander of the Army of the Potomac.

December: Lincoln urges Congress to pass a constitutional amendment allowing gradual, compensated emancipation.

December 13: General Burnside attacks Confederate defenses at Fredericksburg, Virginia, and is badly beaten.

1863   *January 1:* Lincoln issues the Emancipation Proclamation. Later that month, General Joseph Hooker replaces General Burnside as commander of the Army of the Potomac.

February: Congress approves the national banking system.

March: Lincoln signs a law introducing conscription.

April: Lincoln visits the Army of the Potomac and confers with General Hooker. Grant crosses the Mississippi River south of Vicksburg.

May 1–4: At Chancellorsville, Virginia, Lee defeats Hooker.

May 22: Grant begins a siege of Vicksburg.

June: Lee begins a second campaign to invade the North. Lincoln calls for 100,000 militia. General George Meade replaces General Hooker as commander of the Army of the Potomac. West Virginia is admitted to the Union.

July 1–3: At Gettysburg, Meade defeats the Confederates and turns back Lee's invasion of the North.

July 4: Grant captures Vicksburg.

July 9: General Nathaniel P. Banks captures Port Hudson, Louisiana, establishing Union control of the Mississippi River.

July 13–16: Draft riots occur in New York City.

September 19–20: At Chickamauga, the Confederates defeat the Union forces, which retreat to Chattanooga, Tennessee.

October: Lincoln elevates Grant to command all Union forces in the West. Lincoln calls for 300,000 volunteers.

November 19: Lincoln delivers the Gettysburg Address.

December: Lincoln issues the Proclamation of Amnesty and Reconstruction.

1864   *March:* Grant is promoted to general in chief of the army. General William T. Sherman is appointed to command the armies in the West.

May 5–12: At the battles of the Wilderness and Spotsylvania, Grant attacks Lee. Sherman launches campaign against Atlanta.

June: Lincoln is nominated for a second term by the National Union Convention.

June 18: Grant begins a siege of Petersburg. During the month, General Jubal Early initiates a Confederate offensive in the Shenandoah

Valley. Congress approves the National Banking Act, creating national currency.

July: Lincoln refuses to sign the Wade-Davis Bill. He calls for 500,000 volunteers. General Early reaches the outskirts of Washington, D.C., but is forced to retreat.

August: General Philip H. Sheridan takes command of the Union forces in the Shenandoah Valley. The Democrats nominate General George McClellan for president.

September 2: Sherman captures Atlanta.

October 19: At Cedar Creek, Sheridan expels the Confederate forces from the Shenandoah Valley. During the month, Nevada is admitted to the Union.

November 8: Lincoln is re-elected president.

November 15: Sherman begins the March to the Sea.

December: Lincoln calls for 300,000 volunteers.

December 21: Sherman captures Savannah.

1865 *January:* Congress submits the Thirteenth Amendment to the states for ratification.

February 3: Lincoln meets with Confederate representatives at Hampton Roads, Virginia.

February 17: Sherman occupies Columbia, South Carolina.

March 4: Lincoln is inaugurated for a second term.

April 2: Grant captures Petersburg and Lee retreats toward the west, while the Confederate government evacuates Richmond.

April 3: Union forces capture Richmond.

April 4: Lincoln visits Richmond.

April 9: Lee surrenders to Grant at Appomattox Court House, Virginia.

April 14: Lincoln is shot by John Wilkes Booth and dies the next day.

April 26: Booth is killed by federal pursuers.

May 4: Lincoln is buried in Springfield, Illinois.

December 18: The Thirteenth Amendment is ratified.

Questions for Consideration

1. In what ways did Lincoln's early life influence his later ideas and behavior? How did his personal traits shape his performance as president?

2. Why did Lincoln revere the federal Constitution? How did his views of the constitution affect his political and military decisions?

3. Why did Lincoln oppose the extension of slavery into federal territories? According to Lincoln, how did slavery differ from free labor, both in day-to-day practice and in long-term social and political repercussions?

4. Did Lincoln believe in human equality? Why? Did he consider blacks equal to whites? How did his views compare to those of his contemporaries? Should he be considered the white man's president?

5. Why did Lincoln place such a high value on the Union? What were the consequences of his devotion to the Union during his presidency?

6. How did Lincoln view the South? Did his views change? How did his views of the South influence his policies as president?

7. Why did Lincoln become a Republican? How did his leadership of the Republican party shape his actions as president?

8. How did Lincoln's political ideas influence his military strategy? How did military developments shape his presidential policies? What was his understanding of his responsibility as commander in chief?

9. Why was Lincoln often disappointed by the actions of leading generals? What qualities did he value in military commanders?

10. How did Lincoln's ideas about slavery change? Why? Did his ideas about African Americans change? Why? How did Lincoln think freedom would change the lives of slaves?

11. Why did Lincoln issue the Emancipation Proclamation? Did it serve the purposes he intended? What were its short-term and long-term consequences? Does Lincoln deserve to be called the Great Emancipator?

12. How did Lincoln's ideas about the Union and the Constitution mesh with his concepts of freedom, democracy, and equality?

13. To what degree was the Gettysburg Address a departure from Lincoln's previous thinking about the meaning of the Civil War? What messages was Lincoln trying to communicate in the address?

14. What were Lincoln's ideas about religion? Did they influence his thinking about slavery and the Civil War? If so, how?

15. What plans did Lincoln have for Reconstruction? What were his goals for Reconstruction? To what extent would former slaves be equal to whites?

16. In what ways did Lincoln's Second Inaugural Address outline his views of the problems and possibilities of peace and reunion? What were the strengths and weaknesses of his approach to peace and reunion?

17. Do you think Lincoln achieved what was realistically possible during his years as president? Or did he fail to accomplish certain goals that were within reach? If so, what were those goals, and how might he have achieved them?

18. In Lincoln's eyes, what was the significance of the Civil War in the larger realm of world history? What was at stake in the outcome? Were other issues at stake that he neglected to mention or perceive?

19. What was Lincoln's legacy to succeeding generations? How do his thoughts and deeds continue to influence the ways Americans think and act?

20. How do the qualities of Lincoln's writings and speeches compare to those of more recent presidents? What accounts for the differences?

Selected Bibliography

PRIMARY SOURCES AND REFERENCE WORKS

Paul M. Angle, ed., *The Complete Lincoln-Douglas Debates of 1858* (1958, 1991).

Domenica M. Barbuto and Martha Kreisel, *Guide to Civil War Books: An Annotated Selection of Modern Works on the War between the States* (1996).

Roy P. Basler, Marian Dolores Pratt, and Lloyd A. Dunlap, eds., *The Collected Works of Abraham Lincoln* (8 vols.; 1953).

Ira Berlin et al., eds., *Freedom: A Documentary History of Emancipation* (4 vols.; 1982–93).

Mark M. Boatner III, *The Civil War Dictionary* (rev. ed.; 1988).

David J. Eicher, *The Civil War in Books: An Analytical Bibliography* (1997).

Don E. Fehrenbacher and Virginia Fehrenbacher, eds., *Recollected Words of Abraham Lincoln* (1996).

Charles Hamilton and Lloyd Ostendorf, *Lincoln in Photographs: An Album of Every Known Pose* (1985).

Harold Holzer, ed., *Dear Mr. Lincoln: Letters to the President* (1993).

Harold Holzer, ed., *The Lincoln-Douglas Debates: The First Complete, Unexpurgated Text* (1993).

Harold Holzer, ed., *The Lincoln Mailbag: America Writes to the President, 1861–1865* (1998).

Robert W. Johannsen, ed., *The Lincoln-Douglas Debates of 1858* (1965).

David C. Mearns, *The Lincoln Papers* (2 vols.; 1948).

Earl S. Miers, William E. Baringen, and C. Percy Powell, eds., *Lincoln Day by Day: A Chronology* (3 vols.; 1960).

Mark E. Neely Jr., *The Abraham Lincoln Encyclopedia* (1982).

Douglas L. Wilson and Rodney O. Davis, eds., *Herndon's Informants: Letters, Interviews, and Statements about Abraham Lincoln* (1998).

P. M. Zall, *Abe Lincoln Laughing: Humorous Anecdotes from Original Sources by and about Abraham Lincoln* (1982).

BIOGRAPHIES

David Herbert Donald, *Lincoln* (1995).

William H. Herndon and Jesse E. Weik, *Herndon's Lincoln: The True Story of a Great Life* (1890).

Philip B. Kunhardt Jr., Philip B. Kunhardt III, and Peter W. Kunhardt, *Lincoln: An Illustrated Biography* (1992).

Mark E. Neely Jr., *The Last Best Hope of Earth: Abraham Lincoln and the Promise of America* (1993).

John G. Nicolay and John Hay, *Abraham Lincoln: A History* (10 vols.; 1890).

Stephen B. Oates, *With Malice toward None: The Life of Abraham Lincoln* (1977).

J. G. Randall, *Lincoln the President* (4 vols.; 1945–55).

Carl Sandburg, *Abraham Lincoln* (6 vols.; 1926–39).

Benjamin P. Thomas, *Abraham Lincoln: A Biography* (1952).

LINCOLN, SLAVERY, AND THE CIVIL WAR

George Anastaplo, *Abraham Lincoln: A Constitutional Biography* (1999).

Paul M. Angle, *"Here I Have Lived": A History of Lincoln's Springfield, 1812–1865* (1950).

Jean Harvey Baker, *Mary Todd Lincoln: A Biography* (1987).

Herman Belz, *Abraham Lincoln, Constitutionalism, and Equal Rights in the Civil War Era* (1998).

Herman Belz, *A New Birth of Freedom: The Republican Party and Freedmen's Rights, 1861–1866* (1976).

Herman Belz, *Reconstructing the Union: Theory and Practice During the Civil War* (1969).

Michael Les Benedict, *A Compromise of Principle: Congressional Republicans and Reconstruction, 1863–1869* (1974).

James D. Bilotta, *Race and the Rise of the Republican Party, 1848–1865* (1992).

David Blight, *Frederick Douglass' Civil War: Keeping Faith in Jubilee* (1989).

Allan G. Bogue, *The Congressman's Civil War* (1989).

Allan G. Bogue, *The Earnest Men: Republicans of the Civil War Senate* (1981).

Gabor S. Boritt, *Lincoln and the Economics of the American Dream* (1978).

Gabor S. Boritt, ed., *Lincoln the War President: The Gettysburg Lectures* (1992).

Gabor S. Boritt and Norman O. Forness, eds., *The Historian's Lincoln: Pseudohistory, Psychohistory, and History* (1988).

Waldo W. Braden, *Abraham Lincoln, Public Speaker* (1988).

Michael Burlingame, *The Inner World of Abraham Lincoln* (1994).

Bruce Chadwick, *The Two American Presidents: A Dual Biography of Abraham Lincoln and Jefferson Davis* (1999).

Dudley Taylor Cornish, *The Sable Arm: Negro Troops in the Union Army, 1861–1865* (1956).

LaWanda Cox, *Lincoln and Black Freedom: A Study in Presidential Leadership* (1981).

Richard Nelson Current, *Speaking of Abraham Lincoln: The Man and His Meaning for Our Times* (1983).

Cullom Davis, Charles B. Strozier, Rebecca Monroe Veach, and Geoffrey C. Ward, eds., *The Public and the Private Lincoln* (1979).

William C. Davis, *Lincoln's Men: How President Lincoln Became Father to an Army and a Nation* (1999).

David Herbert Donald, *Lincoln Reconsidered: Essays on the Civil War* (1956).

David Herbert Donald, *Lincoln's Herndon* (1948).

John J. Duff, *A. Lincoln: Prairie Lawyer* (1960).

Herbert Joseph Edwards and John Erskine Hankins, *Lincoln the Writer* (1962).

Lois J. Einhorn, *Abraham Lincoln the Orator: Penetrating the Lincoln Legend* (1992).

Don E. Fehrenbacher, *The Dred Scott Case: Its Significance in American Law and Politics* (1978).

Don E. Fehrenbacher, *Lincoln in Text and Context: Collected Essays* (1987).

Don E. Fehrenbacher, *Prelude to Greatness: Lincoln in the 1850s* (1962).

Michael Fellman, *Citizen Sherman: A Life of William Tecumseh Sherman* (1995).

Paul Findley, *A. Lincoln: The Crucible of Congress* (1979).

Eric Foner, *Free Soil, Free Labor, Free Men: The Ideology of the Republican Party before the Civil War* (1970).

Eric Foner, *Reconstruction: America's Unfinished Revolution, 1863–1877* (1988).

George B. Forgie, *Patricide in the House Divided: A Psychological Interpretation of Lincoln and His Age* (1979).

John Hope Franklin, *The Emancipation Proclamation* (1963).

Olivier Fraysség, *Lincoln, Land, and Labor, 1809–1860*, trans. Sylvia Neely (1994).

William W. Freehling, *The Reintegration of American History: Slavery and the Civil War* (1994).

William E. Gienapp, *The Origins of the Republican Party, 1852–1856* (1987).

J. David Greenstone, *The Lincoln Persuasion: Remaking American Liberalism* (1993).

Allen C. Guelzo, *Abraham Lincoln: Redeemer President* (1999).

William Hanchett, *The Lincoln Murder Conspiracies* (1983).

Michael F. Holt, *The Rise and Fall of the American Whig Party: Jacksonian Politics and the Onset of the Civil War* (1999).

Harold Holzer, Gabor S. Baritt, and Mark E. Neely Jr., *The Lincoln Image: Abraham Lincoln and the Popular Print* (1984).

Daniel Walker Howe, *Making the American Self: Jonathan Edwards to Abraham Lincoln* (1997).

Harry V. Jaffa, *Crisis in the House Divided: An Interpretation of the Issues in the Lincoln-Douglas Debates* (1959).

Robert W. Johannsen, *Lincoln, the South, and Slavery* (1991).

Howard Jones, *Abraham Lincoln and a New Birth of Freedom: The Union and Slavery in the Diplomacy of the Civil War* (1999).

Howard Jones, *Union in Peril: The Crisis over British Intervention in the Civil War* (1992).

Philip B. Kunhardt Jr., *A New Birth of Freedom: Lincoln at Gettysburg* (1983).

David E. Long, *The Jewel of Liberty: Abraham Lincoln's Re-election and the End of Slavery* (1994).

John F. Marszalek, *Sherman: A Soldier's Passion for Order* (1993).

Peyton McCrary, *Abraham Lincoln and Reconstruction: The Louisiana Experiment* (1978).

William S. McFeely, *Grant: A Biography* (1981).

James M. McPherson, *Abraham Lincoln and the Second American Revolution* (1990).

James M. McPherson, *Battle Cry of Freedom: The Civil War Era* (1988).

James M. McPherson, *Drawn with the Sword: Reflections on the American Civil War* (1996).

James M. McPherson, *The Negro's Civil War: How American Negroes Felt and Acted during the War for the Union* (1965).

James M. McPherson, *The Struggle for Equality: Abolitionists and the Negro in the Civil War and Reconstruction* (1964).

James M. McPherson, *"We Cannot Escape History": Lincoln and the Last Best Hope of Earth* (1995).

Grady McWhiney, ed., *Grant, Lee, Lincoln and the Radicals* (1964).

Mark E. Neely Jr., *The Fate of Liberty: Abraham Lincoln and Civil Liberties* (1991).

David A. Nichols, *Lincoln and the Indians: Civil War Policy and Politics* (1978).

Phillip S. Paludan, *The Presidency of Abraham Lincoln* (1994).

Merrill D. Peterson, *Lincoln in American Memory* (1994).

David M. Potter, *The South and the Sectional Conflict* (1968).

David M. Potter and Don E. Fehrenbacher, *The Impending Crisis, 1848–1861* (1976).

Benjamin Quarles, *Lincoln and the Negro* (1962).

Benjamin Quarles, *The Negro in the Civil War* (1962).

J. G. Randall, *Constitutional Problems under Lincoln* (rev. ed.; 1951).

Donald W. Riddle, *Congressman Abraham Lincoln* (1979).

Stephen W. Sears, *George B. McClellan: The Young Napoleon* (1988).

Joel H. Silbey, *A Respectable Minority: The Democratic Party in the Civil War Era, 1860–1868* (1978).

Brooks D. Simpson, *Let Us Have Peace: Ulysses S. Grant and the Politics of War and Reconstruction* (1991).

Charles P. Strozier, *Lincoln's Quest for Union: Public and Private Meanings* (1982).

Benjamin P. Thomas. *Lincoln's New Salem* (1954).

John L. Thomas, ed., *Abraham Lincoln and the American Political Tradition* (1986).

Thomas Reed Turner, *Beware the People Weeping: Public Opinion and the Assassination of Abraham Lincoln* (1982).

Jack C. Waugh, *Reelecting Lincoln: The Presidential Election of 1864* (1998).

Frank J. Williams, William D. Pederson, and Vincent J. Mavsala, eds., *Abraham Lincoln: Sources and Styles of Leadership* (1994).

Gary Wills, *Lincoln at Gettysburg: The Words That Remade America* (1992).

Douglas L. Wilson, *Honor's Voice: The Transformation of Abraham Lincoln* (1998).

Douglas L. Wilson, *Lincoln before Washington: New Perspectives on the Illinois Years* (1997).

William J. Wolf, *The Almost Chosen People: A Study of the Religion of Abraham Lincoln* (1959).

David Zarefsky, *Lincoln, Douglas, and Slavery: In the Crucible of Public Debate* (1990).

Index